Culture Shock
and Japanese-American Relations

Culture Shock
and Japanese-American Relations

Historical Essays

Sadao Asada

University of Missouri Press   Columbia and London

Library of Congress Cataloging-in-Publication Data
Asada, Sadao, 1936-
    Culture shock and Japanese-American relations : historical essays / Sadao Asada.
        p.   cm.
    Summary: "Examines historical episodes in the interactions between the United States
and Japan from 1890 to 2006, focusing on naval strategy before and during World War II
and transpacific racism. Asada analyzes both American and Japanese perceptions of Pearl
Harbor and the atomic bomb controversy"—Provided by publisher.
    Includes bibliographical references and index.
    ISBN 978-0-8262-1953-4 (pbk: alk. paper)
  1. United States—Relations—Japan.   2. Japan—Relations—United States.
3. Culture shock—United States.   4. Culture shock—Japan.   5. Racism—United States—
History—20th century.   6. Japan. Kaigun—History—20th century.   7. Pearl Harbor
(Hawaii), Attack on, 1941—Public opinion.   8. Atomic bomb—Public opinion.   9. Public
opinion—Japan.   10. Public opinion—United States.   I. Title.
    E183.8.J3A83 2007
    303.48-2520730904—dc22

                                                                                2007004496

∞™ This paper meets the requirements of the
American National Standard for Permanence of Paper
for Printed Library Materials, Z39.48, 1984.

Designer: Jennifer Cropp
Typesetter: BookComp, Inc.
Printer and binder: Thomson-Shore, Inc.
Typefaces: Palatino, Hiroshige, and Sassafras

To my students, 1963-2006

Contents

Preface

An interesting way of approaching the history of Japanese-American relations is by examining the culture shocks experienced by the main actors, either individually or collectively. And starting with the visit of Commodore Perry's "black ships" to Japan in 1853, the relations between the two countries have been replete with instances of culture shocks. According to Kalervo Oberg, "Culture shock is precipitated by the anxiety that results from losing all our familiar signs and symbols of social intercourse." It involves "a sense of confusion and uncertainty sometimes with feeling of anxiety that may affect people exposed to an alien culture." In this volume I shall employ this term broadly as any situation where an individual or people are forced to adjust to an unfamiliar socio-political situation where previous learning no longer applies.[1]

The theme of culture shock will conveniently bring together such diverse topics as naval strategy, the decision-making process, transpacific racism, and the atomic bomb controversy. I have emphasized mutual perceptions and the interplay of ideas, examining how cognitive dissonance can cause conflict and escalation into crises, even a war. These essays will show that the interplay of ideas and cultural exchange are highly complex and sometimes destructive—contrary to the prevalent notion that cultural exchange is an agent of peace.

It may be an unusual way to open a book on the history of Japanese-American relations, but in response to the request from the director of the University of Missouri Press, I give a brief intellectual autobiography. It is a belated and partial answer to the late Harold Isaacs, the author of *Scratches on our Minds* and a behavioral scientist at MIT. During a visit to Kyoto in 1965, Isaacs discovered that I had spent nine youthful years in America

---

1. Oberg, "Culture Shock: Adjustment to New Cultural Environments"; William A. Smalley, "Culture Shock, Language Shock, and the Shock of Self-Discovery"; Paul Pederson, *The Five Stages of Culture Shock: Critical Incidents around the World,* 1.

and indicated that he wanted to do an in-depth psychological case study of me. I admit that in embarrassment I politely declined.

Seven of the essays in this volume have been previously published in English or Japanese. They are expanded and updated to make them more pertinent or accessible to Western readers by incorporating new research, recent literature, and changing points of view. I decided to reprint "The Shock of the Atomic Bomb and Japan's Decision to Surrender—A Reconsideration" (*Pacific Historical Review,* November 1998), because it has often been cited in a controversy occasioned by Tsuyoshi Hasegawa's *Racing the Enemy: Stalin, Truman, and the Surrender of Japan* (2005). I append to this essay a critical note on *Racing the Enemy.*

The origins of the present book lie in the encouragement of an old and esteemed friend who told me I should put together a collection of my essays. From the beginning the director and editor-in-chief of the Press, Beverly Jarrett, has been enthusiastic about the project.

No historian is an island, and I wish to thank friends who have helped me along the way. I must first mention my graduate teacher, the late Samuel Flagg Bemis, whose memory has been a tower of strength on many occasions. Since my graduate student days, Robert H. Ferrell has constantly supported and encouraged me. Also helpful were Aruga Tadashi, Michael Barnhart, Robert J. C. Butow, Roger Dingman, Waldo H. Heinrichs, Hosoya Chihiro, Ishii Osamu, Charles E. Neu, Ian Nish, Ronald Spector, and the late David A. Titus. I greatly appreciate the enthusiasm of the director and editor-in-chief of the University of Missouri Press, Beverly Jarrett, and the transpacific efforts of my editor, Susan King.

This book is dedicated to my former students at Doshisha University.

Sadao Asada
August 15, 2006
Kyoto, Japan

Abbreviations

BBK	Library, Bōeichō Bōei Kenshūjo (National Institute of Defense Studies), Tokyo
BBKS	Bōeichō Bōei Kenshūjo, *Senshishitsu* (War History Office of the National Institute of Defense Studies, Japanese Ministry of Defense)
DL	National Diet Library, Tokyo
FRUS	*Foreign Relations of the United States*
Gaimushō	Japanese Ministry of Foreign Affairs
ISS-UT	Institute of Social Science, University of Tokyo
JMJ	Office of War Crimes Materials, Japanese Ministry of Justice
JMFA	Japanese Ministry of Foreign Affairs
LC	Manuscripts Division, Library of Congress, Washington, D.C.
NA	National Archives, Washington, D.C.
NGB	*Nihon Gaikō Bunsho* (Documents on Japanese Foreign Policy)
NMSDC	National Maritime Self-Defense College, Tokyo
TSM	*Taiheiyō sensō e no michi* and *Taiheiyō sensō e no michi: Bekkan Shiryōhen* (Supplementary Volume of Documents)

Note on Japanese names

In accordance with the established academic convention, Japanese names are listed with the family name preceding the given name, in the text, footnotes, and bibliography. When Japanese authors who have published in English are referred to in the text, their given names appear first.

Culture Shock
and Japanese-American Relations

Reverse Culture Shock

A Personal Note

This opening essay is a personal account of the culture shocks I have experienced in the United States and Japan. Since I have never kept a diary, the nine youthful years I spent in America are traced from the letters I sent home, some one hundred and fifty of them. These letters were written to inform as much as to reassure my parents, so my reports from America tended to be sanguine, and I unashamedly blew my own horn about my academic achievements. It was precisely because I was so much in my element in America that the "reverse culture shock" I experienced upon my return to Japan was all the more galling. I struggled for many years to overcome the frustrations, alienation, and inner conflict before I was able to eventually reach a measure of accommodation to Japanese society and academe.

Prelude

My exposure to historical revisionism came early in life, at the tender age of nine. On September 20, 1945, a little more than a month after Japan's surrender, the vice minister of education sent out to the heads of all prefectures a notice on "the treatment of textbooks attendant to surrender." It was a hasty attempt to delete those portions that glorified militarism and the emperor's war, before being ordered to do so by the American occupation authorities. Pupils were told to blot out in black ink what were considered objectionable passages, of which there were very many. The teachers who had been inculcating us with kamikaze spirit and a hatred of America almost overnight began extolling American democracy. These experiences, "transvaluation of values," should have taught me that every age must rewrite its own history, but I was too young to understand. Instead, I came to dislike and distrust history as it was taught in school.

Throughout the war years, I had also inwardly hated and dreaded the indoctrination about dying a glorious death for the sake of the emperor. (I was not poisoned by militarism at home because my parents had been educated in Doshisha's liberal schools.) In April 1945 those of us in the third through sixth grades were forced to evacuate to a village facing the Japan Sea, not too far from Maizuru Naval Station. There we witnessed the sinking of a warship in the Miyazu Bay. Wounded sailors were treated in the makeshift hospital set up in the school auditorium. War came close to us when we were strafed by fighters flying just above our heads. I would have been safer back home in Kyoto, which was not bombed. (Thirty years later I learned that Kyoto was spared atomic bombing thanks to Secretary of War Henry L. Stimson's intervention.) At any rate, I saw enough action to make me antimilitaristic. My allergy to history and anything military was to last until I went to study in America in 1954.

To many adults, the American occupation of Japan (1945–1952), with its demilitarization and democratization programs, came as a profound culture shock, but to many of my generation, these programs were "liberating." I vividly remember an air of exhilaration and optimism, especially during the early phase of the occupation, despite the hardships of daily existence. Many of us uncritically embraced what we understood to be "American democracy," and there was an eagerness to learn about the ideas that underlay the occupation reforms.

I was a late bloomer and a shy, introverted boy, but I was catapulted by a chance exposure to an exciting cross-cultural life. During my senior year at Doshisha High School, I was selected to live with Milton L. Bierman, the representative of Carleton College who came to Kyoto in the capacity of a missionary-teacher. This encounter brought about my initial culture shock with its attendant confusions and communication problems, but Milton and I hit it off from the beginning. He gave me a crash course in English. The first book I was assigned to read was John Stuart Mill's *On Liberty*—heady stuff for a high school student. My English proficiency leaped forward, so much so that I won an all-school English recitation contest, reciting a leaf from Thoreau's *Walden*. Milton intellectually awakened and challenged me, and we remained close lifelong friends.

It was natural, then, that upon being awarded a Grew Foundation scholarship in 1954, I chose to attend Carleton. Every year the Grew Foundation selected a few high school graduates to study at quality liberal arts colleges in America for four years.[1] The scholarship, as the name shows, was

1. Sadao Asada, "Gurū kikin no setsuritsu: Grew and Kabayama Aisuke" [The

founded by the former ambassador to Japan, Joseph C. Grew, in 1950. Hoping to better U.S.-Japanese relations, Mr. Grew donated the royalties from the Japanese translation of his diary, *Ten Years in Japan*. It sold seventy-five thousand copies in a year and a half. The Japanese people were starving for information about their prewar leaders.

In August 1954, together with two other Grew students, I boarded the SS *Atami Maru*, a tiny passenger-cargo vessel of a mere four thousand tons. We hit a storm in the mid-Pacific, but otherwise it was a pleasant voyage. Unlike air travel today, there was plenty of time to ponder the experiences to come. After arriving in San Francisco, we took the train straight to New York City where we were met by Akira Iriye, who preceded us by one year as the first Grew scholar and was studying at Haverford College. After a brief stay there, I headed to the Midwest, arriving in Northfield, Minnesota, the site of Carleton College, in early September. Northfield was (and still is) a small college town. It is also the home of Saint Olaf College, which is famous for its choir. As people drive into Northfield, they are greeted by a huge billboard that reads, "Welcome to the Town of Cows, Colleges, and Contentment." Carleton's most illustrious graduate is somewhat incongruously Thorstein Veblen (1857–1929), an acidulous social and economic critic.

Life at Carleton: "Like a Big Family"

Carleton, one of several outstanding colleges in America, was a great adventure, a real challenge, and a truly liberating experience, not just for me, but also for my fellow students. As one of my classmates wrote, "The Carleton Experience challenged me beyond my self-imposed limitations and caused me to aspire to do many things I had previously thought to be beyond my ability."[2]

A small college (about a thousand students), Carleton was "like one huge family." In the words of an alumnus it was "a place where everyone says hello to everyone else." Both students and faculty members went out of their way to make foreign students feel at home. I, and several friends, frequently visited Mrs. Nina Bird—the widow of a distinguished professor of romance languages who was in her late seventies. Mrs. Bird took a personal interest in my welfare, and the Bird House, as we called it, just across the campus, became for me "a home away home." During my Carleton days I cannot recall having ever been homesick. Perhaps it was because I was just too busy

---

Founding of the Grew Foundation: Joseph C. Grew and Kabayama Aisuke], in Asada, trans., *Gurū taishi to Nichi-Bei gaikō,* by Waldo Heinrichs, 401–12.

2. David H. Porter and Merrill E. Jarchow, eds., *Carleton Remembered, 1909–1986,* 126.

and excited to miss home, or perhaps it was because Mrs. Bird treated me like an adopted grandson.

What about culture shocks? Yes, there were some—if you can call them that, for they were all on the pleasant side. The first letter I sent home from Carleton (written shortly before school started) was *forty-one* pages long. It was packed with discoveries, amazements, and excitements—"happy" culture shock.[3] In the opening convocation of the year, President Laurence M. Gould told the freshman class, "You have now matriculated at Carleton College, and your life will never be the same again. You will always be a part of this great institution, and we welcome you to its family."[4] These inspiring words are vividly remembered by this alumnus more than half a century later.

The crash English course I had taken while living with Milton stood me in good stead, and from the beginning I was on the dean's list. This does not mean that I did not have to work very hard, especially during my first year. My classmate Michael Armacost, who served as an ambassador to Japan from 1989 to 1993, used to kid me about how I moved from classroom to classroom carrying my *Webster's Collegiate Dictionary,* Kenkyusha's big *English-Japanese Dictionary, Japanese-English Dictionary,* and an assortment of textbooks. That first year I felt as if I were a sponge absorbing new knowledge, ideas, and experiences.

The introductory history course on the modern world, taught by Lucile Pinkham, was an eye-opener. There were no lectures in this course, only question-and-answer sessions and discussions on the basis of the textbook and assigned readings. I not only rid myself of my childhood allergy to history but considered majoring in it. I am amused that already in my first year I was writing my parents that I hoped to do graduate work in the States and to become a professor of history upon my return to Japan.[5]

English was another favorite subject. In one of the first essays I wrote for my freshman English class, titled "An Innocent Abroad in New York," I sketched my first impressions of the United States. I received an A minus, and my teacher complimented me on my work: "This is splendid description. There are remarkably few errors. Both in choice of words and sentence your writing is fresh and rigorous."[6] I had never expected things would go so well, I reported to the Grew Foundation.[7] On New Year's Day 1955, I

3. It was written in four sittings and posted on September 21, 1954.
4. Porter and Jarchow, eds., *Carleton Remembered,* 81.
5. Asada to parents, March 29, 1955.
6. Asada to parents, October 9, 1954.
7. Asada to Grew Foundation, December 12, 1954.

wrote to my parents: "I feel almost guilty about enjoying my college life here so freely when practically all of the Japanese people are living out daily difficulties."[8]

Exhibits and Talks about Japan

When I was still fresh from Japan, I made a special effort to tell my fellow students and faculty members about my native country and about Japanese culture. Barely a month after I arrived at Carleton, I held an "open house" in my dormitory room. I displayed the various "treasures" I had brought from Japan—wood-block prints (by my famous artist uncle, Asada Benji), a flower basket, a doll, lacquerware, fans, a tea ceremony set, brightly colored wrapping clothes, etc. I hung a large sign on my door saying, "Come and have Japanese tea."[9] The room was packed with visitors. One of the art professors was so impressed with the wood-block prints that he later talked about them in his class. On the following day my friends addressed me, "Hello, Tea Man!" So successful was my "exhibit" that on October 30 I was asked to repeat the display for faculty members and students in Carleton's Great Hall.[10]

The *Carletonian,* the weekly student newspaper, reported, "Freshman Sadao Asada is always eager to tell of his native land and of the beauty of his home town. Visitors to his room are met with an array of Japanese articles which are used by Asada in relating his life and customs in Japan." The article continued, "One of Asada's aims in America is to educate his fellow students about Japan and its present position in world affairs." I had never suspected I could be so sociable and outgoing!

Busy as I was with my studies, I accepted invitations to speak about Japan. In October, I spoke at the "International Night" of the Rotary Club in the next town. And three days later I was invited to a luncheon held by the Northfield Rotary Club. Then there was the United Nations Day speech. Only once did I encounter a fervently anti-Japanese person: he asked me pointed questions about anti-Americanism in Japan. It was triggered by the Bikini incident in which the Japanese fishing boat *Lucky Dragon* was exposed to radioactive fallout from an American hydrogen bomb test. Although I never felt "patriotic," I found myself defending Japan as best I

8. Asada to parents, January 3, 1955.
9. Asada to parents, October 9, 1954.
10. Asada to parents, October 30, 1954.

could. After the meeting a few people came up to me and said, "Good job, young man!"[11]

Afraid of getting out of touch with Japan, I asked my parents to send me magazines and journals, mostly highbrow stuff, which I somehow found time to read.[12] During my first year, aside from two female seniors, there was no presence of Japan at Carleton, and during my third year I was the only Japanese at Carleton. Despite my good intention to follow developments back home, Japan was fast receding from my consciousness as I came to identify more and more with America. Such cultural isolation would be difficult for Japanese students in America today to imagine. They can instantly contact their families through fax or e-mail, enjoy Japanese food, read Japanese newspapers, and watch Japanese television programs or news in real time.

The Americanization of Sadao Asada

In addition to my regular diet of history courses, I made sure to take three good courses in American history taught by Carlton C. Qualey: a survey course, a class in U.S. diplomatic history, and a seminar in American immigration history. I especially enjoyed immigration history, which was Qualey's special field. Perhaps I was attracted to this subject because I was experiencing some of the same things that immigrants had experienced. Outside of class I devoured novels about immigrants in the Midwest such as Ole Rölvaag's *Giants in the Earth* and Willa Cather's *My Antonia.* An advanced course in American literature was an ideal supplement to the American history courses I was taking. We tackled the major writers of the American Renaissance—Hawthorne, Emerson, Thoreau, and Melville.

On an autumn evening, while enjoying a hayride, I saw a large reddish moon rise from the horizon. The country with its vast expanse inspired awe. Minnesota winters were a humbling challenge, and to this day I cannot see how I survived four of them. Otherwise, I was growing into a happy upper midwesterner.[13]

During summer vacations, I developed a special "talent" for long-distance hitchhiking. In my second year I had hoped to hike to the West Coast but got bogged down, so I went to Rocky Mountain National Park and to the Black Hills and Mount Rushmore National Memorial in South

11. Asada to parents, October 20, 1954.
12. Asada to parents, December 4, 1954.
13. Asada to parents, November 10, 1957.

Dakota instead, before returning to Northfield. Later, in September 1959, I hitchhiked from Northfield to New Haven, Connecticut—thirteen hundred miles—in just fifty hours, believe it or not. In Chicago I was picked up by a seemingly shady character who had lost seven hundred dollars in Las Vegas and was hurrying home to Boston at a terrifying speed. Actually, he turned out to be a kindly fellow. He told me that he had fought in the Pacific and described his combat experiences at Rabaul, Saipan, and Guadalcanal, but I sensed no malice as a result of the war.[14]

While hitchhiking I would let myself be engulfed—"lost" is perhaps a better word—in the American continent, forgetting my own national identity. Like panhandling, hitchhiking had a way of becoming a habit. One afternoon I had my right arm up and my thumb pointing in the direction of the Twin Cities forty miles away, and who but President Gould stopped to pick me up.

My job during my first year as a counselor and leader at a boys' camp facing Lake Michigan was healthy, pleasant, and educational. It was one of the largest camps (Miniwanca) supported by the Danforth Foundation. The following summer, the job market was very tight, so I had to settle on a job in a canning factory in southern Minnesota packing peas and corn. It was hard physical labor, sometimes for sixteen hours a day, at the minimum wage, one dollar an hour. During my third summer, I was told by Carleton's employment office that I had landed a job at the Ford auto factory in Ypsilanti, Michigan.[15] But when I showed up, I was told that there was no job. It was a recession year and regular workers had to be laid off. My money was running out and starvation loomed ahead, so after several days of waiting, I decided to take the bus to the head office of the Ford Motor Company. I explained my desperate predicament to the personnel manager, who after making a few telephone calls told me I had a job starting the following morning.[16] This and other experiences would show that in the mid-1950s many Americans went out of their way to be generous to me, a lad from a former enemy country.

That summer I lived in Ann Arbor. I worked the night shift from 4:30 p.m. to 12:30 a.m. at the factory and in the daytime would occasionally visit the University of Michigan library. The assembly line job, recalling Charlie Chaplin's *Modern Times,* was so monotonous that it almost drove me crazy, but I enjoyed working with the kind of people I would never have met at Carleton. The proletarian experience gave me an insight into the seamier

14. Asada to parents, August 25, 1959.
15. Asada to parents, July 3, 1957.
16. Asada to parents, July 24, 1957.

side of American society. It was all a part of my Americanization. I was young enough to take any new experience as a challenge. I didn't have the faintest notion, however, that such unquestioning acculturation to American life would cause me difficulties when I eventually returned to Japan.

The Library Prize

I still take pride in having won the "library prize" during my junior year at Carleton. American colleges generally have such excellent library facilities that students do not have to acquire their own personal libraries. President Gould, a fervent believer in the liberal arts ideal, felt this was deplorable and created a contest for which each entrant was to submit a list of the books in his possession and an essay on the philosophy behind his collection. As a Grew scholar, I received one dollar a day for spending money, and I saved it to buy books specially recommended in classes or in my conversations with professors. In Northfield I missed the used bookstores that I used to frequent in Kyoto, but the Carleton bookstore was well stocked with paperbacks. I entered the contest and to my amazement was awarded the prize! The press release from the Carleton College News Bureau announced that I had "accumulated the most liberal and interesting personal library." My prize was a substantial line of credit at the Carleton bookstore for the purchase of more books.

I dwell on this minor episode because I was unknowingly preparing myself for my first job—essentially a librarianship—that I would hold upon my return to Japan. The Carleton release continued, "Asada told of the necessity of accumulating as many books as possible while he is still in America. Cost alone, he explained, will make further purchases extremely limited, and with this in mind a considerable amount of foresight has gone into the choice of this permanently basic library." (True, in those days the college teacher in Japan was miserably paid. The situation has improved somewhat since.) A nice letter from President Gould said, "I congratulate you heartily on the wisdom and catholicity of your selection. It reveals the kind of educational background which we hope students will take away with them from Carleton College."

The 1950s and the Silent Generation

Carleton was good to me in a personal way, too. When I tried to negotiate a loan of three hundred dollars from the college to defray the cost of

travel expenses for my sister, who was matriculating at Carleton the following year, the dean said the college had never given a loan to a student
without his parents' guarantee. One of my professors came to my aid, offering in loco parentis to be a guarantor with the understanding that I would
repay the loan with the earnings from my summer job. (This was the reason that I so desperately needed a job at Ford.)

These were the days at Carleton. We were happy members of the "silent
generation" of the Eisenhower era. McCarthyism was already on the decline
and had no effect on us. We did not know that during the height of
McCarthyism, President Gould had been under immense pressure to dis-
miss a talented mathematician, Professor Kenneth O. May, who as a former member of the Communist Party had been called before the House
Un-American Activities Committee. But President Gould had held out and
had refused to fire Professor May. To be sure, there were rumblings in the
southern states about Japanese textile imports ("one-dollar blouse"), but
they did not reach Minnesota. As I said, I did not sense any rancor or racial
prejudice as the result of the Pacific War.

We were enjoying the "golden fifties." Perhaps we were smug and self-
satisfied: we accepted the given social covenants of the era. David Halberstam, in his *The Fifties,* wrote that underneath there was social ferment that
was to explode in the 1960s, but we were not aware of it. We celebrated
Pax Americana: the political, economic, and cultural primacy of America
was unquestioned.

Then, I remember vividly, on October 4, 1957, that we were shocked by
the news that the Russians had launched the world's first satellite, *Sputnik.*
The Americans had been beaten by the Russians in science and technology!
Questions were immediately asked about how and why higher education in
America had failed.[17] In retrospect, my four years at Carleton were divided
between pre-*Sputnik* and post-*Sputnik* years. Our complacency was over.

Honors Thesis and Graduation

During my senior year Professor Qualey encouraged me to write an honors thesis under his direction. I chose to write on the American occupation
policy toward Japan—perhaps a natural subject for a youth who had considered the occupation to be liberating. In the course of my research I
acquired a key policy paper from the State Department. I was the first one
to obtain a copy of this paper and this gave me a foretaste of archival

17. Robert A. Divine, *The Sputnik Challenge: Eisenhower's Response to the Soviet Satellite.*

research on the graduate level.[18] By this time I had decided to do graduate work in American history, more specifically in diplomatic history. The choice was perhaps influenced by having received the Grew scholarship as well as a Frank B. Kellogg tuition scholarship, which was named after a former secretary of state.

On June 9, 1958, I graduated from Carleton proudly wearing my Phi Beta Kappa key. On the occasion of my graduation, President Gould wrote me a personal letter:

> Just a little while ago I was talking with Professor Qualey and he spoke with great enthusiasm both of your comprehensive examination and of your honors thesis. Both belong in the realm of scholarly ambition and achievement. We are very sure that the promises of your achievement here at Carleton College will flower into a life of usefulness and service to you and your fellowmen.[19]

Going to Graduate School

The next step was graduate school. My parents wanted me to come back to Japan; four years was long enough. I could understand their concern. I was aware that Japan had undergone such momentous changes that if I stayed another four years in the States I would become a "Rip Van Winkle of the twentieth century."[20] But I strongly felt that my Carleton education, excellent as it was, needed to be complemented by graduate training in order to qualify myself as a college teacher. I explained to my parents that there was no outstanding scholar in my field in Japan under whom I could study and that I wanted to return to Japan with a solid graduate training and as an independent scholar. "If I were to find my life difficult because I had became too Americanized," I wrote my parents, "I hope I will have the strength to live with it for the rest of my life." "Clashes of two cultures will bring about sufferings that only those who actually experience them can understand."[21]

18. "Reforms of the Japanese Governmental System," SWNCC-228, January 7, 1946. This crucial document stated the State Department's view of constitutional reform.
19. Gould to Asada, May 30, 1958.
20. A recent study proposes that in order to avoid "reverse culture shock," foreign students "should return to their home countries for summer vacations at four-year intervals, at a minimum." A fine idea, but who is going to pay for it? See Clyde N. Austin, ed., *Cross-Cultural Reentry: A Book of Readings*.
21. Asada to parents, February 19, 1958; Asada to Grew Foundation, March 3, 1958.

Brave words, indeed, but when it came to applications for graduate fellowships, I was in a conundrum, for national and foundation fellowships were restricted to American citizens. My last hope was the Japan Society in New York, but its fellowship program was limited to those who already had positions in Japan. (Any assistance from home was out of the question, because in those days the yen could not be converted to the dollar.) So it was ironic that I, despite all my achievements at Carleton, was a man without a country when it came to resources for graduate study.[22] For the first time I came close to experiencing a culture shock. Nevertheless, I sent applications to Harvard, Yale, Columbia, Johns Hopkins, Chicago, Pennsylvania, Wisconsin, and Northwestern, all of which accepted me, but no fellowship was forthcoming. (It was a lean year for fellowships.) Finally, Yale came forward with a fellowship of twelve hundred dollars. This was hardly enough, so I appealed to the Grew Foundation for a loan of five hundred dollars.[23] Even then I knew that it would only last half a year, but I was determined to go to Yale. It was going to be "Yale or bust."[24] Yale would not abandon a promising student.

Yale and Sam Bemis

I had decided to study under Samuel Flagg Bemis, known as "the dean of American diplomatic history" and twice the winner of the Pulitzer prize (in history and biography). I shall forever be grateful to Sam Bemis for his instruction and many kindnesses. Bemis's graduate seminar, according to English diplomatic historian H. C. Allen, gave "the widest possible scope for the development of those spiritual successions, sometimes family like, sometimes almost dynastic, of teachers and pupils."[25]

Yes, he was a demanding teacher, but at age sixty-seven was somewhat mellowed. Rumor had it that he was much tougher when he was younger. Bemis's students would complain to the department chairman that his assignments were so heavy that they did not have time to study for other courses. The chairman would call Bemis in and tell him about the complaints, and Bemis would reply that he understood. Then in response he would *double* his students' assignments! The story was perhaps apocryphal but believable.

22. Milton Bierman to Asada, March 12, 1959.
23. Asada to Grew Foundation, May 30, 1958; Grew Foundation to Asada, August 1, 1958.
24. Asada to parents, August 2, 18, 1958.
25. Allen, "Samuel Flagg Bemis," 191–209.

From the beginning I came to know Bemis not as an aloof and august figure, as many did, but as a warm and sympathetic man and a good storyteller. In the words of Bemis's former students, Russell H. Bostert and John A. DeNovo, he was "without pretense, direct, relentless clarity of mind, unaffected honesty of purpose, the force of a New England conscience."[26] Shortly after the semester began I asked Bemis to autograph his majestic two-volume biography of John Quincy Adams,[27] and this is what he wrote: "With kind regards and friendly sentiment to *my fellow student* Sadao Asada." What master would call a mere first-year student a "fellow student"? As I enthusiastically reported to my parents, "For rigorous training, dry sense of humor, and affection for students, he will be the greatest scholar I shall encounter in my life."

I worked hard: my livelihood depended on my grades. For my midyear exam I unexpectedly received a score of ninety-nine. Bemis wrote the following comment on my blue book: "The only reason I didn't give you 100 (not given since 15 years ago) is that I fear it may make you ease up for the future! Bravo! SFB."[28] One day near the end of the year Sam Bemis came to me and asked whether I would like to work under him for an advanced degree. I was overjoyed.

That first year I also took a most stimulating historiography course, Literature of American History—History 180. Four star professors took turns lecturing and conducting seminars for this class: Edmund S. Morgan for the colonial period, David M. Potter for the nineteenth century, John M. Blum for the twentieth century, and Bemis, of course, for diplomatic history. Those were the days of the giants at Yale. Aside from class work, participants were required to write a substantial essay on one of the major historians or historical events. There was a little "contest" in this course: the student who wrote the best essay was to receive as a prize a book written that year by one of the four professors and would have the privilege of reading his essay at the last class session, with all four professors present. I wrote my essay on "American Historians and the Origins of the Pacific War" and to my surprise was the winner. As the prize I received Bemis's *Short History of American Foreign Policy and Diplomacy*, which had just come out in 1959.[29]

---

26. Bostert and DeNovo, "Samuel Flagg Bemis," 125.
27. See Bemis, *John Quincy Adams and the Foundations of American Foreign Policy;* and *John Quincy Adams and the Union.*
28. Blue books in author's possession, February 2, 1959.
29. Asada to parents, May 20, 1959.

I Was Saved by Yale

My first year was not without crisis, however. I lived in abject poverty and had to cut down on food expenses to one dollar a day. My Northfield friends, hearing I was in straits, sent me a check for fifty dollars as a New Year's gift.[30] I felt "homesick" for the family-like atmosphere at Carleton. As I had anticipated, my money ran out midyear. What else could I do but explain my predicament to the director of Graduate Studies. I was saved in the nick of time. On the spot he decided that the university should provide an additional stipend to carry me through the rest of the year, on the condition that I get a thorough checkup at the Yale–New Haven Hospital. I had hitherto thought of Yale as a cold, impersonal place, but I discovered it was a humane institution. From this time forward, I felt as if I belonged at Yale.

I spent the summer of 1959 in Northfield—or to be more precise at Bird House—where I could prepare for my German examination with the least distraction. A summer in Northfield emotionally recharged me.[31] During my first year in New Haven, I had lived alone in a rented room in the house of an old Russian widow, and had felt lonely and isolated. My fellow graduate students were so ferociously competitive—in a struggle for survival—that I formed few friendships. From my second year on, however, I began to receive more financial support from Yale and things began to look up for me.

Joy of Research and Meeting People

The research seminar with Sam Bemis during my second year was exciting. I decided to write my paper on the Washington Conference, on which there existed no recent study. In the spring term we were to go to Washington, D.C., to do archival and manuscript research. When Sam Bemis came to the capital, we joined him at the Cosmos Club for breakfast, and he talked to us about our research strategies.[32] He had connections with the navy department and wrote a strong letter of introduction to Rear Admiral Ernest M. Eller of the Office of Naval History, who specially made available to me some of the classified General Board records. My childhood

30. Asada to parents, February 2, 1959.
31. Asada to parents, August 13, 1959.
32. Asada to parents, December 15, 1959.

antimilitarism had given way to an interest in naval history, first in connection with Washington Conference.

In those days, Yale Graduate School was generous and granted us a travel
grant of four hundred dollars, and I scheduled my research trips to
Washington for the cherry blossom season. On one of those occasions in mid-
March 1960 Sam Bemis introduced me to his friend Stanley K. Hornbeck, long
of the State Department, where he had been chief of the Far Eastern Division
and then Far Eastern adviser to Secretary of State Cordell Hull. From what I
had read about him, I anticipated him being a gruff man, but I found him very
amiable. He not only allowed me to see portions of his personal papers in
his apartment, but upon learning that I was a Grew scholar, he telephoned
Ambassador Grew and took me to his handsome residence near Rock Creek
Park. I was happy to have the opportunity to thank my benefactor, who was
eighty at the time, in person.[33] During the months preceding Pearl Harbor,
Hornbeck in Washington and Grew in Tokyo had clashed over policy toward
Japan, but by 1960 they had reconciled. It was heartwarming to see these
two former ambassadors pleasantly chat about olden days. (I suspect that it
was the Committee of One Million, the anti-Communist Chinese lobby, that
had brought them together.)

Another memorable occasion was my visit, again with a letter of introduction from Sam Bemis, to Mrs. Theodore Roosevelt Jr. in late March 1960.
She invited me to her house ("Old Orchard") in Oyster Bay, Long Island,
to examine the papers and diary of her late husband who served as assistant secretary of the navy at the time of the Washington Conference. Since
I was not able to finish my research in one day, Mrs. Roosevelt invited me
to be an overnight guest. I fondly recall how I entered the world of the
Roosevelts, *pere et fils*. She showed me her old family albums and guided
me around her spacious house. On the walls of the large drawing room
hung the heads of stuffed lions and tigers. Pointing to a large tiger, I said I
presumed President Roosevelt had shot it on one of his African expeditions.
Mrs. Roosevelt, a most gracious lady, matter-of-factly replied that she had
shot the tiger. What I saw was upper-class society of the early twentieth
century that was rapidly vanishing.[34]

From Old Orchard, located on a small hill, there was a magnificent vista
of bays and inlets, and the house was surrounded by apple orchards and
dogwoods. Mrs. Roosevelt told me I must come back in May when the place
would be so lovely. Later she sent me her charming memoir, *Day before
Yesterday*, which was filled with tales of adventures all over the world. I was

33. Asada to parents, March 19, 1960; April 10, 1960.
34. Asada to parents, April 10, 1960.

saddened to hear she died shortly thereafter but felt grateful that I had been her houseguest at Old Orchard.

I was also busy with course work for other classes. I learned much from John Blum's seminar on twentieth-century America. He was still in his thirties, energetic, and brilliant. His command of the field was formidable. It was in his seminar that I wrote the prototype for the second essay in this volume, "Cherry Blossoms and the Yellow Peril." Americans' contacts with and images of Japan offer interesting cases of culture shocks. The interest in images and perceptions that I developed in Blum's seminar to this day colors practically all my writings on Japanese-American relations.[35]

In October 1962 a condensed version of my seminar research paper for Bemis's class was published in the *American Historical Review*.[36] This paper argued that the failure to reach a thorough agreement on the Manchurian question at the Washington Conference proved to be the seed of discord, but now I take a more positive view on the Japanese-American rapprochement, arguing that the convergence of mutual perceptions dispelled the culture shock on the part of the Japanese. This theme is developed in the fourth essay of the present volume, "Between the Old Diplomacy and the New, 1918–1922: The Washington System and the Origins of Japanese-American Rapprochement."

Work on Dissertation

Before I could complete my dissertation I had to cross one hurdle: the Yale history department had a policy that no fellowship would be forthcoming to fourth-year students; they would have to go out and teach, while completing their dissertations. One day Sam Bemis called me to his office and told me not to worry. If necessary, he said, he would talk to Mrs. Bemis and see what they could do to support me financially, for it was important for me to get the degree as soon as possible and return to Japan to teach.[37] I was deeply moved. Fortunately, as an exception, Yale gave me a Junior Sterling Fellowship, the best of all fellowships at Yale.

My dissertation topic was "Japan and the United States, 1914–1925"—a happy choice that was to launch me into a lifelong study of Japanese-American relations between the wars. During the final stage of completing my dissertation, Sam Bemis ordered me to telephone him every morning

---

35. See John Morton Blum, *A Life with History.*
36. Asada, "Japan's 'Special Interests' and the Washington Conference, 1921–1922."
37. Asada to parents, March 10, 1961.

at breakfast time, 8:00 a.m. sharp, to report on my progress. This was the only time he had "ordered" me to do anything. He was perhaps worried that I might break down under the pressure or that I would not finish the thesis in time. What other thesis adviser would go to such trouble?[38]

Decision to Return to Japan

After submitting my dissertation, I was appointed a postdoctoral fellow, and during this eight-month period, the thought crossed my mind of teaching in the United States. Robert Ferrell at Indiana University, who preceded me as a Bemis's student by twelve years, wrote me, "Should you decide, for any reason, to teach in this country for a while, do let me know. There are fine jobs floating around—Duke, Iowa, UCLA."[39] It was a tempting offer, but I felt I must return to Japan as Sam Bemis always expected me to.

The truth was that I had become so thoroughly Americanized that I was afraid of going back to Japan. I had spent one-third of my life in America, and during my nine years, I had not even made a single telephone call to my parents. My Japanese was getting very rusty; in fact, my language training had stopped at the high school level. And, most serious of all, I was not at all sure whether I could readjust to life in Japan, both professionally and personally.

But I felt that being afraid of going back was a negative, pusillanimous, and defeatist reason for remaining in America; I would always have a pang of conscience. So I made a promise with myself: I would do my best to stick it out in Japan for five years, and if I could not readjust, I could come back to America where I would start all over again. When I was getting mentally ready to return to Japan, Sam Bemis wrote my parents a letter with his characteristic kindness:

> Your son Sadao is one of the very best whom I have taught during a long lifetime of teaching. You must have missed him greatly during his eight years' absence in the United States. I wish to assure you that it has been well worth while for him. He has exhibited a fine character and earnest pursuit of learning. I am sure he has a notable career of scholarship ahead of him in his native country.[40]

I was to put to good use at a Japanese university all I had learned at Carleton and Yale. But which university? In Japan "connections" were important

38. Asada to parents, October 6, 1962.
39. Ferrell to Asada, January 22, 1962; Asada to parents, February 6, 1962.
40. Bemis to Mr. and Mrs. Asada, October 24, 1962.

in landing a teaching position. I happened to be a graduate of Doshisha High School, and when Doshisha University was trying to get an American studies program started, my name came up. Its Center for American Studies, recently established within the university, seemed a nice niche.

Back to Japan and Reverse Culture Shock

Upon reentering Japan in May 1963, I was overwhelmed by the shock of contrast with America: I found Japan to be overcrowded with great masses of people and narrow streets. The Japan I had left in 1954 had not completely recovered from the devastations of war; the Japan I came back to in 1963 was a prosperous country with a dizzily growing economy. It is too poignant to recount with what agonies I faced my "reverse culture shock," so I shall quote from some of my letters to Yale and Carleton mentors. In July 1963, a month and a half after I returned, I reported to Bemis:

> At least my "culture shock" of coming home has been eased by superficial Americanization very much in evidence in Japanese city life. But at a deeper level—I mean interpersonal relationships, family life, and the like—the traditional Japanese way has not changed much. My impetuousness, excitability, and impatience with the slow Japanese tempo have exposed me to the charge of being "Americanized."[41]

I was soon to learn that it was precisely these character traits that would antagonize my Japanese superiors. About my reverse culture shock, I found it easier to discuss personally with my Carleton mentor Qualey:

> As a specialist in immigration history, you will understand the kind of "culture shock" one goes through in returning to one's home country after nine long years in America. To confess the truth, during the first few months, it was like coming to a foreign country. . . . I was woefully out of touch with things Japanese, and I sometimes feel like a "stranger" in my own country. There are many things which I feel I can express only in English.[42]

I was particularly critical toward the university's "academic bureaucracy." Promotion was based strictly on seniority, and there was very little mobility. (The situation has somewhat improved since then.) This meant

41. Asada to Bemis, July 11, 1963.
42. Asada to Qualey, December 29, 1963.

that there were an amazing number of phonies among the "old guard." In July 1963 I wrote to Bemis somewhat contritely that "I have to learn to show reverence for seniority and ranks, rather than for ability and initiative."[43] But I found it extremely difficult to put this wisdom into practice. It was Professor Merrill Jensen of Wisconsin who advised me exactly on this point. An authority in the revolutionary era, he had become an old "Japan hand" after making frequent visits to Japan. He was very supportive. In June 1965 he wrote me a long letter in which he said,

> I had a conversation with an American friend of mine after I got back to Tokyo. He asked me if I knew you well enough to give you some advice. He admires you but he says that you made people "sore." As he said, you were right in what you proposed, and thought of the right things to do long before the "old boys" ever get around to thinking of them. This sort of thing is irritating and a young man has to be more tactful, has to make the old boys think they thought of the things first, and so on. . . . Believe me, I sympathize with you. Older Japanese professors are even more stuffy than older American professors, and I am all on the side of the younger ones.[44]

My alienation from the whole "system" was such that I could keep my mental balance only by citing Emily Dickinson on "Pardon my sanity in the world insane." I felt restless and rootless. Two years later on November 5, 1965, I was still writing to Qualey: "I have courted enormous unpopularity among my colleagues by being rather cocky and aggressive, and also by simply being a Yale Ph.D."[45] Rereading these letters, I can now understand why I was so unpopular. I did not even hide the feeling that the education and training I had received in America was superior to that of my Japanese colleagues.

A sociological study of Japanese returnees published in 1958 observes that they "frequently lack the ability to dissemble, to conceal . . . inclinations, or to maintain at least superficial conformity and this constitutes an affront to Japanese tradition."[46] There is no better description of my difficulties. But in my case the difficulties were compounded by the fact that I was trying not only to somehow reacculturate to Japanese life but also to retain my personal and professional commitment to America. In retrospect,

43. Asada to Bemis, July 11, 1963.
44. Jensen to Asada, June 30, 1965.
45. Asada to Qualey, November 5, 1965.
46. John W. Bennett, Herbert Passin, and Robert K. McKnight, *In Search of Identity: The Japanese Overseas Scholar in America and Japan*, 94.

I realize that when I set out for America at eighteen, I had not yet formed a firm self-identity as a Japanese and was taking a great risk. In fact, I was excited, even elated to leave Japan, whose future was under a cloud. Through my nine years at Carleton and Yale, I had gained my identification with America, and I had no intention of "de-Americanizing" myself.

To Build the "Best" American Studies Library

The position I landed at Doshisha University was not a regular teaching job but an administrative post, although I held semifaculty status. The official title given to me was executive secretary of the Center for American Studies. Even though I had understood that I would be "pretty free to run the center as I liked,"[47] it soon became obvious that I had no "executive" power whatsoever and that my status was at the level of a subinstructor. To be the lowest man on the totem pole was a humiliating experience for a newly minted Yale Ph.D. The whole situation was ironical, because I had expected Doshisha to be more "American" than most other Japanese universities. After all, its founder, Joseph Hardy Neesima, was the first Japanese to have graduated from a Western institution of higher learning (Amherst College); it had prided itself on the Doshisha-Amherst relationship; and more recently it was the locale of the Carleton-in-Japan program. Despite all these affiliations with America, I found Doshisha typically Japanese in many ways.

My first assignment at the Center for American Studies was to use up as soon as possible a huge grant from the Rockefeller Foundation to purchase books for the center's library. Here my experience with collecting books at Carleton helped. I spent most of my waking hours ordering books from America. I went on the book-buying splurge of my life. My ambition was to build the best Americana collection in Japan. Already in August 1964 I was proudly reporting to Bemis that the center's Americana collection was "the best-balanced and most comprehensive of its kind in Japan" with roughly nine thousand volumes of standard works.[48] A few years later a distinguished American historian visited the Center for American Studies and inspected our library holdings. He declared, "Upon my word! I shall be happy to appoint to full professor whoever collected this." Lest I embarrass him, I uncharacteristically kept silent: I held only an instructor rank.

47. Asada to parents, March 19, 1963.
48. Asada to Bemis, August 31, 1964.

(Today the center has the best research library, eighty thousand volumes and sizable microfilm and microfiche collections.)

Because I was so preoccupied with building the center's library and attending to my administrative duties, I published very little. So busy did I keep myself that before I knew it, I had survived my initial five years in Japan. During these years I often felt like going back to America. But I doggedly persisted. Japanese society sets great store on consensus and harmony, and rocking the boat is strictly a taboo. As Jensen advised, as the youngest member of the faculty, I had to restrain my Americanized self from speaking out or giving dissenting opinions. Frictions and conflict I often caused, but fortunately none proved fatal. Although it was a rough landing, I did land safely and that was the most important thing.

I already suggested that the Japanese university (as in most other professions) is gerontocratic. In a letter to Qualey I said, "Obviously I cannot reform the system now, but I tell myself that I should patiently wait for twenty years or so until I can attain some position of influence and power. I only hope that I shall never compromise myself, that I shall never lose my rebellious spirit until that time."[49] This last quoted sentence had an aggressive tone, which had never surfaced in my Carleton and Yale days. A psychologist would perhaps explain this as the result of my frustration, alienation, and marginalization.

I found solace in reading works on immigration history. As I wrote to Qualey, "To a large extent, I think, my experiences since my return to Japan have paralleled those of returned immigrants." I was particularly moved by Daniel I. Okimoto's *American in Disguise*, which poignantly recounted the story of a young nisei who came to study at a Japanese graduate school. I also was touched by the plight of returned Greek immigrants as revealed in Theodore Saloutos's *They Remembered America*. Oscar Handlin's classic *The Uprooted* showed that alienation experienced by the immigrant is shared by all men who move either in place or in culture. Reading books such as these were very helpful in relativizing my personal experiences.

My Struggle with the Japanese Language

When I began lecturing, I faced "language handicaps." It was not that I had "forgotten" the Japanese language; I had never been exposed to university-

49. Asada to Qualey, November 5, 1965.

level Japanese. The distance between vernacular Japanese and formal or academic Japanese is great. My first lecture was a disaster. Taking a lesson from this, I would type up my entire lecture in English and look up in the English-Japanese dictionary all the words I did not know in Japanese. I would lecture in Japanese from my English notes. I kept up this time-consuming practice for about seven years until I began to feel more or less confident about lecturing in Japanese. Writing learned articles for Japanese journals was even more arduous. The problem went deeper than mere language; I faced a cultural barrier. I had to acclimatize myself to the Japanese intellectual milieu before I could write anything relevant or significant.

My loneliness was relieved from time to time when distinguished American scholars came to lecture in Kyoto. I particularly enjoyed and benefited from my experience as an interpreter at the Kyoto American Studies Summer Seminar (we would like to think it the Asian counterpart of Salzburg), which was hosted by Doshisha and which met for two weeks every summer. Among the history lecturers were such luminaries as Clinton Rossiter, Merrill Jensen, Ralph Gabriel, John Higham, George Mowry, Edmund S. Morgan, Arthur S. Link, and Robert H. Ferrell. It was a great pleasure to get to know many of them personally.

Bemis Passes Away

In October 1971, when I was a visiting research fellow at Harvard's Charles Warren Center for Study in American History, I visited Sam Bemis in a nursing home in Bridgeport, Connecticut. He had had a stroke in December 1969, which left one leg and his right hand rather immobilized, but he was quite alert mentally. Unexpectedly Ralph Gabriel, Bemis's friend and former Yale colleague, also stopped by that day, and the three of us had a pleasant conversation. That was the last time I saw Bemis. I read in the *New York Times* that he had died on September 26, 1973. Robert Ferrell wrote a moving obituary. Norman Holmes Pearson, the chairman of Yale's American Studies, wrote me, "It was indeed sad to have Sam Bemis die, very much as though a generation had passed away with him."[50] Shortly thereafter I received an unexpected letter from Sam Bemis's son-in-law, Peter K. Bloch. He had been reading our correspondence and graciously sent me a note of appreciation and a copy of the obituary. In response to

---

50. Pearson to Asada, October 24, 1973.

my letter, Mrs. Bloch, Sam Bemis's daughter, wrote me, "Your letter explains why Asada is such a familiar name to us."[51]

Finally on the Right Track

In 1972 I moved to the political science department of Doshisha and shortly thereafter was promoted to professor. I was the youngest faculty member to attain this position. Relieved of the crushing administrative burden and now able to teach in my fields and build my own empire, I came to life. In Japan, diplomatic history is taught in the political science department. This setup has the advantage of combining the disciplines of history and political science or international relations. I immensely enjoyed giving a lecture course in diplomatic history and teaching two seminars in Japanese-American relations and Cold War history. However, I found that teaching seven courses—simultaneously—was a bit too much. From the beginning my seminars were famous among students, because of the amount of readings I assigned. This, I think, was in Bemis's tradition. Also, for seven years starting in 1972, I taught a lecture course in Japanese diplomatic history at Kyoto University, a prestigious institution. Now secure about my career and possessed of a permanent and satisfying role in Japanese society, I gradually began to recover from my reverse culture shock and came more and more to identify myself with Japan.

After several years of preparation I edited and translated a basic bibliographic-historiographical volume: *Japan and the World, 1853–1952: A Bibliographic Guide to Japanese Scholarship in Foreign Relations*, published by Columbia University Press in 1989. It was a big project for the Japan Association of International Relations, funded by the Japanese Ministry of Education and the Suntory Foundation. Editing it made me broadly familiar with the literature of Japanese diplomatic history. James Morley of Columbia University wrote that this book "represents one more important contribution by the Japanese to the building of global community of scholars."[52] I would like to think that it was in the tradition of Sam Bemis's great bibliography of another era, *Guide to the Diplomatic History of the United States, 1775–1921*. Robert Ferrell wrote, "Sam Bemis would have been proud

51. Peter Bloch to Asada, September 30, 1973; Asada to Bloch, October 3, 1973; Mrs. Peter K. Bloch to Asada, October 19, 1973.
52. Blurb in Asada, ed., *Japan and the World, 1853–1952: A Bibliographic Guide to Japanese Scholarship in Foreign Relations*.

of you. He was such a careful scholar that he did not drop things, make wrong citations as so may people have done."[53]

Naval History

My interest in naval history stemmed from my study of the origins of the Pacific War, which was essentially a naval war. But it was in connection with my dissertation that I first began my research in naval history. Any remnants of my boyhood antimilitarism had been wiped out as I studied Admiral Katō Tomosaburō, a navy minister (later prime minister), who successfully concluded the Washington naval treaty. To this day he remains my foremost naval hero. In the long run, the Japanese navy's road to Pearl Harbor can be studied in terms of mounting challenges to and eventual destruction of Katō's legacies.

The occasion to develop this thesis was provided by the now-historic Kawaguchiko Conference of 1969, organized by Hosoya Chihiro ("the dean of Japanese diplomatic history") and his American colleagues to cover the period 1931–1941. At this conference I presented a paper, "The Japanese Navy and the United States," which traced the naval origins of the Pacific War.[54] In revised form, it appears in this volume as "The Japanese Navy's Road to Pearl Harbor, 1931–1941."

In January 1976, Hosoya and his American counterpart organized the Kauai Island Conference on the history of Japanese-American relations during 1918–1931. This gave me an opportunity to do new research on the Washington, Geneva, and London conferences as well as on naval policy and strategy in the intervening years.[55] I was extraordinarily lucky to use a huge collection of official papers preserved by Enomoto Jūji (senior counselor to the Navy Ministry, expert on international law and naval limitation, and onetime professor at the Naval Staff College) who attended all the interwar naval conferences. I was allowed to examine these priceless documents at his house and learned much from my conversations with him. As far as the Japanese navy was concerned, I hold, the origins of the Pacific War can be traced back to the hostile, even violent, reaction of Japanese navy men to the Washington treaty.

53. Ferrell to Asada, March 29, 1988.
54. This essay originally appeared in Dorothy Borg and Shumpei Okamoto, eds., *Pearl Harbor as History: Japanese-American Relations, 1931–1941.*
55. Hosoya Chihiro and Saitō Makoto, eds., *Washinton taisei to Nichi-Bei kankei* [The Washington System and Japanese-American Relations].

In 1977 I published an anthology of Alfred Thayer Mahan for the "Classics in American Culture" series. Editing and translating his arcane and prolific writings was a formidable, but worthwhile, task: Mahan served as the starting point of my naval history.[56] It was also an exercise in transpacific intellectual history and is treated in "Alfred T. Mahan: Navalist, Imperialist, and Racist" in the present volume.

In Japan, where antimilitarism is strong, there are few academic colleagues whose focus is on naval history. My study of naval history was boosted by the visit of the great naval historian Arthur Marder, then working on his *Old Friends, New Enemies*. While he stayed in Kyoto, he befriended me, taught me much, and gave me invaluable advice on the Mahan anthology. He even recruited me to be a last-minute contributor to his Festschrift.[57] I continued to publish in naval history, contributing "Revolt against the Washington Treaty" to the *Naval War College Review* in 1993, for which I was awarded the Edward S. Miller prize from the president of that college. The same year I published "From Washington to London: The Imperial Japanese Navy and the Politics of Naval Limitation, 1921–1930" in *Diplomacy and Statecraft*.[58] This paper appears as the fifth essay in this volume.

These essays set the stage for a collection of monographic essays, *Ryōtaisenkan no Nichi-Bei kankei: Kaigun to seisaku kettei katei* [Japanese-American Relations between the Wars: Naval Policy and the Decision-Making Process], published in 1993 by the University of Tokyo Press. I dedicated the book to the memory of Sam Flagg Bemis. Quite unexpectedly it won the prestigious Yoshino Sakuzō prize. For the acceptance speech (and essay) I chose the title "Karuchā shokku no gaikōshi" [Culture Shock and Diplomatic History]. I explained how I studied naval strategy, the decision-making process, and transpacific racism from the perspective of culture shocks. I felt that perhaps my personal experience with culture shock, instead of being a handicap, could be a vantage point in analyzing cultural interactions. At long last I felt as if I had found my niche in Japanese academe, without having lost my Americanized self. I had worked out a modus vivendi in Japan relatively free of frustration and conflict.

For a dozen years, punctuated by bouts of health problems, I worked on Japanese-American naval relations during the period of 1890–1945 and finally in 2006 published *From Mahan to Pearl Harbor: The Imperial Japanese*

---

56. Asada, ed. and trans., *Arufureddo T. Mahan* [Alfred T. Mahan Anthology].

57. Gerald Jordan, ed., *Naval Warfare in the Twentieth Century, 1900–1945: Essays in Honour of Arthur Marder*, 141–66.

58. This essay was reprinted in Erik Goldstein and John Maurer, eds., *The Washington Conference, 1921–1922: Naval Rivalry, East Asian Stability, and the Road to Pearl Harbor*.

Navy and the United States. I would like to consider this my lifework, as summing up my research in naval history over the years.

Atomic Bomb Controversy

I have had a longstanding interest in the atomic bomb decision of August 1945. In 1953, Dr. Arthur Compton, a Nobel laureate in physics, visited and gave a talk at Doshisha High School, and in March 1955, he gave a lecture at Carleton. After the lecture I went to see him at the college's guest suite and badgered him with questions about the use of the atomic bomb, in whose development he had played an important part.

Since the mid-1960s I followed with dismay the rising influence of Gar Alperovitz's *Atomic Diplomacy: Hiroshima and Nagasaki, the Use of the Atomic Bomb and the American Confrontation with Soviet Power* in the United States as well as in Japan. With little supportive evidence, this "revisionist" work argued that the United States dropped the atomic bomb to intimidate the Soviet Union. Upon the fiftieth anniversary of Hiroshima and Nagasaki in 1995, I had a chance to present my research findings. On three separate occasions, I presented variations of a paper on "The Shock of the Atomic Bomb and Japan's Decision to Surrender": first, in June at the annual meeting of the Society for Historians of American Foreign Relations (SHAFR) at Annapolis, Maryland; second, in August at an international conference at Itō, Japan; and third, in October at the annual meeting of the Japan Association of International Relations in Hiroshima. I published the expanded version of my paper in the *Pacific Historical Review* in November 1998 and won the Louis Knott Koontz Memorial Award from the American Historical Association (PCB). By closely examining the shocks administered to Japan, I believe my article helped move the entire debate in a new direction. I was amused that the *New York Times* called me a "Japanese revisionist"—the Japanese "orthodoxy," of course, being the Alperovitz school of Cold War revisionism.[59]

In 2005 Tsuyoshi Hasegawa of the University of California, Santa Barbara published an ambitious monograph, *Racing the Enemy: Stalin, Truman, and the Surrender of Japan.* He claimed to have totally refuted my interpretations, and I responded by writing a critical review in the *Journal of Strategic Studies* in February 2006, which was followed by Hasegawa's rejoinder and my

59. *New York Times,* August 6 and 9, 1995.

response in June.[60] Hasegawa won the Robert H. Ferrell Book Prize of SHAFR, and for the Japanese edition, *Antō,* he was awarded the more prestigious Yomiuri-Yoshino Sakuzō Prize. I append the gist of my review essay in the addendum to "The Shock of the Atomic Bomb and Japan's Decision to Surrender—A Reconsideration."

For years I have been distressed by the widening gaps in perceptions regarding the atomic bomb decision between the Japanese and American people. The recognition of differences was sometimes such as to bring culture shocks to the Japanese. I initially presented my views on this subject at the Ninth Military History Symposium held at the United States Air Force Academy in Colorado Springs in 1980. Further research went into my "The Mushroom Cloud and National Psyches: Japanese and American Perceptions of the A-Bomb Decision," which was published in the *Journal of American-East Asian Relations* on the fiftieth anniversary of the bombings of Hiroshima and Nagasaki. My effort has been to help narrow the glaring gaps in mutual perceptions and clear the air for meaningful historical dialogue. An updated version of "The Mushroom Cloud and National Psyches," covering the period from 1945 to 2006, is the last essay in this volume. It expands on my "farewell lecture" given in January 2006 to mark the close of forty-three years of teaching at Doshisha.

Looking back on my life since 1954, I have often wondered whether I made the right choice in going to America at such a tender age; in returning to Japan; and finally, in coming to and staying at Doshisha. There were moments of doubt, but I am happy to say now that on all three scores I think I made the right choice. As I write this, the autographed photograph of Sam Bemis is looking over my shoulder. He used to say, "Take your own position and stick to your guns," and I am glad I did just that.

60. See *Journal of Strategic Studies* 29, no. 1 (February 2006): 169–71; 29, no. 3 (June 2006): 565–69.

Cherry Blossoms and the Yellow Peril

American Images of Japan during the 1920s

It is a curious fact that in the 1920s two altogether contradictory images of Japan existed in the United States. These images, which came into focus in the late nineteenth century, continue to the present writing. Both derived from the histories of Japan and the United States—and hence have historical explanations.

The first of these images was a romantic and exotic view of ancient Japan, a far-off island empire that was a fairyland of delicate gardens and paper lanterns. In contrast to this romanticized image was modern Japan, a "progressive" and industrial nation. During the nineteenth century Americans had taken pride in helping modernize Japan. With the Russo-Japanese War of 1904–1905, which suddenly revealed Japan's military and naval prowess, the West grew alarmed of this island nation, a reaction that can be understood in the context of culture shock. By 1920, Americans had two stereotyped images of Japan—cherry blossoms and the yellow peril.[1]

In the early 1920s, these contrasting images not only attracted attention but became controversial. Journal articles appeared with such titles as "The Riddle of Japan"; "Japanese Mystery"; "Ridiculous Stories about

Any early Japanese version of this essay appeared in *Doshisha Amerika kenkyū*, no. 2 (March 1965).

1. The most comprehensive theoretical formulation of image studies is Kenneth E. Boulding, *The Image: Knowledge in Life and Society*. Methodology of social psychology is fully utilized in Harold Isaacs, *Scratches on Our Minds: American Views of China and India*. It is regrettable that Isaacs did not include Japan in his study because there was a "balance of images" between China and Japan (Akira Iriye, ed., *Mutual Images: Essays in American-Japanese Relations*). I draw heavily on an approach developed in John H. Gleason, *Genesis of Russophobia in Great Britain: A Study in the Interaction of Policy and Opinion*.

Japan"; "Japan Real and Imaginary"; and "What the World Wants to Know about Japan." There was speculation as to what made Japan "the best written-up country in the world." Since behavioral science had not yet delved into studies of national character, such inquiries rarely went beyond facile generalizations.

Approaches to Image Studies

In this essay, we are not concerned with evaluating the veracity of image. The aim is to analyze the polarity by relating it, if possible, to the ambivalence felt by Americans of the 1920s—a fascinating period of transition, tensions, and conflicts.[2] The decade lends itself to such an approach. The problem of *national* images became more relevant during this decade that saw a phenomenal rise of mass media.[3] The taste for things Japanese, hitherto a cult among the educated few, became a vogue. During the first half of the decade, American magazines vied with one another to publish special Japan issues.[4]

The images of Japan during this period were particularly stable. The decade from the Washington Conference of 1921–1922 to the Manchurian crisis of 1931 was a tranquil period, with the exception of passage of the Immigration Act of 1924.

A clarification of what we mean by *image* may be in order. Beneath articulated "opinions" (crystallized in public utterances of policy and of media leaders) lie the firm substrata of amorphous, largely subconscious, and often contradictory images. Raw material for more formal views, these images constitute part of diverse stimuli that generate opinions. Thus viewed, the term *image* may be defined as a mirror of the collective experience of a people or a group that is reflected externally. National images serve to fill emotional and societal needs. People tend to project wishes and frustrations into images of far-off places, whether utopias or vicious caricatures. Examinations of American images of Japan can reveal America's own self-images, a segment of its intellectual history.[5]

2. See, in particular, William Leuchtenberg, *Perils of Prosperity, 1914–1932.*
3. Isaacs, *Scratches on Our Minds,* 381, 383, 390–91; Isaacs, "Sources of Images of Countries," in Melvin Small, ed., *Public Opinion and Historians: Interdisciplinary Perspectives* (comments by Athan Theoharis, 106–9). A classic analysis remains Walter Lippmann, *Public Opinion.*
4. From 1914 to 1926 subscriptions to newspapers increased from 28 million to 36 million. The circulation of national magazines multiplied (Frederick L. Allen, *Only Yesterday: An Informal History of the Nineteen Twenties,* 188–90).
5. Isaacs, *Scratches on Our Minds,* passim.

Formation of Images

Harold Isaacs, a journalist specializing in China turned behavioral scientist, maintains that all images are "shaped by the way they are seen, a matter of setting, timing, angle, lighting, distance."[6] We may start by tracing the origins of and the process through which images are formed, then analyze the sets of images and Americans' emotional responses. Finally, we can survey group attitudes toward Japan. How did images differ according to what each group saw in Japan—customers, hypothetical enemy, converts, or the objects of mere exoticism? The concluding part of the essay will explain, within the context of American social history, paradoxes in American images of Japan.

It is futile to isolate images in a given decade, for they embody the images of previous periods. To understand an adult's view of a country it is necessary to go back to half-understood childhood impressions. William E. Griffith, an "old Japan hand" still active in the 1920s, recalled watching Commodore Perry's flagship being launched in 1850 alongside his father's coal wharf in Philadelphia. To adults in the 1920s, those romantic days had not faded into a legend.[7] An exotic Japan, associated in their minds with paper fans and quaint dolls, formed a part of their childhood fancies.

Perhaps as much as any other factor, grade-school geography and world history textbooks stamped the earliest images on impressionable minds.[8] These schoolbooks exhausted the vocabulary of guidebook superlatives in painting "ancient Japan." "The whole country looks like a vast garden, with ponds of silvery-white water." The inhabitants, pupils learned, were all artists and poets. "Young men and maidens, old men and women, wander about through the cherry trees, and, inspired by the sight, write verses of poetry which they tie to the branches." Textbook writers raved about the perfect deportment of Japanese children. "Lit-tle chil-dren in Japan," a second-grade

---

6. Ibid., 390; Isaacs, "Some Concluding Remarks: The Turning Mirrors," in Iriye, ed., *Mutual Images*, 258–65.

7. Griffith, "Japan's Progress in Rebuilding an Empire," 682.

8. To trace formation of images held by adult Americans of the 1920s, I examined a number of geography and history schoolbooks. They include the following: Frank G. Carpenter, *Carpenter's Geographical Reader: Asia*; 15, 16, 26, 63; Arnold H. Guypt, *The Geographical Reader and Primer: A Series of Journeys Round the World*, 175; Ellsworth Huntington, *Asia: A Geography Reader*, 198, 219–20; Frank M. McMurray, *Third Book: Europe and Other Continents*, 407; Frank M. McMurray and A. E. Parkins, *Elementary Geography*, 278–79; Wilber Nichols, *Topics in Geography*, 156; Jacques W. Redway, *All around Asia: Redway's Geography Readers*, 182–83; Mary Cate Smith, *The World and Its People, Book 6: Life in Asia*, 181; and Ralph S. Tarr and Frank M. McMurray, *Third Book: Europe and Other Continents*, 407.

song went, "Are fearfully polite / They always thank their bread and milk [sic] / Before they take a bite." Japan was "the land of Little Children, where the Babies are the Kings."

Flowerlike children, tiny paper houses, and quaint toys drew grade-school children into the world of make-believe. Japan was a topsy-turvy land: the people there not only wrote backward but upside down. The strangeness made this country all the more "wonderful." It was the most "interesting," "delightful," and "charming" country in the world. Children must have been perplexed to be told that inhabitants of this fairy-tale Japan were at the same time "the Yankees of the Orient," noted for their "progressive spirit" and industrial achievements. Of the two images, that of a toyland was bound to leave deeper impressions on children's minds.[9]

Romantic impressions were strengthened by early contacts with things Japanese—dolls with queer, smooth faces, wrapped in bright red kimonos; grandmothers' fans and screens; picture postcards and stamps. Amy Lowell spent her early girlhood surrounded by Oriental objets d'art and books on Japan that her diplomat brother Percival sent home. "All through my childhood," she reminisced, these artifacts "made Japan so vivid to my imagination that I cannot realize that I have never been there." The literary historian Earl Miner has shown how Miss Lowell's poems during the 1910s and 1920s were rife with Japanese themes and similes.[10]

Children learned the stories of Marco Polo and the island of Zipang and how Columbus, hoping to get there, discovered America instead. When they turned to works of fiction, some were fascinated by Lafcadio Hearn's tales of ghostly Japan. Hearn went to Japan in 1890 and was later naturalized. He wrote about ancient Japan until his death in 1904. Because of his polished prose he had a greater effect on the popular American view of Japan than did any other writer. He has been called "one of the great romantic boosters of all that was Japanese." Basking in the mythical moonlight the Japanese people emerged as an embodiment of purer life, the ideal of self-sacrifice, and endless courtesies, and their ancestral land was a country of wonders where the very air was filled with semi-visible spirits.[11]

9. McMurray and Parkins, *Elementary Geography*, 219–20; Carpenter, *Carpenter's Geographical Reader: Asia*, 15; Redway, *All around Asia*, 182–83.

10. Miner, *The Japanese Tradition in British and American Literature*, 162.

11. Here we are discussing Hearn as an admirer of Japan's exotic charms and not as a writer. For in-depth studies of his intercultural experience, see Tsukishima Kenzo, *Rafukadio Hān no Nihonkan* [Hearn's View of Japan]; Makino Yoko, *Rafukadio Hān* [Hearn: Experiences of a Different Culture]; Ōta Yuzo, *Rafukadio Hān: Kyozo to jitsuzo* [Hearn: False and Real Images]; Sheila K. Johnson, *The Japanese through American Eyes*, 1.

Travelers sailed to the Orient with their minds full of such images, and tourists played a role in the formation of images of Japan. With more time and money to spare for travel, Americans visited Japan in increasing numbers: in the 1920s, some 55,364 Americans set off for Japan, and in 1929, travel to this country reached a peak of eighty-five hundred. Travel books and essays, which became the vogue, helped popularize Japan among Americans who did not travel.[12]

Exoticism and the "Inscrutable Oriental Mind"

Travelers' preconceptions about Japan, far from being changed by personal observations, were often reinforced. Visitors found none of the ties binding the Old World to the New—a common heritage and ancestral graves that pilgrims to Europe discovered. They found themselves steeped in a different milieu, the sensations of an alien culture. This quaint Japan was strangely familiar to Americans, for it was the ancient Japan of their childhood fancies. Paradoxically, Japan was a country whose unfamiliarity itself had become familiar.[13]

A sense of unreality ran through the advertisements of shipping and travel agencies. Japan was the island of mystic beauty, strange ceremonies, and sweet maidens dancing to melancholy tunes. "It's a dream come true to life, the Orient stepping out of a delicate and fascinating fan!" Not surprisingly, the traveler upon first setting foot in the country felt as if he had "somehow by mistake walked into a picture book, as Alice had walked into Looking-Glass Land." "The yellow little men" crowding the alleys "seemed to come from some dim void and have no earthy place and habitation." Neat little "paper houses" were dolls' houses "grown big enough for you to live in." The traveler had not yet awakened from his "long dream."[14]

As one tourist wrote, "And the women smiled, and the children smiled, and the cherry blossoms smiled through branches overhead, and the sun smiled through them, casting over the brown roadway and brown houses and brown people a lovely splattering of light and shadow." With such alluring sights and pleasant sounds and a pervasive fragrance, the sentimental pilgrim thought he must be touring "through a celestial suburb, toward the gates of paradise itself." Even the pragmatist philosopher John Dewey, who visited in 1919 to lecture at the University of Tokyo, confessed in a letter to

---

12. Robert S. Schwantes, *Japanese and Americans: A Century of Cultural Relations*, 9.
13. Melvin F. Talbot, "Thoughts on Leaving the Orient," 769.
14. *Missionary Herald* (January 1922), 18.

his daughter that he could not help feeling he was in "a semi-magic country."[15] Such descriptions, of course, were clichés in the late nineteenth century. In 1886, Henry Adams, who represented the best of the contemporary American intellect, referred to *Alice in Wonderland* when he wrote, "This is children's country. Men, Women, children all slipped from children's tales."[16] Earl Miner noted that Lafcadio Hearn "seems to have gone to Japan as if he expected to find a Utopia, and in any case wrote as if he had."[17] Interestingly, such stereotyped exoticism still colored American images during the 1920s.

One tourist, upon landing in Yokohama, made a list of things that were "topsy-turvy." He confessed his childhood fancy that on the other side of the globe everything must be upside down and inside out. Such a notion led to assumption that the Japanese "soul" was constitutionally different from the Occidental mind, that there was no way of penetrating the "inscrutable Oriental mind" that laughed when the Western mind wept and vice versa. A three-part adage about the Japanese said, "One, a smile; Two, a silence; Three, a mystery." Did not even Hearn admit that no westerner could understand the Japanese unless he learned to think like them, that is, to "think backward, to think upside down and inside out, to think in directions totally foreign to Aryan habit?" One wag wisecracked, "the man who says he understands the Japanese is very much like the absurd person who maintains that he understands women."[18]

Such assumptions made it difficult for devotees of exoticism to form relationships with the Japanese. Julian Street, a famed traveler of his day, wrote, "Never have I been so fascinated by a foreign land. Never in so short a time had I seen and heard so much that was new and strange. Yet never had my observations been so fragmentary, so puzzling." Isaac Marcosson of the *Saturday Evening Post* agreed with Hearn that "the longer you remain in the country, the less you know about what is really going on in the people's mind."[19] The travelers' "honeymoon" stage was over.

Whereas the tourist returned satisfied with Japan's charms, many Americans living in Japan—businessmen, journalists, and teachers—underwent "appalling experiences." Their expectations were so high and their

15. Dewey, "Odd Folks and Ways in Japan," 38–44; Dewey, *Letters from China and Japan,* 18; Kawanishi Susumu and Takita Yoshiko, eds. and trans., *Amerikajin no Nihonkan* [American Views on Japan], 207–30.

16. Elizabeth Stevenson, *Henry Adams: A Biography,* 190.

17. Ibid., 100; Ōkubo Toshiaki, ed., *Gaikokujun no mita Nihon, 3: Meiji* [Japan as Seen by Foreigners, Vol. 3: The Meiji Period], 8, 15; Miner, *Japanese Tradition in British and American Literature,* 64.

18. Ellery Sedgwick, "The Japanese Mystery," 289.

19. Street, *Mysterious Japan,* 48, 56–57, 63; Marcosson, "The Changing East," 26.

images so unrealistic that they were bound to be disillusioned by their contact with the Japanese people. The early enthusiasm of many American residents of Japan faded into frustration, giving way to irritation, distrust, and dislike. As the images of exotic Japan disappeared, the "inscrutable" Japanese came to the fore. One disappointed American averred, "Japan is sort of a mirage."[20] This was an instance of delayed culture shock.

American residents found themselves isolated from Japanese life by "a gulf of alien civilization." They admitted that the people of Japan were "nice," "kind," "hospitable," but that it was impossible to "be really pals with them." Temperamental differences—between Japanese "politeness" and reserve and American insistence on "frankness"—proved to be a barrier to personal relationships. "They never let themselves go." A pervading "sense of strain" made many an American feel ill at ease. One thought that the reason for this was that the Japanese completely lacked "expression of human feelings." Travelers' accounts seldom mention the warm, spontaneous intimacy that some Americans, such as the novelist Pearl Buck, found in relationships with the Chinese.[21]

Hugh Wilson, a counselor at the U.S. Embassy, wrote, "I know that comparison between the Chinese and Japanese is always to the disadvantage of the latter. I like the Chinese, too, they laugh when we laugh. . . . The Japanese are as different from the Chinese as black from white." The American naval attaché in Peking said he liked the Chinese because they knew their place; he despised the Japanese because they wanted to be treated as equals.[22] One embassy official observed that the Japanese were insincere, possessed "infinite self-respect," and were too tense. He observed that, to his surprise, irritation with and contempt for the Japanese was especially conspicuous among Americans who had spent years in Japan and could speak Japanese.[23]

---

20. Sydney Greenbie, *Japan, Real and Imaginary,* 16, 437; Joseph I. C. Clarke, *Japan at First Hand,* xix; L. S. Kirtland, *Samurai Trails: A Chronicle of Wanderings on the Japanese High Road,* 79–80; Harry Frank, *Glimpses of Japan and Formosa,* 8; Theodore Geoffrey, *An Immigrant in Japan,* 188; *Saturday Evening Post* (May 2, 1925), 21; William Irvine, "Hybrid Soul of Japan," 1054.

21. "Impressions of the Present Situation in Japan," *Papers Relating to the Pacific and the Far East: Papers for the American Delegation to the Washington Conference,* State Department Archives (hereafter cited as SDA), NA. George F. Kennan also suggested that a tendency to create "hazy and exalted dreams of intimacy particularly characterized American thought about the Chinese" ("The Future of Soviet Communism," 4).

22. Notes on talk with Miss Scidmore, Kyoto, May 7, 1920, in the Papers of Frank A. Vanderlip (file of the Japanese trip of 1920), Japan Society, New York.

23. Harry (?), Embassy of the United States, Tokyo, to William R. Castle Jr., April 18, 1924, William R. Castle Jr. Papers, Herbert Hoover Presidential Library (hereafter cited as Hoover Presidential Library), West Branch, Iowa; Hugh Wilson, *Diplomat between Wars,* 139; Isaacs, *Scratches on Our Minds,* 73, 148–64.

Even those Americans who were disappointed in their association with the Japanese nevertheless voiced admiration for Japanese culture, writing that Americans had much to learn. It was these praises that reached American readers and added to the romantic image. Divorced from a sense of human contact, this image was a highly abstract and intellectualized one. It was to this aesthetic Japan—a silhouette of fantasy and artistic beauty, not real people—that Americans showed a pale, platonic love. Perhaps it was no coincidence that during this period no realistic novel comparable to Pearl Buck's *The Good Earth* (1931) was written about the Japanese, to bring them to life for readers in America.

The above cluster of images called forth contradictory responses from Americans. One prevalent notion associated Japan with primitive simplicity. Americans found particularly admirable the art of living in harmony with nature. These joys of life seemed to be disappearing from the urban America in the machine age. Aversion to the "hideous urge we are pleased to term 'modern progress'" underlay the quest for the old Japan not yet spoiled by the "cruel civilization" of the West. In an idealized Japanese countryside the traveler and reader alike sought "the secret of composure." They felt as if they were in "some old, familiar place." Its symbol was the garden, and the image of the "Chrysanthemum Empire" and "Land of Cherry Blossoms" had an unusually powerful appeal.[24]

Another ingredient was Japan's artistic genius. In contrast to the notion of simplicity, this emphasized a refined, highly complex culture. In the opinion of one textbook writer the Japanese were "the most artistic" and therefore "the most highly civilized" people in the world. "Not since old Greece had Beauty been adored as by the Japanese." The diplomat Hugh Wilson wrote, "in no other race lies so deep-rooted a sense of the beautiful."[25] This aesthetic Japan assumed feminine attributes—delicacy, grace, and a fragility like beautiful porcelain. It was necessarily a peaceful Japan.

The other side of the coin stressed masculine characteristics. It was a Japan of the samurai tradition—of brutal force and iron will, hara-kiri and Mikado worship. Paradoxically, the distance separating the image of an aesthetic Japan and that of a warlike nation was not as great as might appear, for both images, devoid of human qualities, rested on the notions of a "mysterious Japan" and the "inscrutable Oriental mind." As such, it could turn into an object of fear and suspicion. When the images of primitive and sinister

24. Street, *Mysterious Japan*, 21–22; Clarke, *Japan at First Hand*, 70; Harvey Hervey, "The Heavenly City," 624–29; A. Adams Beck, "Unbroken Ways in South Japan," 272–74.
25. Wilson, *Diplomat between Wars*, 140.

Japanese merged with far-fetched notions about an industrialized Japan, the result was the nightmare of the yellow peril.[26]

The Genealogy of the Yellow Peril

A tendency among Americans to see Japan's modern transformation as a "miracle" stemmed from the assumption that Japan before Perry was an entirely primitive country. In little more than half a century Japan had "covered the whole span of Western history from the Middle Ages." Some felt that a kingdom "almost as remote and unusual as one might find on the moon" had stepped into the world spotlight as "one of the foremost progressive powers." This "seemingly impossible" metamorphosis struck Americans as almost a trick of Aladdin's lamp. Some saw Japan as an ancient country "rejuvenated" by a "magic kiss" bestowed by the young American republic.

Interestingly, it was frequently the same individuals who admired Japan's modern advance who felt that it was losing its ancient integrity as it aped Western ways. It was "a tragic disparagement of her own civilization." They regarded as "unfortunate" and "ominous" the signs that Japan was joining a "mad rush for wealth and business supremacy." At heart Americans were attached to the pretty isle in its native kimono.

Within the memory of men still alive, according to a popular view, the Japanese had developed from a primitive country into a twentieth-century nation on a par with the United States and Great Britain. Its people were "a busy, bustling, up-to-date folk getting more western everyday."[27] Against this background was a popular legend that vastly exaggerated Japan's industrial and mechanical efficiency, seeing something even superhuman in it. When linked with the notion of an ancient samurai tradition, this image conjured up the nightmare of the yellow peril. It depicted Japan as possessing all the superior force of the West: a modern fleet, a trained army, and an organizational capacity in government and industry. Manning these mechanisms was a people of iron will, bound by extraordinary unity, lacking in essential

26. Marcosson, "Changing East"; Carl Crow, *Japan and America: A Contrast*, 1; Montaville Flowers, *The Japanese Conquest of American Opinion*, 263. The only scholarly study on the subject is Richard Thompson's Ph.D. dissertation published as *The Yellow Peril, 1890–1924*.

27. Walter B. Pitkin, *Must We Fight Japan?* 46; *Survey* (September 1, 1925), 54; "Japan's Miraculous Commercial Rise," *Literary Digest* (January 7, 1922), 28; Stoddard, "The East Tucks in Its Shirt," 781.

humanity, and subject to primitive savagery. This imagery, which brought about a culture shock to many Americans, was typified in Walter Pitkin's much-talked-about book, *Must We Fight Japan?*[28]

Japanophobia reached a peak during the war scare of 1920–1921, but its symptoms could be observed throughout the 1920s. Outside of California, anti-Japanese sentiments were marked in the Hearst press. Boasting a circulation of 3.4 million, Hearst continued his nationwide campaign to broadcast his prejudices. His anti-Japanese crusade caused concern to editors. The *Literary Digest* decried this "hysterical agitation of phantom issues" and asked why there was "this perennial clamor that Japan is an enemy to be watched, distrusted, armed against and finally fought?" The *New Republic*, the *Nation*, the *Independent*, and the *Outlook* all editorialized on the danger of "Our War-Advertising Campaign." One editor condemned "the studied purpose of the race hatreds, naval ambitions and human greed to bring about a terrific conflict of two civilizations in the Pacific—a clash that might end civilization."[29]

When a newspaper printed a cartoon depicting the future of the white race enslaved by the yellow race, John Dewey was upset. He noted the surprising prevalence of vicious propaganda about a Japanese-American war in the near future. He feared the merging of an anti-Japanese war scare with the ideology of Anglo-Saxon superiority that showed signs of revival in America.[30] He also detected the influence of social Darwinism. For example, Walter Pitkin argued that underlying Japanese-American antagonism was the ruthless race of survival of the fittest, so any number of international agreements could not prevent a violent clash.[31]

The tone of alarmist writings may be gleaned from the titles of books in the early 1920s: *The New Japanese Peril* (Sidney Osborne); *The Japanese Invasion* (Jesse F. Steiner); *Must We Fight Japan?* (Pitkin); and *The Menace of Japan* (Frederick McCormick). These books painted Japan as a world ogre and "a menace, not alone to the United States, but to all civilization." The Japanese, the authors said, could do anything requiring skill and nerve and were "splendidly prepared" to attack the United States. "If we do not check this military

28. Pitkin, *Must We Fight Japan?* 49, 70, 84–86; Crow, *Japan and America*, 55; "Japan's Seventy Dazzling Years," *Literary Digest* (January 7, 1922), 23; Frank, *Glimpses of Japan and Formosa*, 123–24.

29. Ida M. Tarbell, "That War with Japan," 460; *Independent* (May 7, 1921), 481; "Squelching Japanese War Scare," *Literary Digest* (January 3, 1925), 3, 6; "Preparing War with Japan," *Nation* (May 27, 1925), 589.

30. Dewey, "Highly Colored White Lies," 229–30.

31. Pitkin, *Must We Fight Japan?* 346; Sidney Osborne, *The New Japanese Peril.*

colossus, our turn will come next."[32] "Here in the United States," a reporter wrote, "it is in the air. Wherever I have gone, I have met men who told me that they are going to be on the beach with a bomb in each hand for the first Jap who lands." Amory Blaine, the hero of F. Scott Fitzgerald's *This Side of Paradise*, would as a boy dream one of his favorite waking dreams before falling asleep—"the one about the Japanese invasion, when he was rewarded by being made the youngest general in the world."[33] In January 1925, Congressman Fred A. Britten of Illinois created a stir when he introduced a resolution in the House empowering the president to call a conference of white nations to discuss a defense against Japan. "Japan's open preparation for war is a reason why white peoples surrounding the Pacific Ocean should have a definite defense policy." The Tokyo *Asahi* warned that such a proposal "would ultimately lead to a racial war."[34] The Japanese government felt compelled to state "emphatically" that "it does not want or expect war with the United States" nor "is it preparing either in secret or overtly for war." R. P. Hobson, a retired naval captain, hero of the battle of Santiago in the Spanish-American War, and congressman from 1907 to 1915, was dubbed "our leading specialist of Japanese wars," energetically continuing his campaign in the Hearst press and jingoish magazines as well.

The Navy

American admirals painted the most horrendous picture of the Japanese enemy. Ever since 1906 the United States Navy had regarded Japan as its hypothetical enemy number one in its now-famous War Plan Orange ("Orange" being Japan's code name). War with Japan would occur over the Open Door in China, the "inflammable" issue of Japanese immigrants, and the exposed position of Hawaii and the Philippines.[35] Shortly after

32. "Behind the Dreadful Mask," *Sunset* (July 1920), 32; A. Hamilton Gibbs, "Moral Preparedness for the Next War," 10–13; Crow, *Japan and America*, 301–3; Frederick McCormick, *The Menace of Japan*, 346–47.
33. F. Scott Fitzgerald, *This Side of Paradise*, 24.
34. *Independent* (May 7, 1921); "Squelching Japanese War Scare," 3–4; Joseph C. Grew (acting secretary of state) to U.S. Embassy in Tokyo, December 19, 1924, 711.94/523A; Ambassador Edgar A. Bancroft's statement at the Japan-America Society, December 14, 1924, 711.94/531; Ambassador Bancroft to Secretary of State, December 24, 1924, 711.94/525, SDA, NA.
35. Folder 139, op-29, folder no. 4, War Portfolio, no. 2, Asiatic Station, January 1919; Folder 141, op-29, folder no. 6, War Portfolio, no. 3; General Board no. 425, serial no. 425, Strategic Survey of the Pacific, April 26, 1923, Records of the General Board, Modern Military Records (hereafter cited as Records, General Board), Record Group (hereafter

World War I, the U.S. Navy became convinced that the Japanese navy was preparing for war and "the final elimination of the white race from the Far East." On July 14, 1921, a few days *after* the United States sent Japan its invitation to the Washington Conference, Theodore Roosevelt Jr., the assistant secretary of the navy, wrote his wife, "Japan is preparing for war in time of peace more systematically than any other nation in modern history."[36]

In the 1920s the American navy conjured an elaborate picture of the yellow peril in Mahan's tradition. During an acute war scare of 1920–1922, the General Board, the navy's highest advisory body, and the War Plans Division prepared reports, from which it is possible to extract American admirals' Weltanschauung.[37] They saw in Japan a strategic, economic, political, ideological, and racial threat. Japan sought not only territorial expansion and domination of China but also control of East Asia and the Pacific. Unless the United States blocked Japan's march, it would emerge as a colossal power that would *"make the world safe for autocracy for a thousand years."* What seemed to alarm the admirals most was the specter of a gigantic racial conflict. Admirals feared that control and exploitation of Chinese resources and manpower would enable Japan to attain "unification of the yellow race," which would "sweep over the world," creating "a distinct race alignment between East and West." The "rising tide of color," advancing eastward over the Pacific, would threaten not only white supremacy but the security of the United States. This lurid image of yellow peril was a restatement of Alfred T. Mahan's nightmare about the clash of the Eastern and Western civilizations presented in his *Problem of Asia* and other works. Naval alarmists reflected more recent racist writers, Lothrop Stoddard being the most prominent.[38]

---

cited as RG) 45, NA. On the U.S. Navy's views of Japan, see Gerald E. Wheeler, *Prelude to Pearl Harbor: The United States Navy and the Far East, 1921–1931;* Edward S. Miller, *War Plan Orange: The U.S. Strategy to Defeat Japan, 1897–1945.*

36. Albert P. Niblack to the General Board, February 24, 1920, WA-5, Records, General Board, RG 45, NA; Theodore Roosevelt Jr. to Mrs. Roosevelt, July 14, 1921, Theodore Roosevelt Jr. Papers, LC.

37. Report of the General Board on Limitation of Armament, Memoranda for the use of the American delegation, no. 1 (Government Printing Office, 1921), 8–16, 24, a copy in the Charles Evans Hughes Papers (hereafter cited as Hughes Papers), LC; Folder 139, op-29, folder no. 4, War Portfolio no. 2, Asiatic Station, January 1919; The General Board and the Conference on the Limitation of Armament, 2; Director of War Plans C. S. Williams to Chief of Naval Operations, October 28, 1921, 500.A41a/145, folder 141, op-29, folder 6, War Portfolio no. 3, General Board no. 425, Strategic Survey of the Pacific, April 26, 1923, to Chief of Naval Operations, October 28, 1921, Records, General Board, RG 45, NA. Wheeler, "The United States Navy and the Japanese 'Enemy.'"

38. "The Blue-Orange Situation" (secret), lecture of Captain Reginald R. Belnap, 2, 3, 27; Stoddard, *The Rising Tide of Color against White World Supremacy,* 239, 308; William H. Gardiner, "America's Responsibility in the Far East," 88–89.

Supremely confident that they understood the "Oriental mind" best, naval officers contended that the only language the Japanese understood was force. The Japan they saw was a dictatorial nation controlled by the military. Admirals of the General Board attached special importance to differences between the two nations in their political institutions, education, ethics, and "psychological reflexes"; as long as such differences remained, they asserted, war was inevitable.

Even after the Washington Conference brought about naval limitation and stability in the Asia-Pacific area, American admirals did not discard their fear of war. True to Mahan's teaching, they believed that the Washington treaties left the nation exposed in the western Pacific in the face of an aggressive Japan. The 1922 and 1923 versions of the War Plan Orange continued to envisage "an offensive war, primarily naval, directed toward the isolation and harassment of Japan." In July 1923 the General Board defined the initial mission of the navy as "[establishment] at the earliest date [of] American sea power in the western Pacific in strength superior to that of Japan." It seemed as if the treaties had made no difference in the strategic outlook of the navy in the Pacific.[39]

On the heels of the Immigration Act of 1924 that strained relations with Japan, Hector C. Bywater, the most influential naval commentator of his day, published an audacious book entitled *The Great Pacific War: A History of the American-Japanese Campaign of 1931–1933*. A detailed month-by-month account of a hypothetical war, it uncannily predicted the war of 1941–1945. Although an Englishman, the author, an associate member of the United States Naval Institute, was better known in the United States than in his native country. He reflected, perhaps more accurately than any other commentator, the views of the United States Navy.[40]

American admirals kept warning about Japan's aggressive intentions. In 1924, Rear Admiral Bradley A. Fiske declared that "the Japanese and the Americans have taken attitudes that are irreconcilable [regarding the Immigration Act] and that such attitudes have usually preceded wars." He

39. Memorandum from Director of War Plans to Director of Naval Intelligence, "Japanese War Plans," February 17, 1923; Office of the Chief of Naval Operations, Memorandum for the Secretary of the Navy, "Strategic Survey of the Pacific," May 10, 1923, CNO-PD File 198–26, General Records of the Department of the Navy, 1798–1947 (hereafter cited as Records, Department of Navy), RG 80, NA.

40. Bywater, *The Great Pacific War*. He frequently contributed to Naval Institute *Proceedings*. According to the scenario of this book, Japan was to be defeated, Korea to attain independence, and the Sakhalin to become Russian territory, but there was a happy ending: Japan was to rise up from the ruins and establish a truly democratic government. The book was translated into Japanese and attracted considerable attention.

added, "We are prepared for [war] if it does come." Rear Admiral William K. Rodgers stated that Japan was bent on war with America. Secretary of the Navy Curtis D. Wilbur expressed his "belief that the last acts of the drama of civilization will occur in and around the Pacific Ocean." In December 1924, President Calvin Coolidge could not prevent a congressional investigation into the possibility of an "enemy" from Formosa taking the Philippines. In 1927, on the eve of the Geneva Naval Conference, the General Board stated that because Japan's goal was "political, commercial, and military domination of the Western Pacific," a basic clash of interests still existed that could lead to war.[41]

The admirals took for granted that the war with Japan would come over a contest for the China market, oblivious to the government's policy that the United States would never support the Open Door by force of arms.

Businessmen

A war with Japan to defend a limited economic stake in China was the last thing the American businessman desired. American business interests had earlier seen Japan as a commercial competitor and suspected its intention to drive American goods and capital out of Asia,[42] but by 1920 such views had given way to most cordial sentiments. Responding to unprecedented prosperity, trade with Japan rose sharply during the postwar decade, as did capital export to Japan. The 1920s witnessed a growing interest on the part of American bankers in joint Japanese-American enterprises in China. Despairing of China's seemingly interminable civil wars, they had come to see Japan as the "stabilizing force" in East Asia.[43]

Anxious for partnership with Japan, the bankers vigorously denounced war talk. The *Wall Street Journal* demanded that "If Japan went to war with this country, where would she get the money?" In any foreseeable future, the editor asserted, war "is unthinkable to the point of lunacy." Contrary to admirals who saw trade rivalry, businessmen believed that trade constituted "a bond of friendship" in an age when Japan was tied to the New York

41. *New York Times*, June 4, 1924, and September 20, 1924; *Army and Navy Journal*, June 7, 1924; Charles Beard and Mary Beard, "Our War Advertising Campaign," 322–23; Wheeler, "U.S. Navy and the Japanese 'Enemy,'" 65; Gerald E. Wheeler, *Admiral William Veazie Pratt, U.S. Navy,* 260.

42. Akira Iriye, "Japan as a Competitor, 1895–1917," in *Mutual Images,* 73–99.

43. *Commercial and Financial Chronicle* (April 1920), 1581; (November 27, 1920), 2089; Irving National Bank, *Trading with the Far East,* 160–71; *Nation's Business* (February 1929), 173.

money market and the steel grime of Pittsburgh and that the prosperity of thousands of Americans was linked with the functioning of Japan's business machine.[44]

Businessmen viewed Japan as "a great industrial nation" that had come "nearest to ourselves" and expressed admiration for this "progressive and powerful" nation that had proved such "an apt pupil" of the West. Indeed, Japan's "eagerness to learn all that is newest and best in any direction in the West and to adopt it" went far to establish the conviction that "this wonderful nation at the gateway of the East" was destined to play a leading role in the world of tomorrow.[45]

This "enlightened" Japan was a peace-loving Japan. By 1920 a habit of trusting Japan had developed among commercial and banking circles. After a business mission to Japan in the spring of 1920, Frank A. Vanderlip, the president of the National City Bank of New York and of the Japan Society of New York, concluded, "No nation is more ready for frank and friendly intercourse and for fair and honorable efforts to adjust difficulties." He said Japan had "a vital and legitimate interest" in the orderly development of China, Manchuria, and Mongolia so that it could secure from them the raw materials it needed.[46] American businessmen tended to identify Japan's "progress" with the rise of business classes in its national life. Since their contacts with the Japanese were mainly with big business and banks with a Western orientation, they tended to overestimate the "growing liberalism" of Japan: "Japan has a business party." The *Commercial and Financial Chronicle* editorialized, "Our task is to help and not to hinder, to cheer and not to distrust" Japan. In the businessman's view Japan had "moved on through a semi-democracy until she has reached the real rule of the people. . . . It is clear that Japan is to move steadily on the way of a trained and established democracy."[47]

44. "Japanese-American Economic Relations—Statement for the *Japan Advertiser*," Public Statements, Hoover Presidential Library. In the aftermath of the great Tokyo earthquake, Japan floated a large amount of loan in the United States for recovery funds. During this period American investment in the electric power industry was especially noticeable (Kaikoku Hyakunen Kinen Bunka Jigyō Kai, ed., *Nichi-Bei bunka kōshōshi, 2: Tsūshō sangyō hen* [History of Japanese-American Cultural Relations, vol. 2: Commerce and Industry]).

45. "Japanese Civilization" (editorial), *Commercial and Financial Chronicle* (August 16, 1924); (December 24, 1921), 2659; (September 8, 1923), 1057; (August 16, 1924), 742–43; and *Nation's Business* (September 1920), 80; (February 1929), 173; (April 1930), 102.

46. *Commercial and Financial Chronicle* (December 24, 1921), 2659–60; (September 8, 1923), 1057; (August 16, 1924), 742–44; and *Nation's Business* (September 1920), 80.

47. *Commercial and Financial Chronicle* (August 21, 1921), 736–37; *Nation's Business* (September 1923).

Liberal Intellectuals

American intellectuals drew an even brighter picture of a democratic Japan. Oswald Garrison Villard of the *Nation* hoped that before long Japan would become "one of the great strongholds of liberal ideas." Herbert Croly's *New Republic,* Hamilton Holt's *Outlook,* and Lyman Abbott's *Independent* all expressed similar sentiments.[48] "The cause of liberalism in Japan," an excited John Dewey reported during his visit to the Far East in 1919, "has taken a mighty forward step—so mighty as to be almost unbelievable." His articles in the *Dial* and *New Republic* reported every trace of liberalism and democracy in Japanese society.[49] He prophesied that Japan's democratization would make steady and speedy progress if the United States behaved. It was the responsibility of American intellectuals, then, to help their confreres in Japan through directly encouraging and through indirectly advancing the liberal cause at home.

Like businessmen, intellectuals assumed that a liberal Japan was a peace-loving Japan, a notion reinforced by their susceptibility to its artistic charms. They believed that the essence of the Japanese spirit was "love of nature, and of joyous simplicity of life"—the very antithesis of alleged militarism. Yet those intellectuals could not gloss Japan's aggressive foreign policy in the recent past. They often excused Japan by censoring the West. If Japan had indeed been militaristic, the argument went, it was the West that had "forced" militarism on it. Had the West not refused to treat Japan as an equal until it had built a strong army and navy? Japan was denounced for imitating Western imperialists. Even Dewey joined this argument:

> It was European imperialism that taught Japan that the only way in which it could be respected was to be strong in military and naval force. Not its art nor the exquisite courtesy of its people nor its eager curiosity gave Japan the rank of one of the Big Five at [the] Paris [Peace Conference]. Until the world puts less confidence in military force and deals out justice internationally on some other basis than command of force, the progress of democracy in Japan will be uncertain.[50]

48. Villard, "Japan—Enemy or Friend?" 309; *Outlook* (March 17, 1920), 747. *Outlook* and *Independent* were especially pronounced in their pro-Japanese inclination. Hamilton Holt had been decorated by the Japanese government with the order of Commander of the Sacred Treasure for having founded the Japan Society in New York. Ever since he first visited Japan in 1911, he had been an ardent champion of Japan, rationalizing its territorial aggrandizement "in terms which revealed the mind of the military rather than the pacifist" (Warren F. Kuehl, *Hamilton Holt: Journalist, Internationalist, Educator,* 101–2).
49. Jo Ann Boydston, ed., *John Dewey: The Middle Works, 1899–1924, Vol. 2: 1918–1919,* xvii; Dewey, "Japan and America," 502–3.
50. Boydston, ed., *John Dewey: The Middle Works,* 160; Paul Arthur Schilpp, ed., *The*

In the postwar wave of disillusionment following the "betrayal of Versailles," many intellectuals turned their backs on Wilsonian idealism and developed cynicism or a guilty conscience about what they called "American imperialism" and moral hypocrisy in foreign policy. They found an outlet for such emotions in passionate anti-imperialism.[51] As Charles A. Beard, a leading liberal spokesman, wrote, "Hard-boiled Tories who had rejoiced in trampling on the liberties of the Filipino, the Haitians, the Dominicans, the Nicaraguans and other wards of American marines, were visibly pained to see Japan holding a piece of territory [Shandong] belonging to the poor, dear Chinese." When Beard first visited Japan in 1922, he apparently experienced some sort of culture shock. As he recalled twenty-five years later, he received "such a strong impact" that he "became a different person. I have never been the same again." Although we do not know the precise nature of his culture shock, Beard from this time became markedly pro-Japanese.[52]

At times radicals appeared to be more wary of American imperialism than that of Japan. Herbert Croly warned that a victorious America "might seek compensation at China's expense as well as Japan's." Beard had no doubt that "the United States would master the trade of China if it took seven times twenty-one demands." Beard and Villard, refurbishing the old Progressive rhetoric, attacked the bogey of "dollar diplomacy." They wrote that "American traders and concessionaires" plotted to "conquer" the world, forcing commerce and spreading the benefit of American civilization—shiny bathtubs—along the Chinese Eastern Railway. These pacifists were convinced that if there were ever to be war between America and Japan, it must be a war of aggression by America.[53] In 1925 Beard wrote in the *Nation* an essay titled "War with Japan: What Shall We Get Out of It?" He visited Japan again in 1923 to advise the mayor of Tokyo, Gotō Shimpei, on municipal reforms and

Philosophy of John Dewey, 40; Nihon Dewey Gakkai [The Dewey Association of Japan], ed., *Dewey rai-Nichi 50-shūnen kinen ronbunshū: Dewey kenkyū* [Essays in Commemoration of the Fiftieth Anniversary of Dewey's Visit to Japan: Dewey Studies]; Kawanishi and Takita, eds. and trans., *American Views on Japan*, 206–30.

51. Warren I. Cohen, *The American Revisionists: The Lessons of Intervention in World War I*, chaps. 1, 2, and 4; Robert Endicott Osgood, *Ideals and Self-Interest in America's Foreign Relations: The Great Transformation of the Twentieth Century*, 307–32.

52. Charles A. Beard and Mary Beard, "Our View of Japanese-American Relationships," 189; Thomas C. Kennedy, *Charles A. Beard and American Foreign Policy*, 48–51.

53. Charles A. Beard, "The Issues of Pacific Policy," 189; *Nation* (May 25, 1925), 322; *Outlook* (March 17, 1920), 40; *Christian Century* (October 8, 1925), 42; Jabez T. Sunderland, *Rising Japan: Is She a Menace or a Comrade to Be Welcomed in the Fraternity of Nations?* 213.

rehabilitation after the great Tokyo earthquake of 1923.[54] He seemed to speak with an authority on Japan that Dewey lacked.

Missionaries

Missionaries went further than any other group in defending Japan. Although small in number—sixteen hundred in the 1920s[55]—they exercised a far from negligible influence on American images of Japan through church pamphlets, journals, and, of course, contributions at Sunday services. Missionaries were the only group to break down the cultural barrier. Their initial reaction was not much different: "Everything was topsy-turvy, so amusing. How comical the people looked—men in skirts, profuse bowings, accompanied by curious grunts, clogs for shoes, little self-important policemen, obsequious servants."[56] Even Reverend Sidney L. Gulick, who was to become a lifelong friend and defender of Japan, had felt this way upon first setting foot in the country in 1888 as a missionary from the American Board of Commissioners for Foreign Missions.

Missionaries were soon writing to friends and family back home. "How easy it is," exclaimed one missionary, "to make friends with the tired field laborers, boys, girls, men, women. . . . What a wonderful people! But then all people are wonderful when one loves them. But the Japanese are specially wonderful." Missionaries underscored the genuineness of the simple folk, "these eager, quick, responsible kindly people." Said one retired missionary, "There is no real difference in the inhabitants of the Orient and the Occident." They have the same hopes and fears, the same loves and hatreds, the same moral instincts.[57]

Missionaries became, in their own words, "unqualified and outspoken friends of Japan." They took pride in Japan's modern progress. William E. Griffith, who had rendered a notable service as an educational leader in the seedtime of Meiji Japan, had come to have "faith" in the Japanese. The *Missionary Herald* declared, "The Japanese have great capacity for good.

54. Beard, "War with Japan: What Shall We Get Out of It?" 312.
55. According to Sidney L. Gulick, there were 1,594 missionaries (495 of them men) in 1922 (Gulick, *The Winning of the Far East: A Study of the Christian Movement in China, Korea, and Japan,* 116).
56. Sidney L. Gulick, *The East and the West: A Study of Their Psychic and Cultural Characteristics,* 49.
57. *Missionary Herald* (November 1923), 498–99; (April 1924), 163; Rosamond H. Clark, "Getting Home," 29.

Large things are to be expected from them."[58] One missionary even declared that the ideals of the Japanese were "approaching more and more the ideals of America." One might wonder what need there was for missionaries in a country that, according to some of them, "was achieving a height in her ideals which places her side by side with the Western nations to a very remarkable extent."

Missionaries who had a long history of working in Japan had come to identify their own hopes with young Japan's national aspirations. Some even tended to see through Japanese eyes. The most prominent example was Sidney Gulick.[59] His twenty-five years in Japan had made him somewhat out of touch with public opinion in America.[60] To his countrymen the position he took as unofficial spokesman for Japan seemed excessively partisan. He had gone so far as to defend the notorious Twenty-One Demands Japan forced on China in 1915. In 1917 he reluctantly resigned his position at Doshisha University, where he was professor of theology, and returned to America, this time as a "missionary" from Japan to America. During the late 1910s and 1920s he threw himself into a campaign to "educate" the American public, especially with regard to the immigration question. "Japan's militarism was her response to the militarism of the West, which put the mailed fist above justice, reason and humanity."[61]

Many missionaries, however, had difficulty identifying with Gulick's pro-Japanese view. Much like the liberal intellectuals, they defended Japan by denouncing America's past sins. With a past including the Mexican War and the Spanish-American War, asked Griffith, "what American can throw stones at Japan?" As with other groups, missionaries' professional habits influenced their understanding of Japan. Believing that native Christians were "the best friends of America," missionaries advocated an "alliance" between Japanese and American Christians as a solution of "tremendous potency" for difficulties between the two nations. Overestimating Japanese

58. One missionary journal prepared the following question for the use of Sunday school lessons: "WHICH WAY DO *YOU* SPELL JAPAN?

"*Jealous Ambitious Proud Antagonistic Narrow*

"*Just Appreciative Powerful Artistic Noble*"

Griffith, "The Sorrow of a Non-Partisan," 369; Griffith (February 1924), 47, 76.

59. Senate Committee on Immigration, *Japanese Immigration Legislation*, 68th Cong., 1st sess., 1924, 82–84, 89. See Sandra C. Taylor, *Advocate of Understanding: Sidney Gulick and the Search for Peace with Japan*.

60. In addition to Japanese exclusionists, Gulick attacked Percival Lowell, Lafcadio Hearn, and "instant Japan experts" who exalted an exotic Japan.

61. Gulick, *Winning of the Far East*, 139.

Christians as a force for peace, missionaries oversimplified Japanese-American problems.[62]

Triumph of the Inscrutable Image

The above analysis has shown that group images formed through contacts with the Japanese and filtered through professional biases were distorted and one-sided. Commenting on polarized views of Japan, former secretary of state Robert Lansing wrote, "some of these enemies of Japan" said such "preposterous things" that he would think they were "mentally unbalanced but for their sanity on all other subjects."[63] On the other hand, passionate apologia for Japan gave rise to the charge of sinister Japanese propaganda controlled by Tokyo. Memoranda, prepared by the State Department for the American delegates to the Washington Conference, contained a paper on "Japanese propaganda" by East Asian specialists Nelson T. Johnson and Edwin Neville. It claimed that Tokyo was manipulating the "Japan lobby, consisting of church leaders, pacifists, dignitaries, and prominent intellectuals, to conduct large-scale propaganda."[64] An example of typical scare literature was Montaville Flowers's *The Japanese Conquest of American Opinion.*

Complaining about the split in opinion about Japan, Marcosson wrote that "The moment you mention Japan the words 'pro' and 'anti' rise up. There seems to be an unwritten law that everything written about the Island Empire must fall under one or these two heads."[65] This state of affairs reached its height during the controversy over the Immigration Act of 1924. The congressional hearings strayed to the question of Japanese national character: whether the Japanese were inassimilable as exclusionists claimed, or adaptable as pro-Japanese spokesmen insisted.

Interestingly, nearly every proponent of the theory of Japanese inassimilability expressed admiration for Japan and its "wonderful progress." This was in the tradition of Mahan, who, while admiring Japan's modern progress, also believed that "the Japanese racial characteristic could not be changed . . . in two generations, and for this reason Japanese immigrants

---

62. Editorial, *Missionary Herald* (January 1920), 4–5; Fred Smith, in *Christian Work* (February 18, 1922).

63. Lansing's memo, July 31, 1919, Robert Lansing Papers, LC.

64. "Japanese Propaganda," contained in the *Papers Relating to the Pacific and the Far East,* SDA, NA. To be sure, the Japanese Foreign Ministry was engaged in publicity activities, but they were far from being systematic propaganda that the State Department suspected.

65. Marcosson, "Changing East," 4; Griffith, "Sorrow of a Non-Partisan," 369.

remained inassimilable."[66] These ideas were reinforced by imagery of the "inscrutable Japanese" that was broadened into a nationwide stereotype. An exclusionist testified that all one needed to satisfy himself about inassimilability was to live in Japan and to try to enter into full fellowship with the native population. These words reflected the image popularized by travelers' accounts.[67]

The antiexclusionists weakened their case by overstating their defense of Japan. An ardent friend of Japan declared that the nation was "growing into the best of the world's best life today" through "continual bringing into her life of whatever is best in the Western world." Such rapturous outbursts tended to further alienate the Japanese exclusionists. In this sense, the Immigration Act represented a triumph of the exotic image without its romantic contents—mysterious, unchanging—over that of a progressive Japan.

To restore strained relations, in 1926 Gulick opened a campaign called Dolls of Friendship, a program to send American dolls to Japanese children as "messengers of friendship." In a letter to Shibusawa Eiichi, the grand old pro-American businessman, the enthusiastic Gulick wrote, "I believe this project will bring about a groundswell of sentiment among Americans in favor of amending the Immigration Act." Some twelve thousand dolls were ceremoniously presented in 1927 on the Doll's Festival Day (March 3), and Japanese children reciprocated by sending their dolls to America.[68] Gulick's naïve, if well-intentioned, endeavor to counter the yellow peril image with exchange of dolls was symbolic of the dual American image of Japan during 1920s.

Toward More Mature Images

In the 1920s there was a tendency among intellectuals to construct more sophisticated interpretations of Japan, a Japan in transition. Their approaches can be classified into four types. The first was a simple fascination with the isle of contrasts and contradictions. To bring together, in one picture, Japanese gardens and a modern battle fleet demanded a leap of imagination.

---

66. Mahan, *Letters and Papers of Alfred Thayer Mahan*, 3:688–92; Valentine Stuart McClatchy's statement, Senate Committee on Immigration, *Japanese Immigration Legislation*, 68th Cong., 1st sess., 1924, 4.

67. Ulysses S. Webb's statement in ibid., 40–41.

68. JMFA, *NGB: Shōwa jidai I* [Showa Period I], vol. 4, (1927–1931), pt. 2, 539–47; Shibusawa seien kinen zaidan ryūmonsha [Shibusawa Memorial Foundation], ed., *Shibusawa Eiichi denki shiryō* [Materials for a Biography of Shibusawa Eiichi], 616–17, 673; Taylor, *Advocate of Understanding*, 179–80.

For most observers this counterpoint of old and new did not go beyond amusement.[69] Second, American intellectuals responded to pro-American Japanese leaders such as Count Ōkuma Shigenobu, who idealized Japan as the "meeting ground" of East and West. According to this view, Japan was destined to be a bridge or mediator to bring together the two great civilizations. This cosmopolitan ideal, its earlier expression in the writings of Walt Whitman and Ernest Fenollossa, appealed to Americans.[70] The third view, the antithesis of this noble dream, held Japan's experiment to be a pathetic failure. Observers ridiculed the "hybrid soul of Japan" and chided the country for having lost its self-identity in ill-digested Westernism.[71] And fourth, there emerged a more mature view held by informed Americans that gave credit to Japan's progress but sympathetically understood its difficulties. Foremost among them, Dewey noted that no country could continue to adopt Western technological knowledge while clinging to antiquated social and political traditions. He maintained that "Japan shows everywhere the strains of [a deep] split in its life."[72]

Japan is trying, under the leadership of its present rulers, an impossible experiment. It recognizes its dependence on the West for material, technical, and scientific development, and welcomes the introduction of Western ideas and methods so far as they concern these things. But it is trying at the same time to preserve intact its own peculiar moral and political heritage; it is claiming superiority in these respects to anything the West can give it. . . . But no nation can enduringly live a double life; Japan shows everywhere the strain of this split in its life.[73]

Dewey continued, "One finds everywhere in Japan a feeling of uncertainty, hesitation, even of weakness. There is a subtle nervous tension in the atmosphere as of a country on the verge of change but not knowing where the change will take it."

Dewey urged that "America ought to feel sorry for Japan, or at least sympathetic with it, and not afraid. . . . It is very unfortunate for them [Japanese] that they have become a first-class power so rapidly and with so little prepa-

69. *Independent* (January 20, 1923), 43; *Nation* (December 22, 1926), 652; Ellery Sedgwick, "Made in Japan," 463.

70. *Independent* (December 24, 1921), 308; *Nation* (March 25, 1925), 309; Sunderland, *Rising Japan*, 4; Miner, *Japanese Tradition in British and American Literature*, 271; Lawrence W. Chisolm, *Fenollosa: The Far East and American Culture*.

71. Irvine, "Hybrid Soul of Japan," 1049: Greenbie, *Japan, Real and Imaginary*, 422.

72. Boydston, ed., *John Dewey: The Middle Works*, xix; Dewey, *Letters from China and Japan*, 80; Dewey, "Liberalism in Japan I," *Dial* (October 4, 1919), 285; Dewey, "Liberalism in Japan II," *Dial* (October 18, 1919), 334.

73. Boydston, ed., *John Dewey: The Middle Works*, 160–61.

ration in many ways; it is a terrible task for them to live up to their position and they may crash under the strain."[74]

Nelson T. Johnson, a seasoned diplomat in East Asia, wrote in a similar vein, "I cannot see how such a people can meet the conditions of thought now current throughout the world without something in the nature of a crashing occurring. . . . Anything is possible [in Japan] in the next ten or twenty years."[75]

Such insights were rare, however, during the 1920s. The majority of Americans continued either to praise Japan to the sky or to denounce it roundly. Japan remained an ephemeral fantasy, an intellectual abstraction, or an object for hysteria. The popular American images of Japan underwent little significant change as the decade drew to a close.

Conclusion: External Image as Self-Image

How can we account for the fact that American images clung so tenaciously to the notion of "ancient Japan" at a time of rapid industrialization? How can we explain the recurrence of war scares during a decade of tranquility? What were the impulses that underlay the ambivalence of American reaction to Japan's "modern progress"? And how can we interpret the remarkable interest shown in far-off Japan during a decade characterized by what one American historian has called "the isolationist impulse"?[76]

One answer is that American images were conditioned, if not determined, by the ways in which adults of this period reacted to rapid changes that took place during their lifetimes. Within the life span of Americans, Japan had transformed itself from a semilegendary kingdom into one of the foremost twentieth-century powers. The speed of this "almost incredible" transformation seemed to symbolize the "dazzling" tempo of the modern era. The ethos of the 1920s was caught in the following passage that appeared in *Contemporary Review* in 1927:

> For anyone born, as I was, before Japan actually came on the map of the modern world and when her people were still cut off by draconic laws and penalties from intercourse of any kind with foreign nations, few things seem to illustrate more vividly the ceaseless tide of change which sweeps the human race along on the current of time.[77]

74. Ibid., 174.
75. Nelson T. Johnson to Charles MacVeagh, June 24, 1926; Johnson to John V. A. MacMurray, January 15, 1925, Nelson T. Johnson Papers, LC.
76. Selig Adler, *The Isolationist Impulse: Its Twentieth-Century Reaction.*
77. "Japan in World History," *Contemporary Review* (September 1927), 296.

"I am not completely gray, yet Japan as we know it is hardly older than I," one American mused.[78] The photographer Alfred Stieglitz remarked that there was a new generation every five years.[79] The pace of change seemed to require a totally new conception of time.

Some Americans felt that the technological revolution of their era would destroy their comfortable living. If they exaggerated and dreaded Japan's mechanical efficiency, it was perhaps because this industrial image seemed to forecast the brave new world of tomorrow, a dehumanized world of the machine and the robot. (The word *robot* was coined and popularized by the Czech dramatist Karel Capek in 1923, in his attack on technological and material excesses.) It was with a sense of longing that the people of the 1920s cherished the image of old Japan, the Japan of childhood fancies. This image accorded with nostalgia for an earlier, rural America. The romantic images reflected the yearning to recapture the resemblance of things past.[80]

An element in American imagery was a desire to escape not only to the golden past but to the realm of exoticism. Alienated by a drab "materialistic Eden," intellectuals and artists felt that a coldly mechanistic civilization was stifling creativity, imagination, estheticism, and life force itself. Behind America's interest in Japan perhaps lay the same sort of impulse that took expatriate writers to the Left Bank of Paris or drew painters to the primitive arts of Mexico or the Congo. That such an impulse was by no means confined to intellectuals is apparent. A popular song titled "Japanese Sandman" went,

Here is the Japanese Sandman
    Sneaking with the dew,
Just an old second-hand man
    He'll buy your old day for you.[81]

This tune expressed a craving for childhood. For those Americans weary of the hurry and fret of the feverish era, Japan was perhaps their hearts' desire.

The present-day historian Charles E. Neu in an essay on "American Diplomats in East Asia" has shown that a similar nostalgia and exotic

78. Sedgwick, "Japanese Mystery," 293.
79. Cited in Leuchtenberg, *Perils of Prosperity,* 11.
80. Henry May, ed., *The Discontent of the Intellectuals: A Problem of the Twenties;* George E. Mowry, ed., *The Twenties: Fords, Flappers, and Fanatics;* Frederick J. Hoffman, *The 1920s: American Writing in the Postwar Decade;* Harold Stearns, ed., *Civilization in the United States: An Inquiry by Twenty Americans,* vii.
81. In fairy tales or folklore, the Sandman (also called dustman) puts sand in the eyes of children to make them sleepy. The song is quoted twice in Mark Sullivan's popular chronicle, *Our Times: The Twenties,* and also mentioned in Allen's informal account of the 1920s, *Only Yesterday.* (The song is said to have sold three and a half million copies.)

impulse informed diplomats' image of China.[82] This was not a uniquely American reaction. "Our Western world is weary," wrote a German, Serich Everth, in an article entitled "Asia as a Teacher."

> Our Western world is weary of strife and hatred. Indeed, our peculiar society and civilization have been found wanting. . . . Men are looking to the East unconsciously, and therefore sincerely. . . . The World of Asia draws us with its promise of something new and something that will liberate.

Extending dual images to later periods, cultural anthropologist Sheila K. Johnson has observed that "a set of contrasting images have appeared repeatedly, and they concurrently coexist in the minds of the American people—sometimes in the mind of one individual."[83] During the Pacific War, as John W. Dower has shown, American views of Japan were dominated by racial hatred, harking back to the old yellow peril of the 1920s that emphasized barbaric, savage, bloodthirsty, and inhuman aspects.[84] An effort to understand Japan in terms of dual image was typified in a wartime study of Japanese national character by the cultural anthropologist Ruth Benedict, *The Chrysanthemum and the Sword: Patterns of Japanese Culture.*

In the postwar period, as George Kennan wrote, Americans and Japanese were thrown into "a species of intimacy." "I am not speaking of love and admiration. Such things . . . have no place in the real lives of nations. I am speaking of something much deeper: a common recognition that fate—or, if you will, the mistakes of earlier generations—has thrown us in each other's path."[85] Such "intimacy" in Realpolitik was accompanied, on a popular level, by the revival of the romantic, exotic, and aesthetic images of Japan, best represented by James Michener's best seller *Sayonara.* In 1980 the enormously popular TV drama *Shōgun* displayed the scenes of hara-kiri as well as artistic images.

All this changed with trade conflict. In the mid-1980s, well-known journalist Theodore White warned Americans about "the Danger from Japan," once again giving currency to Japanophobia tinged with racism reminiscent of old yellow peril and Pacific War images.[86] "Economic invasion," "trade war," and "war by other means" became clichés in the American mass media.

---

82. Neu, "Higashi Ajia ni okero Amerika gaikōkan," in Hosoya and Saitō, eds., *Washinton taisei to Nichi-Bei kankei,* 214–57.

83. Johnson, *The Japanese through American Eyes,* traces American images from 1941 to 1988 by analyzing American best sellers about Japan.

84. Dower, *War without Mercy: Race and Power in the Pacific War.*

85. Kennan, *The Cloud of Danger: Some Current Problems of American Foreign Policy,* 109.

86. White, "The Danger from Japan," 18–23.

The Pearl Harbor metaphor was much in evidence. When Sony bought out Columbia Pictures, *Newsweek* (October 9, 1989) dramatically announced on its cover "Japan Moves into Hollywood," indicating the threat had become cultural as well.[87] In fact, American images of Japan became so hostile that Ambassador Michael Armacost felt compelled to warn in April 1992 that "Japan bashing" had become "increasingly ugly" and brought about a crisis. The writings of the so-called revisionists who thrived in such a climate seemed to be throwbacks to the old images of the "inscrutable Japanese." Karel van Wolferen, a Dutch journalist who voiced American views, characteristically titled his critical book *The Enigma of Japanese Power: People and Politics in a Stateless Nation*. A book sensationally titled *The Coming War with Japan*, by George Friedman and Meredith LeBard, which was translated into Japanese, became for a short while a best seller, reminding the reader of war-scare literature of the 1920s. The new yellow peril proved transitory, but to this day, as the sociologist Nathan Glazer points out, no one best seller has yet appeared, fiction or nonfiction, that has shaped American popular images on contemporary Japan.[88] The Japan experience and the difficulty of human contacts, reminiscent of the 1920s, still persist.[89]

American images of Japan are still characterized by radical paradoxes, traditionalism and modernity. On the one hand, the ancient image survives in popular culture as the recent film *The Last Samurai* testifies. On the other hand, Japan seems to be quietly gaining global cultural influence as manifested in ubiquitous consumer electronics, fashion, animation, and cuisine.

Ever since the days of Commodore Perry and Townsend Harris, American images of Japan have unfolded like a kaleidoscope. The same can be said about Japanese images of America. During the 1920s there were certain parallels: Japan was also undergoing rapid industrialization, urbanization, and a flowering of mass culture and showed unusual interest in the Model T and New York's skyscrapers. It goes without saying that obsolete and oversimplified images must be straightened in coping with the world undergoing a sea change. For this purpose, it will be first necessary to understand how our images of the external world are formed, how they satisfy our emotional needs, and how they affect our thoughts and behaviors. In the final analysis, these are questions of self-image and self-recognition.

---

87. Ishii Osamu, "Pāru hābā no zanzō: Nichi-bei no keizai, shakai, bunka masatsu, 1982–1992" [The Remnants of Pearl Harbor Image: Economic, Social, and Cultural Frictions between Japan and the United States], 52–70.
88. Glazer, "From Ruth Benedict to Herman Kahn: The Postwar Japanese Image in the American Mind," 152; Ronald Bell, ed., *The Japan Experience*.
89. Bell, ed., *The Japan Experience*.

Alfred T. Mahan

Navalist, Imperialist, and Racist

The Birth of an International Classic

No book has been so extravagantly acclaimed as an instant international classic in the United States, Britain, Germany, and Japan as Alfred Thayer Mahan's *The Influence of Sea Power upon History, 1660–1783*.[1] Overnight its publication transformed an obscure naval officer into a world authority on naval and international affairs. On May 12, 1890, Theodore Roosevelt wrote to Captain Mahan, "During the last two days I have spent half of my time, busy as I am, in reading your book. . . . It is a very good book—admirable; and I am greatly in error if it does not become a naval classic."[2]

The book also caused a sensation among foreign leaders precisely because it was a timely publication that met their respective political needs. The British Admiralty, augmenting the building program of 1889, welcomed Mahan's forceful exposition of the importance of sea power.[3] In Germany, Kaiser William II, who was about to launch on overseas career, wrote that he was "just now not reading but devouring Captain Mahan's book and am trying to learn it by heart. It is a first-class book and classical in all points."

An early Japanese version of this essay was published as "Nichi-bei Kankei no naka no Mahan," in *Ryōtaisenkan no Nichi-Bei kankei*. It is adapted by permission of the Tokyo University Press.

1. Peter Karsten, "The Nature of 'Influence': Roosevelt, Mahan, and the Concept of Sea Power," 585–600.

2. Roosevelt, *Letters of Theodore Roosevelt*, 1:221–22.

3. William D. Puleston, *Mahan: The Life and Work of Captain Alfred Thayer Mahan, U.S.N.*, 145, 154–60.

Recently lured to the sea, the young kaiser was determined to lay the foundations of a great navy, a navy that could challenge British sea supremacy.[4]

Japanese leaders responded to Mahan's work with equal alacrity. Baron Kaneko Kentarō, the former minister of agriculture and commerce, who happened to be in the United States on a fact-finding tour, hastened to peruse it. A graduate of Harvard Law School, Kaneko was a leading Westernizer and importer of American ideas to Japan. He immediately recognized the universal implications of Mahan's sea power doctrine. In the apt words of naval historian Roger Dingman, "it brought to him something akin to a burst of Zen enlightenment."[5] In our context, it may be said to have constituted a culture shock.

Upon his return to Japan, Kaneko had the book's introduction and the first chapter translated, and he showed them to Navy Minister Saigō Tsugumich. When the complete translation came out in 1896, from the Oriental Association in Tokyo, the publisher enthusiastically wrote Mahan that "several thousand volumes were sold in a day or two" and that the Naval and Army Staff Colleges later adopted it as their textbook.[6] Mahan later recollected with pleasure, "[My] theme brought me into pleasant correspondence with several Japanese officials and translators, than whom none, as far as known to me, have shown closer or more interested attention to the general subject."[7]

Mahan also noted that more of his works were translated into Japanese than into any other language. In 1899 he wrote to Minakami Umehiko, the translator of *The Interest of America in Sea Power, Present and Future* (published, significantly, under the title of "On the Sea Power in the Pacific"), "I trust that your undertaking may promote the interest of the Japanese nation in the subject, and so may advance Japan farther in that career of national development, in which she has already made such remarkable progress."[8]

What Mahan did not realize at the time was that the Japanese were quick to appropriate his messages to enhance their own sea power, which would one day come to clash with that of the United States. In the preface to the Japanese translation of *Influence of Sea Power*, Soejima Taneomi, an influential member of the Privy Council, declared, "Japan is a sea power. Japanese leaders must carefully study Mahan's doctrines to secure command of the

4. Poultney Begelow to Mahan, April 12, 1897, A. T. Mahan Papers (hereafter cited as Mahan Papers), LC.

5. Dingman, "Japan and Mahan," 50.

6. Oriental Association to Mahan, April 1, 1897, Mahan Papers, LC. This association had as its officials some of the leading members of Japanese political and economic circles.

7. Mahan, *From Sail to Steam: Recollections of Naval Life*, 303.

8. In all, five of Mahan's books and an anthology have been translated into Japanese.

sea; Japan would then be able to control the commerce and navigation in the Pacific and gain sufficient power to defeat any enemy." Later, in his introduction to Mahan's *Interest of America in Sea Power,* Kaneko proclaimed, "The Japanese empire is the foremost sea power in the Pacific." Like Soejima, he urged that Japanese leaders must obtain the key to command of the sea by assiduously studying Mahan's writings. Ironically, while Mahan expressed pleasure with the attention given to his books in Japan, some Americans (Mahan himself included) were beginning to perceive a menace in a modernized and expanding Japan.

This essay will discuss (1) Mahan's firsthand impressions of Japan; (2) his doctrine of sea power; (3) his views on expansion into the Pacific and East Asia; (4) his yellow peril notion; and (5) Mahan's influence on the Imperial Japanese Navy.

Mahan's First Impressions of Japan: "Love at First Sight"

Mahan's early career showed little promise. It was not as a fighting admiral or even as a competent captain that he was to distinguish himself. Yet in all fairness it must be admitted that he had more than his share of overseas experiences. Of particular interest for our purpose was his cruise to Japan in 1867 on board the steamship USS *Iroquois* when he was twenty-seven years old. It was sheer curiosity and love of adventure that compelled a young Mahan.

The *Iroquois* stayed in Japanese waters for more than one year, protecting American interests and lives in the newly opened treaty ports. In his letters to his family and friends, Mahan vividly described his impressions of Hiogo (Kobe) and Osaka—cities that were in political turmoil following the opening of Japan. He vaguely understood the "revolutionary transition" taking place in Japan; its farseeing leaders realized there was no choice but to "develop the nation to equality with foreigners in material resources."[9]

When conditions eased and he was allowed to go ashore, Mahan found the Japanese people "perfectly civil and respectful." He enjoyed long hikes in the mountains near Kobe and rhapsodized, "The country is more beautiful than anything in our own land." Naval lore had it that the valley Mahan "discovered" came to be known as "Mahan's Valley" to subsequent naval visitors. In his memoirs written some forty years later, he expressed concern that modernization would wipe out the charms of his favorite valley. "If the march of improvement has changed that valley, Japan deserves to be beaten in her

9. Mahan, *From Sail to Steam,* 243–47, 254.

next war." Some reason for "beating" Japan![10] The young Mahan also took an instant liking to the Japanese. "All agree in representing the people as amicable and good-natured to the utmost." He wrote about the "smiling affability characteristic of all classes in Japan." Mahan's general impression of Japan, viewed from the cultural "distance," was "very pretty, like a stage scene."[11]

These idyllic impressions are interesting in light of ambivalent images of Japan that came to dominate his views after the 1890s: a favorable view of Japanese culture and the Japanese people, and the yellow peril notion about Japanese expansionism in the Pacific and immigration to the United States. As the modern Mahan biographer Robert Seager II has written, Mahan's experiences on board the *Iroquois* "led him, for the rest of his life, to fancy himself as a leading authority on Japanese history and American-Japanese relations."[12]

Gospel of Sea Power

In 1885 President Stephen B. Luce of the newly established Naval War College invited Mahan to teach naval history and strategy. His lectures on the rise and fall of sea powers resulted in *The Influence of Sea Power upon History* in 1890. This work's central theme was how England, through sea power, attained its hegemonic position. The lesson for the United States was obvious: "The United States is to all intents an insular power, like Great Britain." This dramatic conceptualization of the United States as one huge island washed by the Atlantic and the Pacific was to become central to his philosophy of sea power. Like Britain, the United States must have an offensive navy and colonies.[13]

It is necessary at this point to summarize salient points of Mahan's sea power doctrine that would come to influence and dominate Japan's strategic thought. Roughly, Mahan's thought fell under two rubrics: a theory of naval strategy, pure and simple, and a theory of commercial expansion backed by sea power.[14] When these two theories converged, Mahan's doc-

---

10. Mahan, *Letters and Papers*, 1:140, 334–35, 337; Mahan, *From Sail to Steam*, 129, 135, 235–36, 247, 335.

11. Mahan, *Letters and Papers*, 1:119–20, 335; Mahan, *From Sail to Steam*, 236, 247.

12. Seager, *Alfred T. Mahan: The Man and His Letters*, 119; Puleston, *Mahan: Life and Work*, 48.

13. Mahan, *Interest of America in Sea Power, Present and Future*, 10; Vincent Davis, *Admirals Lobby*, 110; Baer, *One Hundred Years*, 15.

14. Sprout and Sprout, *The Rise of American Naval Power, 1776–1918*, 203; Russell F. Weigley, *The American Way of War: A History of United States Military Strategy and Policy*, 176, 178.

trine partook of a kind of determinism that postulated that the United States Navy was bound to eventually clash with a competing naval power.

Central to Mahan's strategic thought was the idea that "War, once declared, must be waged offensively, aggressively. The enemy must not be fended off, but smitten down." The aim of a naval engagement was the total annihilation of the enemy fleet in a decisive battle. His strategic doctrine put a premium on command of the sea and the concentration of battleships that alone, he stressed, could destroy the enemy fleet. Steaming out to meet the enemy, with a fleet at least as large as the opposing armada, the American navy would engage in a brief and decisive battle.[15]

Perhaps the most lasting legacy of Mahan's strategy as it bore on Japan was the fixation on the battleship and a decisive fleet engagement. Naval historian Ronald H. Spector has written, "The Japanese navy was a faithful mirror image of its American opponent in strategy. Japanese naval officers, too, had inhaled deeply the heady, if somewhat musty, fumes of Mahan's classic brew of imperialism and salt water."[16] George W. Baer, a naval strategy specialist, goes as far as to say, "Japan's naval strategy was more Mahanian than America's." This resulted in "a mirror image" that would characterize Japanese-American naval confrontation.[17]

To buttress his case for a large battleship navy, Mahan marshaled political-economic arguments. He posited three links on which naval dominance rested: production, shipping, and colonies. In particular, he emphasized the commercial component of sea power.[18] Mahan's theory of commercial and colonial expansion has been reinterpreted by the "new left" school of historians, notably Walter LaFeber.[19] Expansionists like Mahan argued that a vast industrial surplus at home demanded outlets in the form of overseas markets and colonies and that commercial expansion in turn called for sea power. Like many naval officers, Mahan came to believe that economic prosperity at home dictated overseas expansion. Because other powers would also aspire to international economic preeminence, its corollary went, commercial rivalry would inevitably bring the United States into conflict with a competitor.[20]

15. Mahan, *The Influence of Sea Power upon History, 1660–1703,* 287–88; Davis, *Admirals Lobby,* 112; Sprout and Sprout, *Rise of American Naval Power,* v.

16. Spector, *Eagle against the Sun: The American War with Japan,* 43.

17. Baer, *One Hundred Years,* 16, 121.

18. Mahan, *Influence of Sea Power,* 28–53; Mahan, *Interest of America in Sea Power,* 6; Sprout and Sprout, *Rise of American Naval Power,* 219.

19. LaFeber, *The New Empire: An Interpretation of American Expansionism, 1860–1898,* 88–93; LaFeber, "A Note on the 'Mercantilistic Imperialism' of Alfred Thayer Mahan," 32; Mahan, *Influence of Sea Power,* 53. Davis, *Admirals Lobby,* 108.

20. Davis, *Admirals Lobby,* 108; Seager, *Mahan: The Man and His Letters,* 249.

Mahan and America's navalists deduced from this general assumption that they would come to armed conflict with Japan over trade with China. Perpetuating the myth of the China market, navy men believed that the United States would some day fight Japan to support the Open Door in China. (They seemed to be oblivious to the fact that Japan was America's natural trade partners.) As shall later be described, Japan's navalists postulated from Mahan's doctrine a form of economic determinism, which held that irrepressible urge of capitalist America dictated expansion into China, threatening Japan's vital interests. In time it became an article of faith in Japanese naval circles that America's "economic penetration" of China, supported by a superior navy, would some day lead to Japanese-American war.

Expansion in the Pacific

After the publication of his *Influence of Sea Power*, Mahan, while keeping in close touch with Theodore Roosevelt and his fellow expansionists, wrote many articles exhorting the nation to expand in the Pacific.[21] The most comprehensive attempt was a polemical essay titled "The United States Looking Outward" that appeared in December 1890. In this often-quoted article, he called for vigorous efforts to compete in world trade and to penetrate overseas markets to solve the problem of domestic overproduction.[22] And the theater of international action, he emphasized, was moving from the Atlantic to the Pacific.

When the Hawaiian revolution broke out in January 1893, Mahan hastened to publish "Hawaii and Our Future Sea Power," arguing the case for its prompt annexation. A small minority of American residents in Honolulu had seized control of the Hawaiian Islands and formed a provisional government, which immediately sought annexation to the United States. Such a prospect strongly appealed to Mahan. The Hawaiian Islands, only two thousand miles from the American West Coast, were the key to the control of the Pacific. They would also provide stepping-stones to the China market. Mahan wrote that this called for a navy sufficiently large to assert American "preponderance" in the eastern Pacific.[23]

Signs of American expansion in the Pacific naturally alarmed the Japanese government. Tokyo was sensitive to the rights of its nationals in Hawaii

21. Mahan, *Interest of America in Sea Power*, 7–8.
22. Ibid., 31–32; Mahan, *Letters and Papers*, 2:92–93; Akira Iriye, *Pacific Estrangement: Japanese and American Expansion, 1897–1911*, 53–56.
23. Mahan, *Interest of America in Sea Power*, 31–32, 47, 59.

who constituted roughly 40 percent of its population. The Japanese government decided to dispatch its newest and most powerful battle cruiser, *Naniwa*, commanded by Captain Tōgō Heihachirō, to Honolulu as a demonstration to protect the rights of Japanese residents. But this naval action backfired, only provoking American annexationists. However, in the end President Grover Cleveland, an anti-imperialist, repudiated a treaty of Hawaiian annexation. Nevertheless it was portentous that the first clash between American and Japanese expansionism occurred over Hawaii.

When the second crisis over Hawaii erupted in 1897, Mahan was seriously worried about the danger from Japan. By then, Japan stood second only to Britain as a Pacific naval power. The emergence of Japan posed a new threat to American (white) supremacy in the Hawaiian Islands. The Japanese government claimed that maintenance of the status quo in the Pacific was essential to the preservation of friendly Japanese-American relations. Again, Tokyo dispatched the *Naniwa* to Honolulu, and this unwittingly provided Mahan and his fellow expansionists with further ammunition for Hawaiian annexation.

A genuine war scare was in the making. Mahan warned Roosevelt, the assistant secretary of the navy, that there was a "danger of trouble with her [Japan] toward Hawaii, I think beyond doubt." On May 1, 1897, an alarmed Mahan wrote Roosevelt a "personal and private" letter: "The question is are we going to allow her [Japan] to dominate the future of those most important islands because of our lethargy. It may very well happen, if we shut our eyes. . . . Take them [Hawaii] first and solve [political questions] afterwards."[24] Roosevelt replied that he absolutely agreed with Mahan: "If I had my way, we would annex those islands tomorrow." Mahan later restated the case for annexation of Hawaii to counter "military danger" from Japan: "Hawaii is now exposed to pass under foreign domination—notably Japan."[25]

Mahan was called before the Senate Committee on Foreign Relations. Lengthy excerpts from "Hawaii and Our Future Sea Power" were included by Senator Henry Cabot Lodge in the committee's record. Citing Mahan, the committee stated, "The present Hawaiian-Japanese controversy is the preliminary skirmish in the great coming struggle between the civilization and the awakening forces of the East and the civilization of the West.[26] The idea

---

24. Mahan, *Letters and Papers*, 2:506–7.
25. Ibid., 2:538; Puleston, *Mahan: Life and Work*, 182; Richard W. Turk, *The Ambiguous Relationship: Theodore Roosevelt and Alfred Thayer Mahan*, 119.
26. Cited in Julius W. Pratt, *Expansionists of 1898: The Acquisition of Hawaii and the Spanish Islands*, 3; Iriye, *Pacific Estrangement*, 49–52; William E. Livezey, *Mahan on Sea Power*, 170.

of struggle between Western and Eastern civilizations unmistakably bore Mahan's stamp. He had been urging that the United States, as the champion of Western civilization, annex Hawaii to forestall its possession by Japan.

Mahan now emphasized the Pacific Ocean as the arena of America's naval and national destiny. He wrote Roosevelt about "the need of strengthening our Pacific squadron." He added, "In building war ships, build on the Pacific side. . . . Also your best Admiral needs to be in the Pacific, for much more initiative *may* be thrown on him than *can* be on the Atlantic man." Departing from the traditional naval concentration in the Atlantic, Mahan seemed to be prematurely advocating a Pacific-first strategy. In fact, he confided to Roosevelt in May 1897 that "In my opinion we have much more likelihood of trouble on that side [the Pacific] than in the Atlantic. . . . In Asia, not in Europe, is now the greatest danger to our proximate interests." He repeated that there was "a very real present danger of war" with Japan.[27]

In 1897 William McKinley, whose platform was akin to Mahanian expansionism, was inaugurated as president of the United States. That same year Mahan retired from the navy, but he maintained a liaison with the Naval War College, attended conferences, and offered strategic advice.

Mahan the Imperialist

In "A Twentieth Century Outlook" (September 1897), Mahan tried to predict the shape of the coming century by asking "whether the Eastern or Western civilization is to dominate throughout the earth and to control the future." To prepare for such a showdown, he urged the United States to act as a protector of Western civilization by acquiring outposts in Hawaii. Given such a Weltanschauung, it seemed obvious that America's external relations had to revolve around the Pacific Ocean. "It is in the Pacific, where the westward course of empire again meets the East, that their relations to the future of the world becomes most apparent."[28]

In particular, Mahan emphasized that "the appearance of Japan as a strong ambitious state, resting on solid political and military foundations, has fairly startled the world." Mahan applauded Japan's "quick acceptance" of the material civilization of the West but pointed to "the diverse evolution of racial characteristics radically different" from those in the West.[29]

27. Mahan, *Letters and Papers*, 2:506–7. Michael Vlahos, "The Naval War College and the Origins of War-Planning against Japan," 24.
28. Mahan, *Interest of America in Sea Power*, 243, 259.
29. Ibid., 162, 235, 237, 251–52.

In the aftermath of the Spanish-American War in 1898, the United States acquired the Philippines and Guam. The United States was now in a strategic position to expand its oceanic frontier to the western Pacific and assert itself in East Asian international politics. Although Mahan was a leading expansionist of the day, he later confessed that when the Spanish-American War erupted, "the Philippines, with all they mean, had not risen above my mental horizon." "I looked with anxious speculation toward the Chinese hive; but I never dreamed that in my day I should see the U.S. planted at the doors of China."

Although Mahan had vigorously called for the annexation of Hawaii, attained during the Spanish-American War, his feeling as to the Philippines was "much more doubtful." At first, he was skeptical about even the annexation of Luzon.[30] He was realistic enough to fear that if the United States should annex the entire archipelago, it would be impossible to defend it from Japan. The Philippines, which could not be defended by the Pearl Harbor–based squadron, would become a diplomatic pawn, a hostage, or an "Achilles heel" (in Theodore Roosevelt's later words) in the power game with Japan.

Mahan had finally come around to accepting annexation of the entire Philippines because he subordinated realistic strategic considerations to the ideology of Manifest Destiny. He spoke of the Philippines as a "task" or "charge" to which God has "led" the United States. It was out of the question, he declared, to give independence to these backward people.[31] For Mahan the direct occasion for annexation of the entire archipelago was the escalating jungle war with local guerrillas, led by the Philippine leader Emilio Aguinaldo, fighting for independence, which had become totally unmanageable. Thus began America's first involvement in an Asian war that a later generation would call a "war of national liberation."[32]

Once he had reconciled himself to the annexation of the entire Philippines, Mahan saw a magnificent vista of possibilities. In a memorandum to Secretary of the Navy John D. Long he wrote that Manila was "very centrally situated" as a base of operations in the Asia-Pacific regions, "which owing to unsettled political conditions, and our having great political and commercial interests in them, are liable to become scenes of war." The Philippines thus assumed "miraculous importance" strategically, commercially, and politically in defending American interests in China.[33]

30. Mahan, *Letters and Papers,* 2:569, 619.
31. Ibid., 579–80.
32. Ibid.
33. Ibid., 582–83.

At the same time, Mahan noted with satisfaction the remarkable improvement of relations with Japan. Less than four years earlier Japanese leaders were warning the United States that they could not remain indifferent to any annexation of Hawaii, but now they had come around to welcoming American possession of the Philippines. The Japanese government, increasingly concerned about the "slicing" of China by the powers, wanted to cooperate with the United States, to prevent that from happening and, therefore, to see the Philippines in the hands of the United States, rather than any other power.

"The Problem of Asia" and the Open Door

Alarmed at "the collapse of the organization in all its branches [in China] during the late war with Japan [1894–1895]," Mahan concluded that the United States must play a leading role in Chinese affairs. "The future of China is the most interesting commercial question of the Pacific to us at the present moment." *The Problem of Asia and Its Effects upon International Policies*, published in 1900, was a running commentary on current events: Russian-American rivalry in China, John Hay's Open Door notes of 1899–1900, the Boxer Rebellion of 1900, and the siege and relief of foreign legations in Peking.[34]

Mahan's conceptual framework was geopolitics. According to him, the sea power that had dominated world politics since 1500 was now being replaced by a massive land power, the Russian Empire, whose "aggressive advance moves over the inert Asiatics like a steam-roller."[35] To contain Russia, Mahan now emphasized "the solidarity of interests" among the four "maritime states"—the United States, Great Britain, Germany, and Japan. Mahan, once alarmed by the Japanese peril in Hawaii, was now willing to include Japan in the common front against Russia.

Second, Mahan reinforced his geopolitical notion by racial, or more accurately racist, theories. He saw the problem of Asia in terms of three-cornered conflict among the Asiatic, Slavic, and Teutonic races in China. He painted an alarmist picture of "such a vast mass as four hundred million Chinese equipped with modern appliances, and cooped within a territory already narrow for it." For Western civilization, Mahan warned, there would soon be "a day of visitation."[36]

34. Puleston, *Mahan: Life and Work*, 1; Livezey, *Mahan on Sea Power*, 176; Mahan, *The Problem of Asia and Its Effects upon International Policies*, 63–67; Mahan, *Interest of America in Sea Power*, 236; Mahan, *Letters and Papers*, 2:658.

35. Mahan, *Problem of Asia*, 87–90, 154, 165, 167

36. Ibid., 108.

On the other hand, Mahan admired a "progressive" Japan, but his views of Japan were ambivalent. He praised Japan for having accepted not only the "material improvements" of Western civilization but also its "ideals, intellectual and moral." In this respect, Mahan seemed almost willing to regard the Japanese as a Teutonic race, perhaps as an "honorary Aryan" (as Hitler was to call his Axis partner during World War II). Mahan even credited Japan for having participated in "the spirit of the institutions of Christendom." In this "conversion" Japan was "repeating the experience of our Teutonic ancestors, as they came into contact with the Roman policy and the Christian Church."

This is not to say that Mahan held no reservation about Japan's Westernization. He reminded his readers that Japan still suffered from intellectual and moral indigestion in partaking of Western civilization. And Mahan never entirely shed his fear of an eventual racial conflict with Japan. "Differences of race characteristics, original and acquired, entails divergence of ideal and of action, with consequent liability to misunderstanding, or even collision." Yet, in *The Problem of Asia* he minimized the gulf separating the Japanese from the Americans. He rhapsodized, "Japan has established and maintained its place as a fully equipped member of the commonwealth of states, under recognized international law." In other words, Japan was a peaceful "partner" of the family of advanced Western nations. Mahan earnestly hoped Japan would "pass" on to China the "example" of its successful Westernization. In short, Japan was to become the champion of Western civilization in Asia.[37] Such a bland view of Japan suddenly evaporated and gave way to habitual suspicion of Japan with the eruption of the immigration crisis.

Mahan and the Immigration Crisis

When in 1903 the General Board of the U.S. Navy, the highest advisory body for the secretary of the navy, asked Mahan for his views about fleet distribution, he surprised many admirals by recommending fleet concentration on the Pacific coast, not on the Atlantic, as had been the practice. Mahan based this advice on political rather than strategic considerations. A threat from Europe was unlikely, whereas the Far Eastern situation was highly volatile; therefore, it might become necessary to "take the offensive" in the Pacific. He advised the General Board that to remove our fleet—battle fleet—from the Pacific would be a declaration of policy and a confession of weakness.

37. Ibid., 101–2, 106–7, 110, 148–49, 151; Mahan, *Letters and Papers,* 2:707.

"The Pacific and Eastern [Asia?] is the great coming question, as long as we can easily foresee."[38] However prescient Mahan's vision of a transpacific threat may have been, the navy's leaders, wedded to an Atlantic-first strategy, rejected Mahan's advice and kept the fleet concentrated on the Atlantic coast.

The outbreak of the Russo-Japanese War on February 8, 1904, caught Mahan totally by surprise. Regarding Russia as a menace in Manchuria, Mahan cheered for the underdog, Japan. He saw a "brilliant success" in Japan's surprise attack on the Russian fleet at Port Arthur. The Japanese navy, he was pleased to note, had incorporated his doctrines, especially that of tactical concentration. And he had befriended a core of Japanese officers at Annapolis. Admiral Uriu Sotokichi, who distinguished himself in the early phase of the Battle of the Japan Sea, had been an outstanding student at the naval academy when Mahan was teaching there. And Mahan counted among his disciples Lieutenant Commander Akiyama Saneyuki, a brilliant staff officer to Admiral Tōgō's Combined Fleet, who had visited him and sought his personal advice in New York in 1897.

Mahan dashed off a few articles on the naval battles of the Russo-Japanese War, expressing pleasure that his strategic doctrines were vindicated by the Battle of the Japan Sea. The primary lesson to be learned from Tsushima, Mahan wrote in 1906, was never to divide the battle fleet: the Russian navy had made the fatal mistake of dispersing its battleship strength between the Pacific fleet (based at Port Arthur and Vladivostok), the Black Sea fleet, and the Baltic fleet, which had steamed all the way from Europe. Emphasizing his doctrine of concentration, he asked American readers "to substitute therein, in their apprehension, Atlantic for Baltic, and Pacific for Port Arthur." Later in his *Naval Strategy: Compared and Contrasted with the Principles and Practices of Military Operations on Land* (1911), Mahan devoted two chapters to the Russo-Japanese War and praised the Japanese navy for having adhered to his dicta that the sole purpose of the navy was to command the sea and annihilate the enemy navy.[39]

Japan's victory at Tsushima ended the bogey of czarist Russia overrunning China, and replaced it with the fear of Japan's newly enhanced naval power. This fear, when combined with hysterical alarms over Japanese immigration on the Pacific coast, escalated into a major nightmare. Mahan's

38. Mahan, *Letters and Papers*, 3:80.
39. Mahan, "Some Reflections upon the Far Eastern War," *National Review*, 47 (May 1906); and Mahan, "Retrospect upon the War between Japan and Russia," in Mahan, *Naval Strategy Compared and Contrasted with Principles and Practices of Military Operations on Land*, 422–23.

"great coming question" in the Pacific was sparked in 1906, when the San Francisco School Board decided to segregate Japanese pupils into a separate school. The Tokyo government vigorously protested, triggering a war scare. Mahan revived the yellow peril notion. He was in all seriousness concerned about the "Japanizing" of America or at least the western part of it. He sounded almost as shrill as anti-Japanese agitators in California when he wrote, "Open doors to immigration, & all west of the Rocky Mountains would become Japanese or Asiatic. It is not a question of a superior or inferior race; but of races wholly different in physical get-up, and in traditions wholly separate during all time, up to a half-century ago."[40]

The navy's image of Japan as a hypothetical enemy began to congeal in War Plan Orange, first drafted in 1906. War with Japan, which Mahan had been predicting, seemed to have become a real possibility, and the weakness on the Pacific coast because of the fleet's Atlantic concentration became intolerable to Mahan. The problem of strategic fleet movement had become a genuine conundrum.[41] In July 1907, when the Japanese immigration crisis reached a boiling point, President Roosevelt announced the audacious plan to send the entire American battleship fleet, composed of sixteen battleships, on a cruise around the world. It was obviously intended as a demonstration of naval power in the Pacific.

Roosevelt's "big stick" came as a great shock to Tokyo. Japanese naval attaché in Washington, Commander Taniguchi Naomi, sent Tokyo a worried report about the war scare. "Among those military men who openly discuss a Japanese-American war in journals is Admiral Mahan; I have reason to believe that he and other naval officers secretly regard our Empire as an enemy."[42] Mahan, whom, as later narrated, the Japan's Naval Staff College had once considered inviting as a visiting professor, was now regarded as a spearhead of the Japanese-American war scare.

In his article on "The True Significance of the Pacific Cruise" (December 1907), Mahan denied that the cruise of the Great White Fleet (so-called because its ships were painted white) was a hostile demonstration, but like Roosevelt linked sea power in the Pacific to the problem of Japanese immigration. Mahan wrote to an English friend that the conflict over the Japanese immigration question was unsolvable because "there is raw human nature, irrepressible." "So long as you and we have big navies, and Japan is in a

40. Mahan, *Letters and Papers*, 3:221–22.
41. Vlahos, "Naval War College and the Origins of War," 28.
42. Report from the United States, no. 86, no. 89, Taniguchi to Tōgō, April 29, 1907, secret no. 11, U.S., Papers of Saitō Makoto (hereafter cited as Saitō Makoto Papers), DL, Tokyo.

financial hole, the Jap will do his best to keep his people in order; but weaken our navy, and fill the Jap treasury, and it will no longer [be] worth while for them to be unpopular with their own people. When the people of two nations are antagonistic, because of clashing interests, the peace can only be kept by force."[43] Pending the completion of an Isthmian canal, Mahan felt, it was especially urgent for the United States to demonstrate to Japan its ability to move an undivided battle fleet over immense distances from the Atlantic to the Far East quickly and efficiently.

The Tokyo government, fearing the transpacific cruise of the sixteen American battleships would constitute an act of "intimidation," and anxious to defuse the war psychology, decided in a moment of inspiration to invite the Great White Fleet to visit Japan, where the officers and crew would be lavishly entertained. Thus an American "provocation" was happily turned into an occasion for jovial exchange and restoration of friendly relations. But in Japanese naval circles, there were some, like Ōsumi Mineo (a future navy minister), who held rancor against the Great White Fleet.[44]

In Mahan's mind the "threat" presented by the Japanese navy and the "danger" posed by Japanese immigration were inseparably intertwined. In 1910 he wrote, "The Pacific coast intrinsically is more exposed, in greater danger from an enemy, than either of the others. There is also much more imminent danger of hostilities in that sea than in the Atlantic, because of the doubtful issue of the Open Door, and the inflammable prejudice of our Pacific population towards the Japanese resident."[45] This perception of twin dangers from Japan was to persist in the premise of War Plan Orange.

In 1913 the second immigration crisis arose over the California land law that denied the Japanese the right to own land. Mahan's position had been that "free Asiatic immigration to the Pacific coast" would mean "Asiatic occupation—Asia colonized in America." In June 1913 Mahan wrote a lengthy letter to the editor of the *London Times*. Obviously a racist, he asserted that "the Japanese racial characteristics" could not be changed by the Westernization of Japan in two generations, and for this reason Japanese immigrants remained inassimilable. "The virile qualities of the Japanese will still more successfully withstand assimilation."

On the other hand, he fondly recalled his youthful visit to Japan on board the *Iroquois*, during which he saw much of the old Japan then on the point of vanishing. He loved the "charming geniality and courtesy of her peo-

43. Mahan, *Letters and Papers*, 3:277–78; Morris Levy, "Alfred Thayer Mahan and United States Foreign Policy," 281.
44. Ōsumi Taishō Denki Kankōkai, ed., *Danshaku Ōsumi Mineo den*, 382.
45. Mahan, *Letters and Papers*, 3:355.

ple, which has endeared them to my recollection." During the subsequent forty years he had followed Japan's modernization with "sympathy and gladness." The question, he emphasized, was not a matter of superiority or inferiority. Rather, he believed the problem was one of "physical set-up" that prevented assimilation. The presence of a racial group in the United States that was inassimilable remained a perennial source of trouble with Japan. Mahan hoped, "Should these words fall under the eyes of any Japanese, I trust he will accept these sincere assurances, and will himself sympathize, as far as may be, with the difficulties of the United States in the particular instance."[46]

Mahan's racism, prominently published in the *Times,* came as a shock to Japanese readers, and they reacted violently. Tokutomi Sohō, the leading spokesman of the nationalist camp, wrote, "Admiral Mahan says that the Japanese must be excluded because they cannot assimilate. It all boils down to this: The only sin the Japanese have ever committed is that of being Japanese. If this is the case, we must break down the white domination [of the world]."[47]

As noted, at the height of the Californian crisis of 1906, the United States hurriedly drew up War Plan Orange. The next year, Japan formulated the Imperial National Defense Policy, sanctioned by the high command, in which the navy designated the United States as its hypothetical enemy. Here was a mirror image, but there was, however, a certain asymmetry between the outlooks of the two navies. Mahan and Theodore Roosevelt believed that the immigration issue combined with the lack of American naval preparedness would some day trigger a Japanese-American war. In fact, Japanese exclusion was one of the three policies—the others being the Monroe Doctrine and the Open Door—for which naval planners assumed the United Fleet would fight Japan. However, at no time did Tokyo seriously consider war over the immigration question. It was merely a matter of "face," not of vital interest.[48] The Japanese navy's primary concern was to maintain a semblance of naval balance with the U.S. Navy, which would help Japan retain supremacy in the western Pacific and prevent the United States from forceful intervention in China. But the immigration question undeniably exacerbated the Japanese navy's perception regarding the United States.

---

46. Ibid., 3:688–92.
47. Ibid., 3:500; Tokutomi Sohō, *Jimu ikkagen* [My Opinions on Current Affairs], 471–73.
48. Asada, *Ryōtaisen kan no Nichi-Bei Kankei: Kaigun to seisaku kettei katei* [Japanese-American Relations between the Wars: Naval Policy and the Decision-Making Process], 273, 292.

Mahan and the Pacific Strategy

On matters of strategy, the Naval War College and the General Board continued to asked Mahan to comment on war plans, especially War Plan Orange. In September 1910 Mahan advised the General Board, "There is also much more imminent danger of hostilities in that sea [the Pacific] than in the Atlantic, because of the doubtful issue of the Open Door, and the inflammable prejudice of our Pacific population toward the Japanese resident[s]": "To cover the Pacific coast against a landing, and at the same time protect our other interests in the Pacific—the Open Door, the Philippines, Hawaii—Pearl Harbor should receive the development now contemplated, and Guam should be constituted a kind of Gibraltar. . . . No situation in our possession equals Guam to protect every interest in the Pacific." Such a buildup would some day enable the American fleet to defend the Philippines.[49]

In February and March 1911 Admiral Raymond P. Rogers, the president of the Naval War College, asked Mahan to comment on War Plan Orange of that year. The plan assumed that Japan would overrun the Pacific, conquering the Philippines and probably Guam, Samoa, and Hawaii. The strategy favored by Rogers was to advance through the central route to recapture Hawaii; to advance through the central Pacific to seize the Marshalls and the Carolines (in those days German territory); to recapture Manila; and to control Japan's home waters and strangle Japan by blockade.[50]

In his detailed response, Mahan rejected this central route. Instead, this demigod of sea power supported a "northern route": he would move the main force to Kiska in the Aleutians and from there strike Guam, and then use Guam as a base for direct attack on the Ryukyu islands and blockade Japan's home islands. In Mahan's mind, Guam was the key to the Pacific campaign. Underlying this strategy was his conviction that "blows must be straight, rapid, and decisive." Although unstated, the northern route had the advantage of being short, an important factor given Mahan's passion for a short war.[51]

His advice was brilliant. However, the Naval War College rejected his plan, reprimanding its mentor. His northern route was deemed too dangerous and too uncertain. Although Mahan's particular critique was rejected, his broad strategic outlook was in accord with the basic concept of War Plan Orange, which would dominate American naval strategy for the next thirty years.

49. Mahan, *Letters and Papers*, 3:355–56.
50. Ibid., 3:380–83; William R. Braisted, *The United States Navy in the Pacific, 1909–1922*, 33–35.
51. Mahan, *Letters and Papers*, 3:380, 389–93, 439, 480–83.

Mahan repeated his conviction that America's next war must be with Japan. Because of a possible clash with Japan over the Open Door in China, the "inflammable" issue of Japanese immigration, and the exposed position of Hawaii and the Philippines, he warned Secretary of the Navy Meyer and the members of the General Board that "invasion of the Pacific coast is a possibility." To protect the Open Door from violation by Japan, he urged, the United States must reinforce its advance bases and maintain a powerful navy in the Pacific. Interestingly, Mahan warned about Japan's surprise attack: "Orange will not make formal proclamation before striking."[52]

By this time Mahan had realistically come to grasp the global balance of power as a mechanism that underwrote American security. In an essay published in 1910, he explained that the Open Door in China rested on the balance of power in Asia and the Pacific, which—through the Anglo-Japanese Alliance—rested on the balance of power in Europe. In the likelihood of a European war, British and German naval power in the Pacific would be called back to Europe at once, leaving Japan and the United States directly confronting each other across the Pacific. To maintain a commercial Open Door, the two powers would have to create a new regional balance of power. Faced with the new reality of sea power, Mahan retreated from the position he had taken ten years earlier in *The Problem of Asia*. The United States should no longer seek "supremacy" in the Pacific, but secure only its possessions in the Pacific and its approaches to them. He suggested a new balance of naval power in which the United States would dominate the eastern Pacific (Hawaii) and Japan the western Pacific.[53]

After 1913, it was the younger Roosevelt, Franklin D. Roosevelt, the newly appointed assistant secretary of the navy, who turned to Mahan for advice on naval matters. He had been an avid reader of Mahan ever since Christmas 1897, when on his fifteenth birthday he received from Theodore a gift-wrapped copy of *Influence of Sea Power upon History*. For his next birthday he received Mahan's *Interest of America in Sea Power*. The historian William Neumann contends that Mahan understood that "he had an apt pupil in the younger Roosevelt." Soon Roosevelt was citing Mahan in a debate at Groton.[54]

---

52. Ibid., 3:353.
53. Mahan, "Open Door"; Mahan, *Letters and Papers*, 3:353.
54. Neumann, "Franklin Delano Roosevelt: A Disciple of Admiral Mahan," 713–19; Frank Freidel, *Franklin D. Roosevelt: The Apprenticeship*, 46–47. After her husband's death, Mrs. Roosevelt was asked which books her husband considered most influential in his own thinking. She replied that he had always talked of Mahan's history as one of the books he found "most illuminating" (Neumann, "Franklin Delano Roosevelt," 717, 719; Neumann, *America Encounters Japan: From Perry to MacArthur*, 143).

The Mahan-Roosevelt correspondence in 1914 on the eve of World War I was focused on the danger of war with Japan.[55] On June 26 Mahan wrote, "Personally, I feel that our danger in the Pacific much exceeds that in the Atlantic. [Japan] feels as an insult what we regard as essential to national security in forestalling and avoiding a race [immigration] problem." Because of this danger from Japan, Mahan urged that building up military installations on the Pacific coast for the maintenance and repair of the American fleet was of the utmost importance.[56]

Mahan worried that an eruption of a European war would have immediate repercussions on the Pacific, bringing about a dangerous turn in relations with Japan. On August 15, when Japan presented an ultimatum to Germany, he again wrote the younger Roosevelt, expressing concern that once war broke out, Japan would seize the German insular possessions in the central Pacific—the Marianas, the Marshalls, and the Carolines. Some of these islands flanked America's route to the Philippines and Guam. Mahan wrote, "Japan, going to war with Germany, will be at liberty to take the German Islands, Pelew, Marianne, Caroline, and Samoa." It was one thing to have them in the hands of a power whose main strength was in Europe, and quite another to have them passed into the hands of Japan.[57] With regard to China, Mahan warned that Japan might develop "that sense of proprietorship" that "easily glides into the attempt at political control that ultimately means control by force." He thus predicted Japan's forceful presentation of the Twenty-One Demands to China in January 1915 that jeopardized China's sovereignty.

Once the European war broke out, Mahan's Anglophilia drove him into a corner. President Wilson appealed to the American people to remain strictly neutral and blamed rampant "navalism" as one of the causes of the war. Mahan's outspoken support of Britain flew in the face of Wilson's appeal to the American people to be "impartial in thought as well as in action." The president forbade naval officers, active or retired, to publicly discuss the military and political situation of the European war. Mahan's plea for exemption was denied by Secretary of the Navy Josephus Daniels. Mahan's family and close friends believed that this incident hastened his death on December 1, 1914. Others believed that Mahan was inwardly tortured by an awareness that his doctrine of sea power had intensified an

55. Freidel, *Franklin D. Roosevelt*, 234–35; Neumann, "Franklin Delano Roosevelt," 716–17.

56. Miller, *War Plan Orange*, 111.

57. Puleston, *Mahan: Life and Work*, 304; Turk, *Ambiguous Relationship*, 171; Lyle Evans Mahan, "My Parents, Rear Admiral and Mrs. Alfred Thayer Mahan," 91.

Anglo-German naval rivalry that led to war. No doubt, apprehensions about Japanese-American relations also preoccupied Mahan's mind in the months before his death.[58]

In the final analysis, Mahan was a successful—too successful—propagandist of sea power and imperialistic expansion. His influence on England and Germany has been noted, but no scholar has examined, except in passing, his influence on the Imperial Japanese Navy. American historian Richard W. Turk has written, "Nowhere was Mahan's strategic doctrine pursued in purer form than in the Imperial Japanese Navy."[59] My next task is to examine how true such a generalization is.

Nature of Influence

Japanese leaders, civil and military, were quick to note the contemporary relevance of Mahan's *Influence of Sea Power*. The navy found in this book both a uniquely American doctrine (a national policy of greatness through overseas expansion) and universally applicable naval theories (strategic principles). As to the former, Japanese leaders said Mahan's works must be carefully studied for what they revealed about the direction of American national policy. In particular, *Interest of America in Sea Power* was an "ideal weathervane for the secret of America's national power and its future projections abroad."[60] This may be called an "American studies" approach to Mahan.

Naval leaders were also keenly aware that Mahan's works formulated universally applicable strategic doctrines, and they believed they could extract "certain immutable principles" from them. This was what Kaneko Kentarō had in mind when he introduced *Influence of Sea Power* to Japan. Concerning the universality of Mahan's strategic teachings, Fleet Admiral Tōgō Heihachirō of Tsushima fame later paid this homage: "Naval strategists of all nations are of one opinion that Admiral Mahan's works will forever occupy the highest position as a world-wide authority in the study of military science. I express my deep and cordial reverence for his far-reaching knowledge and keen judgment."[61] In addition, Mahan's *Influence of Sea Power* in Japanese translation provided a weighty and sophisticated theory that

58. Turk, *Ambiguous Relationship*, 171; L. E. Mahan, "My Parents," 91.

59. Turk, *Ambiguous Relationship*, 4.

60. Mahan, *Interest of America in Sea Power*; Minakami Umehiko, trans., *Taiheiyō kaiken-ron*, 1–8.

61. Quoted in Charles C. Taylor, *The Life of Admiral Alfred Thayer Mahan: Naval Philosopher, Rear Admiral United States Navy*, 115.

Japan's navalists could utilize as a bureaucratic rationale to assert their primacy in budgetary appropriations in competition with the army.

Mahan's writings became a canon in the Japanese navy, but did its officers really read them? Mahan's convoluted prose must have been formidable. Even Admiral Suzuki Kantarō, one of the most illustrious theorists, who taught in the Naval Staff College from 1905 to 1908, confessed that the English original of *Influence of Sea Power* was beyond him and that he waited for a Japanese translation to appear. But the florid, arcane, and long-winded prose of the Japanese translation was hardly readable.

Most officers absorbed Mahan's doctrines through the lectures and writings of their instructors who had come under Mahan's influence. We shall examine two of them: Akiyama Saneyuki and Satō Tetsutarō. But first it must be pointed out that neither was Mahan's understudy; they brought their own individual and national perspectives to bear on their commentaries on sea power.

While basically agreeing with Ronald Spector that Japanese officers had "inhaled deeply the heady . . . fumes" of Mahan's doctrine,[62] I must caution readers that it is a tricky business to weigh the international "influence" of a seminal thinker such as Mahan. The shared objectives of fleet concentration and a decisive battle forced two maritime powers to think alike, projecting a "mirror image" of the two navies.[63] One must be careful to separate such built-in "mirror images" from the personal and doctrinal "influences" of Mahan. And to be influenced by Mahan's writings was one thing; to use his sea power doctrine to buttress the navy's bureaucratic interests—fleet expansion—was quite another.

Akiyama Saneyuki, the "Disciple" of Mahan

Known as the father of modern Japanese naval strategy, Akiyama began his professional naval career as a "disciple" of Mahan. Brilliant, imaginative, and resourceful, he was not only a seminal naval theorist but also a renowned hero of the Russo-Japanese War. His impact on Japanese strategic thought was such that every important staff officer and fleet commander who fought in the Pacific War was said to have been influenced by his teaching.

Akiyama graduated from the naval academy at the top of his class in 1890, barely ninety days after Mahan's *Influence of Sea Power* was published. In

62. Spector, *Eagle against the Sun,* 43.
63. Baer, *One Hundred Years,* 16, 475.

June 1897 the young lieutenant Akiyama was chosen for a two-year tour of duty in the United States as a part of the navy's program to make its officer corps more professional. Already deeply steeped in Mahan's *Influence of Sea Power* to the point of memorizing portions of it, he naturally wished to go to the Naval War College to study under Mahan. However, the college had closed its doors to foreign students to protect secrecy in areas related to national security, such as war planning. The ever-resourceful Akiyama visited Mahan twice in his New York home to seek his advice on how to advance his professional training. Mahan told him that several months of course work at the Naval War College would hardly suffice; instead, he urged Akiyama to read as widely as possible in the literature of Western naval and military history, both classical and modern. Mahan also introduced him to the navy library, then on the third floor of the Navy Department in Washington. In its spacious reading room, Akiyama immersed himself in books on military and naval history and strategy.[64]

Reporting on the progress of his work, Akiyama wrote to Captain Katō Tomosaburō (acting head of the Naval Affairs Section), "Captain Mahan says the subject of naval strategy is too profound to be grasped by mere academic studies. I agree with him that it is all important to observe combat action." A splendid opportunity presented itself when the Spanish-American War broke out in April 1898. With the intercession of the Japanese legation, Akiyama was allowed to join the American forces, and in Santiago he observed how Admiral William T. Sampson blocked Admiral Pascual Cervera's Spanish fleet and destroyed it.[65] (Later, during the Russo-Japanese War, Akiyama drew upon the lesson of Santiago when he drafted the plan to sink the Russian Pacific Fleet by blocking the entrance to Port Arthur Harbor.)

Upon his return to Washington, Akiyama learned that the Japanese Naval Staff College was considering hiring Mahan for a three-year term, from 1898 to 1901, as visiting professor of strategy. Akiyama received a letter from his friend Lieutenant Commander Yamaya Tanin, an instructor at the Naval Staff College, asking him for his candid opinion of Mahan. Akiyama replied,

Although I do not necessarily admire all of his views, judging from his words and deeds, he appears to be a meticulous nervous strategist who

---

64. Shimada Kinji, *Amerika ni okeru Akiyama Saneyui* [Akiyama Saneyuki in America], 43–57; Akiyama Saneyuki Kai, *Akiyama Saneyuki*, 99. Mark R. Peattie, "Akiyama Saneyuki and Emergence of Modern Japanese Naval Doctrine," 61–69; Koyama Hirotake, *Zōho gunji shisō no kenkyū* [A Study on Military Thought], 253–56; Dingman, "Japan and Mahan," 49–66; Yamanashi Katsunoshin Sensei Kinen Shuppan Iinkai, ed., *Yamanashi Katsunoshin ihōroku* [Legacies of Yamanashi Katsunoshin], 23–24.

65. Shimada, *Amerika ni okeru Akiyama Saneyui*, passim.

combines a philosophical brain with a logical mind; he is a spiritualist—a pretty rare bird among Americans. . . . Mahan has come a long way since he authored *The Influence of Sea Power;* he has deepened his knowledge and ideals. There is much to be learned from his recent writings.[66]

Akiyama was alluding to Mahan's influential articles that were recently collected in his *Interest of America in Sea Power.* Akiyama continued, "Mahan entertains definite strategies and national ambitions, and I believe we must keep a watchful eye on this old man." Keeping in mind the recent American annexation of Hawaii and the decision to acquire the Philippines, Akiyama had become wary of the American ambition to advance into East Asia.

Although the plan to invite Mahan to the Naval War College never materialized, the episode shows how highly he was regarded in Japanese naval circles. It is interesting to speculate how different the course of Japanese-American relations would have been in the unlikely event that Mahan had come to teach at the Naval Staff College.

Akiyama's Theory of Strategy

Akiyama returned to Japan in 1900, and following a stint as a staff officer, he was appointed a senior instructor of the newly established course on naval tactics and strategy at the Naval Staff College in 1902. In his lectures on fundamental strategy, he categorically stated, "The main object of battle is attack. The main element of fighting power is offensive power. The battleship is the fighting unit that controls naval battles."[67] Akiyama's strategic thought became the basis of the Naval Battle Instructions (*kaisen yōmurei*) of 1910, which through five revisions remained the fundamental manual for naval actions until the mid-1930s. The instructions declared, "Decisive engagement is the essence of battles. Battles must be offensive. The aim of a battle is to annihilate the enemy speedily. . . . The essential points of the battle are forestalling and concentration." Mahanian doctrines resounded throughout.[68]

During the Russo-Japanese War, Commander Akiyama played the central role as a senior staff officer to Admiral Tōgō Heihachirō's Combined

66. Ibid., 3, 498–500.
67. Mizuno Hironori, "Ā Akiyama kaigun chūjō," 19; Yasui Sōmei, "Yo no mitaru Akiyama Saneyuki kaigun chūjō" [Vice Admiral Akiyama as I Saw Him], 137; Sakurai, *Teitoku Akiyama Saneyuki,* 307–9; Shimadai Kinji, *Roshia sensō zen'ya no Akiyama Saneyuki* [Akiyama Saneyuki on the Eve of the War with Russia], 2:714, 722, 764.
68. BBKS, *Senshi sōsho: Kaigun gunsenbi* [War History Series: Naval Armaments and Preparations; hereafter cited as *Kaigun gunsenbi*], 1:125–29, 135–42.

Fleet. When the Japanese navy concentrated its fleets and won a decisive battle in the Tsushima Strait that annihilated Russia's Baltic Fleet, Mahan acclaimed the Japanese strategy as vindication of his principle of fleet concentration.[69]

From December 1905 to February 1908, Akiyama again taught naval strategy at the Naval Staff College. He devoted his full attention to devising a strategy vis-à-vis the United States, which was then emerging as the Japanese navy's hypothetical enemy. Formulating a war plan against the United States, separated by nine thousand miles of the Pacific Ocean, so severely taxed his resources that his colleague Satō Tetsutarō began to worry that Akiyama had become mentally deranged.[70]

No uncritical follower of Mahan, Akiyama took into account Japan's peculiar geopolitical condition and modified Mahan's teachings with ideas drawn from Japan's maritime tradition as well as his own battle experiences. He contended that Mahan's concept of command of the sea was too vague, in that it failed to take into consideration the practical difficulties involved in securing complete control of the vast expanses of the Pacific. He also departed from Mahan's overriding emphasis on annihilation of the enemy fleet, arguing on the authority of the ancient Chinese strategist Sun Tzu that victory could be achieved by "breaking the enemy's will to fight and forcing it to succumb rather than literally annihilating its fleet."[71] The strategy that brilliantly succeeded at Tsushima was "ambush operations" against Russia's Baltic Fleet that had steamed all the way from Europe in 220 days. But how could an ambush strategy work against the superior American fleet that had only seven thousand miles to steam from a base in Hawaii? Akiyama and his colleagues devised a prototype of "interceptive operations." As later refined, interceptive operations involved lying in wait for the American fleet to reach Japan's home waters and then engaging in a climactic all-out fleet encounter. Interceptive operations would become the centerpiece of Japanese strategy for more than three decades.

Akiyama died in 1918 at the age of fifty, leaving behind a rich legacy of strategic thought. He was a unique individual: he was the only Japanese naval officer to have enjoyed extensive contact with American naval officers, and he became the first Japanese naval officer to observe Western sea power in action.

---

69. Akiyama Saneyuki Kai, *Akiyama Saneyuki*, 309.

70. *Yamanashi Katsunoshin ihōroku*, 23–24; Sakurai, *Teitoku Akiyama Saneyuki*, 236–37, 388.

71. Akiyama Saneyuki, *Senjutsu ronshū* (secret); Akiyama Saneyuki Kai, *Akiyama Saneyuki*, 300; Shimada, *Roshia sensō zen'ya*, 2:893–95.

Satō Tetsutarō, the "Mahan of Japan"

Satō Tetsutarō adapted Mahan's sea power theory to Japan's geopolitical situation and strategic realities, recasting it as Japan's own doctrine of naval defense. Just as Mahan had been handpicked by Admiral Stephen B. Luce, the president of the Naval War College, to become an ideologue of sea power, so was Satō chosen by Navy Minister Yamamoto Gombei to become a leading theorist and propagandist for a navy-first policy. Traditionally, the navy was distinctly subordinate to the army in power and influence, and Yamamoto's aim was to reverse the priority of defense spending.

In May 1899 Yamamoto dispatched Lieutenant Commander Satō Tetsutarō to England to study naval strategy and history. After a year and a half in London, Satō traveled to the United States, where he stayed for eight months and fell under the "decisive influence" of Mahanian navalism.[72] He returned to Japan in October 1900 and was appointed instructor at the Naval Staff College. In November 1901, on Yamamoto's order, Satō presented the fruits of his study abroad in a strategic manifesto titled *Teikoku kokubōron* [On Imperial National Defense]. In this volume he negated the army's continental expansion and argued the navy's case for obtaining equality with the army in budgetary appropriation. He emphasized that Japan must avail itself of its insular position to become a maritime power. The book backfired, however, by provoking the army's strong antagonism.

After having served as the senior staff officer during the Russo-Japanese War, Satō was again appointed instructor at the Naval Staff College, where he taught a course on the history of naval defense. One of his former students, Admiral Yamanashi Katsunoshin (himself an avid reader of Mahan), later recalled,

> Admiral Satō in his lectures frequently referred to Captain Mahan's doctrine, often quoting from his writings. Mahan may have been a great scholar, but he had no real combat experience. On the other hand, Admiral Satō was both an excellent scholar and an able staff officer and commander. This is where he differed from Captain Mahan. . . . He interfused his history with his actual battle experiences.[73]

72. Tsunoda Jun, *Manshū mondai to kokubō hōshin: Meiji kōki ni okeru kokubō kankyō no hendō* [The Manchurian Question and Japan's Defense Policy: Changes in the Defense Setting of Japan in the Late Meiji Period], 648–50.

73. Quoted in Shinohara Hiroshi, *Kaigun Sōsetsushi: Igirisu gunji komondan no kage* [History of the Founding of the Japanese Navy: The Shadow of the British Naval Advisory Mission], 451.

On Mahan's authority Satō warned that no nation, however rich, could maintain both a first-class army and a first-class navy. Declaring the navy to be Japan's "first line of defense," he attacked the army's program of continental expansion even to the extent of suggesting the withdrawal of troops from Korea and Manchuria. "History proves that since time immemorial there has been no nation that became a world power without oceanic expansion."[74]

In 1908 Satō expanded his lectures, adding profuse historical illustrations and spicing them with his own battle experiences to write his massive tome *Teikoku kokubō shiron* [On the History of Imperial Defense]. David Evans and Mark Peattie rightly call this volume "the most extended and comprehensive essay ever formulated by the Japanese on the relationship of sea power to the Japanese situation."[75] It is no exaggeration to say that few Japanese officers of importance failed to come under Satō's influence, whether in person or in print.

To buttress his arguments, he copiously quoted from Mahan on the importance of command of the sea, fleet concentration, the decisive fleet encounter, and the need to take the offensive.[76] Citing Mahan almost verbatim, he wrote, "The object of a wartime navy is, first and foremost, to break up the enemy fleet, thus securing command of the sea. For this purpose, our navy must concentrate its sea power to annihilate the enemy fleet."[77]

Satō's Regional Navalism

Although Satō talked about the importance of taking the offensive, his strategy was different from Mahan's. The Japanese navy's planning for war against the United States was essentially defensive: waiting for the approach of the American fleet into the western Pacific, where Japan would seek a decisive fleet encounter. This "ambush strategy" was predicated on the regional advantages of the Japanese navy in East Asian waters.

At times, however, Satō was carried away by Mahan's vision of imperial navalism and wrote about global "oceanic expansion." "Now is the time for our Empire to attempt world-wide expansion, and our world-wide expansion must of necessity depend on oceanic expansion." He also argued that

74. Satō, *Teikoku kokubō shiron* [On the History of Imperial National Defense], 78–79, 337, 456, 758, 831, 870, 877–78. See also Satō, *Teikoku kokubō shironshō* [Abbreviated History of Imperial National Defense], passim; *Yamanashi Katsunoshin ihōroku*, 23.
75. Evans and Peattie, *Kaigun: Strategy, Tactics, and Technology in the Imperial Japanese Navy, 1887–1941*, 137.
76. Satō, *Teikoku kokubō shiron*, 70–71, 160, 718, 752, 758.
77. Ibid., 350, 752, 756–59.

"Japan must control world trade, and this in turn necessitates the building of sea power capable of annihilating the enemy fleet."[78] Brave words indeed, but Japan simply did not possess the "three links" Mahan had postulated for a great sea power: production, commerce, and colonies. It is unlikely that Satō seriously thought about global maritime expansion, but he believed that contending for it would serve as a rationale for establishing the navy's budgetary primacy over the army. In reality, Satō's vision of maritime expansion was limited to East Asia and, later, Southeast Asia (especially the Dutch East Indies).

Satō and the Idea of War with the United States

In *Teikoku kokubō shiron*, Satō had not yet conceived of the United States as a *probable* enemy. Referring to the crisis over the immigration question and the war scare in the United States in 1906–1908, Satō wrote, "There are signs, it is said, that the American people are looking at our country with belligerent feelings. But I wish to believe that there is no possibility of war with the United States in the near future." In view of America's great national strength, Satō believed it unwise to "maintain a naval power on a par with such a rich nation." *"Therefore, it is absolutely necessary to continue the friendly relations with that power that exist today."*[79]

Satō's views on the United States suddenly took a pessimistic turn in 1912, when he wrote "Kokubō sakugi" [Plans for National Defense], a confidential memorandum for limited circulation within the Navy Ministry. He argued that Japanese-American antagonism had become serious because of the immigration crisis in California and clash of policy in China. He felt bitter about the Mahanian version of the yellow peril, which held that because Japanese immigrants could not assimilate, the two nations would sooner or later come to blows. Satō now came to see anti-Japanese agitations in California in the context of a war with the United States.

The more recent cause of conflict was America's "dollar diplomacy," which challenged Japan's position in Manchuria. Projecting neo-Mahanian economic determinism, Satō was now convinced that the United States "absolutely requires expansion of its China market." He warned that if the "United States freely exerts its power in the Orient, a clash of interests with Japan will become inevitable."[80]

78. Ibid., 160.
79. Ibid., 760, 814–15 (emphasis Satō's).
80. Satō, "Kokubō sakugi" (secret) [A Proposal for National Defense], 21–24; Satō, *Teikoku kokubō shironshō*, 509, 512–13.

In 1913 Satō and three associates wrote *Kokubō mondai no kenkyū* [A Study of the National Defense Problem]. He argued that "the first nation that will obstruct our trade in China will be the United States, and only our navy can prevent it from doing so."[81] Satō's arguments repeated neo-Mahanian economic determinism that postulated an inevitable war over China. The United States seemed "intent on monopolizing the interests in the Pacific basin, making it an American lake by means of naval and commercial expansion." It was for this purpose, he observed, that the United States was "building up Hawaii as a base and fortifying the Philippines, and it may be that there is no way to avoid war unless we abandon our China market and interests in the South Seas."[82] He had come a long way since 1908, when he denied the possibility of war with the United States.

Satō is often called "the Mahan of Japan," but there were decisive differences between the two. Mahan advocated worldwide expansion backed by a "preponderant navy" that would share global command of the sea with Britain, whereas Satō championed "a naval force sufficient to control Far Eastern waters." Satō was aware of the great disparity in economic and military strength between the two nations. It may be concluded that because Japanese and American visions for sea power and overseas expansion were fundamentally different, the applicability of the Mahan doctrines to the Japanese navy was limited.

Unlike Mahan, Satō climbed to a high position: in August 1915 he was appointed vice chief of the Naval General Staff. But his overzealous navalism irritated Navy Minister Katō Tomosaburō. When he harassed Katō to speedily complete the ambitious "eight-eight fleet" plan (consisting of eight battleships and eight battle cruisers), the latter snapped back sharply, "That I can't do; you do it when you become navy minister."[83] He later incurred Katō's wrath by plotting (during the absence of his chief Shimomura Hayato) to expand the authority of the Naval General Staff at the expense of the navy minister. That angered Katō so much that he demoted Satō to president of the Naval Staff College.[84] Unlike some of his colleagues, Satō never had a chance to go on a fact-finding tour to Europe and the United States, so he missed the opportunity to observe the revolutionary changes in technology abroad. His outlook on naval warfare remained embedded in the "lessons" of the Russo-Japanese War. At the time of the Washington

---

81. Satō et al, *Kokubō mondai no kenkyū* [A Study of the National Defense Problem].

82. Satō, *Teikoku kokubōshi ronshō*, 509; Satō, "Kokubō sakugi," 25–26, 34.

83. Kurihara Hirota, ed., *Gensui Katō Tomosaburō den* [Biography of Fleet Admiral Katō Tomosaburō], 259.

84. Record of interview with Takahashi Sankichi, BBK.

Conference of 1921–1922, Satō clamored that Japan, instead of succumbing to the "unreasonable demands" of the United States, must "throw in the sponge and return home." Incensed by Satō's intransigent public posture, Katō placed him on the reserve list in the personnel retrenchment that followed the Washington Conference.[85]

Throughout his life Satō remained a staunch naval lobbyist for a greater naval budget. In 1936, after the Washington and London treaties expired, the Navy Ministry quoted from his *Teikoku kokubō shiron:* "in the course of history one cannot find an instance of a nation ever having gone bankrupt and ruined as the result of excessive expenditure on naval armaments."[86] Thus Satō abetted the ensuing naval race with the United States that was to place Japan in an increasingly difficult bind.

Mahanian Strategy in Triumph

The Mahanian strategy that put a premium on the battleship fleet and a decisive engagement dominated Japanese naval thinking in the interwar period. For example, Navy Minister Ōsumi Mineo's memorandum, prepared in connection with the 1935 London Naval Conference, stated, "Some argue that in the future a decisive fleet engagement will never take place, but didn't Admiral Mahan, venerated by Americans, declare that the primary aim of naval power is annihilation of the enemy fleet in a decisive encounter?"[87]

In the 1920s and 1930s Mahan continued to be perused by Japanese naval officers. A selected translation of his *Naval Strategy* was prepared by the Naval General Staff in 1924 and the full translation appeared in 1932 at the height of the crisis over the Manchurian Incident. The translator, Ozaki Chikara on the Naval General Staff, wrote in the preface, "The publication of this book is most timely and significant; it gives a good idea of naval strategy according to which the offensive actions of the United States navy will be conducted."[88]

Interestingly, this book was reprinted in July 1942. In the preface of the reprinted edition, Lieutenant Commander Tominaga Kengo of the Publicity Division of the Naval General Staff asserted, "If there had been no Mahan, perhaps the Greater East Asian War would never have taken place. At least

85. Ishikawa Yasushi, *Satō Tetsutarō kaigun chūjō den* [Biography], 356, 358.

86. Satō, *Teikoku kokubō shiron*, 144.

87. Memo prepared for the 1935 conference of naval limitation, no. 1, Navy Ministry, BBK.

88. Mahan, trans. *Kaigun senryaku*, 1–2.

there would have been no Hawaii operation." Tominaga quoted Mahan as saying, "Hawaii was the starting point of America's attempt to make the Pacific its own lake." Since the annexation of Hawaii, Tominaga wrote, "American extension of bases, so essential for command of the sea, has faithfully followed Mahan's wise counsels." Then Tominaga wildly speculated on how Mahan would have reacted to the Pearl Harbor attack had he been alive, concluding that he would have been "thrown into consternation" and soliloquized, "The object of the navy is to destroy the enemy fleet. There never was and there never will be such perfect success [as the Pearl Harbor attack]."[89] By the time Tominaga wrote that "Mahan's book is a required reading to reconfirm our understanding of the importance of command of the sea," the Japanese navy had been defeated in the battle of Midway. Mahan's disciple President Franklin D. Roosevelt was having his mentor's strategic doctrine applied by Admiral Ernest King in his transpacific operations. Military historian Russell F. Weigley wrote, "The American victory over Japan was a Mahanian triumph of sea power, that power rendered immensely more formidable through its acquisition of aerial and amphibious dimensions."[90] The United States Navy fought the Pacific War essentially in accordance with Mahan's sea power doctrine, which held that it was necessary first to secure undisputed command of the sea by defeating the enemy fleet.

Mahan and the Mirror Image

It is possible to argue that precisely because the Japanese and American navies shared the same Mahanian strategic doctrine—fixation with the battleship and obsession with the main fleet engagement—they pursued a collision course leading to Pearl Harbor. The American navy was quite aware of Mahan's influence on the Japanese navy. For example, William H. Gardner, the president of the powerful Navy League, who had access to the inner circles of the navy's officialdom, wrote in a letter to Admiral William S. Sims, the president of the Naval War College, in 1920–1921:

> I warrant every Japanese flag officer knows [Mahan's books]. . . . Mahan is a perfect guidebook to the imperial policy of Japan and to me the wonder is that we are blind to the fact that her overseas expansion is an exquisite adaptation to her entourage of the overseas expansion of England—

89. Ibid.
90. Weigley, *American Way of War*, 286, 293, 311, 334.

without England's mistakes. We talk about her Prussianized army, but of what infinitesimal danger is that to us or even to continental Asia, without her sea power, naval and mercantile?[91]

About the same time, the American naval attaché in Tokyo was reporting with some exaggeration, "Through the writings of Admiral Mahan it has become common knowledge not only to the man on the street but even the schoolboy, that to an Island Kingdom a foreign war is only possible by having command of the seas."[92] That American naval circles were uneasy about Japan's adoption of Mahan's doctrines presents an interesting case of mirror image.

The United States and Britain saw a periodic recurrence of the devil theory of Mahan that indicted him as an "incendiary," a philosopher of death and destruction, the mastermind behind the naval race between Britain and Germany before World War I.[93] But it would seem that Mahan's influence in Japan was most devastating.

One middle-echelon Japanese officer who carried Mahanian navalism to the extreme during the late 1930s was Captain Nakahara Yoshimasa, nicknamed "the King of the South Seas" for his ardor for southern expansion. On September 3, 1939, the day Britain declared war against Germany, Nakahara wrote in his diary in large letters, "The important thing now is to take this opportunity to reorient Japan as a sea power and concentrate its efforts on naval expansion." He essentially restated Satō Tetsutarō's brand of navy-first ideology: "If our sea power is expanded, the East Asian Continent will automatically be stabilized and Japan will be able to expand its interests there. However, even if continental interests are expanded, there is no way to increase production unless sea communications are secured."[94]

Nakahara continued, "The history of the East and West, both ancient and modern, more than amply testifies that expansion of continental interests, not based on sea power, is ephemeral. Nay, the existence of continental interests itself depends on sea power." In September 1939 he declared that the most important thing for Japan was to take advantage of the European war to forcibly expand its sea power and consolidate its foundations. For this purpose Japan "like lightning must advance to South Seas," specifically to

91. Gardiner to Sims, July 17, 1921, and September 27, 1921, William Howard Gardiner Papers, Houghton Library, Harvard University.
92. "Some Observations on the Navy of Japan," received February 25, 1920, U.S. Navy Department Policies, "The Navy of Japan," Records, General Board, RG 45, NA .
93. Louis Hacker, "The Incendiary Mahan: A Biography."
94. Nakahara Diary, December 3 and 29, 1939, January 15, 1940, Nakahara, "Dainiji sekai taisenshi" [A History of the Second World War], vol. 1, unpublished, BBK.

the Philippines, Borneo, Celebes, New Guinea, and the Solomon Islands. "Today is the moment for maritime Japan to carry its flag as far as to the Bay of Bengal." To attain this objective, Japan "should not flinch from even fighting Britain and the United States." Although such a drastic policy change did not find acceptance among the cautious leaders of the Navy Ministry, it revealed Mahanian navalism run amok, eventually playing havoc with relations with the United States.

As the example of Nakahara shows, the Japanese navy's adoption of Mahan's ideas was highly one-sided, arbitrary, and extremist. The Japanese navy also used Mahan's sea power theory as a rationale for naval appropriation. Those who originally introduced Mahan to Japan were careful to point out that there were two aspects to his doctrine: a uniquely American doctrine of overseas expansion and a universally applicable strategic theory. However, such an understanding was not that of later Japanese navalists, who read into Mahan's writings whatever they wanted to. Misuse and misapplication of Mahan's doctrines, ignoring differences in geopolitical positions of the two nations, was of course a recipe for catastrophe. For example, Admiral Inoue Shigeyoshi, one of the Japanese navy's few "liberal" leaders, wrote after the war that Japan lacked most of the elements of a great sea power, as spelled out by Mahan, that were required to wage war with the United States, namely (1) a secure territorial position; (2) human resources (size of population, national character, etc.); and (3) material resources (natural resources, industrial power, etc.).[95]

It is often suggested that the more extensive the intellectual and cultural contacts that take place between nations, the greater the chances are for peace. Cultural exchanges, it is argued, make war less likely. Although it is comforting to believe this, Mahan's influence on the Japanese navy is proof of the contrary.[96] And the "mirror image" prepared the navy's road to Pearl Harbor. The exchange of ideas in international relations is often too complex and destructive to allow complacency about its inherent peaceful tendency, as impacts of Mahan's navalism, imperialism, and racism have shown.

95. Inoue Shigeyoshi Denki Kankō Kai, *Inoue Shigeyoshi*, 295.
96. John Lewis Gaddis, *The Long Peace: Inquiries into the History of the Cold War*, 224.

Between the Old Diplomacy and the New, 1918-1922

The Washington System and the Origins of Japanese-American Rapprochement

The period from the end of World War I to the Washington Conference of 1921–1922 was a great turning point in Japanese-American relations. Leaders of both nations, but especially of Japan, were quite conscious of the contrast between the Old Diplomacy and the New. During the war President Woodrow Wilson emerged as the champion of the New Diplomacy, repudiating military alliances, the scramble for colonies, and the arms race—evils associated with the Old Diplomacy. He spelled out his vision of international idealism in his address on the Fourteen Points in January 1918, which proclaimed self-determination, removal of economic barriers, reduction of armaments, peaceful settlement of disputes, and, above all, the creation of a League of Nations.[1] More concretely, the emerging Wilsonian world order was predicated on the vision of "liberal-capitalistic internationalism" to be led by the United States and supported by cooperation among the leading industrial nations.[2]

For analytical purposes this essay uses the paradigms of the Old Diplomacy and New Diplomacy.[3] Attempting to eschew simple dichotomies, the essay shows the complex manner in which the Old Diplomacy and the New

This essay originally appeared in *Diplomatic History* 30 (April 2006): 211–30, and is reprinted by permission of Blackwell Publishing. I am indebted to Robert H. Ferrell, Charles E. Neu, and Michael A. Barnhart for commenting on this essay.

1. Thomas J. Knock, *To End All Wars: Woodrow Wilson and the Quest for a New World Order.*
2. N. Gordon Levine Jr., *Woodrow Wilson and World Politics: America's Response to War and Revolution.*
3. Robert L. Beisner in his *From the Old Diplomacy to the New, 1865–1900* uses a similar paradigm but in a totally different context.

interacted with each other and between two nations, both before and during the Washington Conference. There was no linear progression from the Old Diplomacy to the New; as the title says, it was *between* the Old Diplomacy and the New.

Initially, Wilson's ideological offensive was directed at Europe, but his call to international democracy inevitably had a universalistic appeal to Japanese leaders.[4] One of the first to respond was Yoshino Sakuzō, the intellectual leader of the democratic movement in Japan, who "greatly admired" Wilson's Fourteen Points. Yoshino held that Japan must join the new peaceful order in which "the rule of morality" was to replace "the rule of naked power." He argued that the regime of international cooperation that Wilson advocated "is to the common interest of the world and also of Japan as a member of the world."[5] Ukita Kazutami, the editor of the journal *Taiyō*, excitedly wrote about "Wilson's great diplomatic revolution." He hoped that "the ideals of liberalism and democracy be expanded to apply to [non-Western] peoples so that they will be realized internationally."[6] Hasegawa Nyozekan, an influential liberal journalist, understood the great transformation of the world in terms of change from the Old Diplomacy to the New Diplomacy. Now that Wilson's cooperative policy was prevailing over the Machiavellian forces of "exclusive, militant nationalism, militarism, and imperialism," Hasegawa contended that only democratic nations were allowed to participate in the new moral world order.[7]

Some government leaders enthusiastically responded to Wilson's New Diplomacy. Hara Kei, Japan's prime minister from 1918 to 1921, believed it vitally important to cooperate with the United States, the nation he considered to be the leader of the democratization of the world.[8] Makino Nobuaki, a former foreign minister and a liberal, was even more emphatic in his support of Wilsonianism. In December 1918, before his departure as one of the delegates to the Paris Peace Conference, Makino spoke at the Advisory Council on Foreign Relations (the highest foreign policy advisory

4. For Japan's intellectual response to Wilsonianism, see Asada, "Nichi-Bei kankei no imēji (Senzen)" [The Image of Prewar Japanese-American Relations], 307–59.

5. Yoshino, "Sekai kaizōn no risō" [The Ideal of Reconstructing the World], 87–91; Yoshino, "Taigaiteki ryōshin no hakki" [Manifestation of International Conscience], 101–3.

6. Ukita, "Daitōryō Wiruson togaikōjō no daikakumei" [Wilson and the Great Diplomatic Revolution], 352; Ukita, "Beikoku daitōryō no kyōsho o yomu" [Wilson's Presidential Message], 24.

7. Hasegawa, "Osaka *Asahi* kara *Warerae*" [From Osaka *Asahi* to *Warera*], 6–16; Hasegawa, "Minzoku shugi to kokusaishugu" [Nationalism and Internationalism], 9.

8. Mitani Taichirō, "'Tenkanki' (1918–1921) no gaikō shidō: Hara Kei oyobi Tanaka Giichi o chūshin to shite" [Diplomatic Leadership during "the Transitional Period" [1918–1921] with Particular Reference to Hara Kei and Tanaka Giichi], 2:331–36.

body), urging that Japan must abandon the Old Diplomacy and embrace the New:

> The so-called Americanism is unanimously advocated all over the world. The situation has completely changed since the days of the Old Diplomacy. . . . The New Diplomacy aims at fair play, justice, and humanity. Now that the New Diplomacy is gaining a complete victory, I conjecture that the peace conference in Paris will attach greatest importance to eradicating the Old Diplomacy.[9]

Makino insisted that Japan must forsake the Old Diplomacy of intimidating and coercing China.

Those who supported Makino's advocacy of the New Diplomacy were, however, a small minority. The majority of leaders clung to the old habits of thought. Itō Miyoji, who was left behind by the march of internationalist thought, was a captive of the Old Diplomacy. A powerful member of the Advisory Council on Foreign Relations, he scathingly attacked Makino. According to Itō, the League of Nations was "nothing more than a stratagem in the hands of the strongest powers to suppress the second-rank countries like Japan."[10] To the old guard the impact of Wilsonian appeal, undermining the very basis of their thought and policy, came as a profound culture shock. Gotō Shinpei, Japan's foreign minister from 1916 to 1918, called Wilson's diplomacy that of "moralistic aggressiveness." "It is nothing but a great hypocritical monster under the cloak of justice and humanity."[11] In a similar vein Lieutenant General Ugaki Kazushige of the General Staff wrote in his diary that Japan must be on guard against "America's real designs that are masqueraded under the name of peace and justice."[12]

The best-known and most thoroughgoing attack on Wilsonianism came from future prime minister Konoe Fumimaro, then twenty-seven years old, who published a powerful treatise entitled "Ei-Bei hon'i no heiwashugi o haisu" [Rebutting Pacifism That Only Serves the Interest of the Anglo-American Powers]. He claimed that the gospel of peace preached by their leaders was simply a rationalization of "the status quo that favors only the Anglo-American powers." He saw Japanese-American relations in terms of a conflict between a "have" (the United States) and a "have-not" (Japan),

9. Kobayashi Tatsuo, ed., *Suiusō nikki: Rinji Gaikō Chōsa Iinkai kaigi hikki nado* [Record of the Advisory Council on Foreign Relations], 326–27, 333–35; Makino, "Kokusai rennmei to Nihon no taido" [The League of Nations and Japan's Attitude], 50–51.

10. Kobayashi, ed., *Suiusō nikki*, 310, 339.

11. Ibid., 309.

12. Ugaki, *Ugaki Kazushige nikki* [Diary], 1:225.

protesting that American "economic imperialism" was threatening Japan's right to survive.[13] (When he became prime minister in 1937, he set out to actualize his vision in a China policy.)

Meanwhile, Japanese advocates of the Old Diplomacy had come to fear that Wilson's ideological offensive would undermine Japan's national polity. Ugaki described the depth of the culture shock when he wrote in his diary,

> Recently Americans are vehemently attacking the Japanese people as militarists and aggressors. They used precisely this ruse to destroy Germany's national spirit and bring about the collapse of the monarchical polity of Germany and Austria. Now, Americans are using this same tactic against us in order to destroy our Empire's strength and essential character.[14]

All this time Wilson had been mounting a series of diplomatic offensives. He bombarded Japanese leaders with protests against the continued occupation of Siberia and North Sakhalin, fought a pitched diplomatic battle at the Paris Peace Conference over Shandong, and attempted to contain Japan's China policy through a new four-power financial consortium. In the end, Wilson was forced to retreat because America had neither the power, the interest, nor the commitment sufficient to enforce his views. But it is important to note that Japanese leaders keenly felt the pressure of Wilson's New Diplomacy. He had directed world public opinion against Japan and censured its militaristic policy, trying to coerce the Japanese government into a more moderate China policy. Japan's foremost task from this time forward was to extricate itself from diplomatic isolation. At the same time, the escalating naval arms race in the Pacific brought about a crisis in Japanese-American relations, even a war scare.

Such was the background of the Washington Conference. The conference brought an across-the-board détente by redirecting naval confrontation to a new order of peaceful cooperation. Arguably, after Wilson had left the scene, some of his principles (arms reduction, peaceful settlement of international disputes, international cooperation, etc.) were partly realized at the Washington Conference by the more pragmatic Harding administration. The conference succeeded in creating in East Asia a neo-Wilsonian order of cooperation under a liberal-capitalism system. The resulting international order, the Washington System, was to consist of naval limitation in

13. Konoe, "Ei-Bei hon'i no heiwashugi o haisu," 23–25; Yabe Teiji, *Konoe Fumimaro,* 1:81–85.
14. Ugaki, *Ugaki Kazushige nikki,* 1:304–5, 311–12.

the Pacific and a regime of political cooperation in East Asia.[15] This study focuses on questions regarding the latter, and I will examine the naval aspects in my chapter on "The Imperial Japanese Navy and the Politics of Naval Limitation, 1921–1930." The two were, of course, interrelated.

The American invitation to the Washington Conference, arriving on July 11, 1921, came to Japan as a "bolt from the sky." This was another case of culture shock. A sense of crisis gripped the nation. Its shock can be gleaned from the headline of the Tokyo *Asahi*: "THE DAY OF THE FINAL ACCOUNTING OF FAR EASTERN QUESTIONS; JAPAN IN GRAVE DIF-FICULTIES." There was a fear that the United States and Britain were "col-luding" to use the naval conference to drag Japan to an international court, to roll back its wartime expansion in the Far East, and even to deprive it of its special interests in Manchuria.[16] Such extravagant expressions of culture shock struck Prime Minister Hara Kei as unseemly. He wrote in his diary that the "panic" was "jeopardizing Japan's national dignity."[17]

The alarm can be explained by Japan's deepening sense of isolation. A widespread view held that because of the cataclysmic changes in Japan's international environment—the Russian Revolution, Germany's defeat, and dissension among the victorious powers—the emerging world order would be Pax Americana. The Anglo-Japanese Alliance, which since 1902 had been the "pivot" of Japanese diplomacy, seemed destined to disappear because of American opposition. As far as Washington was concerned, the Anglo-Japanese Alliance, an exclusive military alliance recognizing and guarantee-ing spheres of influence, was a symbol of the Old Diplomacy that must go.[18]

From the outset the Japanese government assumed that the United States would dominate the Washington Conference.[19] Matsudaira Tsuneo, the chief of the Europe-America Bureau of the Foreign Ministry, wrote that prevention of war with the United States was "the pressing need of the moment." A Foreign Ministry memorandum crisply stated, "Necessity to turn around our

15. See Hosoya and Saitō, eds., *Washinton taisei to Nichi-Bei kankei*. Cf. Ian Nish, *Japanese Foreign Policy, 1869–1942: From Kasumigaseki to Miyakezaka*, 141–42. Nish argues that the Washington treaties, resulting from a series of hasty compromises, hardly amounted to a "masterpiece," and that each power had a different perception of what had been accomplished at Washington. But I contend that the United States and Japan shared the view that the Washinton Conference gave birth to a new international system (regime or order) in the Asia-Pacific based on across-the-board adjustment of major issues and cooperation among Japan, the United States, and Britain.

16. Tokyo *Asahi*, July 13, 1921; Ishii Itarō, *Gaikōkan no isshō* [Life of a Diplomat], 81–82.

17. Hara, ed. *Hara Kei nikki* [Diary of Hara Kei], 4:415.

18. Kobayashi, ed., *Suiusō nikki*, 611; Ian Nish, *Alliance in Decline: A Study in Anglo-Japanese Relations, 1908–1923*, chap. 21.

19. About Japan's reaction, see Satō Seizaburō, "Kyōchō to jiritsu tono aida: Nihon" [Between Cooperation and Autonomy: The Case of Japan], 108–14.

policy. Otherwise the fear of total isolation and a Japanese-American war."[20] Government leaders hoped that "by seizing an opportunity at the coming conference Japan can remove the fear of Japanese-American war." For the forces of the New Diplomacy, the invitation to the conference was welcomed as an occasion to reorient Japan's policy, assert a cooperative stance, and save the nation from isolation. Foreign Ministry files bulge with policy papers to the effect that "we must opt for a liberal policy and turn the conference to our advantage and improve our Empire's international position."[21]

Shidehara Kijūrō, Japan's ambassador to Washington, soon to become a delegate to the Washington Conference, was a foremost advocate of cooperation with the United States; he pleaded for a "constructive" policy to stabilize the Asia-Pacific. It simply would not do to defend past policy or cling to the status quo.[22] This was a clarion call for the New Diplomacy. Accepting such counsel, the Foreign Ministry worked out a policy of "taking the initiative to propose exactly what other powers are about to." Its memorandum on fundamental policy (July 16, 1921) stated that "Japan must turn this occasion to its good advantage by rectifying the past mistakes of dual diplomacy [military intervention in diplomacy], militaristic politics, and diplomacy dominated by military cliques."[23]

Underlying such a policy turnabout was the idea of economic diplomacy. It was thought that the only course open to Japan was peaceful economic development. For this purpose it was necessary to maintain friendly relations with both the United States and China, the two major importers of Japanese products. Japan must therefore adhere to the Open Door and territorial integrity of China. Close economic relations with the United States became vitally important, because from World War I to the postwar years trade with that power had rapidly increased Japan's exports by fourfold and its imports by sevenfold.[24]

20. Matsudaira Tsuneo's memo on the policy to be adopted by the Japanese government concerning the Pacific Conference, July 7, 1921; Memo on the urgency of Japanese-British-American naval agreement, n.d.; Memo on the Anglo-Japanese Alliance and Japanese-American cooperation, July 6, 1921; Memo on policy toward the Pacific Conference centering on the China question, JMFA.

21. See, for example, memo on the fundamental policy [toward the Washington Conference], decided on July 16, 1921; Asia Bureau's memo on policy . . . centering on the China question; Memo on the fundamental policy, JMFA.

22. Shidehara to Uchida, July 27 and 30, 1921, JMFA; Shidehara Heiwa Zaidan, ed., Shidehara Kijūrō, 225–26, 238–41; Shidehara Kijūrō, Gaikō 50-nen [Fifty Years of My Diplomacy], 84–85. Documents cited in notes 18 and 19; Memo on Sino-Japanese relations and Japanese-American relations, JMFA.

23. Foreign Ministry memorandum on fundamental policy, July 16, 1921, JMFA.

24. Ibid.; Memorandum on Sino-Japanese and Japanese-American relations, microfilm PVM Reel 47: 1449–52, JMFA .

Shidehara clarified his thinking as he prepared for the conference. And as he did so, basic differences between him and Foreign Minister Uchida Yasuya came to the fore. Shidehara opposed Uchida's regressive policy of trying to exclude "problems of sole concern to Japan and China" and "faits accomplis" from the conference agenda. These problems included, especially, the Shandong question. He asserted that insofar as the Washington Conference was aimed at general détente in the Pacific, "it would naturally require revision of the status quo" in East Asia.[25]

Shidehara's forward-looking policy, leaning toward the New Diplomacy, was tentatively approved by the cabinet on July 22, but the cabinet had to contend with the forces of the Old Diplomacy.[26] Even Prime Minister Hara, who had accepted the tenets of Shidehara's diplomacy and wanted to remake China policy, had difficulties overcoming an "insurmountable historical obstacle," namely, the traditional claim to special interests in Manchuria.[27] Foreign Minister Uchida, who was a captive of the Old Diplomacy, had long been convinced that "the keynote of our Manchurian-Mongolian policy is to plant our influence there." In the summer of 1919 he reasserted his belief at a meeting of the Advisory Council on Foreign Relations that Manchuria was not part of China proper and hence must be "controlled" by Japan.[28] Had Japan not received a "firm recognition" of its special interests in Manchuria in the Lansing-Ishii Agreement of 1917? Had Japan not obtained from the three powers an agreement "to exclude Manchuria and Mongolia" from its activities when the new China consortium was formed by Japan, the United States, Britain, and France in 1920?[29]

But it was not just Uchida who tried to maintain "the special position and interest in Manchuria." The Hara ministry had in the cabinet decision of May 1921 reconfirmed the traditional claim that special interests in Manchuria were "required for our national defense and economic necessities of our people," and that Japan must "endeavor to expand them in the future."[30] As we shall presently see, Uchida's position on the special interests in Manchuria clashed with Shidehara's at the Washington Conference. Devoted to the Open Door principles, Shidehara tried to minimize the

25. Shidehara to Uchida, July 17, 24, and 26, and August 1, 1921, JMFA.

26. Cabinet decision on policy toward the conference, July 22, 1921, JMFA.

27. Mitani, "'Tenkanki' (1918–1921) no gaikō shidō," 2:345–68.

28. Uchida Yasuya Denki Hensan Iinkai, ed., Uchida Yasuya, 197–99, 310, 334–35, 392; Kobayashi, ed., Suiusō nikki, 520, 543, 634.

29. Kurihara, ed., Tai-Mammō seisakushi no ichimen, 223–35.

30. Gaimushō, Nihon gaikō nenpyō narabini shuyō bunsho, 1840–1945 [Chronology and Major Documents on Japanese Foreign Policy, 1840–1945], 1:523–24; Uchida to Shidehara, September 27, 1921, JMFA.

importance of Japan's claim to special interests. Uchida, not known for strong leadership, was simply not capable of bringing together these two conflicting approaches to the China question.

The Foreign Ministry began to formulate its conference strategy with utmost caution in stages. First, as stated, it tried to remove from the agenda "faits accomplis" and "problems of sole concern to Japan and China," but this effort failed because Secretary of State Charles Evans Hughes opposed it on the ground of general principle. Second, the ministry endeavored to limit the agenda through preliminary negotiations with Washington, but this measure also met with Hughes's refusal. (Japan's demand would have meant excluding from the conference the Manchurian question, the Shandong question, the troubles stemming from the Twenty-One Demands of 1915, and the Siberian expedition.) As a last desperate resort, the ministry came up with a "counteroffensive plan" in case Japan's special interests should be attacked. It was after Hughes presented his conference agenda on September 8 that Japan's counteroffensive plan came to be seriously discussed at cabinet meetings and the Advisory Council on Foreign Relations.[31] The American agenda was a shopping list of all the issues that were to the detriment of Japan. Although not revealed to Japan, even more thoroughgoing was the plan drawn up by John V. A. MacMurray, the chief of the State Department's Far Eastern Division. It foresaw an indictment of Japan: spheres of influence (South Manchuria, Guangdong, Shandong, and Fujian); the status of the South Manchurian and Shandong railways; rights obtained by the Twenty-One Demands; and troops stationed in China that were not supported by international treaties.[32]

To prepare for the worst contingency, the Japanese government deliberated on its trump card, "The Open Door in the Pacific." Japan was to demand that the Open Door must be applied not only to China and Siberia but to the whole Pacific region, where Western powers possessed colonies. The plan included motley questions such as the economic and commercial Open Door (complete removal of economic barriers and free access to resources) in the Pacific, especially Southeast Asia, and the "freedom to immigrate to the United States, Canada, and Australia." If these proposals were not enough to deter the United States, Japan would denounce the Central America policy of the United States, namely, its Panama policy and

31. *FRUS (1921)*, 1:67–68.

32. Tentative Schedule of Far Eastern Matters Suggested for Discussion, Division of Far Eastern Affairs, n.d., 500.A41a/161, SDA, NA; "Suggested Agenda for Discussion," John V. A. MacMurray to Charles Evans Hughes, August 6, 1921, Leland Harrison Papers, Manuscript Division, LC.

intervention in Mexico. If this did not suffice, the Foreign Ministry would assert "the independence of Hawaii and the Philippines" and "restoration of conditions in the Orient (Pacific) as they existed one hundred years ago."[33] This was a counsel of sheer desperation upon which the whole conference would have been wrecked. That such a plan was considered in all seriousness is clear from the memoirs of Sugimura Yōtarō, a member of the delegation, who shortly after the conference wrote, "If the United States censured Japan's past deeds, we were determined to counter it by raising the question of American annexation of Hawaii and the Philippines."[34]

Prime Minister Hara knew that introducing the immigration question would alienate the United States, so he hoped it would not be necessary to raise this question. Hanihara Masanao, an expert on American affairs who was soon to join the delegates, warned that if the immigration question was raised, Japan "would have to fight all the participating powers."[35] Despite these caveats, the substance of the "counteroffensive plan" was retained. In anticipation of the worst contingency, the delegates and Shidehara (on October 13 and 14) received the following instructions:

> The problem [of the Open Door in the Pacific] is a strong weapon in our hands to defend our Empire's position at the conference and to bring about a thoroughgoing realization of our demands, while it is also meant as a means of restraining [the Anglo-American powers] from raising and discussing problems of China and Siberia.[36]

That the Japanese government was grimly prepared, if necessary, to resort to such an extreme course attests to the tenacity with which it held to special interests and faits accomplis. The "Open Door in the Pacific," ostensibly purporting the language of the New Diplomacy, was in actuality the last gasp of the Old Diplomacy. The policy-making process described above shows that those who envisaged initial steps for "positive" and cooperative

33. Memo on fundamental policy; Memo on policy to cope with the Washington Conference; Memo on the agenda on Pacific questions. See other memoranda prepared by the Asia Bureau, Foreign Ministry, cited above.

34. Sugimura Yōtarō, *Hatashite kyōkoku wa sametariya* [Have Great Powers Awakened?], 65.

35. The Third Section of the Europe-America Bureau, "Opinion regarding the immigration question that might be proposed at the Washington Conference"; Draft telegram to Ambassador Shidehara, October 10, 1921; The sixth meeting of the Foreign-Army-Navy Ministry consultation (December 9, 1921), JMFA.

36. Uchida to Shidehara, October 13, 1921, JMFA. The instructions to the delegates are printed in Gaimushō, *NGB: Washinton kaigi* [Washington Conference], 1:81–118. Their explanations are printed in 1:196–218.

foreign policy—the New Diplomacy—were compelled to retreat because of standpattism on special interests in Manchuria—the Old Diplomacy. It was fortunate for the success of the Washington Conference that American policy at the conference turned out to be so "friendly" that the Japanese never had the occasion to raise "the Open Door in the Pacific."

In deciding policy toward Japan, Secretary Hughes assumed unusual leadership in taking a friendly posture and easing Japan of any culture shocks it might have initially felt. The Republican administration, with ties to business interests, was concerned with economic relations and desired international cooperation with Japan. Hughes frankly told Shidehara, "The United States wanted to eliminate all the sources of conflict and misunderstanding in the Far East in a fresh and friendly spirit."[37] Shidehara trusted Hughes and cabled home, "Hughes is not the kind of person whose judgment is easily swayed by what his subordinates say." Hughes would come to his own conclusions based on broader political considerations.[38] Justice Louis Brandeis is said to have once called Hughes "the most enlightened mind of the eighteenth century." Hughes brought his rationalist and legalistic approach to bear on his policy. In this respect, his policy may be said to have partaken of the New Diplomacy. His view of world order was basically Wilsonian in that it sought internationalist cooperation among liberal-capitalist nations and considered Japan an important partner. Thus he came to harbor a friendly sentiment toward Japan. Unlike Wilson's policy, however, Hughes's diplomacy was realistic in the sense that it pursued "concrete and achievable goals" and aimed at reasonable settlement of disputes through compromise. This augured well of adjustment with Japan at the conference.[39]

Hughes's views were in many ways similar to those of Shidehara. Shidehara also believed in economic internationalism: the road to peace lay in an interdependent economic order. Shidehara aimed at peaceful cooperation through a policy of "live and let live."[40] This fundamental identity of views between the two protagonists reinforced their mutual trust and became an important human factor in the settlements achieved at the Washington Conference.

37. Memo of conversation with British ambassador, September 20, 1921, 500.A4/1902 1/2, SDA, NA; David J. Danelski and Joseph S. Tulchin, eds., *The Autobiographical Notes of Charles Evans Hughes*, passim.

38. Shidehara to Uchida, August 14, 1921, JMFA.

39. For Hughes's foreign policy, see Betty Glad, *Charles Evans Hughes and the Illusion of American Innocence: A Study in American Diplomacy;* John Chalmers Vinson, "Charles Evans Hughes," 128–48.

40. Shidehara Zaidan, ed., *Shidehara Kijūrō*, 252–56.

On the American side, a crucial factor for rapprochement with Japan was a partial retreat from Wilsonian New Diplomacy and a partial return to the realist tradition of Theodore Roosevelt, a master of the Old Diplomacy. Hughes's primary aims were to reconfirm the Open Door principles and to write them into a multilateral treaty, but he faced the problem of how to handle Japan's anticipated opposition. He had been warned by State Department officials that Japan would strenuously demand that its special interests in Manchuria be recognized. It was an old conflict between America's "milieu goal" (the Open Door principles) and Japan's "possessive goal" (special interests in Manchuria).[41] The U.S. government aimed to establish rules of conduct, the equality of commercial opportunity, and to create an international environment that would allow China to establish a stable, unified, and autonomous government free from fear of foreign intervention—the principles that accorded with the New Diplomacy. The United States government feared that this "milieu goal" would come into conflict with Japan's "possessive goal," its special interests in Manchuria—in short, the Old Diplomacy.

Cables from Far Eastern posts as well as memoranda prepared by the Far Eastern Division had been warning Hughes that since Japan regarded as "vital" the protection of resources and economic control of Manchuria, it might take forceful measures to defend its "paramount position." In a perceptive memorandum to the American delegation, Edwin L. Neville, a Japan specialist in the Far Eastern Division, pinpointed America's weak position: "Our Open Door policy . . . cannot be sustained without force. . . . The United States has never been willing to supply force [to defend the Open Door]. . . . Besides, we have at different times openly acknowledged the *status quo,* when we knew what that involved, and even recognized the special interests of Japan."[42] Neville was referring to the Lansing-Ishii Agreement of 1917. Chandler P. Anderson, a former counselor of the State Department and a member of the American delegation, handed Hughes a copy of a letter President Theodore Roosevelt had written to his successor William H. Taft in 1910, when the latter provoked Japan by proposing to neutralize Manchurian railways:

It is peculiarly our interest not to take any steps as regards Manchuria which would give the Japanese cause to feel, with or without reason, that

41. For a theoretical analysis of "possessive goals" vs. "milieu goals," see Arnold Wolfers, *Discord and Collaboration: Essays on International Politics,* 73–76.
42. Neville's memo for Hughes, June 15, 1921, 790.94/5; Neville's memo for Hughes, October 8, 1921, 500.A41a/163; MacMurray to Hughes, October 10 and 11, 1921; MacMurray's confidential rider, October 12, 1921; Neville's memo, "Japan in the Far East," in *Papers Relating to the Pacific and the Far East,* SDA, NA.

we are hostiles to them, or a menace—in however slight a degree—to their interests. And as regards Manchuria, if the Japanese choose to follow a course of conduct to which we are adverse, we cannot stop it unless we are prepared for war.[43]

This realist legacy of the past master of the Old Diplomacy must have been a powerful reminder to Hughes. Paying attention to these recommendations, Hughes forged a policy of his own. He was sensitive to public opinion, and the polls showed that the American people overwhelmingly demanded naval limitation, while few had an interest in Far Eastern issues. It followed that he could not afford to antagonize Japan for fear of jeopardizing naval limitation. On the other hand, the United States Senate might not approve a naval treaty if Far Eastern issues were left unresolved. Hughes had to strike a balance.

Recommendations pointed to a cautious approach. Hughes would oppose, in his words, Japan's "aggressive" policy of "political domination or a discrimination in her favor," but he was willing to recognize "natural and *legitimate* economic opportunities for Japan."[44] Regarding Japan's "legitimate interests," there were differences among the American delegates and representatives. Herbert Hoover, the secretary of commerce and a member of the advisory committee with whom Hughes conferred on the China question, emphasized that given dependence on Chinese resources, "Japan certainly had legitimate reasons" for its continental policy. Having lived in China as an engineer, he had doubts about China's potentiality for Westernization. On the other hand, he admired the Japanese and sympathized with their plight. He felt that faced with the chaotic condition in China, Japan needed to protect its special interests.[45]

Elihu Root, one of the American delegates and the genro of the Republican Party, was outspoken in defense of Japan's "legitimate interest." Having served as Theodore Roosevelt's secretary of state, he was a masterful practitioner of the Old Diplomacy. In 1908 he concluded the Root-Takahira Agreement, which implicitly recognized Japan's special interests in Manchuria. He regarded Japan as a peacekeeping power in the Far East.

---

43. The Diary of Chandler P. Anderson, October 28, 1921, Chandler P. Anderson Papers (hereafter cited as Anderson Papers), LC; Roosevelt to Taft, December 22, 1910, cited in Arthur Whitney Griswold, *Far Eastern Policy of the United States,* 131–32. See also Henry Cabot Lodge, "Journal of the Washington Conference," November 1, 3, and 6, 1921, Henry Cabot Lodge Papers, Massachusetts Historical Society, Boston.

44. *FRUS, 1922,* 1:1–2 (italics added).

45. Hoover, *Memoirs of Herbert Hoover: The Cabinet and the Presidency, 1920–1933,* 180; Robert Gordon Kaufman, *Arms Control during the Pre-Nuclear Era,* 115.

He sympathized with Japan's feeling that the Western powers had thwarted its legitimate claims. And he felt Americans must graduate from their sentimental beliefs about protecting China and recognize the cold logic of Japan's position in East Asia. As Richard W. Leopold, Root's biographer, has written, Root "hoped . . . that Japan would become the England of the Orient, with a constitutional form of government, a freedom from excessive territorial ambition, and a desire to promote stability and equality of commercial opportunity in a troubled area." Believing that the "moderate" and "liberal" elements were in control of the Tokyo government, Root advocated a manifestly friendly policy calculated to give strength to these elements.[46] Root's pro-Japanese views were not entirely shared by Hughes and State Department officials. On his part, Root, a throwback to the days of the Old Diplomacy, did not fully appreciate the changes that had take place in American policy during the Wilson era. He often negotiated personally with the Japanese delegates or through his intermediary without telling his American colleagues or State Department specialists.

The most comprehensive recommendation was presented by J. Reuben Clark, who was special counsel to the State Department and Hughes's assistant. Injected into his lengthy memorandum was Rooseveltian realism. Here is a synopsis of his recommendation:

(1) America's "only prime and great concern" is the "security" of the United States in the Pacific region. While the problem of naval limitation is of vital importance, Far Eastern questions are only secondary.

(2) Balance of power must be maintained in the Pacific and the Far East. If one power (Japan) becomes overwhelmingly dominant, it will threaten the American territories (the Philippines, Guam, Hawaii, etc.).

(3) Mutual recognition of territorial and political status quo in the Pacific and the Far East.

(4) "The doctrine of special relationship must be agreed upon. Japan is right in her claim that she has a special relationship in China." He added that it was important that the conference "not busy itself with an attempt to expose and punish the individual wrongs of the past."

(5) Every effort must be made to remove Japanese suspicion and fear of the United States.[47]

46. Anderson Diary, November 26 and December 27, 1921, Anderson Papers, LC; Leopold, *Elihu Root and the Conservative Tradition*, 60; Philip Jessup, *Elihu Root*, 2: 447–48.

47. Clark, "Some Basic Reflections on the Far Eastern Problems," September 28, 1921; "Preliminary Suggestions," n.d., 500.41a/58, SDA, NA; Hughes to Clark, June 10, 1922, Hughes Papers, LC.

In giving priority to America's security in the Pacific and openly calling for recognition of Japan's special interests, Clark's memorandum was clearly in line with Roosevelt's realism. This memorandum appears here because most of the points were incorporated into Hughes's policy at the conference.

However, one point, Japan's special interests, baffled Hughes. He tended to relate issues simply, because of his legal approach, and was prone to ignore ambiguity not easily defined in international law. He opposed reconfirming or even bringing up in the negotiations Japan's special interests. For the moment, he would proceed on the basis of the status quo. He gave his views in his instructions to the American delegation:

> That the only real yellow peril lay in the exploitation of China by an imperialistic Japanese government; that he had gone along on the theory always that this country would never go to war over any aggression on the part of Japan in China, and that consequently the most that could be done would be to stay Japan's hand, and that . . . nothing should be done in such a way as to offer a pretext for Japan to enter upon any further acts of aggression.[48]

Such was the extent of Hughes's Far Eastern policy. Like Root, Hughes also rejected a hard-line policy that might provoke Japan's "military party"; instead, he would pursue a friendly policy that would bolster Japan's liberal-moderate elements and promote Japanese-American cooperation.

On November 12, at the opening session of the Washington Conference, Hughes resorted to a technique of the New Diplomacy. In his initial address he dramatically presented the famous "bombshell proposal" stipulating a drastic naval limitation. To many at the meeting, it seemed like an adventure in Wilsonian diplomacy ("an open covenant openly arrived at").[49] Sugimura, a member of the Japanese delegation, wrote with some exaggeration, "Court diplomacy and bureaucratic diplomacy have become things of the distant past. The new age is no longer satisfied even with people's diplomacy; it demands public diplomacy."[50] What Hughes, and his fellow American delegates, calculated was that his drastic proposal for naval

48. Minutes of the thirteenth meeting of the United States delegation, December 7, 1921, *Papers of the American Delegation to the Washington Conference*, 500.A41/12, SDA, NA.

49. Inaba Masao, Kobayashi Tatsuo, Shimada Toshihiko, and Tsunoda Jun, eds., *TSM: Bekkan Shiryōhen* [Japan's Road to the Pacific War: Separate Volume on Documents], 3. For a detailed treatment of the Japanese delegates' response to Hughes's proposal, see Asada, "Japan and the United States, 1915–1925," chaps. 5–7.

50. Sugimura, *Hatashite kyōkoku wa sametariya*, 3–4.

limitation would instantly receive such an overwhelming support not only from the American people but from world public opinion that Japan would have no choice but to accept it. Hughes also linked the naval question with Far Eastern issues. If naval limitation should be jeopardized by Japan's obstructionism regarding Far Eastern problems, it would be condemned by the whole world, so Japan would perforce have to take a conciliatory position. On both accounts Hughes proved correct, as a look at the Japanese side of the picture would show. The most urgent and important task for the Japanese delegates was to wipe out the stigma of a "militaristic" and "aggressive" nation and salvage it from diplomatic isolation. They did their very best to persuade the Tokyo government time and again to accept compromise solutions in the interest of a successful conference.[51]

Hughes's design was to start the whole process of Pacific détente. For this purpose the United States would take the initiative by demonstrating its friendly attitude toward Japan. Root secretly apprised the Japanese delegate Hanihara that the United States had proposed drastic naval limitation at the outset to assure Japan that it had no hostile intentions. Hughes was careful to avoid any threat; he would rely on persuasion and the moral force of public opinion.[52] This relieved the Japanese enormously.

Hughes liberally sprinkled his opening address and public discussions with the rhetoric of the New Diplomacy—that of peace and liberal democracy—but his secret negotiations on Far Eastern problems were none too different from the give-and-take and mutual compromise that characterized the Old Diplomacy. With regard to Asian-Pacific questions, he avoided public appeals, which could have only clashed and exacerbated relations with Japan. Instead, he would reach compromise solutions through quiet behind-the-scenes negotiations.

Root kept close liaison with his friend Hanihara, one of the Japanese delegates, and Root played a crucial role. A veteran of Old Diplomacy, Root told Hanihara that he saw Japan's China policy as similar to America's "big stick" diplomacy in Central America. He also told him that "I fully understand that Japan's expedition to China, like American expeditions to Cuba and Haiti, had some good reasons, but it is difficult to make the American people understand this." Root advised expeditiously withdrawing, handling the matter adroitly. (Hughes, not to mention the Far Eastern Division of the State Department, would have been surprised to hear what he was

51. For a detailed treatment of the Japanese delegates' response to Hughes's proposal, see Asada, "Japan and the United States," chaps. 5–7.
52. Hanihara to Uchida, December 5, 1921, JMFA; Anderson Diary, November 26, 1921, Anderson Papers, LC.

confiding to Hanihara.) Root counted on the statesmanship of Japan's enlightened leaders who appreciated the interrelatedness of nations. He told Hanihara that he was "willing to offer as much sympathetic assistance to Japan as possible." He thought that every one of the Japanese delegates ran the risk of assassination when they returned if they agreed to anything that might be regarded as inimical to the interests of Japan.[53]

But there was a limit beyond which Root could not go as an American delegate, so he employed Stanley Washburn, the secretary of the American delegation and a pro-Japanese journalist, as a confidential go-between. Hanihara told Washburn that Japan would absolutely oppose any attempt to undermine the status quo in Manchuria or weaken Japan's special interests and influence there.[54]

The resolution that Root introduced to the Far Eastern Committee of the conference on November 21 became the nucleus of the Nine-Power Treaty relating to China, so it is necessary to examine its genesis. A. Whitney Griswold in his classical study, *Far Eastern Policy of the United States*, wrote that the Nine-Power Treaty was "the most dynamic and the most comprehensive attempt" to confine "the hungry expansionism of Japan."[55] However, Japanese archival evidence shows that the treaty was nothing of the sort: it represented yet another example of ambiguous Japanese-American compromise in the tradition of the Root-Takahira Agreement and the Lansing-Ishii Agreement—with one important difference: this time the Open Door principles were to be written into a multilateral treaty.

While drafting his resolution, Root anticipated that the Japanese "would undoubtedly insist upon maintaining their hold on Manchuria," and he admitted that "a good deal was to be said" in favor of Japan's attempt to strengthen its position there. With this in mind Root phrased the fourth clause of his resolution that pledged the signatories to refrain "from countenancing *action inimical to the security of [signatory] powers.*"[56] Whose "security" could be threatened in China? As we have seen, it had been Japan's traditional contention that its special interests in Manchuria were vital to

53. Hanihara to Uchida, December 5, 1921, and January 24, 1922, JMFA.

54. Stanley Washburn to Root, October 30 and November 26, 1921; Washburn's memo for Root, "Japanese Situation," November 26, 1921, Interview with Stanley Washburn (hereafter cited as Washburn interview), Oral History Project, Butler Library, Columbia University.

55. Griswold, *Far Eastern Policy*, 331.

56. Hanihara to Uchida, December 5, 1921, JMFA; Anderson Diary, December 5, 1921, Anderson Papers, LC. For details on the drafting of the Root Resolution, see Asada, "Japan and the United States," 270–78. The Root Resolution is printed in U.S. Department of State, *Conference on the Limitation of Armament: Washington, November 12, 1921–February 6, 1922*, 890.

its "national defense and economic existence." The "security clause," then, is to be understood as America's implicit recognition of Japanese claims to special interests. This impression was reinforced by Root's having lifted the clause from the American note to Japan of March 16, 1920, at the time of formation of the four-power China consortium. This note stated in part,

> There would appear to be no occasion [for Japan] to apprehend on the part of the Consortium any activities directed against *the economic life or national defense of Japan*. It is therefore felt that Japan could with entire assurance rely upon the good faith of the United States and of the other two Powers associated in the Consortium [Britain and France] *to refuse their countenance to any operation inimical to the vital interests of Japan*.[57]

One detects here a thread of continuity running from the Root-Takahira Agreement of 1908 through the Lansing-Ishii Agreement of 1917 to the Nine-Power Treaty of 1922, so far as Japan's "special interests" were concerned. It was hardly an instrument of the New Diplomacy. Not surprisingly, Root assured Japanese delegates through a secret channel that "There will be no change whatsoever in Japan's present position in Manchuria."[58]

Not satisfied with an *implicit* recognition contained in the "security clause," Foreign Minister Uchida instructed Shidehara to rephrase the Root Resolution "so that it would not restrain Japan's rightful actions accruing from its special interests based on its geographic propinquity to China"—Japan's "possessive goal."[59] This instruction, calling for a public reconfirmation of the "Manchurian-Mongolian reservation" (read "exclusion"), seemed to be another attempt to write the Lansing-Ishii Agreement, a document of the Old Diplomacy, into a new treaty. Shidehara protested that such a demarche would run counter to the Open Door principles (America's "milieu goal") to which the Japanese delegates had already openly subscribed "without condition or reservation." He cabled, "It is not the guiding principle of our diplomacy to establish a definite exception to the principle of the Open Door and

---

57. *FRUS, 1920*, 1:512–13 (italics added). This note was in response to the Japanese demand of March 2, 1920: "In matters . . . relating to loans affecting *South Manchuria and Eastern Inner Mongolia* which in their opinion are calculated to create a serious impediment to *the security of the economic life and national defense* of Japan, the Japanese Government reserves the right to take the necessary steps to guarantee such security" (*FRUS, 1920*, 1:500–503, italics added). For a detailed treatment of formation of the new four-power China consortium, see Asada, "Japan and the United States," 83–109.

58. Anderson Diary, November 18, 19, 20, and 26, and December 27, 1921, Anderson Papers, LC; Japanese delegates to Uchida, December 11, 1921, and January 16, 1922, JMFA; Asada, "Japan and the United States," 280–81; Jessup, *Elihu Root*, 2:562.

59. Uchida to the delegates, December 3, 1921, JMFA.

equality of opportunity." If Japan demanded the "Manchurian-Mongolian reservation," Shidehara warned, the United States and China would denounce it as an attempt to reassert monopolistic and exclusive rights and establish a sphere of influence in Manchuria and Mongolia.[60] The conflict between the Old Diplomacy and the New, never resolved in Tokyo in pre-conference days, reappeared at the Washington meeting, and a clash seemed imminent between Shidehara's policy of cooperating with the United States and Uchida's policy of having special interests acknowledged. However, Shidehara adroitly persuaded Uchida by assuring him that the Root Resolution's security clause would serve the same purpose as an explicit reference to special interest. On his part, Root, who never thought much of his resolution, said that this would have "the advantage of making the Nine-Power Treaty look *as if the Conference had accomplished something.*"[61]

Other Far Eastern questions need to be briefly sketched. The Shandong question, according to Japan's original position, was "a problem of sole concern" to Japan and China—Old Diplomacy. Japan opposed any American interference or mediation. Root was aware of the strong stand Japan had taken on Shandong. Shidehara, however, cabled Uchida that the question had become a Japanese-American issue "because of the Senate controversy over the ratification of the Versailles treaty."[62] On the other hand, Hanihara forcefully warned Washburn that "If Japan should succumb to American pressure, the Japanese government would collapse within twenty-four hours." In reporting to Root, Washburn emphatically stated that Japan must be "helped to extricate itself from the present difficulty." It was important to give Japan an opportunity to withdraw with honor. Above all, the conference must avoid provoking or isolating Japan.[63]

The Republican Party had attacked the "rape of Shandong" during the Senate controversy over the ratification of the Versailles Treaty, so the settlement of this question was a political imperative for the Harding administration, without which the ratification of the naval treaty was in doubt. It was fortunate that at this juncture both Hughes and Shidehara could put themselves in each other's shoes. Shidehara understood that the Shandong issue was more important politically to the United States than to Japan. Keenly aware of the American government's predicament and to help it out, he urged Tokyo to make one compromise after another.[64] Like Hughes,

60. Delegates to Uchida, January 22, 1922, JMFA.
61. Anderson Diary, December 27, 1921 (italics added), Anderson Papers, LC.
62. Shidehara to Uchida, July 24, 1921, JMFA; Ujita, *Shidehara Kijūrō*, 70.
63. Washburn to Root, October 30, 1921; Washburn's memo to Root, November 26, 1921, Washburn interview, Butler Library, Columbia University.
64. Delegates to Uchida, December 20 and 31, 1921, and January 9, 1922, JMFA.

Shidehara linked Shandong with naval limitation and tried to solve both in the context of Japanese-American détente.

During the last stage of the Japanese-Chinese negotiations, after the Japanese had made their "final concession," Hughes, siding with Japan, turned to put pressure on China. When Stanley K. Hornbeck, a pro-Chinese and anti-Japanese member of the Far Eastern Division protested, Hughes retorted, "Japan has felt the full pressure that the situation admits. It should be remembered that she has her own opinion and the prestige and position of her Government to consider. . . . There are certain limits beyond which she will not go."[65] Hughes ruled that Japan should withdraw from Shandong with honor and on its own initiative. And this Japan faithfully did after the conference, in late October 1922. Whereas Wilson, the champion of the New Diplomacy, had fought a diplomatic feud with Japan and lost at Paris, the more pragmatic Harding administration carefully avoided confrontation with Japan and obtained a settlement that satisfied the Senate.

One remaining issue was the withdrawal of troops from Siberia. Members of the Russian Division of the State Department urged Hughes to apply "strong moral pressure," but Hughes, just as he had regarding the Shandong question, rejected this recommendation, saying that there was no means of "driving the Japanese troops out of Siberia without going to war."[66] He quietly settled the matter with Shidehara so that Japan could pledge the troop withdrawal on its own initiative, a pledge that was honored in October 1922.

Abrogation of the Anglo-Japanese Alliance—a prime symbol of the Old Diplomacy—was a prerequisite for a treaty of naval limitation, but it would have been delicate for a third party to demand termination. Working on the drafts presented by Shidehara and British delegate Arthur Balfour, Hughes transformed them into "a general and harmless international agreement."[67] First, he limited the scope of its application to the Pacific islands, so that it would guarantee the status quo of the Pacific, which meant the security of the Philippines. Second, he made it a four-power treaty by including France. This was intended to remove any impression of an exclusive political pact with Japan and Britain, the Old Diplomacy in new form. The result was the Four-Power Treaty. For the United States it was a diplomatic triumph, in that it terminated the Anglo-Japanese Alliance, the hated symbol of the Old Diplomacy, and demilitarized the western Pacific. Japan and Britain accepted

65. Hughes's memo for information of E. T. Williams and Stanley K. Hornbeck, January 26, 1922, 793.94/1265, SDA, NA.

66. DeWitt Poole's memo for Hughes, January 10 and 11, 1922; Hughes to Root, January 31, 1922, Hughes Papers, LC; Delegates to Uchida, January 25, 1922, JMFA.

67. Anderson Diary, November 20 and 27, 1921, Anderson Papers, LC; FRUS, 1922, 2:7–8.

the new treaty because Japan and Britain gave priority to naval arms limitation and good relations with the United States. Although Japan lost the
alliance, it was saved from diplomatic isolation and had its security and economic development assured by the new system of interrelated treaties—the
Washington System—that consisted of the Five-Power Treaty of naval limitation, the Four-Power Treaty, and the Nine-Power Treaty.[68]

All in all, the Japanese government positively responded to America's
détente diplomacy and gladly joined the Washington System. Peaceful economic cooperation, embodied in Shidehara diplomacy, became the main
stream of Japanese foreign policy. This turnabout could be noted in the
remarkable improvement in the Japanese attitude toward the United States.
The culture shock that the Japanese had initially experienced when they
received the invitation to the conference was removed by the unexpectedly "sympathetic attitude" of the American delegates, and Japan's delegates appreciated American efforts "not to hurt our feelings or honor."
According to the delegates, "American attitude toward Japan is surprisingly friendly and favorable when compared with the Japanese-American
confrontation at the Paris Peace Conference." "We have ascertained," the
Japanese happily reported toward the end of the conference, "that the policy of the American government is on the whole pro-Japanese." Shidehara
declared, "There is no doubt that Hughes has respected Japan's position
as much as possible."[69]

Chief delegate Katō Tomosaburō, who as head delegate masterfully handled the naval negotiations, cabled, "Here in Washington we delegates have
hardly imagined any such thing as Anglo-American oppression." He especially wanted to emphasize this point, for upon return to Tokyo he publicly declared, "I hear that some people are prejudiced and think that Japan
was subjected to Anglo-American coercion at the conference, but as one who
directly participated in the negotiations, I can categorically state that this
was not the case."[70]

It is clear that both Shidehara and Hughes held a broad and long-range
vision of cooperative relations that went beyond individual treaties and
agreements of the conference. What was important, they believed, was trust,
rapport, and mutual confidence that alone could ensure treaties and agreements. Hughes proclaimed that the conference had dissipated the war

68. Delegates to Uchida, December 2, 1921, JMFA.
69. Delegates to Uchida, December 5, 1921; and Shidehara to Uchida, January 26, 1922,
JMFA.
70. Navy Minister Katō to Vice Minister Ide, January 16, 1922, JMFA; Tokyo *Asahi*,
March 13, 1922.

clouds with a "new atmosphere" of peace and harmony, which he called "the spirit of the Washington Conference."[71] For the Japanese, the conference became the starting point of "Shidehara diplomacy." When later appointed foreign minister in June 1924, he exclaimed his diplomatic stance in the following words:

> Machiavellian stratagem and aggressive policy are now things of the past. Our diplomacy must follow the path of justice and peace. . . . In short, Japan hopes to adhere to and enlarge the lofty spirits that are shown both explicitly and implicitly in the Paris Peace Treaty and the treaties and agreements of the Washington Conference.[72]

Admiral Katō Tomosaburō, known for his reticence, spoke eloquently about the New Diplomacy: "The conference succeeded because the participating nations agreed on the pressing need to establish world peace and alleviate the burden [of armaments]. And these two aims can be accomplished only by freeing ourselves from the old world of exclusive competition among the powers and by creating the new world of international cooperation."[73]

The Japanese leaders of the democratic movement blessed the Washington System in hyperbolic terms. The leading Wilsonian thinker, Yoshino Sakuzō, wrote while the conference was still in session that "It is almost certain that a fair and just peaceful position will in the end morally triumph." To him the Washington Conference signaled the arrival of a new age in world history. "The Four-Power Treaty was concluded as the result of a complete change in men's minds. The important thing is this renovation of the spirit, in comparison with which individual treaties are not important." He saw the Washington Conference as "an irrepressive manifestation of international democracy."[74] There were abundant expressions of a conviction that the era of New Diplomacy had arrived. Hayashi Kiroku, a diplomatic historian who accompanied the delegation as the Foreign Ministry's counselor, wrote, "We must be resolved to conduct the New Diplomacy in accord with the new era." Sugimura Yōtarō wrote that although there remained "considerable differences between the government's diplomacy

71. Memo of Hughes's interview with Charles Addis, March 30, 1922, Hughes Papers, LC; Hughes, *The Pathway of Peace*, 575–83.

72. Shidehara Zaidan, ed., *Shidehara Kijūrō*, 255–56.

73. Tokyo *Asahi*, March 13, 1922.

74. Yoshino Sakuzō, "Jiron" [Current Opinions], (January 1922) 303, 310; Oka Yoshitake, ed., *Yoshino Sakuzō hyōronshū* [Collected Current Commentaries of Yoshino Sakuzō], 331–32.

and the people's diplomacy," Japan must try to walk in the path of New Diplomacy like Europe and the United States.[75]

In conclusion, in this essay we have examined the making of Japanese-American rapprochement from 1918 to 1922. Japanese policy moved from the Old Diplomacy of the World War I era to the New Diplomacy represented by Shidehara, while American policy somewhat receded from Wilsonian New Diplomacy in the direction of the Old Diplomacy in Theodore Roosevelt's tradition. The Washington System emerged when the two movements intersected.

75. Hayashi Kiroku, "Kafu kaigi to waga teikoku" [The Washington Conference and Our Empire], 2.

From Washington to London

The Imperial Japanese Navy and the Politics of Naval Limitation, 1921-1930

The 1920s seemed a tranquil decade of arms limitation defined by the three naval conferences: at Washington in 1921–1922, Geneva in 1927, and London in 1930. Within the Japanese navy, however, there was strong and growing opposition among officers, particularly those on the Naval General Staff, to the policy of arms limitation pursued by the leadership of the Navy Ministry. This essay explores, on the basis of hitherto unused Japanese naval records,[1] the hidden moves and countermoves in the years after the Washington Conference that climaxed in a violent collision within Japanese naval circles in 1930 over the London naval treaty. In short, it examines the Japanese side of the "prelude to Pearl Harbor."[2]

Japanese Naval Traditions

The Five-Power Treaty of the Washington Conference, signed on February 6, 1922, received a chilly, even hostile reception from professional navy men among all the signatories, but none harbored as great an antipathy and

This essay is adapted from an article bearing the same title that appeared in *Diplomacy and Statecraft* 4 (November 1993). It was reprinted in *The Washington Conference, 1921–1922: Naval Rivalry, East Asian Stability, and the Road to Pearl Harbor,* edited by Erik Goldstein and John Maurer. In preparing this essay I am greatly indebted to the late Nomura Minoru, the late Suekuni Masao (BBKS), the late Arthur Marder, and especially the late Enomoto Jūji. It is reprinted here by permission of the Taylor and Francis Group, LLC http://www.taylorandfrancis.com.
1. The single most important record for the purpose of this essay is the enormous collection of papers of the late Enomoto Jūji (hereafter cited as Enomoto Papers) at the BBK. (See above, p. 23).
2. Cf. Wheeler, *Prelude to Pearl Harbor.*

indignation as those in the Japanese navy. They viewed the Washington treaty, which "imposed" on Japan an "inferior fleet ratio" of 60 percent vis-à-vis the United States and Great Britain, as nothing short of a total negation of Japanese naval traditions, dating back to 1907, the year in which "Teikoku kokubō hōshin" [The Imperial National Defense Policy] was sanctioned by the high command. By this time the navy's views had been formulated into the following basic guidelines: (1) the need for a 70 percent naval fleet ratio as a strategic imperative; (2) its corollary, a building plan for an "eight-eight fleet" (consisting of eight battleships and eight battle cruisers); and (3) the concept of the United States as the Japanese navy's "hypothetical enemy." These doctrines were of course interrelated, and the abandonment of the first guideline at the Washington Conference jeopardized the other two. Therefore, a brief discussion of these doctrines is in order here, to understand Japanese naval policy during the 1920s.

The idea of the United States as the navy's "hypothetical enemy" had first appeared in the Imperial National Defense Policy of 1907. It stipulated that "of all hypothetical enemies the most important from the viewpoint of naval operations is the United States." At that time, however, it amounted to little more than a "budgetary enemy," a target for building a large fleet. It will be recalled that Satō Tetsutarō in his treatise *Teikoku kokubō shiron* [On the History of Imperial National Defense] (1908) employed the term *hypothetical enemy* as a "standard for armaments," a bureaucratically convenient pretext for demanding greater building appropriations.[3] This manner of defining a hypothetical enemy reflected the sea power theories of Alfred T. Mahan, who wrote that the standard of naval preparedness should take into account "not the most probable of dangers, but the most formidable."[4] Similarly, Japanese naval strategists defined their hypothetical enemy as "any one power, whether friendly or hostile, that can confront Japan with the greatest force of arms."

The idea of a 70 percent ratio as Japan's minimum defense requirement vis-à-vis the United States rested on the premise that the approaching enemy armada would need a margin of at least 50 percent superiority over the defending fleet.[5] On the American side, distance, as Mahan said, was a

3. Satō, *Teikoku kokubō shiron*, 724, 748, 760.
4. Mahan, *Interest of America in Sea Power*, 180.
5. If the Japanese navy had 70 percent strength vis-à-vis the United States, it would correspond to 143 percent for the United States Navy—not quite enough for launching an attack on Japan with prospect of success. If the Japanese navy had 60 percent, the American navy's strength would amount to 166, deemed sufficient to attack Japan. BBKS, *Senshi sōsho: Daihon'ei kaigunbu: Rengō kantai* [War History Series: Navy Section of the Imperial Headquarters: Combined Fleet; hereafter cited as *Rengō kantai*], 1:156–59; Nomura Minoru, "Tai-Bei-Ei kaisen to tai-Bei 7-wari shisō" [The Outbreak of War with the United States and Britain, and the Idea of a 70 Percent Ratio], 26–27.

factor equivalent to the number of ships.[6] It was a rule of thumb among American naval planners that for every one thousand miles from its advance base a battle fleet steamed, it lost 10 percent of its fighting efficiency, because of wear and tear, bottom fouling, or enemy attacks en route. The Philippines are three thousand miles from Hawaii; therefore, the U.S. naval fleet would have an operational strength of 70 percent upon its arrival in the western Pacific.[7]

To the Japanese navy, therefore, the seemingly minor difference between 60 and 70 percent made the difference between victory and defeat. The great importance it attached to this issue explains the tenacity with which Japan demanded a 70 percent ratio at the three naval conferences held during the 1920s. The idea of a 70 percent ratio, reinforced by war games and maneuvers in the Pacific, was in time crystallized into a firmly held consensus— even an obsession—within the Japanese navy.

With an eye to attaining a 70 percent ratio, the Japanese navy drafted the "eight-eight fleet" plan, an ambitious program consisting of eight battleships and eight armored cruisers (later, battle cruisers), all no more than eight years old. With this force level, Japanese planners believed that the United States was not likely to risk war. The eight years spanning 1914–1921 may be called "the age of the eight-eight fleet"; through the navy's public relations efforts, the "eight-eight fleet" plan became widely known and supported by the Japanese people.

The outbreak of the European war in August 1914 proved Mahan's predictions correct: the great war destroyed the multilateral balance of power in East Asia and left Japan and the United States directly confronting each other across the Pacific. Japan occupied German islands in Micronesia upon declaration of war on Germany, and in January 1915 Japan presented to China the Twenty-One Demands, jeopardizing China's integrity. This resulted in serious aggravation of Japanese-American relations. In January 1917, to counter the perceived Japanese threat, the General Board of the United States Navy urged that the navy must strive "for American domination of the western Pacific" that would, in the words of William R. Braisted, "practically deprive Japan of the capacity of independent self-defense."[8] Given the official U.S. policy of never using force to support the Open Door in China, the American naval buildup seemed entirely excessive.

By this time an increasing number of Japanese officers had come to regard the United States as more than a mere "budgetary enemy." A significant

6. Quoted in Harold Sprout and Margaret Sprout, *Toward a New Order of Sea Power: American Naval Policy and the World Scene, 1918–1922,* 23.
7. Miller, *War Plan Orange,* 32; Itō Masanori, *Gunshuku?* [Naval Limitation?], 242–74.
8. Braisted, *The United States Navy in the Pacific, 1897–1909,* 208.

memorandum prepared in March 1916 by Rear Admiral Takeshita Isamu, the head of the Operations Division, stated, "The nation with which a clash of arms is most likely *in the near future* is the United States." He concluded with a neo-Mahanian brand of economic determinism:

> With its vast resources and newly acquired colossal financial power, the United States is invading the Oriental market. It is blocking our national expansion and depriving us of our interests [in Asia]. In addition, it is rapidly expanding its naval strength and completing military facilities in the Pacific, thus imposing its national policy on us.[9]

Takeshita's memorandum was important, for he was to participate in the revision of the Imperial National Defense Policy, which was sanctioned in June 1918. Although its text has not yet been discovered, it is likely, in light of Takeshita's memorandum, that the United States came to be regarded as the hypothetical enemy with which a clash was probable "in the near future." This is corroborated by a working paper prepared by the Naval Staff College in June 1918, which stated, "the rivaling nation with which the clash is most probable on account of the China question has become the United States."[10] Japan's frankly expansionist policy in China and Siberia had critically aggravated relations with the United States. Against this backdrop the conviction grew in the Naval General Staff that "the rival nation with which a clash of interests is most probable—in other words, the potential enemy—is the United States."[11]

However, Navy Minister Katō Tomosaburō reiterated at a cabinet meeting the conventional view that it was *"from the viewpoint of naval armaments* that America is regarded as hypothetical enemy number one."[12] Katō's statement, in line with the traditional idea of a "budgetary enemy," is to be understood as an expression of Japan's effort to maintain a semblance of naval balance with the United States. The ambitious American plan to build a "navy second to none" in 1916 had almost come as a culture shock to the Japanese navy. In November 1918, shortly after the Armistice, Katō observed at the Advisory Council on Foreign Relations (the highest foreign policy advisory body) that if the United States carried out its plan to

9. Hatano Masaru, ed., *Kaigun no gaikōkan Takeshita Isamu nikki* [Diary of Takeshita Isamu, the Naval Diplomat], 48 (italics added).

10. Kaigun Daigakkō [Naval Staff College], "Taishō 4 naishi 9-nen sen'eki kaigun senshi Furoku dai-6 hen kimitsu hoshū" [Confidential Supplement, Vol. 6, to the Naval War History of World War I], BBK.

11. Ibid.

12. Kaigun Daijin Kanbō [Navy minister's secretariat], ed., *Kaigun gunbi enkaku* [Developments of Naval Armaments], 1:220 (italics added).

expand the navy, "it will result in such extreme disparity as to reduce the Pacific Ocean to an American lake."[13] To counter such a fear, the Naval Strength Requirement that accompanied the revised national defense policy of 1918 provided for an "eight-eight-eight fleet" plan that was to add eight capital ships or battle cruisers to the existing "eight-eight" program. But from the beginning there was little hope of obtaining the budgetary appropriation for such a grand program. The share of the naval appropriations in the total national budget for 1921 was 31.6 percent.

In October 1920 Tokyo obtained a copy of an operational paper jointly drafted by three brilliant young planners—Harry E. Yarnell, Holloway H. Frost, and William S. Pye—outlining a transpacific offensive. The Naval General Staff gathered, correctly, that the American navy required at least a three-to-two superiority over Japan's navy in order to advance its main fleet to the western Pacific and cut off Japan's vital seaborne traffic for an economic blockade that would lead to final victory.[14] To counter such a strategy the Japanese navy spelled out in more detail its war plans in the Principles of Strategy that accompanied the 1918 national defense policy. It stipulated that after having captured the American naval base in Luzon in the initial phase of hostilities, the Japanese fleet must "intercept" the approaching American fleet in the western Pacific and annihilate it in an all-out decisive encounter recalling the battle of Tsushima.

Offensive operations, early engagement of the enemy in a main encounter, and a quick and decisive showdown—these were to remain the precepts of Japanese naval strategy throughout the 1920s and beyond, and they had a definite Mahanian stamp. Indeed, Admiral Katō Kanji, who was to be the chief opponent to the Washington treaty, took special note of the fact that "the Japanese navy's studies on strategy tallied exactly with their American counterparts." It was only natural, he explained, "that strategic planning, even that bearing on the most secret aspects of national defense, should lead to identical conclusions if based on the same premises and reliable data. . . . It was precisely because of these shared naval doctrines that a fundamental conflict arose between the two navies over a 60 or 70 percent ratio."[15] The Japanese and American strategies were mirror images of each other.

13. Kobayashi, ed., *Suiusō nikki*, 299, 303.
14. Takagi Sōkichi, *Shikan Taiheiyō sensō* [A Personal Interpretation of the Pacific War], 64–66. My search in the U.S. naval records has failed to pinpoint the document in question, but its contents are very similar to Admiral R. E. Coontz to secretary of the navy, February 17, 1920, P.D. 198–2, Records, Department of Navy, RG 80, NA.
15. Katō Kanji, "Gunshuku shoken" [My Views on Naval Limitation], January 1930, Saitō Makoto Papers, DL.

The Lessons of World War I

Taking account of the "lessons" of World War I, the new national defense policy stipulated that "the determination and preparations for enduring a long drawn-out war will be required."[16] What kinds of armaments would Japan need in this new age of total war? The fundamental conflict over arms limitation was at the heart of the dissension within the Japanese navy.

The "clash of the two Katōs" at the Washington Conference, with all its drama and poignancy, has been narrated elsewhere; a summary account of their respective positions should suffice here.[17] Cognizant of the new realities of total war, Navy Minister Katō Tomosaburō held that no amount of armament would be adequate unless it was backed by overall national strength, the essence of which was in Japan's industrial and commercial power. Squarely facing Japan's limitations in this respect, he concluded that it would have to be content with "a peacetime armament commensurate with its national strength."[18]

In sharp contrast, Vice Admiral Katō Kanji (then president of the Naval Staff College), representing staff and line officers, gave the highest priority to military-strategic considerations. The "lessons" he drew from the recent war were markedly different. He maintained that the United States, with its "huge wealth, resources, and gigantic industrial power," could quickly mobilize naval forces as soon as hostilities broke out. Hence, it could meet its security needs with peacetime preparations on a par with a "have-not" nation such as Japan. Conversely, Japan required a large peacetime armament. The strategic lesson of World War I, he held, was the need to bring about a decisive encounter early in the war; failure to do so would turn the conflict into a drawn-out war of economic attrition, to Japan's disadvantage.[19] Thus the Japanese navy faced the dilemma of "expecting" any future war to be prolonged, while at the same time realizing that its chance of victory rested on a quick showdown. This predicament prompted Japan to accelerate its naval buildup, which in turn aggravated the vicious circle of the arms race with the United States.

It was Navy Minister Katō Tomosaburō—the architect of the "eight-eight fleet" plan—who was the first to recognize that this program was destined

16. BBKS, *Rengō kantai*, 1:168; BBKS, *Kaigun gunsenbi*, 1:146.
17. Asada, "Japanese Admirals and the Politics of Naval Limitation: Katō Tomosaburō vs. Katō Kanji," 141–66.
18. *TSM: Bekkan Shiryōhen*, 3–7; Terashima Ken Denki Kankōkai, ed., *Terashima Ken den* [Biography], 147.
19. Katō Kanji Hensankai, comp., *Katō Kanji den* [Biography of Admiral Katō Kanji], 756–57.

to be a plan on paper only. In 1919–1921 Japan was chafing under a post-war recession. At a meeting of the Diet budget subcommittee in February 1919, Katō frankly admitted, "Even if we should try to compete with the United States, it is a foregone conclusion that we are simply not up to it."[20] He knew very well that a continued naval race spelled financial ruin for Japan. For Katō, who was hoping for a convenient occasion to halt the dangerous armaments race, the invitation to the Washington Conference must have been a godsend.[21]

Washington Conference

As was to be expected, however, violent objections came from the navy men in charge of operational matters. An important "resolution" of the navy's special committee on arms limitation, submitted to Navy Minister Katō in late July 1921, categorically stated that Japan "absolutely requires a naval ratio of 70 per cent or above vis-à-vis the American navy," thus reconfirming the navy's long-standing consensus.[22] But Katō simply ignored this position paper because he was determined to maintain a completely free hand in his negotiations at Washington. He had been appointed chief Japanese delegate because Prime Minister Hara Kei believed that he was the only naval leader capable of restraining the demands of the naval establishment; civilian delegates would be unequal to the task.[23] Paradoxically, Katō—the navy minister and a full admiral on active duty—was expected to exercise what might be termed "civilian" control by proxy.

At the Washington Conference, Katō was prepared for any contingency and was ready to take a flexible position. Even so, at the opening session of the conference on November 12, 1921, he was "utterly dumbfounded" by Charles Evans Hughes's "bombshell proposal" offering an itemized plan for the drastic reduction of capital ship strength according to the ratio of 10:10:6

---

20. Minutes (February 5, 1919) of the Fourth Subcommittee for Budget, Lower House of the Imperial Diet (Forty-first session), BBK; *Yamanashi Katsunoshin ihōroku*, 66–7; Yamanashi Katsunoshin, *Katō Tomosaburō gensui o shinobu* [Fleet Admiral Katō Tomosaburō in Reminiscence], 8; Kurihara, ed., *Gensui Katō Tomosaburō den*, 87–88.

21. For the Washington Conference, see Braisted, *United States Navy in the Pacific, 1909–1922*, chaps. 28–41; Roger Dingman, *Power in the Pacific: The Origins of Naval Arms Limitation, 1914–1922*; Asada, "Japan and the United States," chap. 5.

22. Kaigun Kokusai Remmei Kankei Jikō Kenkyūkai [Navy Ministry's Committee to Investigate League of Nations Affairs], "Kafu kaigi gunbi seigen mondai ni kansuru kenkyū" [Studies on the Arms Limitation Question at the Washington Conference], July 21, 1921, Enomoto Papers.

23. Hara, ed., *Hara Kei nikki*, 5: 435.

for the United States, Britain, and Japan. Katō at once decided that Japan had no choice but to accept it. His was an "intuitive decision" aimed first and foremost at improving Japanese-American relations. Defining security in broad terms, he held that "avoidance of war with America through diplomatic means is the essence of national defense." The prudent course, then, was to accept the American proposal and stop the risky naval competition.[24] Katō thus subordinated military-strategic needs, however imperative, to higher political considerations. In return for the status quo regarding fortifications in the Philippines and Guam, he accepted the 60 percent fleet ratio.

This decision was vehemently opposed by Vice Admiral Katō Kanji, the chief naval expert. A typical "sea warrior" of the blue-water school, he adamantly opposed any compromise and pressed for a 70 percent ratio from a strategic standpoint, and he fortified his view with the doctrine of "the equality of armament" and "points of national honor." He held that Japan, as a sovereign nation, was inherently entitled to parity—a "ratio of 10:10." Thus viewed, the 70 percent ratio already represented Japan's maximum concession and 60 percent was totally unacceptable.[25] Further, Katō Kanji saw behind America's proposal an ulterior motive to freeze the status quo and to "deprive the Imperial Navy of its supremacy in the Far East," substituting America's own "hegemony." Embittered to see the British delegates aligning with the Americans, Katō Kanji warned the naval authorities in Tokyo that submission to "Anglo-American oppression" would be an "unbearable humiliation" and would result in "the most serious threat" to Japan's security.[26]

These views were, of course, contrary to those held by Katō Tomosaburō. He had wired Tokyo that "Anglo-American coercion is a fantasy which has never even occurred to us delegates in Washington."[27] The senior Katō, a controlling figure who exercised charismatic leadership, simply defied any challenge from his subordinates, forcefully overruling and silencing the junior Katō.

24. Navy minister to navy vice minister, November 12, 1921 (strictly confidential), Enomoto Papers; *TSM: Bekkan Shiryōhen*, 3–4.

25. Vice Admiral Katō Kanji to navy minister and chief of the Naval General Staff, November 24, 1921, BBK; Katō Kanji Hensankai, comp., *Katō Kanji den*, 746–49.

26. Katō Kanji to navy vice minister and vice chief of the Naval General Staff, December 4, 1921, BBK. Ian Gow's *Military Intervention in Pre-War Japanese Politics: Admiral Katō Kanji and the "Washington System"* is deeply flawed because Gow failed to use the Japanese archives, naval or diplomatic, although he claims to have made "an extensive search of archival materials."

27. Navy minister to navy vice minister, January 16, 1922, BBK; *TSM: Bekkan Shiryōhen*, 7.

The relentless Kanji, however, attempted to subvert his chief's decision: going behind Tomosaburō's back, he disregarded regular procedure and directly ordered the telegraph officer to wire to the Naval General Staff his dissenting views.[28] Such backstairs machinations did not confuse or mislead the naval authorities in Tokyo. With his usual foresight, the senior Katō had already wired them through a direct pipeline to his vice minister, Ide Kenji, and obtained the approval of the government and the naval genro, especially Fleet Admiral Tōgō, for his decision to accept a 60 percent ratio.[29]

The most notable feature of Katō Tomosaburō's decision-making style was the extent to which he ignored or suppressed his unruly subordinates at Washington. Such a mode of policy making, quite unusual in Japan where consensus building was the norm, was especially effective in coping with a crisis situation, which Katō saw in the accelerated naval race. In short, it was triumph of rational decision making over bureaucratic politics.[30]

On the other hand, there was the drawback of overburdening an individual leader. Already suffering from colon cancer, Katō had to endure almost superhuman strains that were to shorten his life. Another disadvantage was that no matter how powerful a leader he was, his individualized decision making, which went against the strongly held bureaucratic norms of the naval establishment, was destined sooner or later to be undermined. As "the clash of the two Katōs" showed, the senior Katō squashed the junior Katō's spirited opposition, but he could never persuade the latter who remained unreconciled to the 60 percent ratio. On the day Japan accepted the 60 percent ratio, Katō Kanji shouted, with tears of chagrin in his eyes, "As far as I am concerned, war with America starts now. We'll get our revenge over this, by God!"[31] Thus the *political* decision to accept the compromise settlement failed to take root in Japan's subsequent naval policy; on the contrary, the reaction from naval men, if anything, reinforced their obsession with the 70 percent ratio.

Foreseeing this development, Katō Tomosaburō had already begun while attending the Washington Conference to contemplate drastic institutional reforms, including a system of civilian navy ministers. Apparently, he had

28. Hori Teikichi's memo on the Washington Naval Conference, n.d., Hori Teikichi Papers (hereafter cited as Hori Papers), National Maritime Self Defense College (hereafter cited as NMSDC).

29. Navy minister to navy vice minister, December 4, 1921; Captain Nomura to navy vice minister, November 15, 18, and 28, and December 9, 1921, Enomoto Papers.

30. A theoretical analysis of Katō's negotiation and decision-making behavior is Asada, "Washinton kaigi o meguru Nichi-Bei seisaku kettei katei no hikaku" [A Comparative Study of the Japanese and American Decision-Making Process at the Washington Conference], 419–64.

31. Mori Shōzō, *Sempū nijūnen* [Twenty Tumultuous Years], 50.

been contrasting the Anglo-American brand of civilian control with Japan's anomalous system, which imposed on him, a full admiral and navy minister, the onerous task of going against the organizational mission of the service that he himself headed. The second institutional reform Katō had in mind was to subordinate the Naval General Staff to the navy minister.[32] Did Katō foresee the collision between the navy and the government, as well as an internal conflict between the Navy Ministry and the Naval General Staff, which would result at the time of the 1930 London Naval Conference?

The officers who had faithfully supported Katō Tomosaburō—Commander Hori Teikichi, Captain Yamanashi Katsunoshin, and Captain Nomura—all occupied Navy Ministry posts. These heirs to Katō Tomosaburō remained firmly committed during the 1920s and beyond to what has become known as the Washington treaty system.[33]

The conventional interpretation (to which the present writer has contributed in the past) holds that the senior Katō's views of national security and naval limitation were handed down through these heirs as "naval orthodoxy" into the 1920s and 1930s. It is true that they held on to the "orthodoxy," but they became a minority in the 1930s. When viewed in the context of the foregoing analysis, however, quite a different picture emerges. After all, was it not Katō Tomosaburō himself who abandoned the Imperial Japanese Navy's three basic guidelines—a 70 percent ratio, the "eight-eight fleet" plan, and the notion of the United States as the "hypothetical enemy"? Rather, it was Katō Kanji and his followers in the Naval General Staff and the fleets who soon claimed to occupy the "mainstream" of the naval establishment.

From Washington to Geneva, 1922–1927

Appointed prime minister in June 1922, Katō Tomosaburō served concurrently as navy minister for nearly a year. His immediate task was to implement the Washington treaties, but he faced an even more difficult problem in carrying out the navy's institutional reforms and revising the national defense policy to accord with the new course he had set at Washington. But alas, his health, so severely taxed at Washington, failed him at this critical juncture, and his premature death was to doom all but the first of these tasks to failure.

Katō's second attempt at institutional reform backfired because Katō Kanji was of course absolutely opposed to any system of civilian navy

32. *TSM: Bekkan Shiryōhen*, 7.
33. *Yamanashi Katsunoshin ihōroku*, passim.

ministers. This is evident in the third and most important task, the revision of the national defense policy. It was only after the Navy and Army General Staffs had reached an agreement that they showed the new national defense policy to the ailing Katō Tomosaburō, who had no choice but to give his reluctant consent.[34]

Officially sanctioned in February 1923, the revised national defense policy negated the senior Katō's basic principle of "avoidance of war with America" and instead adopted the junior Katō's notion of inevitable war. This document singled out the United States as the common hypothetical enemy number one for *both* the navy and the army (which had hitherto placed priority on Russia). Its underlying perception of the international situation went directly counter to the views of the senior Katō and the liberal diplomat Shidehara Kijūrō, soon to become foreign minister, who envisaged an era of peaceful cooperation under the Washington treaty system. The new national defense policy, in line with the neo-Mahanian economic determinism, saw the East Asian scene as still riddled with "sources of conflict."

> The United States, following a policy of economic invasion in China, menaces the position of our Empire and threatens to exceed the limits of our endurance. . . . The longstanding embroilments, rooted in economic problems and racial prejudice [discrimination against Japanese immigrants], are extremely difficult to solve. . . . Such being the Asiatic policy of the United States, sooner or later a clash with our Empire, will become inevitable.[35]

Reflecting a fatalistic belief in the coming of war, the new defense policy unmistakably bore Katō Kanji's stamp. For him the United States was the archantagonist with whom hostilities were unavoidable in "the near future." It is an irony of history that such an idea was officially adopted in the top-level policy document just when the Washington naval treaty made it strategically infeasible for either navy to wage offensive warfare in the Pacific.

The background of these developments was the remarkable ascendancy of Katō Kanji in the Naval General Staff. Outweighing his mild-mannered chief, Admiral Yamashita Gentarō, he wielded such great power that he "often tended to overwhelm the administrative branch [the Navy Ministry]," according to his official biography.[36]

---

34. BBKS, *Rengō kantai,* 1:196, 202–3, 234; BBKS, *Kaigun gunsenbi,* 1:68–73.
35. Shimanuki Takeharu, "Daiichiji sekai taisen igo no kokubō hōshin, shoyō heiryoku, yōhei kōryō no hensen" [The Development of the Imperial National Defense Policy, the Naval Strength Requirement, and the Principles of Strategy since World War I], 65–74.
36. Katō Kanji Hensankai, comp., *Katō Kanji den,* 767–68, 770–72.

Katō Tomosaburō's untimely death in August 1923, removing effective control over the insurgent elements, caused a crack in the Washington treaty system as far as the Japanese navy was concerned. Significantly, the profound effect of Katō Tomosaburō's death on Japanese-American relations was seen most clearly by the American admiral William V. Pratt.[37] Upon hearing about Katō's death, a "greatly shocked" Pratt hastened to send his old friend, Rear Admiral Nomura Kichisaburō, who had served as a faithful aide to Katō at Washington, a moving letter of condolence:

> During the course of the conference in Washington I watched Baron Kato very closely; I wanted, if possible, to find out the kind of a man he was. . . . I became thoroughly convinced in my mind at that time that Baron Kato was one of the finest, biggest, and most courteous gentlemen that I ever had the honor of meeting. I felt that so long as he [Katō Tomosaburō] had the direction of affairs in his hands no misunderstanding could arise between your country and mine which could not be settled through amicable arrangements.[38]

The succeeding navy minister, Takarabe Takeshi, simply did not possess the kind of charismatic leadership, broad internationalist outlook, and powerful personality that distinguished Katō Tomosaburō. With Katō's towering presence gone, the vagaries of bureaucratic politics and "competition among mediocrities" came to the fore. For his part, Katō Kanji had been building a cohesive faction. He and Suetsugu cultivated a strong following among "hot-blooded young officers" in the Naval General Staff.[39] It was against such a power lineup that policy regarding naval limitation unfolded in the mid-1920s.

Strategy against the United States Navy

The effort to break the strategic deadlock in the Pacific under the Washington treaty had resulted in major innovations in Japan's naval technology and strategic planning. A new feature added to the Principles of Strategy (accompanying the 1923 version of the national defense policy)

37. Wheeler, *Admiral William Veazie Pratt*, 182–87.

38. Pratt to Nomura, August 25, 1923, Papers of William V. Pratt, Operational Archives, Naval History Division, Washington Navy Yard.

39. Katō Kanji Hensankai, comp., *Katō Kanji den*, 768; Yamaji Kazuyoshi, *Nihon kaigun no kōbō to sekininsha tachi* [The Rise and Fall of the Japanese Navy and Its Leaders], 175.

was an "attrition strategy" that was to precede the interceptive operations. This strategy assigned to large, high-speed submarines the important mission of wearing down the enemy's main fleet on its transpacific passage. In addition to patrolling and defending the western Pacific, the submarine squadrons were to engage in relentless attacks on the enemy's approaching main fleet. It was Rear Admiral Suetsugu who worked out this strategy, as commander of the First Submarine Squadron in 1923–1925.[40]

As the radius of action and line of naval defense had been extended for both navies by rapid advances in technology and weaponry, war plans began to take more concrete shape on both sides of the Pacific in the mid-1920s. The Japanese navy hypothesized, correctly, that America's main fleet would in all probability advance by the central route from Pearl Harbor to the Gilbert Islands, Guam, and then to Manila Bay. On this transoceanic passage the American forces would try first to seize the islands under Japanese mandate—the Marshall and Caroline islands—and then carry their offensive into Japan's home waters.[41] It was on such a scenario that Japan's interceptive operations were predicated.

There was, however, some speculation among Japanese planners as to America's timing in sending its main fleet to the western Pacific. The dominant view in the Naval General Staff held that the Japanese capture of the Philippines would so provoke the American people as to compel immediate dispatch of the American main fleet to relieve Manila. Katō Kanji observed, "The fundamental guideline of American strategy is the principle of the quick-and-decisive battle. It is bent on promptly forcing an encounter with the Japanese fleet and deciding the issue in one stroke."[42] There were those in the Japanese navy, however, who feared that the United States would choose to hold back its main fleet until it had secured overwhelming strength and the essential logistic support. In that case, Japanese efforts to keep up the naval ratio vis-à-vis the United States would all come to naught.

40. Yamaji, *Nihon kaigun no kōbō,* 148–49, 152–58; Naval General Staff, "Kōjutsu oboe-gaki," [1930], apparently prepared by Katō Kanji, BBK; Nagai Sumitaka, "Kokubō hōshin to kaigun yōhei shisō no hensen" [The Development of the Imperial National Defense Policy and Naval Strategic Thought], 3329–31, BBK; Ikeda, Kiyoshi, *Nihon no kaigun* [A History of the Japanese Navy], 2:137–39.

41. Nagai, "Kokubō hōshin to kaigun yōhei shisō no hensen," 3329–31; BBKS, *Kaigun gunsenbi,* 1:150–51; Naval General Staff (Katō Kanji), "Kōjutsu oboegaki," BBK; Katō Kanji, "Gunshuku shoken," Saitō Makoto Papers, DL; Naval General Staff, Memo on American armaments since the Washington Conference, presented by Katō Kanji to Saitō Makoto, December 14, 1929, Saitō Makoto Papers. Cf. William R. Braisted, "On the United States Navy's Operational Outlook in the Pacific, 1919–1931"; Wheeler, *Prelude to Pearl Harbor,* 77–91.

42. Katō Kanji, "Gunshuku shoken," Saitō Makoto Papers, DL; BBKS, *Kaigun gunsenbi,* 1:150. For the Pacific strategy of the United States Navy, see Miller, *War Plan Orange.*

To overcome such strategic weaknesses, Katō Kanji, appointed commander in chief of the Combined Fleet in December 1926, ordered his fleet to conduct relentless night drills. Such were the risks involved that a double collision of four cruisers occurred one moonless night in August 1927, resulting in 120 casualties. After this disaster Admiral Katō grimly addressed the assembled commanders: "We must devote ourselves more and more to this kind of drill, to which our navy has applied all its energies ever since the acceptance of the 10:10:6 ratio." This was language calculated to inflame antipathy to the Washington naval treaty. The mounting indignation with the 60 percent ratio had crystallized into the conviction that "only through these hard drills can we expect to beat America!"[43]

The discontent that had been building among fleet officers ever since the Washington Conference found hyperbolic expression in a letter of protest written later by Admiral Yamamoto Eisuke (not to be confused with Yamamoto Isoroku), the commander in chief of the Combined Fleet at the time of the 1930 London Naval Conference. He wrote that as the nation's "first line of defense," the fleet was engaged in relentless exercises to overcome an inferior ratio, but the top leaders of the Navy Ministry were all too ready to make "political compromises" when confronted with budgetary problems. These "moderate leaders" in Tokyo had "come to resemble civilian desk officers rather than real sailor-warriors." Venting his "violent resentment," he traced this "deplorable" condition to the Washington Conference and Katō Tomosaburō's "despotic" rule and "emasculation" of the navy.[44]

Such strong sentiments bespoke a deep split that plagued the navy. The late 1920s saw the confluence of two undercurrents that had been building ever since the Washington Conference. First, there was the rivalry between the "command group" in the Naval General Staff led by Katō Kanji and the "administrative group" who adhered to Katō Tomosaburō's legacy and who occupied some of the key posts in the Navy Ministry.

Second, there was a growing sense of crisis, among fleet officers and the Naval General Staff, concerning the "grave defects in national defense" caused by the policy of naval limitation pursued by the "administrative group." This conflict along organizational lines would suddenly explode over the London treaty of 1930. Previous to this denouement, however, Japan participated in a second naval conference at Geneva.

43. Katō Kanji Hensankai, comp., *Katō Kanji den*, 846–57, 918–19; Katō Kanji's posthumous writing, "Rondon Kaigun jōyaku hiroku" [A Secret Record of the London Naval Treaty], BBK; Katō to Makino Nobuaki, January 29, 1930, Makino Nobuaki Papers (hereafter cited as Makino Papers), DL.
44. *Kido Kōichi kankei bunshō*, 263–66.

The Geneva Naval Conference, 1927

When the American invitation to the Geneva Conference came in February 1927, the Japanese government, headed by Wakatsuki Reijirō, decided to participate because Tokyo put a premium on the political necessity of cooperating with the United States. Japan replied that it would be happy to join a conference "calculated to complete the work of the Washington Conference." But the navy was opposed to extension of the Washington ratios of 10:10:6 to auxiliary vessels. Since the United States would demand the 60 percent ratio in auxiliary ships (cruisers and destroyers), a head-on collision between Japan and the United States seemed unavoidable.[45]

As it turned out, the entire parley at Geneva was so plagued with Anglo-American differences over the question of cruiser types and tonnage that a Japanese-American conflict never came to the surface. As the civilian delegate Ishii Kikujirō later reflected, "Had the negotiations continued for a little while longer, at the least a violent controversy with America over the ratio issue would have become inescapable." This statement is corroborated by Commander Nomura Naokuni, a naval member of the delegation: "Although Japan had taken a very rigid stand [on the ratio issue], Anglo-American antagonism so dominated the conference that it broke up without going into the issues at stake with Japan."[46] As far as the Japanese navy was concerned, therefore, the historical significance of the Geneva Conference was that it amounted to a preliminary skirmish with the United States, a prelude to the major confrontation at the London Naval Conference of 1930.[47]

The general instructions given to the Japanese delegates contained no specific mention of the ratio matter, but the instructions handed to the chief naval adviser, Vice Admiral Kobayashi Seizō, revealed that the naval authorities in Tokyo maintained a rigid stand on the 70 percent ratio. However, the chief delegates—Admiral Saitō Makoto and the veteran diplomat Ishii—interpreted the 70 percent formula rather flexibly, as "a mere criterion for negotiations," not as a "strict mathematical figure absolutely required for national defense."[48] As had been the case at the Washington Conference, much would depend on the head delegate.

45. BBKS, *Rengō kantai*, 1:218; *FRUS, 1927*, 1:4, 13–14, 28.
46. Ishii Kikujirō, *Gaikō yoroku* [Diplomatic Commentaries], 234; Nakamura Kikuo, ed., *Shōwa kaigun hishi* [Secret History of the Navy during the Showa Era], 33–34.
47. Unno Yoshirō's *Nihon gaikōshi, Vol. 16: Kaigun gunshuku kōshō, fusen jōyaku* [Japanese Diplomatic History, Vol. 16: Naval Limitation Negotiations/the Kellogg-Briand Pact] is based on the Foreign Ministry archives and does not address itself to naval policy and politics.
48. Instructions to the chief delegates to the Geneva Conference, cabinet decision, April 15, 1927, JMFA; Navy minister's instructions to chief naval aide, April 19, 1927, Enomoto Papers.

The great importance that Prime Minister Wakatsuki attached to the success of the forthcoming conference, rendered all the more urgent by the financial crisis of March 1927, was clear from his selection of Admiral Saitō as head delegate. One-time navy minister and the incumbent governor-general of Korea, he was regarded as "a great figure of superdreadnought caliber."[49] The move to appoint Saitō greatly alarmed Katō Kanji, then commander in chief of the Combined Fleet. He hastened to write Saitō a long, presumptuous letter, urging him to withdraw his acceptance. Katō invoked the "bitter lesson" of the Washington Conference. "From the navy's standpoint," Katō opined, "it is undesirable to appoint a great naval figure as the chief delegate to discuss naval questions." Obviously, Katō feared that an "admiral-statesman" like Saitō might overrule strategic views to reach a political compromise, just as Katō Tomosaburō had done at Washington. Rather condescendingly, Kanji explained that a free and extemporaneous give-and-take in international conferences required a certain practical experience and skill, which, he insinuated, Saitō lacked. Matters of substance were best left to naval experts in the delegation.[50] Katō vastly underestimated Saitō's diplomatic acumen.

In the negotiations at Geneva, as it turned out, Admiral Saitō showed that he was a master of diplomacy and that he commanded the respect of the American and British delegates. Under the leadership of Saitō, who was ably assisted by his chief naval adviser, Vice Admiral Kobayashi, the naval members of the Japanese delegation worked "in a shipshape manner."[51]

Saitō's views are reminiscent of Katō Tomosaburō's broad views on national defense. "The essence of preparedness" consisted in "gradually enhancing our national strength—our economic and industrial power—while winning greater respect and understanding from the rest of the world." In view of Japan's limited resources, Saitō warned, "we should not opportunistically attempt a sudden expansion of our navy in one conference or two."[52]

49. Navy Minister Takarabe Takeshi to Saitō, March 17, 1927, Saitō Makoto Papers, DL.

50. Katō Kanji to Saitō Makoto, March 23, 1927, Saitō Makoto Papers, DL. Because of the "most delicate nature of the problem," Katō requested Saitō to "destroy this letter upon reading."

51. Kobayashi Seizō, Report on the Geneva Conference on Naval Limitation, submitted to the navy minister and the chief of the Naval General Staff (hereafter cited as Kobayashi report), [1927], 191–92, Enomoto Papers; *Yamanashi Katsunoshin ihōroku*, 119; Aritake Shūji, *Saitō Makoto*, 107–9; Saitō Shishaku Kinenkai, ed., *Shishaku Saitō Makoto den*, 3:78–9, 90–91.

52. *Shishaku Saitō Makoto den*, 3:91–93.

However, Saitō's decision making at Geneva was hampered by the lack of coordination with the naval authorities in Tokyo. Departing from the procedure set at the time of the Washington Conference, the navy decided that instructions should be sent from the navy vice minister to the chief naval adviser, not to the head delegates.[53] Furthermore, Navy Vice Minister Ōsumi Mineo was Katō Kanji's confidant. Regarding the Washington Conference as a "most flagrant oppression" of Japan, Ōsumi harbored a deep distrust of the United States.[54] On the other hand, Vice Admiral Kobayashi, the chief naval adviser, was a nephew of Katō Tomosaburō, and he desired to complete the work of his illustrious uncle. Thus a clash of views between the delegates in Geneva and the naval leaders in Tokyo was inevitable.

The greatest obstacle the Japanese faced at Geneva was, of course, the rigid position taken by the American delegates on the 10:10:6 ratio. From the beginning, the Japanese delegates proposed to take as the standard of naval reduction Japan's existing strength plus its authorized building program, which would place its ratio somewhat above 70 percent of the United States, but about 65 percent of Britain. Afraid that the Anglo-American powers would jointly try to impose a 60 percent ratio on Japan—a fear fueled by their subjective memory of the Washington Conference[55]—the Japanese delegates entered into bilateral talks with the British, who seemed more accommodating on the ratio issue. On July 16 a broad Anglo-Japanese "compromise formula" emerged out of informal exchanges between Vice Admiral Kobayashi and the British delegate Vice Admiral Frederick Field. Most notably, in this compromise formula the Japanese conceded the lowering of the acceptable ratio to 65 percent in "surface auxiliary vessels."[56] Why was it that the Japanese delegates proposed this important concession, despite renewed instructions from Ōsumi "to do their utmost" to obtain the 70 percent ratio? The Japanese delegates believed it to be most urgent to remove the Anglo-American "fixation" with the Washington ratio system and reach any agreement, be it 62 or 63 percent, that would do away with the 60 percent ratio.[57] Computing from a 65 percent ratio for surface auxiliaries and the parity of sixty thousand tons for submarines, the delegates

53. A senior adjutant to the navy minister, Memo on procedural matters relating to naval limitation conferences, n.d., Enomoto Papers.

54. Ōsumi Taishō Denki Kankōkai, ed., *Danshaku Ōsumi Mineo den*, 407, 484–6, 760; Kiba Kōsuke, *Nomura Kichisaburō*, 856.

55. Delegates to foreign minister, June 25, July 7, 16, 1927; Kobayashi report, 127.

56. Kobayashi to Ōsumi, July 15, 1927; Kobayashi report, 127.

57. Delegates to foreign minister, June 25 and July 6, 16, 1927, JMFA; Kobayashi report, 101–2, 115–16, 127, Enomoto Papers; *FRUS, 1927*, 1:76.

showed that Japan would attain the overall figure of 68.7 percent for auxiliary vessels—only 1.3 percent short of their original instructions. On Saitō's
behalf, Kobayashi hastened to wire to Navy Vice Minister Ōsumi an important policy recommendation, listing four reasons for speedy acceptance of
the proposed compromise:

(1) Naval limitation on the basis of the Anglo-Japanese plan would not
be disadvantageous to Japan's national defense.
(2) Rupture of the conference would inevitably accelerate a naval race,
causing international instability.
(3) If Japan were to be held responsible for the breakup, its international
position would be adversely affected.
(4) A more favorable opportunity for naval limitation would not recur in
the near future.[58]

This "wide view," which emphasized compromise in the interest of larger
political considerations, was quite similar to Kato Tomosaburō's view at the
Washington Conference. But Ōsumi rejected out of hand any formula that
deviated from their original instructions. Ōsumi directed the delegates to
withdraw the "compromise formula" at once and cabled Kobayashi:

We feel it most deplorable that the delegates have proposed to sacrifice
the 70 percent ratio which has been Japan's long-cherished desire. Such
a concession would be especially painful from the standpoint of our relations with the United States. . . . The delegates must persist to the bitter
end in their demand for a 70 percent ratio. If this demand cannot be met,
public opinion will certainly be aroused, and the resultant treaty will have
little chance of being approved by the cabinet or being ratified. . . .
Depending on the attitude of Britain and the United States, a worst case
scenario might arise, ultimately forcing us to *resolve to fight to the death*.[59]

In these scathing words, as Kobayashi later wrote, Ōsumi "rebuked and
denounced Kobayashi as if he were a traitor who endangered Japan's
national defense."[60]

58. Kobayashi to navy vice minister and vice chief of the Naval General Staff, July 15,
18, 1927, Enomoto Papers.
59. Navy vice minister to Kobayashi, July 6, 17, 20, 22, 1927; Kobayashi to navy vice
minister and vice chief of the Naval General Staff, July 18, 1927; Kobayashi report, 101–
3, 115, 128–32, Enomoto Papers (italics added).
60. Kobayashi Seizō, *Kaigun taishō Kobayashi Seizō oboegaki* [Memos of Kobayashi Seizō],
62; Terashima Kankōkai, ed., *Terashima Ken den*, 134.

From the beginning the Anglo-Japanese compromise was doomed to failure, because it encountered stiff opposition not only from Tokyo, but also
from the American naval advisers who rejected the 65 percent ratio as
"gravely endangering America's position in the western Pacific."[61] On July
24 Saitō and Ishii cabled Tokyo that the time was fast approaching when
Japan would be forced into a confrontation with the United States over the
ratio issue. (Their alarm was well founded, for two days earlier Gibson had
wired Washington that discussion of the ratios with the Japanese would
be necessary "at a very early date.")[62]

As was to be expected, Ōsumi's reply was a flat refusal: "If such is the
case, the game is up; there will be no room for further negotiations whatsoever." If Japanese demands should be rejected, "the resentment of our
people would become an eternal source of future trouble, and it would also
destroy the morale of our navy."[63]

Yet the worst did not materialize, and a head-on collision with the United
States was narrowly avoided, because irreconcilable Anglo-American differences over the cruiser issue submerged the explosive ratio question. On
the public scene in Geneva, the Japanese delegates managed to hold on to
the legacy of Katō Tomosaburō, but within the navy the forces of opposition personified by Katō Kanji and Ōsumi were gaining momentum.
Although many high-ranking naval leaders belonged to the "moderate
group" who supported the Washington naval treaty, their collective leadership could not match the overwhelming control exercised by Katō
Tomosaburō at the time of the Washington Conference. The balance between
the two camps—the one committed to the Washington naval treaty and the
other to overturning it—was, indeed, a precarious one. Before it came to a
showdown at the London Naval Conference in 1930, the former attempted
to reiterate their position.

The Road to London, 1928–1930

Only two months after the debacle of the Geneva Conference, Navy
Minister Okada Keisuke ordered the committee on arms limitation to make

61. Kobayashi report, 113–32, 134–40, Enomoto Papers; Delegates to the foreign minister, July 24, 1927, JMFA; W. H. Medlicott, Douglas Dakin, and M. E. Lambert, eds.,
Documents on British Foreign Policy, 1st ser., 3:686–7, 691–3; *FRUS, 1927*, 1:113–14, 123–
24, 130–31.
62. Delegates to foreign minister, July 24, 1927, JMFA; *FRUS, 1927*, 1:130–34.
63. Navy vice minister to Kobayashi, July 28, 1927; Foreign minister to the delegates,
July 27, 1927, JMFA.

a comprehensive study that would guide not only preparation for the next naval conference but also building programs in the broad context of Japanese-American relations, present and future. Headed by Vice Admiral Nomura Kichisaburō, this committee (referred to as the Nomura Committee) was dominated by the supporters of naval limitation. The strictly confidential report of the committee, submitted to the navy minister in September 1928, was an authoritative document that was to provide the basis for future naval policy.[64]

The first point to be noted in this report is the reaffirmation of the Washington naval treaty, which was said to be "on the whole advantageous" to Japan, financially as well as strategically. Katō Tomosaburō's philosophy of naval security was restated in the following passages:

> Since Japan's national strength in relation to the Anglo-American power is vastly inferior, it would be to our advantage to keep them tied down to the capital ship ratio of 10:10:6, even though Japan was assigned an inferior strength. . . . Vis-à-vis great industrial powers like the United States and Britain, the utmost effort must be made to avoid a war whose outcome would be decided by an all-out contest of national strength.[65]

The report saw Japan's naval armament as a "silent power" with which to deter the United States from "obstructing" Japanese policy in China,[66] again reiterating Katō's view of the navy as an instrument of deterrence. Second, the Nomura Committee's report presented a highly optimistic view of Japanese-American relations. It stated that ever since the Washington Conference mutual relations had been "so greatly improved" that there no longer existed any problems that would provoke a war. As to China, Americans were finally awakening to its "chaotic and hopeless condition" and therefore becoming more sympathetic and cooperative toward Japanese policy. "Therefore the United States is quite unlikely to collide head-on with our efforts to make peaceable inroads into China."[67] Such views were almost identical with the liberal outlook that informed Foreign Minister Shidehara's policy.

In sharp contrast, the dissenting opinion attached to the committee's report reechoed Katō Kanji's convictions. In strong language similar to that

64. Kaigun Daijin Kanbō, Gunbi Seigen Kenkyū Iinkai [Investigatory Committee on Naval Limitation], "Studies on policy regarding naval limitation," prepared in August 1928, bk. 1, BBK; BBKS, *Kaigun gunsenbi*, 1:350–67.
65. Gunbi Seigen Kenkyū Iinkai, reports, pt. B, 133–4, 169–71, BBK.
66. Ibid., pt. A-l, 1.
67. Ibid., pt. B, 10; pt. C-l, 49–50.

of the 1923 national defense policy and evoking Mahanian economic deter-minism, the dissenting view held that conflict over the China market must "lead to the outbreak of war between Japan and the United States." At the zenith of its prosperity, the United States was "increasingly showing its true colors as an economic imperialist" in China.[68]

While the report of the Nomura Committee and the dissenting opinion were diametrically opposed in their estimates of Japanese-American rela-tions, both agreed on the necessity for a 70 percent ratio for auxiliary ves-sels. The committee's report reconfirmed that a 70 percent ratio for auxiliary vessels was "absolutely necessary for the nation's defense, nay, for its very existence"; there must be no bargaining over this at the next conference.[69]

The Nomura report attached great importance to the emergence of ten thousand–ton cruisers carrying eight-inch guns (the maximum allowed under the Washington treaty) as the main prop of auxiliary strength. The Japanese navy had come to recognize the superiority of these high-speed, armored heavy cruisers, regarding them as "quasi-capital ships." In attri-tion and interceptive operations, the Naval General Staff assigned heavy cruisers the crucial mission of wearing down America's main fleet in its transpacific passage.[70]

A staff study, prepared in late 1929 by the Operations Division, spelled out in detail the "formidable power" of the class of heavy cruisers. First, they excelled in speed; second, they were equipped with great striking power (eight-inch guns had twice the firepower of six-inch guns); third, and most important, their great cruising capacity was a vital element in transoceanic operations. Thus the Pacific had been "seemingly reduced to an American lake." For these reasons Japanese naval planners emphasized that their demand for a 70 percent ratio in heavy cruisers left "absolutely no room for compromise."[71]

Whereas *relative* strength, or ratio, was all-important with regard to the heavy cruiser, *absolute* strength (total tonnage irrespective of the ratio) was the paramount consideration with respect to the submarine. The submarine was to be deployed to wear down the enemy's main fleet. At the coming London Conference, therefore, the navy decided to demand seventy-eight

68. Ibid., pt. B, 10; pt. C-l, 48–49, 53.

69. Ibid., pt. A-2, 15–16, 36, 38; pt. B-l, 41–42, 58, 68–69, 76.

70. Katō Kanji, "Rondon jōyaku hiroku," BBK; Gunbi Seigen Kenkyū Iinkai, reports, pt. A-l, 4–5; pt. A-2; pt. B-l, 65–66, 99, 206–7, BBK; BBKS, *Rengō kantai,* 1:218.

71. Operations Division, Memo on the power of ten thousand–ton, eight-inch-gun cruisers, December 1, 1929, BBK; "The value of 10,000-ton, 8-inch-gun cruisers and the need to secure 70 per cent," n.d., BBK; Saitō Makoto Papers, DL; *Kaigun gunbi enkaku,* 162, 177.

thousand tons—Japan's submarine strength upon the completion of the building program at the end of fiscal 1931.[72]

The Denouement: The 1930 London Naval Conference

Preparations for the London Conference began as early as June 1929, when Navy Minister Okada obtained the cabinet's approval for the navy's "Three Basic Principles": (1) a 70 percent ratio with the United States in total auxiliary tonnage; (2) the special importance of the 70 percent ratio with regard to ten thousand–ton, eight-inch-gun cruisers; and (3) the submarine tonnage of seventy-eight thousand.[73] The key figure in insisting on these demands was, of course, the chief of the Naval General Staff, Katō Kanji.

On November 18 Katō pressed upon Prime Minister Hamaguchi Osachi that the 70 percent ratio was "the rock-bottom ratio" and constituted "a matter of life or death for our navy." This overriding goal had "stiffened the navy's morale and sustained its determination through unspeakable hardships" ever since the Washington Conference. Japan would "rather do without any new agreement" than yield on this. In his conversations with Foreign Minister Shidehara, Katō urged the "pressing need of obtaining a prior commitment to a 70 percent ratio" for auxiliaries in preliminary negotiations with the United States and Britain. Uppermost in his mind was a determination "never to repeat the mistake of the Washington Conference."[74] However, preliminary diplomatic efforts in Washington and London, which continued until the eve of the conference, failed to yield any prior understanding.

As the chief delegate to the conference Prime Minister Hamaguchi chose Wakatsuki Reijirō, twice finance minister, and prime minister at the time of the Geneva Naval Conference, trusting that he would carry out the government's twin goals of fiscal retrenchment and friendly cooperation with the Anglo-American powers. Wakatsuki knew full well that Japan's limited financial capabilities ruled out a naval race. At the coming conference, he believed, it would be "unwise to persist uncompromisingly in the 70 percent ratio"; he favored "concluding a treaty within negotiable limits, say 65 or 67 per cent."[75]

72. Katō Kanji, "Gunshuku shoken," Saitō Makoto Papers, DL.
73. Cabinet decision on policy regarding naval limitation, June 28, 1929, JMFA.
74. Katō Kanji to Makino Nobuaki, January 29, 1930, Makino Papers, DL.
75. Wakatsuki was to be assisted by another civilian delegate Matsudaira Tsuneo, then ambassador to London. At the time of the Washington Conference, Matsudaira had supported Katō Tomosaburō as secretary general of the Japanese delegation. Wakatsuki, *Kofūan kaikoroku* [Memoirs], 334–35.

The choice of Wakatsuki as the civilian delegate posed a problem for the navy. Navy Minister Takarabe was all too willing to go to London, but within the navy he had the reputation of being "unreliable." Katō Kanji therefore consulted Fleet Admiral Tōgō and decided to send as "the highest naval adviser" Admiral Abo Kiyokazu—his intimate friend, hard-liner, and member of the Supreme Military Council. The second-ranking naval expert member, Rear Admiral Yamamoto Isoroku, was counted on to take a firm stand in London. Among junior naval members Katō took special care to include Captain Nakamura Kamesaburō, the chief of the Operations Section and a steadfast "hawk."[76]

During Takarabe's absence, Vice Minister Yamanashi assumed the onerous responsibility of controlling the navy and keeping close contact with the government.[77] Yamanashi was ably assisted by Rear Admiral Hori Teikichi, the head of the Naval Affairs Bureau, but these moderate leaders were simply no match for Katō Kanji. Later, when the fate of the naval treaty hung in the air, Navy Ministry leaders relied on naval elder Admiral Okada Keisuke to be a mediator between the government and the navy on the one hand and between the two branches of the navy on the other. It was believed that Okada was the only man available to restrain the impetuous Katō Kanji.[78]

Yamanashi and his subordinates in the ministry took a flexible position. "Armament plans, drafted by the Naval General Staff from strategic-operational viewpoints, are not fixed absolutes; they must be agreed upon between the Navy Ministry and the Naval General Staff, on the basis of a broad consideration." Hori, the head of the Naval Affairs Bureau, went further, believing that decisions on armament were *political* matters involving budgetary appropriations; therefore, he maintained that the responsibility for these decisions lay with the government.[79] The leaders of the Naval General Staff, for their part, believed that they were performing their assigned duty in pressing for their estimated security needs. Taking an absolute stand on the Three Basic Principles, these leaders burned their

76. Koga Mineichi's Diary (hereafter cited as Koga Diary), entry of September 27, 1929, copy contained in the Hori Papers, NMSDC; Katō Kanji Hensankai, comp., *Katō Kanji den*, 887.

77. *Yamanashi Katsunoshin ihōroku*, 129.

78. Wakatsuki, *Kofūan kaikoroku*, 365–66; Okada Taishō Kiroku Hensankai, ed., *Okada Keisuke*, 50–68; James W. Morley, ed., *Japan Erupts: The London Naval Conference and the Manchurian Incident, 1928–1932*, 28–29.

79. Hori Teikichi, Memo on the London Conference and the problem of the right of the supreme command, July 11, 1946, Hori Papers, NMSDC; Arima, "Takarabe denki shiryō," bks. 5 and 6, BBK; Okada Hensankai, ed., *Okada Keisuke*, 59; my interviews with Enomoto Jūji, August 1975.

bridges when they clamorously appealed to public opinion. Their public campaign annoyed and embarrassed the chief delegate, Wakatsuki, whose diplomatic hands were thus tied.[80]

Harking back to the view he had held since the Washington Conference, Katō invoked twin "convictions": the doctrine of "the equality of armament" and the dictate of "national prestige." He held that a 70 percent ratio would already be a substantial concession on Japan's part. "The more humbly Japan acquiesces in the 70 per cent ratio *despite its sovereign right of equality,* the more flagrant the United States becomes in flaunting its high-handed and coercive attitude."[81]

Behind all these convictions was neo-Mahanian determinism, which Katō believed guided American policy. He held that American ambitions in China must "inevitably lead its diehards to clamor for forcible settlement of the China question by naval strength." The United States was being inhibited "only by Japan's armament and by America's lack of offensive capability." America's real design was to bind Japan to an inferior naval ratio so that it could "dominate" China without hindrance.

Similarly, Katō wrote on February 5 to Admiral Abo in London: "The real issue at stake is no longer our naval power per se but *our national prestige and credibility.*" In these emotional outbursts Katō subordinated the material factor of ratios and tonnage figures to such intangibles as national dignity and a valiant self-image. In the same letter he requested Abo to send home "more and more telegrams about Anglo-American oppression," which he assured him would stir up public sentiment and "force the government to stiffen its attitude."[82]

In London, however, the prospect of attaining the Japanese terms seemed to be getting dimmer and dimmer. Soon after the conference opened on January 21, Matsudaira Tsuneo, one of the Japanese delegates, warned Shidehara that if Japan should insist, to the bitter end, on a 70 percent ratio, clashes with the United States and Britain were inevitable, and the two powers would conclude a bilateral treaty to the exclusion of Japan. In reply,

80. Naval Affairs Bureau, "A Report on the 1930 London Naval Conference and Related Papers," Vol. 10, prepared in December 1930, Enomoto Papers; Harada Kumao, *Saionjikō to seikyoku* [Prince Saionji and Politics], 1:1, 74; Nakamura Kikuo, *Shōwa kaigun hishi,* 9, 34.

81. Katō Kanji, "Rondon jōyaku hiroku," BBK; Katō Kanji, "Gunshuku shoken," Saitō Makoto Papers, DL; Naval General Staff (Katō Kanji), "Kōjutsu oboegaki" (italics added); Naval General Staff, Memo on American armaments since the Washington Conference, Saitō Makoto Papers.

82. Katō Kanji to Makino Nobuaki, January 29, 1930, Makino Papers, DL; Katō Kanji Hensankai, comp., *Katō Kanji den,* 890–92 (italics added).

Shidehara "strictly forbade" the ambassador to take a defeatist view, urging him to redouble his efforts to win the 70 percent ratio. Chief delegate Wakatsuki had also concluded that "further perseverance in the same hard-line demands must inevitably result in an angry parting with America and Britain." On January 25, 1930, he drafted a telegram to this effect: "We are at our rope's end; the time has now come to request the government to apprise us of the terms of compromise." Meeting staunch opposition from Admiral Takarabe and his naval advisers, this telegram was shelved.

In mid-February, when the conference seemed to flounder on the reef of a Japanese-American deadlock, Wakatsuki confidentially wired Foreign Minister Shidehara, urging the government to take the utmost precautions "so as not to drive the issue to the last extremity." The breakup of the conference would place Japan in an "extremely difficult position internationally."[83]

Shidehara and Hamaguchi, faced with the intransigent stand of the Naval General Staff, directed Wakatsuki to follow "the logical steps of first consulting with delegate Takarabe and jointly working out some appropriate solution." For Wakatsuki, however, such "consultation" with Takarabe had become totally impossible. In fact, the civilian and naval delegates had become locked in irreconcilable differences. Later, when the Japanese-American negotiations reached a critical point, Wakatsuki complained to Shidehara about Takarabe's intransigence in these bitter words:

> Although I have urged delegate Takarabe to rise resolutely to the occasion as a statesman and take broad-minded measures to save the situation, he disagrees with me in every instance and has instead aligned himself with Admiral Abo and naval advisers. . . . To my great distress, it has proved beyond my power to persuade him despite my repeated efforts.[84]

Members of the delegation felt Takarabe was "indecisive and vacillating." In appointing the navy minister as a delegate, the precedent of the Washington Conference had been followed without much thought; Takarabe was simply not of the caliber to reenact Katō Tomosaburō's role at Washington.

---

83. Matsudaira to Foreign Minister Shidehara, February 20, 1930 (strictly confidential dispatch with a note: "Please destroy upon reading"), JMFA; Sakonji, Report on the 1930 London Naval Conference (hereafter cited as Sakonji's report), 1, 22, 41–42, Enomoto Papers; Captain Nakamura, "Seikun ni itarishi jijō" [Report on the Circumstances Leading to the Request for the Final Instructions from the Government; hereafter cited as Nakamura's report], April 1930, Hori Papers, NMSDC.

84. Shidehara to Matsudaira, February 21 and 22, 1930; Matsudaira to Shidehara, March 24, 1930, JMFA; Arima Kaoru, "Takarabe denki shiryō" [Manuscript Materials for the Biography of Takarabe Takeshi], bk. 7; Koga Diary, entries of March 6 and 15, 1930, Hori Papers, NMSDC; *TSM: Bekkan Shiryōhen*, 10–11, 31.

To find a way out of the Japanese-American deadlock, two civilian delegates—Matsudaira and David A. Reed, the chairman of the Senate Naval
Appropriations Committee—entered into informal talks, but Wakatsuki
reassured the naval advisers that any formula produced by these conversations would be merely a "private plan" that he would decide on "only
after consulting with the navy side." Meanwhile, however, the negotiations
had forced the Japanese civilian delegates to commit themselves to the
Reed-Matsudaira compromise on March 13. To the naval representatives
this compromise plan came as "a bolt from the blue." It conferred on Japan
(1) an overall ratio of 69:75 percent; (2) a 60 percent ratio in heavy cruisers,
with a proviso that assured Japan of a ratio slightly above 70 percent (the
United States promising not to complete three of its heavy cruisers during
the life of the treaty, that is until 1936); and (3) parity in submarine tonnage, which was set at 52,700 tons.[85]

Wakatsuki hastened to wire Foreign Minister Shidehara, categorically
stating that there was "no prospect of obtaining more favorable terms" and
pleading with the government to "make the final determination" to accept
them. On the other hand, Takarabe—ever mindful of the stiff stand taken
by Katō, and faced with the strong position taken by his naval advisers—
demurred, saying that the compromise plan would not be acceptable to
the Naval General Staff. However, on March 14 Takarabe reluctantly joined
the civilian delegates in sending an important dispatch to Tokyo over all
their signatures. In effect, this dispatch requested the government to accept
the Reed-Matsudaira compromise. Uppermost in Wakatsuki's mind was
the importance of preventing the failure of the conference, which would
lead to a ruinous naval race, and on this stand he would stake not only "his
position as chief delegate but also his life itself."[86]

However noble Wakatsuki's resolve may have been, the fact remains that
the Reed-Matsudaira compromise did not satisfy the navy's demands.
Wakatsuki honestly believed that this plan was not only acceptable but also
advantageous to Japan. After all, did it not to all intents and purposes meet
the demand for a 70 percent ratio? Did the United States not make "an

85. Nakamura's report, March 7, 10, 13, 14, and 23, 1930, Hori Papers, NMSDC; Andō
Yoshio, ed., *Shōwa keizaishi e no shōgen* [Witness Accounts of the Economic History of
the Showa Period], 2:267.

86. Sakonji's report, 46–7, 63–5, 73, 88, 93, Enomoto Papers; Nakamura's report, March
13 and 15, and April 2, 1930, Hori Papers, NMSDC; Wakatsuki, "Rondon kaigun kaigi"
[Memoirs of the London Naval Conference], JMFA; Wakatsuki, *Kofūan kaikoroku*, 350–
54; *TSM: Bekkan Shiryōhen*, 12; *Gendaishi shiryō* [Documents on Contemporary History;
hereafter cited as *GS*], Vol. 7, *Manshū jihen* [The Manchurian Incident], 35; Satō Naotake,
Kaiko hachijūnen [Eighty Years in Reminiscence], 246–49; Okada Hensankai, ed., *Okada
Keisuke*, 33.

enormous concession" by agreeing to parity in submarines? Wakatsuki was prepared to resign if the Japanese government disapproved of the compromise plan or sent a new instruction at variance with it.[87]

But Wakatsuki overlooked the fact that according to the Reed-Matsudaira compromise Japan was not allowed to build any new heavy cruisers and submarines for the duration of the treaty. In the expert eyes of the navy men, Wakatsuki's "amateurish" reasoning ignored Japan's strategic imperatives. Chief naval adviser Sakonji, although a supporter of the treaty, nonetheless opposed the Reed-Matsudaira compromise. It gave Japan, he said, a mere token—an overall 70 percent ratio, the least important of its demands—while denying the "essence" regarding the all-important categories of the heavy cruiser and the submarine. Furious at the compromise, Yamamoto vented his opposing views on Takarabe. So vehement did Yamamoto feel toward the civilian representatives that, one witness noted, he "almost seemed intent to do them in."[88] When Kaya Okinori, a ministry of finance representative, emphasized financial considerations for naval limitation, Yamamoto shouted, "Say another word, Kaya, and you will get a smack in the face."

In Tokyo, Katō Kanji angrily declared, "The American [Reed-Matsudaira] plan is a most high-handed one, offering us, as it were, only the crust of a pie without filling."[89] On March 19 he visited Prime Minister Hamaguchi and in a most unbending manner harangued for more than an hour, insisting that he was "absolutely opposed" to the compromise. Katō emphasized that its acceptance would undermine Japan's operational plans since (1) the shortage in submarine strength would impede Japan's capture of the Philippines and cripple its patrolling as far as Hawaiian waters, not to mention its attrition strategy in the Pacific, and (2) the concession on heavy cruisers would cause "grave defects" in a main fleet encounter, making it impossible to make up for the 60 percent strength in battleships. Katō was powerfully backed by Fleet Admiral Tōgō, deified as "the Nelson of Japan," who said he would rather break up the conference and walk out than yield one iota. These strong words Katō hastened to send to Takarabe in London to put further pressure on him.[90]

87. Wakatsuki, *Kofūan kaikoroku*, 356–57.

88. Ibid., 354–56; Sakonji's report, 72, Enomoto Papers; Nakamura's report, March 13, 1930, Hori Papers, NMSDC; Sorimachi Eiichi, *Ningen Yamamoto Isoroku: Gensui no shōgai* [Personal Biography of Yamamoto Isoroku], 301–2.

89. Harada, *Saionjikō*, 1:27; "Katō Kanji hiroku"; Naval General Staff (Katō Kanji), "Kōjutsu oboegaki," BBK; Koga Diary, March 24, 1930, Hori Papers, NMSDC; *TSM: Bekkan Shiryōhen*, 17.

90. Sakonji's report, 76, Enomoto Papers; Nakamura's report, March 13–16, 1930; Rear Admiral Yamamoto's memo, "Personal views on conference strategy," March 10, 1930;

From London, Sakonji (perhaps on behalf of Takarabe who had second thoughts about the Reed-Matsudaira compromise) cabled the naval authorities in Tokyo that acceptance of the compromise plan, entailing a "crisis" in naval defense, was "simply out of the question." On March 15 an incensed Admiral Abo blew up at Takarabe, accusing him of having been brought over to the side of the civilian delegates. He threatened to resign from the Supreme Military Council if the compromise should be accepted. Yamamoto was equally vehement in his opposition to "any unwarranted political retreat." Even more extreme were junior officers such as Captain Nakamura, who directly appealed to Takarabe and Wakatsuki for "a firm and resolute stand." These young officers proposed, as the last resort, to send their strongly worded dissenting views directly to the chief of the Naval General Staff, Katō, and the navy vice minister, Yamanashi. Their aim was to force some "drastic" new instructions from Tokyo that would turn the tables and reverse the "defeatist policy" of Wakatsuki and his colleagues.

It must be emphasized that the naval leaders in Tokyo, such as Yamanashi and Hori, were by no means entirely satisfied with the Reed-Matsudaira compromise, but it was their responsibility to take careful measure of the diplomatic, political, and fiscal considerations that compelled a compromise settlement. To bring about a successful naval treaty, Admiral Okada backed these moderate leaders, using his considerable political influence and tact to mediate between the Navy Ministry and the Naval General Staff on the one hand, and between the navy and the government on the other. Okada, whose views on naval limitation were in the tradition of Katō Tomosaburō, took a flexible stand on the ratio matter and naval armament.[91]

At the conference of naval leaders on March 25, Prime Minister Hamaguchi told Yamanashi that the government had made up its mind not to run the risk of breaking up the conference: "Though I lose the prime ministership, though I lose my life itself, this decision is unshakable." When Hamaguchi had an audience with the emperor on March 27, His Majesty told him "to make every effort to speedily conclude [the London treaty] in the interest of world peace." These words had an electrifying effect on Hamaguchi. Later in the day, Hamaguchi called Katō Kanji, Okada Keisuke, and Yamanashi to his official residence and alluded to the source of his renewed resolve.[92]

---

and Yamamoto to Hori, March 17, 1930, Hori Papers, NMSDC; *TSM: Bekkan Shiryōhen,* 15, 264; Nomura Minoru, *Tennō, Fushimi no miya to Nihon kaigun* [The Emperor, Prince Fushimi, and the Japanese Navy], 142–54.

91. Okada Hensankai, ed., *Okada Keisuke,* passim; Okada Sadahiro, ed., *Okada Keisuke kaikoroku* [Memoirs of Okada Keisuke], passim.

92. Ikei Masaru, Hatano Masaru, and Kurosawa Fumitaka, eds., *Hamaguchi Osachi nikki, zuikanroku* [Diary and Memos of Hamaguchi Osachi], 318.

Until March 26 there still remained a modicum of harmony, but the arrival on that day of two separate and conflicting telegrams from Wakatsuki and Takarabe caused great confusion in Tokyo. Wakatsuki once again urged a speedy and full acceptance of the compromise plan, while Takarabe withdrew what he had said in the joint telegram of March 14 and urged the government to push one more time for better terms at the risk of breaking up the conference. These dispatches from London precipitated a violent split within the Japanese navy as well as one between the government and the navy. In the words of leading naval historian Ikeda Kiyoshi, thus began "an upheaval unprecedented in the history of the Imperial Japanese Navy."[93]

How it became politicized and developed into a national political crisis, involving the "right of supreme command," needs no retelling here.[94] Suffice it to say that Takarabe, placed in a dilemma between his duty as navy minister and his political responsibility as a member of the Hamaguchi cabinet, continued to vacillate to the last. His contradictory behavior bewildered Tokyo and compounded the confusion. Even as the government's "final instructions"—directing the delegates to accept the treaty along the lines of the Reed-Matsudaira compromise—were being dispatched to the delegates in London, an apprehensive Yamanashi wired Takarabe to urge "utmost prudence" and "circumspection":

> It is feared that in the event that you should take actions at odds with Wakatsuki, they will divide our delegation in London to the detriment of its negotiating power, and at home such actions will cause grave political difficulties, driving the navy into a most inimical and self-damaging predicament.[95]

Yamanashi's warning against any rash action betrayed his fear that at the last moment Takarabe might yet be swayed by his intransigent naval advisers, who demanded "one final thrust" to wrench further concessions from the United States. Takarabe finally accepted the treaty.

Tokyo's final instruction, arriving in London on April 1, produced quite a commotion among naval representatives. Suddenly informed of the gov-

93. Ikeda, *Nihon no kaigun,* 2:99.
94. See, most notably, Morley, ed., *Japan Erupts,* 27–117. "The right of supreme command" revolved around article 12 of the Japanese constitution, which stipulated an imperial prerogative for the organization of the military forces. This became a point of contention between the Navy Ministry and the government and the high command (the Naval General Staff); Ikeda, "Rondon gunshuku joyaku to tōsuiken mondai" [The London Naval Treaty and the Problem of the Right of the Supreme Command], 1–35.
95. Sakonji's report, 101–5, 111, Enomoto Papers; *TSM: Bekkan Shiryōhen,* 22, 37; *GS,* Vol. 7, *Manshū jihen,* 4.

ernment's decision for compromise, excited young officers denounced and reviled Wakatsuki and plotted to storm Takarabe's suite. On the following day, Yamamoto admonished his subordinates "not to commit a breach of service discipline," but he himself proceeded to contradict his orders to his subordinates. He put extraordinary pressure on his chief, even asking Navy Minister Takarabe to take responsibility by resigning immediately: "The last and the only way left for the navy minister to preserve honor after this defeat at the conference is to resign in protest as befits the occasion and to prove to the Japanese people that 'the navy has not betrayed' their trust." He warned that public surrender to the American demands would "shock our entire navy, destroy its morale, and bring about some untoward incident." (The above account should modify the prevalent notion of Yamamoto as a member of the "treaty faction.")[96]

Prelude to Catastrophe

On April 22 the London naval treaty was signed at the Court of St. James's. Success in steering this treaty safely to its signature and ratification meant victory for the "administrative group" and defeat for the "command group." Ironically, however, the outcome of the domestic commotions it triggered actually enhanced the power of the latter group. The struggle over the London naval treaty brought into the open a violent split within the navy between the protreaty and antitreaty camps. How the treaty issue was made a football of party politics; how it brought about a head-on collision between the government and the navy; and how it triggered a series of political assassinations, starting with the fatal attack on Prime Minister Hamaguchi in November 1930—these are questions that fall outside the purview of this study of naval policy.

For our purpose, however, it is important to underscore that the London treaty, just at the time when Japan concluded it, was regarded by the antitreaty forces as short-lived. The navy held that the London treaty, "seriously jeopardizing national defense, must not be allowed to last long." The emperor astutely surmised the navy's intent and tried to obtain an assurance that the "navy's policy would not bind Japan's position at the next naval conference of 1935." This caveat notwithstanding, the Supreme

96. Yamamoto's oral presentation, April 2, 1930; Yamamoto's memo on the problem of submarine strength (summary of oral presentation to the navy minister), April 9, 1930; and Nakamura's report, April 2, 1930, Hori Papers, NMSDC; Nakamura Takafusa et al., eds., *Gendai o tsukuru hitobito* [Men Who Shaped Contemporary Japan], 3:51.

Military Council stated in its "official reply to the Throne" on July 23 that the navy was opposed to the continuation of the London naval treaty beyond its expiration in 1936.[97]

With the advantage of historical hindsight, the tragedy of the London Conference may be said to have been that it contained the seeds of subsequent tragedies during the 1930s. First, the so-called Ōsumi purge prematurely retired brilliant senior officers who had assiduously worked for the London treaty. Second, Japan abrogated the Washington naval treaty in 1935 and withdrew from the second London Naval Conference in 1936. This led to the resumption and escalation of the naval race, which one American historian has called "the Race to Pearl Harbor."[98] These problems will be treated in the following essay.

When one traces the historical origins of the navy's collision course, however, the forces of opposition that had been building since the Washington Conference loom large. In 1933 Prime Minister Saitō Makoto stated succinctly, "The present commotions have their roots in Katō Kanji's antipathy toward [the policy of] Admiral Katō Tomosaburō, the chief delegate at Washington."[99] No contemporary Japanese leader was better qualified to make this assessment. Katō Tomosaburō's success in 1921–1922 proved to be a Pyrrhic victory. Heralded at the time as "a new order of sea power,"[100] the Washington and London treaties—or rather Japan's response to them— were signposts on the Japanese navy's road to the Pacific War.

97. The emperor's statement, July 22, 1930, Hori Papers, NMSDC; Harada, *Saionjikō*, 1:40.

98. Stephen E. Pelz, *Race to Pearl Harbor: The Failure of the Second London Naval Conference and the Onset of World War II.*

99. Harada, *Saionjikō*, 3:147.

100. Sprout and Sprout, *Toward a New Order of Sea Power.*

The Japanese Navy's Road to Pearl Harbor, 1931-1941

In the 1930s the Japanese navy underwent momentous transformations that went far to explain its road to Pearl Harbor. The process may be viewed as a gradual breakdown, under mounting challenges from within, of the Japanese naval tradition and the moderate leadership that inherited it.

Institutionally, the traditional navy was a relatively well-ordered, unitary organization. While operational and tactical matters fell within the jurisdiction of the chief of the Naval General Staff, policy-making power was centralized in the hands of the navy minister. All this changed in the turbulent, crisis-ridden 1930s: the decade witnessed a steady erosion of the Navy Ministry leadership from the Naval General Staff and the middle echelons (commanders and captains of section chief rank). And with the rise of fervently pro-German, anti-British, and anti-American elements in the middle echelons, naval policy became increasingly dominated by an emotional mode of thinking and myopic strategic preoccupations. And naval leaders became preoccupied with the navy's bureaucratic interest and expansion of armaments vis-à-vis the United States.

The first part of this essay briefly surveys (1) the various groupings of naval officers; (2) their respective influence on naval policy[1] and its institutional

This essay is adapted from Asada, "The Japanese Navy and the United States," in *Pearl Harbor as History: Japanese American Relations, 1931–1941*, edited by Dorothy Borg and Shumpei Okamoto. It is reprinted here by permission of the Columbia University Press. In preparing its earlier version I was greatly indebted to Nomura Minoru and Suekuni Masao (BBK), Toyoda Kumao (JMJ), and Rear Admiral Tomioka Sadatoshi (Documentary Research Society), all of whom served in the Imperial Navy. I benefited from comments on earlier drafts of this essay by Arthur Marder, Ian H. Nish, and D.C. Watt.

1. Throughout this essay the term *naval policy* is used in the dual sense in which the Japanese navy employed it: (1) the management of the military-professional affairs of

framework; and (3) the conflicting images, values, and strategic visions that conditioned their attitudes toward the United States.

Naval Factions and Their Influence

The navy's elite officers were recruited from top-ranking graduates of the naval academy. Starting about the time of World War I, the academy increasingly emphasized spartan regimentation and rote memory. The Naval Staff College, though designed to train high-ranking commanders, functioned as a nursery for staff officers. The fixation at the college, day in and day out, on annihilation of the American fleet in a main encounter caused intellectual atrophy.

The most readily apparent groupings of naval officers were the "administrative group" in the Navy Ministry and the "command group" in the Naval General Staff. Traditionally, the key policy-making posts in the Navy Ministry went to elite officers with political and administrative abilities, while the pivotal positions in the Naval General Staff were occupied by "sea warriors." The differences between these two groups of officers were brought out in full relief by the issue of naval limitation. As had been stated, the basic split dated back to the Washington Conference of 1921–1922.

At Washington, Navy Minister Admiral Katō Tomosaburō, the head of the Japanese delegation, had chosen to avoid a dangerous naval race with the United States by accepting a 60 percent fleet ratio. On the other hand, Vice Admiral Katō Kanji, the chief naval representative, clamored for a 70 percent ratio as a strategic imperative, but his spirited opposition was squelched by the elder Katō. A charismatic leader, Katō Tomosaburō defied any challenge from his subordinates, but with his untimely death in 1923, effective control over the insurgent elements within the navy began to falter.

The origins of the two opposing groups during the 1930s can be traced to the two Katōs, in terms of both the direct personal patronage and their influence. The leaders who steered the London treaty safely to final ratification—"the treaty faction"—were protégés of or heirs to Katō Tomosaburō. Among later inheritors of his legacy one may count Yonai Mitsumasa and a handful of senior officers who loyally supported him—Yamamoto Isoroku, Inoue Shigeyoshi, Nomura Kichisaburō, and Yoshida Zengo.

Turning to the opposite camp—"the command group"—Katō Kanji remained an ever-powerful force as a member of the Supreme Military

---

the navy itself; and (2) national policy that the navy urged on the government. In view of the peculiar nature of Japanese policy making during the 1930s, I have chosen to stress the latter aspects; cf. Robert G. Albion, *Makers of Naval Policy.*

Council after his resignation as chief of the Naval General Staff. In February 1932 he managed to have his protégé Takahashi Sankichi appointed vice chief of the Naval General Staff, and in November 1933 his confidant Admiral Suetsugu Nobumasa became commander in chief of the Combined Fleet. Suetsugu was succeeded by Takahashi the following year. But it was among the spirited young officers that Katō and Suetsugu wielded their greatest influence.

The 1930s also gave rise to a third group of naval officers: a "German (later Axis) faction" and an "American (or Anglo-American) faction." Traditionally, the navy sent its most promising junior officers—the top graduates of the naval academy—to Washington as attachés, and its best naval architects to Greenwich, England, for training at the Royal Naval College. But in the 1930s, Germany became the preferred nation. This shift occurred in the years immediately after World War I, when many Japanese naval officers bitterly resented Great Britain's sudden abandonment of its alliance with Japan after having fully exploited Japan as a "watchdog of the British Empire."

After the termination of the Anglo-Japanese Alliance at the Washington Conference, the Royal Naval College ceased to admit Japanese naval architects. Therefore, Japan increasingly turned to Germany for technology. In 1920, during his fact-finding tour of Europe, Katō Kanji was so impressed with Germany's naval technology, especially the submarine,[2] that he concluded a clandestine submarine agreement with Germany. (It almost wrecked his career when Navy Minister Katō Tomosaburō peremptorily ordered Kanji to cancel the agreement for fear that it violated the Versailles Treaty.[3]) After 1936—the year the Anti-Comintern Pact with Germany was concluded—Japanese naval officers at the attaché office in Berlin outnumbered those working in Japan's Washington or London offices. Upon returning from Berlin, these junior officers formed the influential "nucleus group" of the pro-German and anti-American elements. By 1940, the "German faction" had come to occupy some of the key middle-echelon posts that provided the driving force in naval policy making.

Transformation of the Policy-Making Mechanism

The violent split over the London treaty gave the Katō-Suetsugu group a chance to expand its own influence, with the strong support of the venerable Fleet Admiral Tōgō Heihachirō, "the Nelson of Japan." Its aim was to wrest control from the "administrative group."

2. Katō Kanji Hensankai, comp., *Katō Kanji den,* 714–27.
3. Nagai Kansei, "Katō Kanji Shōshō ikkō no hō-Doku chōsa," 1.

Their first step was to install a member of the imperial family, Prince Fushimi Hiroyasu, a cousin of Hirohito, as chief of the Naval General Staff. Prince Fushimi had supported Katō Kanji and the fleet faction at the time of the London Naval Conference. During Prince Fushimi's long and undistinguished tenure, from January 1932 to March 1941, his vice chiefs often evoked the august name of the imperial prince to pressure and intimidate the navy minister into acquiescing to the demands of the Naval General Staff. Things were not much better when Prince Fushimi was actually in command, for as a member of the imperial family, he could not be held accountable for any error or misjudgment. As relations with the United States worsened in the late 1930s, Prince Fushimi recommended a belligerent policy, to the great distress of the emperor.

The second important move to strengthen the "command group" was to expand the authority of the Naval General Staff. In 1922 Katō Kanji, then vice chief, had ordered his confidant Takahashi Sankichi to draft a plan, but it was shelved, as Kanji did not dare submit it to the elder Katō. When Takahashi became vice chief in February 1932, the plan was revived.[4]

Acting on behalf of Prince Fushimi, Takahashi presented to the Navy Ministry demands designed (in his own words) to "reduce the navy minister's authority to a minimum." When the demands met with the staunch resistance of Captain Inoue Shigeyoshi, Takahashi forced a confrontation with Navy Minister Ōsumi Mineo, threatening that Prince Fushimi would resign. Next, Fushimi himself directly pressured Ōsumi, who hastily complied. The change that went into effect in September 1933, going against naval tradition, established the Naval General Staff's supremacy over the Navy Ministry. Captain Iwamura Seiichi, the senior aide to the navy minister, confided to his friend Inoue that he feared the danger of war had been increased by weakening the ability of the navy minister to rein in the Naval General Staff.[5] The revision was against the wishes of the emperor.

The so-called Ōsumi purge was the third step taken to strengthen the "command group." From 1933 to 1934, senior officers of moderate persuasion who led the treaty faction were systematically retired. Among its victims were Yamanashi Katsunoshin, Hori Teikichi, Sakonji Seizō, and others. In particular, the retirement of Hori, celebrated as "the most brilliant brain ever produced by the navy," greatly distressed his friend Rear Admiral

---

4. Katō Kanji Hensankai, comp. *Katō Kanji den*, 770–72; Harada, *Saionjikō*, 3:1, 14–15, 173–74.

5. Memorandum on "Regulations Concerning the Mutual Jurisdiction of the Navy Ministry and the Naval General Staff," n.d., BBK; Ōsumi Taishō Denki Kankōkai, ed., *Danshaku Ōsumi Mineo den*, 586–89.

Yamamoto Isoroku. The far-reaching consequences of the Ōsumi purge cannot be overemphasized. It decimated navy leadership and fatally weakened the moderate forces that might have exercised a measure of rational restraint over the Katō-Suetsugu group and, later, over the fire-eaters in the middle echelons.

Ishikawa Shingo and the First Committee

In November 1940 an important restructuring took place in the Naval Affairs Bureau, the nucleus of the navy's policy functions. Many of its duties were transferred to the newly created Naval Ordnance Bureau, and a Second Section was established in the Naval Affairs Bureau to specialize in foreign and defense policy. The reshuffling was aimed at overcoming the crisis resulting from the conclusion of the Tripartite Pact with Germany and Italy in September 1940. The crisis demanded that the navy "resolutely place itself at the center of activities of the state."

By the very nature of its assigned task, the Second Section assumed a bellicose posture toward the United States and Britain. Its chief, Captain Ishikawa Shingo, was known as "the direct heir to the Katō-Suetsugu line." As the "spearhead of anti-Anglo-American hard-liners," Ishikawa took the toughest stand of all among the middle-echelon officers during the Japanese-American crises of 1940–1941.[6]

Another institutional change was the creation in late 1940 of the First Committee. A controversy exists among historians about the role of this committee, but recent documentation seems to confirm its importance.[7] The First Committee was created to cope with "an unprecedented crisis" resulting from the Tripartite Pact. The committee was to be "the central organ" to "enable the Imperial Navy to take the lead and guide the government." The central figure in this committee was Captain Ishikawa. Other members were Tomioka Sadatoshi, the chief of the Operations Section; Ōno Takeji, the war guidance officer; and Takada Toshitane, the chief of the First Section of the Naval Affairs Bureau. They were the crème de la crème in

6. Ishikawa, *Shinjuwan made no keii,* 237 and passim; Takagi, *Shikan Teiheiyō sensō,* 181.

7. Tsunoda, "Nihon no tai-Bei kaisen, 1940–1941," *TSM,* vol. 7, passim, emphasizes the importance of the First Committee. On the other hand, the author of the official history, in particular Nomura Minoru, denies its importance. He argues that "in reality the First Committee was merely the synonym for Ishikawa" (BBKS, *Rengō kantai,* 1:325). But Admiral Inoue Shigeyoshi stresses the importance of this committee (*TSM,* 7:495 [new edition]).

the middle echelons; all had graduated at the top of the Naval War College or received awards from the emperor.[8]

These energetic and supremely confident men naturally tended to view Japanese-American relations from the perspective of war planning and preparations and were ready to take risks when dealing with the United States. Yet, the First Committee was engaged only in policy planning and never in decision making. The problem was that the committee members' recommendations were almost automatically accepted by their superiors and became the basis of national policies. Because of the weak leadership at the top, the navy's policy making came to "revolve around the First Committee," as one member of the committee recalled.[9] The Ōsumi purge had effectively crippled the navy's leadership.

Katō's "Spiritualism"

The almost fatalistic belief in the inevitability of war with the United States, which pervaded the ranks of these middle echelons, can best be understood by looking again at Admiral Katō Kanji and the negation of the Washington treaty system that he personified.

At the heart of Katō's doctrine lay neo-Mahanian economic determinism that the "irresistible lure of the Pacific" spelled an eventual naval showdown with the United States, in which each side would contend for its economic stake in China. As a "capitalistic-imperialistic nation," the United States would find an outlet for its expansive energies in the Pacific Ocean.[10] Naval limitation was merely a humanitarian veil to hide America's desire for economic domination over East Asia, and the Washington and London Conferences were simply steps in this direction. The resulting treaty system was an instrument for perpetuating America's naval supremacy and preserving a status quo that favored that power.

These ideas, of course, were not original or peculiar to Katō Kanji, but the way in which he related them to his worldview brought out certain ideo-

8. Among middle echalons who staffed the First Committee, Captain Takada and Commander Shiba had served in Germany, Commander Fujii was an outspoken Axis sympathizer, and Onoda was known as a "hardliner."

9. BBKS, *Senshi soshō: Daihon'ei Kaigunbu: Daitōa sensō kaisen keii* [War History Series: Navy Section of the Imperial Headquarters: Circumstances Leading to the Commencement of the Greater East Asian War], 3:310.

10. Apparently Katō had absorbed the Mahanian sea power theory from his immediate predecessor as president of the Naval Staff College, Rear Admiral Satō Tetsutarō, the leading exponent of Mahanian doctrine in Japan.

logical strains alien to Japanese naval tradition. According to his reading of history, the westward advance of American civilization across the Pacific, with all its "poisonous" effects on Japan, was the grand culmination of four centuries of steady expansion of "materialistic Western civilization." In this overall framework, his anti-Americanism merged into a general revulsion against Westernism, capitalism, and materialism—"isms" he identified externally with the Washington treaty system and domestically with the established political and social order.[11]

Viewed in another way, Katō's brand of "spiritualism" may be regarded as a psychological compensation for the inferior battleship ratio of 60 percent accorded Japan in the Washington treaty. One way to overcome the handicap, he held, was to pit Japan's "willpower against America's physical superiority." As soon as he was appointed its commander in chief in 1926, he ordered the Combined Fleet to engage in relentless drills under simulated combat conditions. These drills finally led to a double collision of four cruisers off Mihogaseki in 1927.[12] In time his obsession with drilling bred a mental habit of slighting the material basis of national power. And his idée fixe that Japan must have a ratio amounting to 70 percent of the American fleet strength fostered the delusion that once this ratio was attained, Japan would prevail in war.

Suetsugu's Attrition-Interceptive Strategy

The Japanese navy's answer to the strategic deadlock it faced was to devise submarine tactics that would offset the "deficiencies" of the 60 percent capital ship ratio. Developed by Admiral Suetsugu in 1923–1925, when he commanded the First Submarine Squadron, the plan was perfected in the "strategy of interceptive operations" after he became commander in chief of the Combined Fleet in 1933. Simply stated, this strategy was two-pronged: first, it sought through repeated submarine attacks to "gradually reduce" by about 30 percent the fighting capabilities of the United States fleet on its transpacific passage; and second, to seek an all-out decisive encounter with the enemy armada after it had advanced to the western Pacific.

The Naval Operational Plan of 1936, the oldest extant document, stipulated that "a portion of the Combined Fleet's submarine forces will advance, as soon as hostilities commenced, to Hawaii and the Pacific Coast of the United States." They would scout the moves of the enemy main fleet, attack

11. Katō Kanji Hensankai, comp., *Katō Kanji den*, 792–93, 809, 816–34, 924–29.
12. Ibid., 846–67, 918–19.

it on its transpacific passage, and eventually join the Combined Fleet in the main decisive encounter.[13]

Such a combat mission was a unique feature of the Japanese submarine strategy. (In foreign navies the mission assigned to the submarine was commerce raiding.) For this purpose, large, high-speed submarines were built in great numbers.[14] Suetsugu was supremely confident that with his strategy the Japanese navy would overcome the U.S. Navy, but he vastly underestimated the capability of American submarines. Assuming that Americans were inherently unsuited to strenuous submarine duty, Japanese strategists commonly regarded two weeks as being the limit of American endurance.[15]

The basic concept of interceptive operations embodied the traditional "principle of big battleships and big guns" (taikan kyohō shugi) and remained intact throughout the decade. Based on the "lesson of history" derived from the battle of the Japan Sea in 1905, this Mahanian doctrine of the decisive battle had hardened into a dogma that continued to govern conservative strategic thinking throughout the 1930s and even beyond.[16]

The strategy of interceptive operations raised questions that were never solved. Would the United States Navy opt for a Mahanian decisive fleet encounter early in the war? Or would it not be more likely to husband its fleet until it had built up an overwhelming strength? What if a quick and decisive engagement should fail to materialize and the conflict turned into a drawn-out war of attrition? Yet, strangely enough, it seems as if Japanese naval planners did not consider such a prospect until hostilities loomed immediately ahead.

This fixation with a main fleet encounter blinded conservative naval officers to technological innovations that were rapidly transforming naval warfare and necessitating a fundamental reassessment of their strategic concepts.

Yamamoto-Inoue Strategy: Naval Aviation

In sharp contrast to the conservative majority stood men such as Admirals Yamamoto Isoroku and Inoue Shigeyoshi, who had successfully readjusted their strategic thinking to the realities of the air age.

13. BBKS, Shiryōshū: Kaigun nendo sakusen keikaku [Collected Documents: The Navy's Annual Operational Plans], 24.

14. BBKS, Kaigun gunsenbi, 1:160–62, 174–77; BBKS, Senshi sōsho: Sensuikanshi [War History Series: History of the Submarine; hereafter cited as Sensuikanshi], 20, 32.

15. BBKS, Sensuikanshi, 27–54; Naval General Staff (Katō Kanji), "Kōjutsu oboegaki," BBK; JMJ interview records; Ikeda, Nihon no kaigun, 2:11–12, 137–38; Fukudome Shigeru, Shikan: Shinjuwan kōgeki [Pearl Harbor Attack: A Historical Interpretation], 124.

16. BBKS, Senshi sōsho: Hawai sakusen [War History Series: Hawaii Operations], 6, 38–39; BBKS, Kaigun gunsenbi, 1:130–32.

Yamamoto's views were informed with firsthand observations and experiences in the United States. He was at Harvard in 1919–1921, revisited the country on a fact-finding tour in 1923–1924, and served as naval attaché in 1925–1927. He often warned against the mistake of dismissing the American people as "weak-willed and spoiled by material luxuries"; on the contrary, he asserted, they were infused with "a fierce fighting spirit and an adventurous temperament."

America's industrial might and matchless resources convinced Yamamoto of the manifest impossibility of a naval race. "Anyone who has seen the auto factories in Detroit and the oil fields in Texas," he observed, "knows that Japan lacks the national power for a naval race." Concerning the existing naval arrangement, he declared, "The 5:5:3 ratio works just fine for us; it [the Washington naval treaty] is a treaty to restrict the *other* parties [the United States and Britain]."[17]

As early as 1928 Yamamoto had predicted that airpower would become the mainstay of the navy. Upon his return from the London Naval Conference of 1930, he asked to be appointed chief of the Technical Division of Naval Aviation, and in 1935–1936 he headed the Naval Aviation Department. Sharply critical of "hardheaded gunners" and Admiral Suetsugu's strategy of interceptive operations, Yamamoto argued that a frontal engagement of battleships was a thing of the past. By 1940 he was convinced that the airpower age he had foreseen in 1928 had become a reality.[18]

Vice Admiral Inoue Shigeyoshi, who had been the head of the Naval Aviation Department since October 1940, was an even more thoroughgoing and outspoken advocate of airpower: he envisaged nothing less than a virtual conversion of the navy into an air force. In a cogently argued memorandum to Navy Minister Oikawa Koshirō ("On New National Defense"), he pointed out with alarm how anachronistic Japan's armaments had been rendered. He mercilessly derided the Japanese navy's fixation with fleet ratios, scathingly terming it a "ratio neurosis." And he insisted that it was simply a waste of money to build battleships that were no match for planes. Asserting "who commands the air commands the sea," he declared that American naval leaders would not be "so stupid or reckless" as to mount offensive operations in the western Pacific as long as Japan controlled the air. And, he added, mastery of the air would in turn require adequately fortified air bases on the islands of the South Pacific. With a prophetic note, Inoue stated that any future war with the United States would revolve around a contest for those islands. In conclusion, he again urged rational

17. Sorimachi, *Ningen Yamamoto Isoroku*, 450–51; Agawa Hiroyuki, *Yamamoto Isoroku*, 131.
18. BBKS, *Hawai sakusen*, 7, 73–75.

armaments plans based on a redefinition of the nature, form, and strategic objective of a possible war with the United States.[19]

In view of the fact that both in the United States and in Britain the battleship was still commonly regarded as the backbone of the navy, the aviation-oriented Yamamoto-Inoue group must be credited with unusual farsightedness. But they were a decided minority, and their ideas were too advanced to find acceptance among the conservative mainstream. Inoue became a nuisance and was sent to the South Pacific as commander in chief of the Fourth Fleet in August 1941. Having built their careers on battleships and gunnery, the mainstream remained committed to the Mahanian axiom that "the battleship was the core of naval force."[20]

Having surveyed the factional, institutional, and strategic backgrounds, we shall now examine major issues in relation to the United States that paved the navy's road to Pearl Harbor.

Toward Abrogation of the Naval Treaties

By the fall of 1933 the navy had come to the view that the "unequal" treaties must be terminated, because of aggravated relations with the United States resulting from the Manchurian Incident and an anticipated crisis over the submission of the Lytton Report on Manchuria. Captain Shimomura Shōsuke, the Japanese naval attaché in Washington, cabled Tokyo a series of overly alarmist forecasts of an impending armed clash with the United States. He was worried about the U.S. Navy's decision to retain its Scouting Force on the Pacific coast after its annual maneuvers were finished.[21] Japan's sense of isolation deepened in the aftermath of its withdrawal from the League of Nations in March 1933. And there was uneasiness about the U.S. naval expansion commenced by President Franklin D. Roosevelt. All these factors crystallized a naval resolution to terminate the Washington treaty and demand parity at the forthcoming London naval talks.[22]

19. "On New Armaments Plan" submitted to the navy minister on January 30, 1941. Full text is printed in BBKS, *Hawai sakusen*, 42–48; Inoue Kankō Kai, *Inoue Shigeyoshi, Shiryō*, 34–38, 126–32.

20. BBKS, *Kaigun gunsenbi* 1:174, 198–99, 452, 581; BBKS, *Rengō kantai*, 1:404–5; Chihaya Masataka, *Nihon kaigun no senryaku hassō* [The Strategic Thought of the Japanese Navy], 294–95.

21. Naval attaché Captain Shimomura to vice chief of the Naval General Staff, nos. 57, 84, 85, June 10 and August 20, 1932; Shimomura to Navy Ministry, no. 67, July 14, 1932, Kōbun bikō file, BBK; Kido Kōichi Kenkyūkai, ed., *Kido Kōichi nikki*, 1:198.

22. Chief of the Naval General Staff to navy minister, confidential no. 154, May 6, 1933; Navy Ministry memorandum, strictly confidential, no. 1, October 3, 1933, Saitō Makoto

This was the course vigorously advocated by Commander Ishikawa Shingo, then principal officer in charge of armaments in the Naval General Staff. The foremost disciple of Katō Kanji, he held, as the reason for demanding parity, that the right of armament among sovereign states was equal—Katō's conviction since the Washington Conference. In an October 1933 memorandum to Katō, Ishikawa argued that parity was indispensable to Japan's security since nothing less would prevent the United States from mounting a transpacific offensive.[23] Suetsugu, the Combined Fleet commander, also asserted that the parity issue and the Manchurian question were two sides of the same coin. Was it not, he asked, the forbidding presence of the Imperial Japanese Navy that had enabled Japan to ward off American efforts at intimidation by covering the ocean flanks while the army completed the conquest of Manchuria?[24]

Katō denounced the inferior fleet ratio particularly for its pernicious effects on the navy's morale. In his statement to Navy Minister Ōsumi on behalf of commanders in chief and military councilors, Katō declared that if only the "cancer" of the Washington naval treaty could be excised, "the morale and self-confidence of our navy would be so bolstered that we can count on certain victory over our hypothetical enemy, no matter how overwhelming the physical odds against us."[25] This sweeping assertion, which disregarded the limits of national power, typified the highly emotional, all-or-nothing psychology that was seizing naval circles. The Ōsumi purge had made such a clean sweep of moderate leaders that there remained no counterforce to restrain the Katō-Suetsugu group.

At the Five Ministers Conference (which included the prime minister, the foreign minister, and the ministers of navy, army, and finance) in October 1933, Ōsumi declared, "If the United States should take a strong stand in opposition to our fundamental policy, we must resolutely repel it and proceed to complete our preparedness." To do so required "freeing ourselves of the disadvantageous restrictions imposed by the existing naval treaties."[26]

The initiative in restraining the navy came from Army Ministry leaders ever sensitive to a diversion of anti-Soviet armaments to a large-scale naval

Papers, DL; Navy minister's draft statement at Five Ministers Conference, September 21, 1933; Navy minister's draft statement at cabinet meeting, October 6, 1933, BBK; GS, Vol. 10, *Nitchū sensō* 3 [China War 3], 4, 35.

23. Katō Kanji, *Zoku gendaishi shiryō, Vol. 5: Kaigun Katō Kanji nikki* [Sequel to GS, Vol. 5: The Diary of Katō Kanji; hereafter cited as *Katō Kanji nikki*], 480–81.

24. Ibid., 480–83, 534–36.

25. Ibid., 538–41.

26. Navy Minister, "My view on the Empire's foreign policy to cope with coming international situation," October 16, 1933; "The navy's revised draft: Policy toward the United States," JMFA.

race with the United States. In a series of army-navy parleys beginning in the spring of 1934, the representatives of the two services tried to iron out their differences. By early summer Ōsumi was demanding "out-and-out parity, ratio of 10 to 10," although he admitted there was not the slightest chance that this demand would be accepted. On July 20, Army Minister Hayashi Senjūrō urged Ōsumi to reconsider, saying that the announcement of Japan's abrogation of the Washington treaty would provoke a joint Anglo-American front. Ōsumi retorted, Had it not been the practice of the United States to gang up with Britain to browbeat Japan with the specter of a naval arms race to impose an inferior fleet ratio? Ōsumi concluded that if its parity demand was not met, "rupture of the conference could not be helped."[27]

On July 8, 1934, Admiral Okada Keisuke—a naval genro squarely in the orthodox tradition, who had worked for the London treaty—was appointed prime minister. He had been chosen in the expectation that he would check the Katō-Suetsugu group, control the navy, and conclude a new treaty. As soon as the Okada cabinet was formed, Ōsumi threatened Okada that he would resign unless the parity demand was accepted. This demand, Ōsumi declared ominously, had already been privately presented to the emperor by Chief of the Naval General Staff Fushimi and had won His Majesty's approval. Indeed, Prince Fushimi had submitted to the throne a sealed letter containing the "wishes" of the navy. The document stated, "There is no other choice but to discard the existing system of [discriminatory] ratios and vigorously pursue a policy of equality [of armaments]; otherwise, *the navy will not be able to control its officers.*" As it turned out, the emperor had indignantly rejected the document, stating with unusual severity that he would not permit Prince Fushimi, not in a position of responsibility, to behave in such an irregular manner.[28]

At the Five Ministers Conference of July 24, Okada said that he "more than anything else wanted to conclude a treaty, so the notice to abrogate the Washington treaty could be delayed at least pending the preliminary London talks." He received the solid support of the army, foreign, and finance ministers, but his argument failed to move Ōsumi, who objected that naval subordinates could "hardly be pacified by such explanations."[29]

27. GS, Vol. 12, *Nitchū sensō* 4 [China War, 4], 16–18, 25–26, 28–29, 30–36; Harada, *Saionjikō*, 4:24; Tōgō Shigenori, *Jidai no ichimen* [An Aspect of the Showa Period], 92–93.

28. Ōkubo Tatsumasa et al., eds., *Shōwa shakai keizai shiryō shūsei: Kaigunshō shiryō* [Collection of Documents on Social and Economic History of the Shōwa Period: Navy Ministry Documents; hereafter cited as *Kaigunshō shiryō*], 1:101; Kido, ed., *Kido nikki,* 1:328, 330, 346–47; Harada, *Saionjikō*, 4:16–19, 22–23; Honjō Shigeru, *Honjō nikki* [Honjō Diary], 191, 192 (italics added).

29. Minutes of Five Ministers Conference, July 24, 1934, JMFA; Harada, *Saionjikō*, 4:20, 24, 27–28; Honjō, *Honjō nikki,* 192; Kido, ed., *Kido nikki,* 1:347.

Ōsumi's response was an allusion to the backstage maneuverings of Katō Kanji and Suetsugu. The two men had been trying to get commanders of the Combined Fleet to support the demand for parity. Katō had induced some sixty commanders to draft a joint memorial, which was submitted by Suetsugu to Ōsumi and Prince Fushimi. Moreover, Katō asserted that the demand for parity was "absolute" and that the entire navy had "burned its bridges behind it." Katō and Suetsugu incited younger officers and then threatened that unless the cabinet at once decided for parity, it would *"endanger control over naval subordinates."*[30]

Finally, on September 7, Okada admitted defeat when the cabinet decided that before the end of the year it would issue the required two years' notice of the abrogation of the Washington naval treaty.[31]

General conditions and the climate of opinion in 1934 were essentially different from those that prevailed at the time of the London Naval Conference of 1930. The deterioration of Japan's international situation has been noted. At home, party government had come to an end. Within the navy the Ōsumi purge had made such a clean sweep of the treaty faction that few voices of caution remained in the upper echelons. The emperor worried that the navy was "jeopardizing vital diplomatic problems for the sake of placating subordinate officers."[32]

Above all, the nightmarish memory of the May 15 Incident, in which a group of young officers played a part in the assassination of Prime Minister Inukai Tsuyoshi, practically immobilized government leaders, who were haunted by the fear that another wrangle over naval limitation would rekindle domestic violence that would surpass the earlier "incident." In that event jingoists and right-wing malcontents might well exploit insurgent young naval officers to destroy the existing social order. Admiral Suetsugu had warned that such would be the consequences of any concession made at the coming naval talks.[33]

How did the navy expect its aim of security to be served by withdrawing from the existing system of naval limitation? Deeply disturbed, the emperor queried Prince Fushimi: would the demand for parity not result

30. Suetsugu to Katō, July 7, 1934, Katō Kanji Papers, ISS-UT; Harada, *Saionjikō*, 3:321–22, and 4:33–36; Kido, ed., *Kido nikki*, 1:350; Katō Kanji Hensankai, comp., *Katō Kanji den*, 903–4 (italics added).

31. Kido, ed., *Kido nikki*, 1:354; Memorandum by navy minister, revised draft of January 2, 1934, JMFA; *GS*, Vol. 12, *Nitchū sensō* 4, 4–9.

32. Honjō, *Honjō nikki*, 194, 198.

33. Harada, *Saionjikō*, 4:20, 27, 44–45; Finance Ministry memorandum, [1934], sent to former prime minister Saitō with a rider by the head of the Budget Bureau, Saitō Makoto Papers, DL.

only in wrecking the naval conference and reopening the arms race, and in that event would Japan not be outbuilt by the United States? Prince Fushimi merely repeated the navy's stock answer: there was nothing to fear from an arms race. Going further, the Naval General Staff contended that unrestrained naval construction would actually be *more economical*, for Japan would be free to concentrate on ship categories "best suited to its peculiar national requirements."[34]

The key to the navy's seemingly paradoxical position was, of course, the monster battleship of the *Yamato* class, displacing fifty thousand tons and carrying eighteen-inch guns. With a rough plan of such a ship ready in October 1934, the Naval General Staff counted on getting a head start of at least five years on the United States. Even if the latter should in due course attempt to catch up, any comparable ships it built would be too large to pass through the Panama Canal. Ishikawa, one of the early enthusiasts for the plan, wrote Katō that the mammoth battleships would "at one bound raise our [capital ship] strength from the present ratio of 60 percent of the U.S. strength to a position of absolute supremacy."[35] Here was an inverted expression of the "ratio neurosis" discussed earlier. The *Yamato* plan rested on—in fact, improved on—the conventional precept of "big battleships and big guns." From the moment of its inception, air-power advocates such as Yamamoto mercilessly derided the plan as anachronistic.[36]

As had been anticipated, the preliminary London talks that began in October 1934 were shipwrecked on the rock of the Japanese demand for parity. The United States and Britain insisted on retention of the Washington-London system. Yamamoto, who represented Japan, subtly registered his disagreement with his superiors when he stated in his report to the throne that "there was no appearance whatsoever of two powers [the United States and Britain] combining to oppress the third [Japan] at these talks."[37] In January 1936, Admiral Nagano Osami walked out of the main conference, thus signaling the demise of naval limitation and resumption of the naval arms race.[38]

With the lapse of the Five-Power Treaty, the United States was no longer bound by article 19 to the status quo to fortifications in regard in the

34. Honjō, *Honjō nikki*, 193; *GS*, Vol. 12, *Nitchū sensō* 4, 28–29, 60–61.
35. Ishikawa memorandum, October 12, 1933, Katō Kanji Papers, ISS-UT; Katō, *Katō Kanji nikki*, 482; Ishikawa, *Shinjuwan made no keii*, 78–81; Shizuo Fukui, *Nihon no gunkan* [Japanese Warships], 72–76; BBKS, *Kaigun gunsenbi*, 1:466, 482–89.
36. Toyama Saburō, *Daitōa sensō to senshi no kyōkun* [The Greater East Asian War and the Lessons of War History], 21.
37. *GS*, Vol. 12, *Nitchū sensō* 4, 83–85; Takagi Sōkichi, *Yamamorto Isoroku to Yonai Mitsumasa*, 46–49.
38. For the Second London Naval Conference, see Pelz, *Race to Pearl Harbor*.

Philippines and Guam. The Japanese navy held that although the clause restricting their fortifications was to Japan's advantage, it did not compensate for the inferior ratio of 10:6. The lapse of the nonfortification clause was important, for in 1941 the building of American airpower in the Philippines was to pose a threat to Japan.[39]

Under the impetus of the Vinson-Trammell bill passed by Congress in March 1934, which allowed the U.S. Navy to build up its fleet to treaty limits, the Japanese navy embarked on its "second building program" (to span the years 1934–1937). By the end of 1935, Japan had exceeded the quotas set by the Washington and London treaties. The pamphlet the Navy Ministry published, titled *International Situation and Naval Limitation,* quoted from Satō Tetsutarō: "There are some countries that were ruined as the result of defeat, but there has not been a single country in history that was ruined as the result of spending excessively for armaments."[40] As we shall see, after 1936 the navy faced one crisis after another as a result of the arms race with the United States.

Preparations for Southward Advance

In 1936 Commander Ishikawa, then staff officer in the Second Fleet, returned from a fact-finding tour of Southeast Asia with the vivid impression that "an ABCD [American, British, Chinese, and Dutch] encirclement" was in the making to the south of Japan.[41] He reported to naval leaders that this "encirclement," led by the United States, was oppressing Japan militarily, politically, and economically. These fears and anxieties were greatly exaggerated and premature, but the fact remained that the geographical advantages that Japan had hitherto enjoyed in Far Eastern waters were beginning to disappear as the result of rapid advances in weaponry. That elusive goal of naval security, which Japan had sought to attain by withdrawing from the existing treaty system, was further away than ever.

In July 1935 the navy had established the Committee to Study Southern Policy.[42] The navy was searching for a rationale for fleet expansion after the demise of the treaties. The policy, laid out in the "Outline of National Policy" (April 1936), advocated to "defend the north, advance to the south." In expanding into the south, it noted, Japan must "as a matter of course

39. *GS,* Vol. 12, *Nitchū senso* 4, 28, 37.
40. Kaigunshō Kaigun Gunji Fukyūbu [Publicity Department, Navy Ministry], *Kokumin no seikatsu to gunshuku* [National Life and Naval Limitation].
41. BBKS, *Senshi soshō: Daihon'ei rikugunbu,* 1:415–16.
42. Ōkubo et al., eds., *Kaigunshō shiryō,* 1:282–310.

anticipate obstruction and coercion by the United States, Britain, and the Netherlands, etc. and must therefore provide for the worst by completing preparations for a resort to force." It also stated that "sufficient armaments must be prepared to cope with the traditional Far Eastern policy of the United States."[43]

Rejecting the army's demand for priority in anti-Soviet armaments, the navy adamantly demanded precedence in armaments against the United States. Unable to decide on priority, the government on August 7, 1936, settled on an interservice compromise: the now famous "Fundamentals of National Policy," which stipulated expansion toward *both* south and north.[44] The document did contain a provision to "strengthen naval armaments in order to ensure the command of the western Pacific against the United States Navy." On the basis of this stipulation, Navy Minister Nagano obtained appropriations for a huge "Third Replenishment Program," providing for sixty-six new ships, including two *Yamato*-class super-battleships and fourteen flying corps within five years.[45]

With the adoption of the "Fundamentals of National Policy," the navy's program of southward advance entered a new stage, under the guidance of Captain Nakahara Yoshimasa (dubbed "the King of the South Seas") and Captain Ishikawa, who demanded to secure advance bases for operations in the South China Sea. The China War that broke out in July 1937 kindled the navy's hope of acquiring Hainan, an inland rich in iron ore and strategically located for moves south. The views of the Naval General Staff prevailed, and in February 1939 Japan occupied Hainan, and one month later the Spratly Islands.

The Tripartite Pact and the Navy, 1938–1940

The first and foremost task that Navy Minister Yonai Mitsumasa had set for himself upon assuming office in February 1937 was to restore order and control within the navy, which had been allowed to all but disintegrate during the Ōsumi-Nagano era because of Katō Kanji's and Suetsugu's political activities. He strictly forbade naval officers to meddle in political matters and assumed full responsibility for handling the problem of a German alliance. In this endeavor he had the loyal support of his vice minister, Yamamoto Isoroku, and the head of the Naval Affairs Bureau, Inoue

---

43. Ibid., 361–65; BBKS, *Kaigun gunsenbi*, 1:477–82.
44. Gaimushō, *Nihon gaikō nenpyō narabini shuyō bunsho*, 2:344–45
45. Hirota Kōki Denki Kankō Kai, ed., *Hirota Kōki*, 212–16.

Shigeyoshi. For Yamamoto, here was an opportunity to "rebuild" the navy along the orthodox line. And Inoue, a man of determination, did his best to control his subordinates.[46]

From the outset, however, this celebrated "trio" was beset with difficulties; they had to contend not only with the army but also with German sympathizers within the navy. Among the middle echelons, pro-German forces were Captain Takada Toshitane, Commanders Kami Shigenori and Shiba Katsuo, Fujii Shigeru, and War Guidance Officer Yokoi Tadao. (Kami, Shiba, and Yokoi had recently returned from the attaché office in Berlin.)[47] Their advocacy of an alliance was fired with anti-British feelings.

Oka Takazumi revealed the navy's bureaucratic motive for an anti-British alliance when he argued that if the pact were to be directed against the Soviet Union alone, it could not "be used for the pursuit of national policy (*expanding to the South Seas*, etc.)."[48] In other words, a strictly anti-Russian alliance would concede the army's priority in armaments, whereas a broader pact against Britain as well would serve to direct national policy to a southward course, thereby strengthening the navy's demand for armaments against the Anglo-American powers. The budget-minded advocacy of an Axis alliance found a more explicit expression in a memorandum prepared by Captain Takagi Sōkichi, the chief of the Research Section:

> We have set Britain and America as the targets of our fleet expansion program . . . and have not hesitated to demand naval appropriations amounting to a billion and a half yen. By reversing this stand and agreeing to confine our target to the Soviet Union, we would not only expose contradictions and inconsistencies in our naval policy, but also cause the army to draw the erroneous conclusion that the navy, though ready to use Britain and America as "pretexts" for securing a [large] budget, does not really intend to confront these powers.[49]

As is well known, Navy Minister Yonai's objection to a military alliance with Germany was that such an alliance would most likely cause the United States to join hands with Britain, that together they would apply economic

---

46. Ogata Taketora, *Ichi gunjin no shōgai* [The Life of a Sailor, Yonai Mitsumasa], 19, 36–38.

47. Harada, *Saionjikō,* 7:39; *GS,* Vol. 10, *Nitchū sensō,* 3:153–54, 174–76.

48. *GS,* Vol. 10, *Nitchū sensō,* 3:176 (italics added).

49. Harada, *Saionjikō,* 7:267–69; Takagi Sōkichi, "My view on Japanese-German-Italian pact," December 17, 1938, in *Takagi Sōkichi nikki: Nichi-Doku-I sangoku dōmei to Tōjō naikaku datō* [Takagi Sōkichi Diary: The Japanese-German-Italian Tripartite Pact and the Overthrow of the Tōjō Cabinet], 197.

pressure on Japan, and that eventually Japan would be dragged into war. At the Five Ministers Conference of August 8, 1938, Yonai flatly declared that there was no chance of Japan's winning a conflict of this nature—the Japanese navy was "simply not designed to fight a war with America and Britain."[50] Yamamoto's stated reason for opposing the alliance was that "alignment with Germany that aimed at a new world order means inevitably being dragged into war for the overthrow of the old order of the Anglo-American powers. With the present strength of naval armament, especially aircraft, there is no chance of winning a war with the United States."[51]

In the course of some seventy-five sessions of the Five Ministers Conference, Yonai, opposing a German alliance, fought a verbal duel with Army Minister Itagaki Seishirō. Yamamoto ably supported Yonai at the risk of assassination. And Inoue held down recalcitrant subordination. Yet the Yonai-Yamamoto-Inoue leadership was highly personal, and therein lay its main weakness. Control over pro-German elements began to falter as soon as the three men left their posts after the Hiranuma cabinet fell in the bewildering aftermath of the Nazi-Soviet Pact of August 1939.

Shortly after the succeeding navy minister, Yoshida Zengo, took office, middle-echelon officers presented to him a policy paper ("Outline of Policy toward America") that indicated that their attitude was stiffening. In view of "the inseparable connection between Britain and America," it stated, an anti-British policy would inevitably lead to a deterioration of relations with the United States; therefore, the program of naval preparedness must be stepped up to guard against "a sudden unpredictable turn in American diplomacy."[52]

The German blitzkrieg in the spring of 1940 dazzled Japanese naval circles and further enhanced their admiration for Germany and disdain for Anglo-American powers. Among the middle echelons the expectation of a German landing on the British Isles was rampant. No longer confined to middle-echelon ranks, the rekindled pro-Axis fervor came to infect bureau and division chiefs.[53] Although increasingly isolated, Navy Minister Yoshida continued to resist the trend of events, but in late August he suffered a physical and mental collapse and resigned.

The appointment of Admiral Oikawa Koshirō as the new navy minister and Toyoda Teijirō as vice minister on September 5 tipped the balance in favor of the Tripartite Pact. A scholarly type devoted to Chinese classics and

50. Ogata, *Ichi gunjin*, 40–43, 54, 58.
51. Navy memorandum, October 20, 1939, Papers of Konoe Fumimaro, photocopy at BBK; Ōkubo, ed., *Kaigunshō shiryō*, 8:557.
52. Ōkubo, ed., *Kaigunshō shiryō*, 8:557.
53. Okada Sadahiro, ed., *Okada Keisuke kaikoroku*, 133; Inoue Kankō Kai, "Omoide no ki" [Reminiscences], in private hands.

a man of few words, Oikawa was not a very powerful leader. The only reservation he demanded in the treaty provisions was that Japan retain the right to determine the time and circumstances under which to extend military assistance. Once this condition was met, he promptly gave his formal consent to the Tripartite Pact at the Liaison Conference of September 14.

But why was it that the navy, which had so staunchly blocked the German alliance for more than two years, finally reversed its position? The major consideration, according to a version later given by Oikawa and his aggressive vice minister Toyoda, was "political": they feared a frontal clash with the army might occasion an army coup d'état.[54] Disappointed by the navy's volte-face, Prime Minister Konoe Fumimaro queried Toyoda. Toyoda replied, "It is for political reasons that the navy supports [the Tripartite Pact]. From a military viewpoint, the navy does not have confidence in fighting a war with the United States." A dumbfounded Konoe retorted, "We politicians can take care of domestic politics. The navy should have examined [the question of the Tripartite Pact] from a strictly military viewpoint, and should have opposed the pact to the end if it is not confident [about fighting the United States]."[55] Oikawa failed in his duty as navy minister to advise political leaders about the navy's military capability from a technical-professional standpoint.

Furthermore, the pressures from naval subordinates could not be ignored.[56] As stated, the majority in the navy from division and bureau chiefs on down now supported the Tripartite Pact, and Oikawa was vulnerable to their pressure. Above all, he put the navy's sectional and organizational interests before the nation's security. He did not dare to openly admit, as Yonai had done earlier, that the navy was not capable of fighting the United States and Britain, because he felt that such a confession of weakness would seriously jeopardize the morale of naval officers and call into question the raison d'être of the navy itself.

The navy's perennial concern for a larger share of the budget and war matériel was another unstated but important factor. The navy desired to reverse the priority the army had enjoyed since the outbreak of the China War. This purpose could be served by an emphasis on southward advance and a military alliance aimed at Britain and the United States. At the Liaison Conference of September 14, Oikawa coupled his consent to the Tripartite Pact with a request that special consideration be given to the navy's request

54. Shinmyō Takeo, ed., *Kaigun sensō kentō kaigi kiroku: Taiheiyō sensō kaisen no keii* [A Record of the Conference of Former Naval Leaders: Examining the Circumstances Leading to the Opening of the Pacific War], 79; BBKS, *Kaigun keii,* 2:107.

55. Yabe, *Konoe Fumimaro,* 2:161–62.

56. *TSM,* 5:194–95, 203–6.

for matériel.[57] Years later, Vice Minister Toyoda described the navy's basic position: "The navy accepted the Tripartite Pact, but it desired as far as possible to avoid war with the United States. . . . However, we had to be adequately prepared to meet the worst contingency; we therefore demanded further reinforcement of naval armaments." "The navy does not want to go to war but it demands acceleration of war preparations vis-à-vis the United States." This underlying bureaucratic opportunism, as we shall see, was to prove the undoing of the Japanese navy.[58]

The navy's assessment of the war in Europe was one additional key factor. From early summer into the fall of 1940, naval officers, especially in the middle echelons, expected the prospect of successful German cross-channel operations against Britain. The Intelligence Division (headed by Oka Takazumi) stated on September 7, 1940, "There is a great likelihood of Germany proceeding to invasion of Britain."[59] On the basis of this assessment the navy apparently began to see the Tripartite Pact as an instrument to restrain the United States from going to war with Germany before the end of 1940, by which time, the Japanese hoped, Britain would have been disposed of and the war in Europe ended. The fact was that in mid-September Hitler had given the order to indefinitely postpone (virtually give up) the invasion of Britain. The navy's wishful thinking was to prove a terribly costly miscalculation.[60]

Advance to Southern Indochina, 1941

In the end it was the decision on the "southern advance"—or rather the stringent American reaction to it—that precipitated the navy's "determination" to go to war. Yet it is difficult to pinpoint exactly when this "determination" was reached. Lacking firm leadership and racked by confusion, dissension, and misperception about America, the navy failed to foresee the ultimate outcome of a southward advance and to realistically assess the chance of war. Having no clear sense of direction, the navy was preoccupied with obtaining a greater share of the budget and war matériel, with the result that it lost the opportunity to stem the drift into "termination" for war.

57. *TSM: Bekkan Shiryōhen*, 333.
58. Record of interview with Toyoda Teijirō, BBK.
59. Intelligence Division, "Estimate of the European war situation," September 7, 1940, BBK.
60. Harada, *Saionjikō*, 8:198; Toyoda Soemu, *Saigo no teikoku kaigun* [The Last of the Imperial Navy], 51; Shigemitsu Mamoru, *Shōwa no dōran* [Showa: Years of Upheaval], 1: 259; Nomura Naokuni's testimony in Nakamura, *Shōwa kaigun hishi*, 28–31, 41–42.

In September 1939, with Britain, France, and the Netherlands—all with colonies in Southeast Asia—pinned down in Europe, Japan had the opportunity to make a forceful southward advance. The day Britain declared war with Germany, Captain Nakahara wrote in his diary that the important thing was "to restore Japan's position as a maritime nation and concentrate our efforts on naval expansion (for this purpose we shall not desist from fighting Britain or America)."[61] However, such a radical plan to switch national policy was not acceptable to senior naval leaders.

German victories in May and June 1940 in the West dazzled the Japanese navy, which saw an opportunity to forcefully advance south. Thus, in April 1940, a conference of section chiefs concluded that now was "the finest chance to occupy the Dutch East Indies." After the fall of France in June, French Indochina seemed to be rapidly becoming "a ripe persimmon." Navy Minister Yoshida almost single-handedly resisted these pressures. He was more convinced of the need for caution because the war games conducted in May had shown conclusively that a surprise attack on the East Indies would inevitably lead Japan into a war with the Netherlands, Britain, and the United States simultaneously.[62] Henceforth, America rather than Britain was to loom large athwart Japan's southward path.

Yet the rising tide of impatience, summed up in the slogan "Don't miss the bus," could not be contained and in July 1940 found expression in a national policy paper drafted by army staff officers and bearing the ponderous title "Main Principles for Coping with the Changing World Situation." It called for preparations to "resort to force" against the Dutch East Indies, French Indochina, and the British possessions in the Far East. The navy objected, saying that the army draft "did not consider relations with the United States seriously enough." While the army thought that Japan would fight with Britain alone in case of an armed advance southward, the navy made much of the danger of war with the United States.[63]

What attracts our attention is the particular importance the navy attached to preparations vis-à-vis the United States: "Since war with the United States may become unavoidable, sufficient preparations for it must be made." Of course, the navy was not yet confident about war with the United States, but, as Commander Kawai Iwao of the Operations Section confessed, "if we

61. Nakahara Diary, September 3, 29, 1940, and January 15, 1941, BKK; James W. Morley, ed., *The Fateful Choice: Japan's Advance into Southeast Asia, 1939–1941*, 242.
62. *TSM*, 7:19; Nakazawa Tasuku Kankō Kai, ed., *Kaigun chūjō Nakazawa Tasuku: Sakusen buchō, jinji kyokuchō* [Vice Admiral Nakazawa Tasuku: Chief of the Operations Division and Personal Bureau], 42–47.
63. BBKS, *Kaigun kaisen keii*, 2: 41; BBKS, *Rikugun Kaisen keii*, 1:390; *TSM: Bekkan Shiryōhen*, 315–18, 322–24.

say so, we were vulnerable to the army's demand to take away our war matériel and reduce the naval budget." Behind the navy's hard-line posture lay the navy's desire to expand its armaments "by leaps and bounds."

The navy was greatly alarmed by the huge building plans the United States had recently announced. The second Vinson plan of May 1938 authorized an increase of 20 percent. Japan responded with the huge "Fourth Replenishment Program" of 1939, which involved the construction of eighty ships including two more *Yamato*-class super-battleships and a doubling of its naval aviation over a five-year period.[64] Then in June 1940, Congress, faced with the threat of German conquest and with Japan's imminent southward advance, agreed to an 11 percent increase of naval strength over a two-year period. This was followed on July 19 by the Stark Plan, the so-called two-ocean navy, that provided for a 70 percent increase. This astronomical arms expansion came as a great shock to the Japanese navy. According to the Naval General Staff's estimate, Japan's capital ship ratio vis-à-vis the United States would be reduced to about 50 percent in 1943 and 30 percent or below by 1944. As for aircraft, American production capacity would be more than ten times that of Japan.[65] Thus caught in the straits of an ever-escalating arms race, the navy desperately needed a rationale to establish its priority in defense appropriations. Viewed in this context, the "Main Principles" may be said to have been a mere verbal show of strength, more budget-minded than war-minded.

On July 26, the day before the "Main Principles" were officially approved by the Liaison Conference, President Roosevelt signed an executive order placing aviation gasoline, high-grade iron, and steel scrap under an export licensing system. The Japanese navy seized the occasion to step up its plans of southward expansion. On August 1 the Operations Section produced a notable scenario concerning an armed advance into French Indochina. This document contained a peculiar style of circular reasoning based on the premise that war with the United States was inevitable: (1) to prepare for hostilities with the United States, Japan would have to march into Indochina, obtaining raw materials and strategic vantage points there; (2) the United States would retaliate by imposing a total trade embargo; (3) this in turn would compel Japan to seize the Dutch East Indies to secure vital oil resources; and (4) this step would involve a "determination to initiate hostilities" against the United States.[66] This was a stark expression of the logic of mutual escalation pointing to war. However, it was not until the spring

64. Inoue Kankō Kai, *Inoue Shigeyoshi*, 286–87.
65. *TSM*, 7:324.
66. *GS*, Vol. 10, *Nitchū sensō*, 3:361–71, 497–501, 504–7; *TSM*, 7:47.

of 1941 that advocacy of southward advance, predicated on war with the United States, became dominant in the navy.

In return for the informal agreement by which the navy had consented to the Tripartite Pact, the navy had gained precedence over the army in the materials mobilization program. Thenceforth, the navy could take a more confident view of its preparedness against the United States. But the improvement in the navy's position did not calm the clamor for a belligerent policy motivated by the need for matériel; on the contrary, the improvement in the navy's position, ironically, encouraged the advocates of war in the middle echelons. In October 1940 Commander Kami Shigenori of the Operations Section told the Army General Staff that by April of the following year—when Japan would have attained 75 percent (actual operational strength) of the U.S. fleet strength—a war should be initiated in the south, adding that otherwise it would be difficult to control restless officers.[67] Such a view was by no means confined to the ranks of the middle echelons. The vice chief of the Naval General Staff, Kondō Nobutake, also argued that as war preparations would be completed by the following April, it would be to Japan's advantage to strike at the United States before the ratio differential between the two navies grew even greater.[68] Here was another instance of the "ratio neurosis."

In retrospect, the replacement in April 1941 of the ailing Prince Fushimi with Admiral Nagano Osami as chief of the Naval General Staff was a milestone in the drift toward the final catastrophe. Nagano had already come to view war with the United States as inevitable. Despite his stately appearance, his attaché experience in Washington, and his seniority, Nagano was an impulsive and ineffective man. Lacking the energy to lead, he nonchalantly remarked that he relied on his section chiefs because they were in the know. Ministry leaders could hardly restrain Nagano. Navy Minister Oikawa was opposed to war but remained silent. Vice Minister Sawamoto Yorio was a cautious bureaucrat, and Oka, the head of Naval Affairs, served as a mediator between Oikawa and Nagano.

It was hardly surprising that the middle echelons, now asserting a sort of collective leadership through the First Committee, came to the fore. As their policy recommendations were almost automatically approved by their superiors, strategic requirements came to dominate national policy. Their demand for war preparations drove ranking naval leaders into an impasse that finally forced their "determination" for war. The decision to march into southern Indochina was a case in point.

67. BBKS, *Rikugun kaisen keii*, 3:304.
68. Taped interviews with Shiba Katsuo, BBK; JMJ interview records.

By April 1941 the section chiefs conference had voiced its support for going to war with the United States. Captains Tomioka and Ishikawa were heard to say, "Now is the time to strike; we won't be defeated."[69] On June 5 the First Committee produced a notable policy paper, drafted under the direction of Captain Ishikawa, titled the "Attitude to Be Adopted by the Imperial Navy under Present Circumstances." Underlying this document was confidence that resulted from progress in war preparations since the previous summer. The authors of this policy paper demanded an end to the nagging uncertainty and vacillation of their superiors, which made it impossible to push war preparations to the final stage. And it expressed the fear that, as long as the issue of war or peace hung in the balance, Japan might lose the favorable moment to strike decisively. They therefore urged that the navy immediately *"make clear its determination in favor of war"* with the United States, "lead" the government to commit itself, and carry out an armed advance into Indochina and Thailand "without a day's delay."[70]

The First Committee justified these moves as "preemptive" measures against the Anglo-American "military offensive." It maintained that inasmuch as the United States was rapidly reinforcing its airpower in the Philippines and steadily consolidating its strategic, political, and economic position in Southeast Asia in collusion with Britain, Japan would find itself forestalled unless it moved quickly into Indochina. Admittedly, there was no evidence that such a danger actually existed. But the subjective notion of being oppressed by an "ABCD encirclement" cast a powerful spell on Japan's naval planners who therefore argued the case for breaking through it for the sake of "self-existence and self-defense."[71]

The outbreak of Nazi-Soviet hostilities on June 22 spurred the army's demand for war with Russia, and the navy tried to restrain the army by clamoring for a southward drive. At the Imperial Conference of July 2, the navy representative confirmed the policy of marching into southern Indochina, proposing to insert the significant phrase, "[Japan] will not desist from war with Britain and the United States." This belligerent position surprised Vice Minister Sawamoto, to whom Oikawa explained, "My idea is to avoid war, but the army is insisting on advancing both to the north and south, so it was utterly impossible to restrain the army unless we made that statement." The navy's real stand was that "As the matter stood, the army would get hold of both the budget and matériel, so that the navy had

---

69. *TSM*, 7:241.
70. *TSM: Bekkan Shiryōhen*, 427–40; *TSM*, 6: 268–71; JMJ interview records (italics added).
71. Ishikawa, *Shinjuwan made no keii*, 294–97; JMJ interview records; *TSM: Bekkan Shiryōhen*, 427–40.

no choice but to prepare for a southern drive in order to complete war prepa-rations. But we did not really mean to go to war." Here again the navy was putting priority on its organizational interest in deciding on national pol-icy. Without having thoroughly examined the risk of war and Japan's chances of winning or losing, the navy was deciding on crucial national pol-icy in "contention, rivalry, and bargains" with the army.[72]

The visible stiffening of Nagano's stance in mid-June was due to the rec-ommendations of the First Committee. At the Liaison Conference he stated, "Now we have a chance of victory over the United States, but as time passes this chance will decrease." Although the majority in the Naval General Staff had become convinced of the inevitability of war, the top leaders of the min-istry remained cautious. All this time Navy Minister Oikawa maintained his silence, but he hoped that a southward drive could somehow be accom-plished without inciting a war with the United States.[73]

Total American Embargo and "War Determination"

Whatever the inner thoughts of the navy minister may have been, it seems clear that Nagano and some of his subordinates anticipated a sharp American reprisal in the form of a total embargo when it was decided to send thousands of Japanese troops marching into southern Indochina.[74] As Nagano put the stamp of approval on the navy's decision for the drive, he muttered, "This will mean war with America." At the Liaison Conference of June 11 and 12, he declared in a belligerent tone that surprised even army leaders that if the United States and Britain should stand in the way, "we must attack them."[75]

On July 25, the United States government, which had surmised Japan's advance into southern Indochina through interceptive diplomatic dis-patches, issued an order freezing Japanese assets in America. The day *before*, Nagano was heard to say that there was "no choice left but to break the iron fetters strangling Japan."[76] The de facto oil embargo that went into effect on August 1 completed this "strangulation." The logic of escalation,

72. Yoshizawa Minami, *Sensō kakudai no kōzu: Nihongun no Futsu-in shinchū* [The Structure of War Escalation: Japanese Troops' Advance into French Indochina], 211.
73. *TSM: Bekkan Shiryōhen*, 481; BBKS, *Rikugun kaisen keii*, 4:124; Oka Takazumi, JMJ interview records; staff studies, BBK.
74. Tomioka, *Kaisen to shūsen*, 59; BBKS, *Rengō kantai*, 1:528.
75. Daihon'ei Rikugunbu Sensō Shidōhan [War Guidance Office of the Imperial Japanese Headquarters: The Army Section], *Kimutsu sensō nisshi* [Confidential War Journal], 1:115; *TSM: Bekkan Shiryōhen*, 442–43, 468–69, 474, 481.
76. Kobayashi, *Kobayashi Seizō oboegaki*, 93, 102.

foreseen for a year, was now being activated. A policy predicated on the necessity for war preparations had thus trapped the Japanese navy in a predicament that would soon force its leaders to determine for war.[77]

As far as the navy was concerned, the point of no return was reached when Japanese troops marched into southern Indochina on July 28. Yet there is no evidence that the Liaison Conference or cabinet meeting carefully considered the risk of a total embargo before deciding to take this fateful step. More difficult to account for is the fact that some members of the First Committee were "stunned" by the severity of the American reaction. The shock of the total embargo was profound. As Captain Ōno Takeji later stated, he and some of his colleagues in the committee underestimated the risk of an embargo because they did not expect Washington to resort to such a drastic measure; Americans must have realized that Japan would be compelled to strike, and the United States was hardly ready to face a two-ocean war.[78]

In fact, the United States was not prepared for war in the Pacific. In response to President Roosevelt's query, Harold R. Stark, the chief of Naval Operations, had stated on July 21 that he opposed an oil embargo, fearing that it would prompt a Japanese invasion of the Dutch East Indies and "possibly would involve the United States in early war in the Pacific." (The intercepted Japanese message gave the false sign about Japan's impending drive toward the Dutch East Indies.)[79] Already engaged in "an undeclared war" with Germany in the Atlantic, the United States wanted to avoid war with Japan. It was to deter Japan from further advance southward that the United States resorted to a total embargo. This attempt backfired: instead of deterring Japan, the embargo drove Japan into a decision to open hostilities with the United States for "self-existence and self-defense."

The Decision for War, August–November 1941

Whatever the reasons for their miscalculation, it was too late for the navy minister and ranking ministry officials to reassert their influence for peace. Having long since abnegated their leadership, they hardly could have overruled Nagano who pressed for prompt commencement of war. With the lifeblood of the fleet—fuel oil stocks—being drained at the rate of twelve

77. Hattori Takushirō, *Daitōa sensō zenshi* [The Complete History of the Great East Asian War], 1:142.

78. Record of interview with Takada Toshitane, JMJ; Tomioka Sadatoshi, "Taiheiyō sensō zenshi," 3:57.

79. Quoted in William L. Langer and S. Everett Gleason, *The Undeclared War: The World Crisis and American Foreign Policy*, 645–54.

thousand tons daily, time was running out. The navy feared that America's delaying tactic would bring out, in the navy parlance, "gradual pauperization." On July 30, Nagano reported to the throne that Japan's "Oil stockpile would last only for two years, and in case of war they would be exhausted in a year and a half, so there is no way but to sally out."[80]

From this time forward the navy's slogan was "Strike quickly if there is to be a war." On August 3 the First Committee drafted a policy paper that stated that if a diplomatic breakthrough was not forthcoming until mid-October, war should be initiated. The revised version of this paper became the critical decision of the Imperial Conference of September 6: "We must immediately determine for war with the United States (Britain, the Netherlands) if we cannot carry through our demands in early October."[81]

Nagano's statements at this conference recall a "spritualism" Katō Kanji had advocated earlier. Driven to the "last extremity," Nagano reverted to a brand of "spiritualism." He maintained that if Japan faced national ruin whether it decided to fight the United States or to submit to American demands, it must by all means choose to fight. He would rather go down fighting than surrender without a struggle, for surrender would mean "spiritual as well as physical ruin for the nation."[82]

Admiral Okada Keisuke later noted in his memoirs that Nagano was scolded by the emperor for saying, "We must fight, although we shall lose."[83] Of course, Nagano had not despaired of the chance of victory. But by "chance" he meant the advantages he could count on at the initial stage of hostilities. Obviously affected by the "ratio neurosis," he based his hopes on Japan's current fleet strength of slightly over 70 percent (75 percent in actual operational capability) of that of the United States. When queried about Japan's prospect in a protracted war, he equivocated: he could say "nothing for certain" beyond the first two years. The fullest exposition he ever gave of his war plan is in his statements at the Imperial Conference of September 6. He contended that Japan would be able to wage a protracted war by speedily establishing an "impregnable sphere" in the South to control raw materials.

In reality, this plan was hardly feasible. For one thing, little had been accomplished to adequately fortify the islands in Micronesia, despite Vice Admiral Inoue's urgent request. Second, the airpower to defend the "impregnable sphere" was not provided by the "Fourth Replenishment Program," and the "Fifth Replenishment Program," hurriedly drawn up

80. Kido, ed., Kido nikki, 2:895–96.

81. TSM: Bekkan Shiryōhen, 510; Daihon'ei, Sensō Shidōhan, Kimutsu sensō nisshi, 1:148.

82. Fukudome, Shikan: Shinjuwan kōgeki, 136–37; TSM: Bekkan Shiryōhen, 508–12; Yabe, Konoe Fumimaro, 2:361; Fujii Diary, September 6, 1941 (in private possession).

83. Okada Sadahiro, ed., Okada Keisuke kaikoroku, 136.

at the eleventh hour, involved huge figures clearly beyond the nation's capacity. Third, there was a serious shortage of vessels to transport the essential oil resources from the South and of ships to convoy them. Pre-occupied with a Mahanian decisive encounter, the navy completely neg-lected its convoy operation. In sum, there was little to substantiate Nagano's plan from an operational standpoint.

Perceiving the fatal flaws in Nagano's plan, Combined Fleet Commander Yamamoto met with him on September 26, but he could not dissuade Nagano from his "determination" for war. The war games had convinced Yamamoto that Japan could never hope for victory in interceptive opera-tions. He believed that in the light of the recent strategic thought of the U.S. Navy, there was little chance of its main fleet waging a frontal attack in a decisive encounter.[84] Yamamoto's plan of air attack on Pearl Harbor at the start of the hostilities was a supreme gamble, but he argued that it was the only strategy that, however desperate, held a flicker of hope of ending the war before it became prolonged. In his letters to Oikawa and Shimada he emphasized the importance of destroying the morale of the American peo-ple at the outset,[85] but given his familiarity with the American national char-acter, it is difficult to believe he shared with his countrymen such underestimation of the American morale. It is probably more accurate to say that his plan was "conceived in desperation" as he himself admitted.[86]

The Naval General Staff, deeply committed to the conventional strategy of interceptive operations and concerned with the great risks involved in Yamamoto's bold plan, strenuously opposed it. But Nagano reluctantly accepted it on October 19 because Yamamoto threatened to resign as com-mander in chief of the Combined Fleet.[87]

The last chance for Navy Minister Oikawa to register opposition to war was lost, when at the Five Ministers Conference of October 12 he failed to state that the navy lacked confidence in a war against the United States. Instead, he merely said that he would leave to the prime minister the deci-sion on war or peace. Oikawa later explained the navy's "true intention": "After so many years of clamoring about its 'invincible fleet,' the navy was hardly in a position to say it could not fight the United States. It cannot single-handedly accept the blame for being a coward, for the navy would have no ground to stand on both internally and externally!"[88]

84. *TSM: Bekkan Shiryōhen*, 512; *TSM*, 7:322–37.
85. BBK, *Hawai sakusen*, 74, 78.
86. Ibid., 81–87.
87. BBKS, *Hawai sakusen*, 82–85, 113–14; Fukudome, *Shikan: Shinjuwan kōgeki*, 144–59.
88. *TSM: Bekkan Shiryōhen*, 531–33; Sanbō Honbu [Army General Staff], ed., *Sugiyama memo* [Liaison Conference Records of Chief of Staff Sugiyama], 1:116–18; Yabe, *Konoe*

Vice Minister Sawamoto also cited three reasons: (1) the navy would lose its raison d'étre; (2) it would adversely affect the navy's morale; and (3) "the army said there was no need to give war matériel to a navy that could not fight."[89] Again, the navy's bureaucratic concern was given precedence over Japan's national interest. Another explanation emphasizes the fear of domestic upheaval.

Regarding the psychic environment in which the navy made decisions leading to war, Operations Division head Fukudome recalled after the war, "When we took our position as individuals, we were all in favor of avoiding a Japanese-American war by all means, but when we held a conference the conclusion always moved step by step in the direction of war. It was all very strange." In a similar vein, Nagano said, "The truth of the matter was that we came step by step to war determination by force of circumstances."[90] It is, of course, easier to make decisions in the face of great uncertainty if one is a fatalist. What characterized this mode of decision making by consensus was an almost pathological lethargy, abandonment of independent thinking, evasion of responsibility, and swimming with the tide. According to psychologist Irvin L. Janis, this type of decision making may be called "groupthink" or even "collective irrationality."[91]

From this time on, strategic imperatives and operational requirements governed naval (and national) policy. On October 18, Shimada Shigetarō was appointed navy minister, with the strong backing of Prince Fushimi. Having served exclusively in the fleets and the Naval General Staff, Shimada had no experience or interest in politics. When he took over from Oikawa, he was not briefed and upon assumption of office was "greatly shocked" to learn about the decisions of the Imperial Conferences of July 2 and September 6. Prince Fushimi pressured Shimada, saying "we shall lose time unless we promptly start a war."

Finally on October 30, Shimada reached the decision to go to war. He informed Vice Minister Sawamoto and Oka, "As it is, there is no telling when the United States will make a preemptive strike." His fear was that the American fleet would steam across the Pacific in full force as soon as

Fumimaro, 2: 379–81, 386–91, 394; Toyoda, *Saigo no teikoku kaigun*, 62; Itō Masanori, *Rengō kantai no saigo* [The Last of the Combined Fleet], 255–56; Shinmyō Takeo, ed., *Kaigun sensō kentō kaigi kiroku*, 169, 178–79.

89. Sawamoto Yorio, "Sawamoto Yorio kaigun jikan nikki: Nichi-Bei kaisen zen'ya" [Diary of Navy Vice Minister Sawamoto Yorio: On the Eve of the Japanese-American War], 474.

90. Fukudome, *Shikan: Shinjuwan kōgeki*, 97–98; Shinmyō, *Kaigun sensō kentō kaigi kiroku*, 26.

91. Irvin Janis, *Groupthink: Psychological Studies of Policy Decisions and Fiascoes*, 37, 39.

Japan ran out of oil and its fleet was stranded.[92] How totally Shimada misread U.S. strategy is clear from what Admiral Harold Stark and General George Marshall wrote to President Roosevelt on November 5:

> At the present time the United States Fleet in the Pacific is inferior to the Japanese Fleet and cannot undertake an unlimited strategic offensive in the Western Pacific. . . . War between the United States and Japan should be avoided while building defensive forces in the Far East, until such time as Japan attacks or directly threatens territories whose security to the United States is of great importance.[93]

In short, the United States would not fight unless Japan directly attacked American, British, or Dutch territories. But Shimada's distrust of the United States ran too deep to make an objective assessment. Internally, Shimada emphasized the risk of a domestic crisis: "We had no choice but to agree [to commence hostilities] in order to avoid the worst situation of the army and navy fighting each other."[94]

When Shimada finally expressed his "determination" to Army Minister (Prime Minister) Tōjō Hideki and Army Chief of Staff Sugiyama Hajime on November 1, he also requested an increased allotment of steel. The navy needed a large amount of additional steel for the "Fifth Replenishment Program." Even at this climactic moment, the navy was preoccupied with a larger share of matériel. Sugiyma asked Shimada, "Will you decide for war, Shimada-san, if the navy gets the steel it demands?" The navy minister nodded in assent. As a result, in the materials mobilization plan for 1942, the navy was to receive 1.1 million tons of steel and the army 790,000 tons.[95]

At the Imperial Conference of November 5, it was decided that if Japanese-American negotiations did not succeed by the beginning of December, Japan would declare war on the United States. Finally, on December 8, the declaration was issued. The imperial rescript stated that faced with the American embargo, Japan had resolutely arisen for "self-

---

92. Sanbō Honbu, ed., *Sugiyama memo*, 1:370–71; *TSM: Bekkan Shiryōhen*, 550, 560–61, 568. Shimada, "Shimada nikki," 360, 362 (entry of November 29, 1941); Shimada, biboroku [memoranda] of October 29 and November 1, 1941; Shimada Shigetarō shuki [Notes and manuscript], Suikō Kai, Tokyo.

93. Chief of staff and chief of naval operations, Memorandum for president, November 5, 1941, *Hearings before the Joint Committee of Investigation of the Pearl Harbor Attack*, 79th Cong., pt. 12, 1061–62.

94. Sanbō Honbu, ed., *Sugiyama memo*, 1:370–71; Shimada, "Shimada nikki," November 1, 1941.

95. Sanbō Honbu, ed., *Sugiyama memo*, 1, 372; Gaimushō, *Nihon gaikō nenpyō narabini shuyō bunsho*, 2:573.

existence and self-defense."[96] This fulfilled the logic of armed escalation that had been first articulated by the Naval General Staff on August 1, 1940, and sanctioned in the Imperial Conferences of July 1 and September 6, 1941.

The night before the Pearl Harbor raid, a staff officer of the Eighth Squadron, Commander Fujita Kikuichi, wrote in his diary, "We have endured British and American tyranny under the fetters of the Washington treaty and for twenty years have sharpened our swords to fight against heavy odds." On December 8, upon hearing about the success of the Pearl Harbor attack, Admiral Suetsugu said, "Ever since the 10:6 ratio was imposed by the Washington treaty, we have endured unspeakable naval drills for twenty years. . . . We may say that these efforts and the resentment accumulated until today have exploded to produce this success." Suetsugu's first thoughts were of Katō Kanji.[97] It is significant that these men went all the way back to the Washington Naval Conference to identify the underlying cause of the war with the United States.

It is possible to argue that the ghost of Katō Kanji (he died in 1939) hovered over Japanese naval leaders on their course to Pearl Harbor.[98] His legacies included negation of the Washington system, decimation of the naval leadership, supremacy of the Naval General Staff over the Navy Ministry, the idée fixe with a 70 percent ratio and the inevitability of war with the United States, the demise of the Washington-London system of naval limitation, and the reopening of the arms race. All of these had their origins in decisions made under Katō's influence, by men such as Suetsugu, Prince Fushimi, Takahashi, Ōsumi, Nagano, and others. And these decisions were implemented by Katō's disciples, Ishikawa Shingo and his kindred spirits.

I have also written that the ghost of Alfred T. Mahan hung over Japanese leaders.[99] For almost half a century they uncritically held to Mahan's theories as they understood them: preoccupation with the battleship, a decisive fleet encounter and annihilation of the enemy's armada, neglect of convoy escort, and, above all, a fatalistic belief in the coming of a Japanese-American war. Equally disastrous was the Japanese navy's bureaucratic use (or misuse) of Mahan's sea power doctrine for budgetary precedence over the army. By the 1930s the perceived lessons of Mahanian doctrines had hardened into unquestioned dogmas, an article of faith.

---

96. *TSM: Bekkan Shiryōhen*, 565, 571; Gaimushō, *Nihon gaikō nenpyō narabini shuyō bunsho*, 2:573.

97. BBKS, *Hawai sakusen*, 13, 114, 318; Itō Kinjirō, *Ikiteiru kaishō Katō Kanji* [Living Admiral Katō], 222, 261–62.

98. Asada, "Japanese Navy and the United States," 259.

99. Ibid.

Institutional Defects

Although operating in an age of total war, the Japanese navy conceived of the coming conflict in terms of a limited war. Banking heavily on German victory, the navy expected that the collapse of Great Britain (and China) would so cripple America's fighting spirit that it would agree to terminate hostilities on the basis of some compromise settlement rather than continue to pay heavy sacrifices in the South Pacific. Beyond this the navy had no plan for ending the war.[100]

Moreover, its operational plans could hardly be said to constitute a grand strategy. The traditional strategy was based on the premise of a single hypothetical enemy, the United States, and not until June 1941 did the Operations Division draft a plan for simultaneous operations against a coalition of enemies—the United States, Britain, and the Netherlands. Completed in rough form in late August, this plan merely added to the war with the United States operations to seize the "southern resource areas."[101]

The second point to be noted is that there was no master plan for conducting the war, based on an overall and long-range estimate of national resources. Reliable data on the nation's war resources could not be obtained from the Cabinet Planning Board because of bureaucratic rivalry. For example, the army and the navy were so suspicious of each other that they refused to pool information on their respective oil holdings until late October 1941.[102]

Within the Navy Ministry, mobilization and allocation of war matériel was handled by the Naval Ordnance Bureau, but its assessments were sometimes vitiated by pressures, bordering on intimidation, from middle-echelon officers in charge of operations. When Rear Admiral Hoshina Zenshirō stated at a bureau chiefs conference that it was impossible to prepare adequately for war with the United States, Captain Ishikawa, furious that "such an opinion will make war impossible," pressured him into reversing his conclusion. Again, when Hashimoto Shōzō, a chief of the Armaments Section, expressed his fear about the oil shortage, Ishikawa came up with his own optimistic estimate to support his advocacy of war. In October 1941, Kurihara Etsuzō, a chief of the Mobilization Section, expressed his appre-

---

100. *TSM: Bekkan Shiryōhen*, 560–61; Tomioka, *Kaisen to shūsen*, 53–56.

101. BBKS, *Hawai sakusen*, 94, 96; BBKS, *Rengō kantai*, 1:500–508; Tomioka, "Taiheiyō sensō zenshi," 4:2–5, 9–11.

102. Testimony of Obata Tadayoshi, vice president of the Cabinet Planning Board, in Andō, ed., *Shōwa keizaishi e no shōgen*, 2: 121, 287–88; Ōkubo et al., eds., *Kaigunshō shiryō*, 12: 33; Ishikawa, *Shinjuwan made no keii*, 338–41; Hoshina Zenshirō, *Daitōwa sensō hishi* [A Secret History of the Great East Asian War], 21–22.

hension that "from the viewpoint of materials mobilization, a protracted war with the United States is totally impossible." He protested that the hypothetical conclusions of the Cabinet Planning Board were being concocted to make it appear possible to wage war. Captain Tomioka of the Operations Section called Kurihara to task for voicing a "counsel of defeatism" and told him that his duty was to devise ways of fighting with limited resources at hand.[103]

If the Japanese navy's estimates of Japan's national power were faulty, its calculations regarding the United States were even more so. The Naval General Staff tended to vastly underestimate American war potential while overestimating that of Germany. It was not that the navy lacked adequate information. The reports of the naval attaché in Washington (after October 1940 Captain Yokoyama Ichirō) were of high caliber. Until the virtual breakdown of the Japanese-American negotiations in mid-October 1941, he maintained close contact with Rear Admiral Richmond Kelly Turner, the U.S. director of war plans, with whom he had been on friendly terms ever since Turner's visit to Japan in 1939. In March 1941 Yokoyama had a "violent argument" about American national strength with Yamaguchi Bunshirō, the chief of the Fifth (America) Section of the Intelligence Division, who was visiting Washington. Shocked to learn about the warlike stance of the Naval General Staff, Yokoyama urged caution, calling his attention to the formidable industrial power of the United States.[104]

The Operations Division tended to slight attaché reports, for it maintained independent sources of information including reports from its scouting force, intercepted messages of foreign navies and chancelleries, and contacts with the army. The Intelligence Division did not enjoy anything like the privileged position of the U.S. Office of Naval Intelligence. Its members derided themselves, calling their office "the dumping ground for third-rate officers." The division was headed by Nomura Naokuni (1936–1938), Abe Katsuo (1938–1939), and Oka Takazumi (1939–1940), all of whom were pro-German. And their successor, Maeda Minoru (1940–1942) was a follower of Katō Kanji and a self-styled "leading war advocate."

Perhaps middle-echelon strategists were misled by their overconfident assumption that the Japanese navy was well informed about its traditional hypothetical enemy. The leading war advocate, Captain Ishikawa, boasted, on the basis of his intensive study at the Naval Staff College, that he was

103. Naval Ordnance Bureau's memorandum to the chief of the Naval General Staff, October 31, 1941, BBK; JMJ interview records.
104. Yokoyama, *Umi e kaeru: Kaigun shōshō Yokoyama Ichirō kaikoroku* [Returning to the Sea: Memoirs of Rear Admiral Yokoyama Ichirō], 114–20; JMJ interview records.

better versed in the history of American Far Eastern policy "than any specialist in the Foreign Ministry." In 1936 he had visited the United States on the last leg of a fact-finding tour of Southeast Asia (where he became alarmed at the "encirclement" led by the United States) and Europe (where he busied himself gathering data on Germany's rising strength). How much he learned during his stay in the United States may be gathered from his own nonchalant statement: "I passed through America in a relaxed tourist mood, because the Japanese navy was constantly in possession of detailed information about that country."[105] As Admiral Inoue later observed, the truth of the matter was that middle-echelon officers "neglected to inform themselves adequately about the United States."

Army-navy rivalry was an important bureaucratic factor in Japan's drift toward war. The navy's middle echelons urged speedy completion of war preparations regardless of the outcome of the Nomura-Hull negotiations in Washington and demanded "war determination." The more cautious leaders of the Navy Ministry tried to draw a line between "war preparations" and "war determination." The navy could proceed with "preparations" without having to make any real "determination" for war, expecting that preparations (fleet mobilization and its concentration of ships and aircraft in bases) could be cancelled should a diplomatic settlement be reached. For the army, however, "preparations" and "determination" were synonyms, since "preparations" involved the large-scale mobilization of manpower and its deployment toward the south—a process which, once set in motion, could not easily be cancelled. This basic organizational difference lay at the heart of the interservice bickering that accompanied the formulation and discussion of national policy.[106]

Indeed, until November 1941 the navy's advocacy of "preparations without determination" seemed to army staff officers a "political trick" to procure war matériel at the army's expense. A disgusted army staff officer scrawled the following entries in the Confidential War Journal: "If the navy is advocating war with the United States in order to increase its armaments, is not the navy a traitor to the country?" (February 17); "The navy is as unprincipled as a woman!" (February 23); "The navy's whole attitude and preparations to date have been directed toward the single aim of expanding itself" (October 16); and "Is the navy a warrior and samurai? At this critical moment that will decide the nation's fate, the navy is begging for

105. Ishikawa, *Shinjuwan made no keii*, 114–29.
106. Sawamoto, "Sawamoto nikki," 471; Hoshina, *Daitōwa sensō hishi*, 28, 46; Toyoda, *Saigo no teikoku kaigun*, 57; Naval Ordnance Bureau to chief of the Naval General Staff, October 31, 1941, BBK; JMJ interview records.

matériel like a panhandler. Is it not the navy's usual trick to get matériel without determining to go to war?" (November 1).[107]

It was not just middle-echelon officers who were preoccupied with scrambling for budget appropriations and matériel. Even a senior officer like Admiral Inoue, whose sound judgment on many matters we have noted throughout, was not above the bureaucratic game. He wrote, "The army is like a mad man, almost pillaging domestic resources. . . . As far as matériel is concerned, a state of anarchy prevails."[108]

Of course, army-navy differences also existed in the U.S. Navy, but nowhere did interservice conflict reach such intensity as in Japan. Hara Shirō, a former officer of the Army General Staff, has cited four reasons for this:

(1) The geopolitical situation of Japan as a maritime as well as continental power;
(2) The idea of parity between the army and the navy;
(3) Inability of the emperor under the Meiji Constitution to directly intervene and dissolve army-navy differences;
(4) Existence of an organ for intra-government "coordination"—the Liaison Conference—which on the contrary exacerbated interservice differences.[109]

The fundamental difficulty, as Inoue stated, was that "the army's armament against the Soviet Union was incompatible with the navy's armament against Britain and America."[110] Tragically, the navy lacked strong leaders who were able to transcend sectional and bureaucratic differences and declare, as Katō Tomosaburō did at the Washington Naval Conference, that "national defense is not a monopoly of the military."

The Army General Staff's denunciation of the navy's "irresponsibility" was also inspired by its own bureaucratic concerns, but it contained a grain of truth. The navy's all-too-frequent invocation of such slogans as "War with America" and "Our Enemy the U.S." to fortify claims to appropriations had so vulgarized these terms that many of its officers—especially in the middle and lower echelons—had grown insensitive to their grave import.[111]

107. Daihon'ei, Sensō Shidōhan, *Kimutsu sensō nisshi,* 1:75, 77, 86, 121, 147, 163, 179; BBKS, *Daihon'ei rikugunbu,* 2:409–21.
108. Inoue Kankō Kai, *Inoue Shigeyoshi,* 310–11.
109. Hara Shirō, *Senryaku naki kaisen: Kyū Daihon'ei Rikugunbu ichi bakuryō no kaisō* [Starting a War without Grand Strategy: A Memoir of a Staff Officer of the Army Section, Imperial Headquarters], 64, 66.
110. Inoue Kankō Kai, *Inoue Shigeyoshi,* 310–11.
111. Takagi, *Yamamoto Isoroku to Yonai Mitsumasa,* 247.

A former officer put in a nutshell the central dilemma that naval leaders faced: "Although the navy demands priority to complete its armaments against the United States in order to prepare for the worst, it does not desire to go to war with that country. But it cannot say it is absolutely opposed to war either, for others will retort that in that event armaments against the United States are not necessary."[112]

Such an ambivalent policy became bankrupt as soon as it confronted a real crisis. Middle- and lower-echelon officers, trained to fight America as "*the* enemy," had become obsessed with the idea of war. In the end, concern for the "morale of our fleet" became a matter of overriding importance that immobilized Navy Minister Oikawa and overcame his inner reservations about the Tripartite Pact and, finally, his opposition to war.

Failure of Leadership

Shimada said after the war, "If Hori Teikichi had been navy minister, the outcome would have been quite different." Obviously, he meant that if Hori had been at the helm of the navy, perhaps the war could have been averted. But Hori, a disciple of Katō Tomosaburō, had been retired by the Ōsumi purge. Aside from the Yonai-Yamamoto-Inoue triumvirate that had successfully blocked the Tripartite Pact, there were few leaders who could effectively control unruly subordinates. After the war, Sawamoto, who had served as navy vice minister from 1941 to 1944, reflectively wrote,

(1) What prevailed was a competition of mediocrities; there was no leader of outstanding ability. Pressures from subordinates was the order of the day. Younger officers would not respect their seniors and this made the matter even more difficult.
(2) Everybody wanted to evade responsibility and no one had the grit to sacrifice himself to do his duty.
(3) The atmosphere was such that it put a premium on parochial and selfish concerns for either the army or the navy; considerations of the nation and the world were secondary.[113]

Admiral Inoue was even more outspoken in his attack on senior naval leaders:

112. Taped interview with Miyo Kazunari, BBK.
113. Cited in Yoshida Toshio, *Kaigun sanbō* [Naval staff officers], 312–13.

As subordinates in the Navy Ministry and the Naval General Staff began preparations and mobilization, they were governed by the idea of inevitable war, whipping up a belligerent spirit in their speeches and actions. Senior leaders of the Navy Ministry and the Naval General Staff did not have the courage and resources to control their subordinates, thus moving step by step toward the crisis.[114]

Generally, in a crisis situation the decision-making process is limited to only a few top leaders. The participation of subordinates—with attendant preoccupation with bureaucratic politics—is kept to the minimum. National interest and security become the overriding concern of the central policy makers.[115] But Japan's decision to go to war with the United States constitutes a conspicuous exception to this generalization. Naval leaders failed in "crisis management." Externally, they failed to control the crisis with the United States; on the contrary, their actions tended to magnify it. Internally, they failed to contain rivalry with the army as well as to control their own subordinates. In the navy of 1941, central decision makers hardly existed. Chief of the Naval General Staff Nagano even acted as the mouthpiece of belligerent middle-echelon officers. Pleas for rationality and stronger leadership in Tokyo did come from men such as Yamamoto and Inoue, but they were not in central decision-making positions. Viewed from the standpoint of the decision-making process, therefore, the Japanese navy's road to Pearl Harbor can best be studied in terms of the failure of leadership.

114. *TSM*, 7:494 (new edition).
115. See, for example, Ole R. Holsti, "Theories of Crisis Decision Making," 101–2.

The Shock of the Atomic Bomb and Japan's Decision to Surrender—A Reconsideration

On the morning of August 6, 1945, the B-29 Superfortress *Enola Gay* released a single bomb that substantially destroyed the city of Hiroshima. Its power was vividly, though inaccurately, described in the flash report transmitted from the nearby Kure Naval Station to the navy minister:

> (1) Today 3 B-29s flew over Hiroshima at a high altitude at about 08:25 and dropped several bombs. . . . A terrific explosion accompanied by flame and smoke occurred at an altitude of 500 to 600 meters. The concussion was beyond imagination and demolished practically every house in the city. (2) Present estimate of damage. About 80 percent of the city was wiped out, destroyed, or burned. . . . Casualties have been estimated at 100,000 persons.[1]

Later on the same day Lieutenant General Miyazaki Shūichi, the head of the Operations Division of the Army General Staff, wrote in his diary that "it may be the so-called atomic bomb."[2] His conjecture was confirmed shortly after 1:00 a.m. on August 7 when the Domei News Agency received President Truman's statement by shortwave broadcast. In it the president announced that the atomic bomb dropped on Hiroshima was more powerful than twenty thousand tons of TNT, and he warned that if Japan failed to immediately

This essay first appeared in *Pacific Historical Review* 67, no. 4 (November 1998). It was reprinted in Ellis Krauss and Benjamin Nyblade, eds. *Japan and North America*, Vol. 1: *First Contacts to the Pacific War* (London: RoutledgeCurzon, 2004). It is reproduced here with minor changes. I am grateful to the following friends for their valuable suggestions: Barton J. Bernstein, Robert Butow, Roger Dingman, Robert H. Ferrell, Richard B. Frank, Hata Ikuhiko, Hatano Sumio, Hosoya Chihiro, Osamu Ishii, D. C. Watt, and Russell Weigley.
1. Edward J. Drea, "Previews of Hell: The End of the War with Japan," 79.
2. Diary of Lieutenant General Miyazaki Shūichi (hereafter cited as Miyazaki Diary), August 6, 1945, BBK.

accept the terms of the Potsdam Declaration of July 26, 1945, it "may expect a rain of ruin from the air, the like of which has never been seen on this earth."[3]

This essay reexamines how the shock of the atomic bombing galvanized the "peace party"—Emperor Hirohito himself, Lord Keeper of the Privy Seal Kido Kōichi, Foreign Minister Tōgō Shigenori, Navy Minister Yonai Mitsumasa, and—with some reservations—Prime Minister Suzuki Kantarō—to take actions that led to the termination of the Pacific War. Their efforts met implacable opposition from the military chiefs—Army Minister Anami Korechika, Chief of the Army General Staff Umezu Yoshijirō, and Chief of the Naval General Staff Toyoda Soemu—who refused to admit defeat and clamored for a decisive homeland battle against invading American forces. It was these military chiefs, especially Anami, who constituted the most volatile forces arrayed against Japan's surrender.

In both the United States and Japan, it is often argued that Japan was virtually a defeated nation in August 1945 and thus the atomic bombings were not necessary. This argument confuses "defeat" with "surrender": Defeat is a military fait accompli, whereas surrender is the formal acceptance of defeat by the nation's leaders—an act of decision making. After the loss of Saipan in early July 1944 brought Japan within range of B-29 bombers, its defeat had become certain, and Japan's leaders knew this. But because its governmental machinery was, to a large extent, controlled by the military and hampered by a cumbersome system that required unanimity of views for any decision, Japanese leaders had failed to translate defeat into surrender.[4] In the end it was the atomic bomb, closely followed by the Soviet Union's entry into the war, that compelled Japan to surrender. This essay, focusing microscopically on August 6 through 14, 1945, reconstructs the Japanese decision-making process in the aftermath of Hiroshima.

Historians and the Sources

There is an enormous literature on the A-bomb decision, yet relatively little has been written about the impact of the bomb on Japan's leaders.[5] Robert J. C. Butow's classic monograph, *Japan's Decision to Surrender* (1954), has

---

3. *FRUS, 1945 (Potsdam)*, 2:376–77.

4. The cabinet system, as inaugurated in 1889, in practice required a unanimity of views among its members for any decision making. The army and navy ministers were privileged members and, by resigning and refusing to name their successors, they could overthrow the government.

5. A recent historiographical essay is J. Samuel Walker, "The Decision to Use the Bomb: A Historiographical Update," 11–37

largely stood the test of time.[6] In fact, his work seemed so definitive that few historians have attempted to go over the same ground.[7] To my knowledge, there are only two recent studies that focus on the decision to surrender utilizing Japanese sources. Herbert P. Bix's 1995 article, "Japan's Delayed Surrender," focuses on Emperor Hirohito's responsibility for *delaying* Japan's surrender primarily during the months before Hiroshima, in contrast to this essay's argument that the emperor's "sacred decision" in the aftermath of the bombs made it finally possible for a divided government to surrender. Lawrence Freedman and Saki Dockrill, in "Hiroshima: A Strategy of Shock" (1994), argue that the United States pursued "a clear and coherent strategy of 'shock,'" which was successful.[8] The present essay attempts to provide a much more detailed and comprehensive analysis of the decision-making process in Japan leading to its surrender.

Other broader works that are germane to this essay include Barton J. Bernstein's three reflective essays that appeared on the fiftieth anniversary of Hiroshima and Nagasaki.[9] "The Atomic Bombs Reconsidered," in particular, attracted considerable attention in Japan when its translation appeared in the respected monthly journal *Chūō Kōron* in February 1995. Leon V. Sigal, in *Fighting to a Finish* (1988), presents a good analysis of bureaucratic politics but minimizes the "psychological impact of the atomic bomb."[10]

The review above shows that there are few recent American historians who deal with the impact of the bomb on the Japanese government. Instead they have been preoccupied with the historiographical controversy between "orthodox historians," typified by Herbert Feis[11] (1961), and "revisionists,"

6. Butow's *Japan's Decision to Surrender* was translated into Japanese and was well received.

7. Since this article was published two monographs have appeared: Richard B. Frank, *Downfall: The End of the Imperial Japanese Empire,* and Tsuyoshi Hasegawa, *Racing the Enemy: Stalin, Truman, and the Surrender of Japan.* For the latter, see the addendum. See also my critical review of Hasegawa in *Journal of Strategic Studies,* 29 (February 2006): 169–71 (my exchange with Hasegawa is in the June 2006 issue of this journal [565–69]). Frank's work makes effective use of Japanese sources through an able translator, providing a balanced narrative on the termination of the Pacific War.

8. In Saki Dockrill, ed., *From Pearl Harbor to Hiroshima: The Second World War in Asia and the Pacific.*

9. Barton J. Bernstein, "The Atomic Bombings Reconsidered"; "Understanding the Atomic Bomb and the Japanese Surrender: Missed Opportunities, Little Known Near Disasters, and Modern Memory"; "The Struggle over History: Defining the Hiroshima Narrative"; "The Perils and Politics of Surrender: Ending the War with Japan and Avoiding the Third Atomic Bomb."

10. Sigal, *Fighting to a Finish: The Politics of War Termination in the United States and Japan, 1945,* 225.

11. Herbert Feis, *Japan Subdued: The Atomic Bomb and the End of the War in the Pacific.* In his revised version, *The Atomic Bomb and the End of World War II,* Feis tentatively and partially incorporates some thoughts on anti-Soviet motives of the bombing.

led by Gar Alperovitz and more recently Martin Sherwin.[12] The former contends that the bomb was necessary as a military means to hasten the end
of the war with Japan, while scholars of the latter—the "atomic diplomacy"
school—claim the bomb was meant as a political-diplomatic threat aimed
against the Soviet Union in the emerging Cold War. Bernstein advances a
third interpretation, arguing that the bomb, although primarily aimed at
the speedy surrender of Japan, had the "bonus" effect of intimidating the
Soviet Union. In the heat generated by this debate, American historians have
neglected the Japanese side of the picture. Concentrating on the *motives*
behind the use of the bombs, they have slighted the *effects* of the bomb.

Strange as it may seem, Japanese historians have written little on this subject. Because of a strong sense of nuclear victimization, it has been difficult
until recently for Japanese scholars to discuss the atomic bombing in the
context of ending the Pacific War. The "orthodox" interpretation in Japan
is close to the American "revisionist" view. Long before Alperovitz's *Atomic
Diplomacy* appeared in 1965, Japanese historians had come under the influence of British Nobel laureate physicist P. M. S. Blackett, whose *Fear, War,
and the Bomb* (1949) anticipated the main thrust of Alperovitz's arguments.
Blackett contends that "the dropping of the atomic bombs was not so much
the last military act of the Second World War, as the first major operation
of the Cold War with Russia now in progress." *Fear, War, and the Bomb* was
translated into Japanese in 1951 and has often been cited.[13] Finally, on
August 6, 1995, a Japanese translation of Alperovitz's *The Decision to Use the
Atomic Bomb and the Architecture of an American Myth*[14] appeared, but the
Japanese reading public paid more attention to the translation of Robert Jay
Lifton and Greg Mitchell's *Hiroshima in America: Fifty Years of Denial* (1995),
which appealed to the emotionally charged atmosphere of the fiftieth
anniversary of Hiroshima and Nagasaki.

Let us sample what Japanese historians have written. A widely read survey by Tōyama Shigeki, Imai Seiichi, and Fujiwara Akira, *Shōwashi* [History
of the Showa Period] (1959), quotes Blackett approvingly: "The dropping
of the atomic bombs was not so much the last military act of the Second
World War as the first major operation of the Cold War with Russia."[15] The
"atomic diplomacy" thesis has filtered down even to junior high school history textbooks. A typical sample reads, "As the Soviet Union's entry into

---

12. Alperovitz, *Atomic Diplomacy*. Martin Sherwin's most recent position is stated in
"Hiroshima at Fifty: The Politics of History and Memory."
13. Blackett, *Fear, War, and the Bomb: Military and Political Consequences of Atomic Energy*.
14. Alperovitz's use of Japanese sources via a translator is inadequate to say the least.
15. Tōyama, Imai, Fujiwara, *Shōwashi*, 238.

the war became imminent, the United States dropped the atomic bombs to gain supremacy over the Soviet Union after the war."[16]

Among monographs, perhaps the most quoted book is Nishijima Ariatsu's *Gembaku wa naze tōka saretaka? Nihon kōfuku o meguru senryaku to gaikō* [Why Were the Atomic Bombs Dropped? The Strategy and Diplomacy of Japanese Surrender], originally published in 1968 and reissued in 1985. Recapitulating the Blackett thesis, Nishijima argues that "the most important thing" was that Hiroshima-Nagasaki residents were "killed as human guinea pigs for the sake of [America's] anti-Communist, hegemonic policy."[17] Similarly, *Taiheiyō sensōshi* [A History of the Pacific War] (1973), compiled by a group of left-wing historians, states that "500,000 citizens [of Hiroshima and Nagasaki] were utterly meaninglessly sacrificed for America's cruel political purposes."[18]

This is not to say that more objective scholarship has been absent.[19] In an early collaborative work edited by Hayashi Shigeru, *Nihon shūsenshi* [History of Japan's Surrender] (1962), the authors reveal an interesting ambivalence. They quote extensively from Herbert Feis (1961) for their narratives of the Manhattan Project and the decision to use the bomb, but, when it comes to assessing the significance of the bomb, they base their interpretation on Blackett.[20] Arai Shin'ichi has drawn on American works and the unpublished Stimson diaries for *Gembaku tōka e no michi* [The Road to the Use of the Atomic Bomb] (1985), which leans toward the "atomic diplomacy" thesis and is the only scholarly monograph written by a Japanese historian.

One thing is clear: Like their American colleagues, Japanese historians have not studied sufficiently the crucial period from Hiroshima to the surrender.[21] It may well be that while the "atomic diplomacy" thesis heightens the Japanese sense of victimization, it also accords with their general unwillingness to come to grips with their responsibility for the Pacific War and its consequences. Consciously or unconsciously, historians have been

16. Kodama Kōta et al., *Chūgaku shakai: Rekishiteki bun'ya* [Junior High School/Social Studies-History], 197; Kawata Tadashi et al., *Atarashii shakai: Rekishi* [New Society: History], 24.

17. Nishijima, *Gembaku wa naze tōka saretaka*, 146–48. The author does not seem to have used English-language sources.

18. Rekishigaku Kenkyūkai, comp., *Taiheiyō sensōshi*, 5:363–66.

19. A massive collection of American archival materials is Yamagiwa Akira and Tachibana Seiitsu, eds., *Shiryō Manhattan keikaku* [Documents on the Manhattan Project].

20. Hayashi Shigeru, ed., *Nihon shūsenshi*, 2:84–93, 94–95.

21. For further discussion on the subject, see Hatano Sumio's thoughtful historiographical essay and his exhaustive bibliography, both contained in volume 6 of Gaimushō, *Shūsen shiroku* [Historical Record Relating to the Termination of the War], 6:230–53, 259–93.

affected by this climate of opinion—until recently. On August 6, 1995, on the fiftieth anniversary of Hiroshima, the *New York Times* quoted from the embryonic version of this essay, calling me, in an ironic twist of logic, a "Japanese revisionist." It observed that such "revisionists" are still "a tiny minority" but "the taboos are breaking down in Japan."[22] The disappearance of the "taboos" coincided, domestically, with Emperor Hirohito's death in 1989 and, externally, with the end of the Cold War.

Because of the nature of Japanese documentary source materials concerning the decision to surrender, historians face enormous handicaps and frustrations. In the weeks before General Douglas MacArthur's arrival, the Japanese government destroyed most of its diplomatic and military archives for fear that the materials might be used in the trials of war criminals. In addition to few surviving official records, historians are forced to utilize such materials as postsurrender memoirs, testaments, and postwar "interrogations" of Japanese officials. Problematic manuscript sources include "Interrogations" and "Statements" (interviews) of Japanese military and civilian officials conducted from 1948 to 1950 by the Military History Section of G-2 of General MacArthur's General Headquarters (the United States Army, Far East Command).[23] In these "statements," Japanese officials often contradicted themselves and were eager to defend the emperor.

Among published sources, Kido Kōichi's diaries, meticulously edited by a group of scholars at the University of Tokyo, are the most reliable. Kido, as Lord Keeper of the Privy Seal, had special access to the emperor. He was a realist par excellence; some would call him an opportunist. In this essay he figures as the foremost "peacemonger," in Kase Toshikazu's words.[24] A wealth of various printed materials—contemporaneous government documents, diaries, memoranda, and excerpts from memoirs—are conveniently collected in Gaimushō [Japanese Ministry of Foreign Affairs], ed., *Shūsen shiroku* [Historical Record of the End of the War], published in 1952 and republished with additions and new annotations in six volumes in 1977–1978.[25] A more critical collection of documents is Kurihara Ken and Hatano Sumio, eds., *Shūsen kōsaku no kiroku* [Record of the Efforts to End the War]. A useful work

22. Nicholas D. Kristof, "The Bomb: An Act That Haunts Japan and America," *New York Times*, August 6, 1995.

23. The Japanese version, edited by Satō Motoei and Kurosawa Fumitaka, is *GHQ Rekishika jutsuroku* [Statements to History Section, General Headquarters: Materials on the Termination of the War].

24. Kido, ed., *Kido nikki; Kido Kōichi nikki: Tokyo saibanki* [Diaries of Kido Kōichi during the Period of the Tokyo Trials]; and *Kido Kōichi kankei bunsho* [Papers Relating to Kido Kōichi]; Kase Toshikazu, *Journey to the Missouri*, 55.

25. Gaimushō, *Shūsen shiroku* (new edition), especially vols. 3–5, which are carefully edited by Kurihara Ken, an archivist par excellence of the Foreign Ministry.

based on oral history is volume 4 of Yomiuri Shimbunsha, ed., *Shōwashi no tennō* [The Emperor in the History of the Showa Period].

The Japanese army's mentality is revealed in the Sanbō Honbu [Army General Staff], comp., *Haisen no kiroku* [A Record of the Defeat] (1979). Finally, the most important memoir is one by Foreign Minister Tōgō Shigenori, which has been translated into English.[26] These and other materials enable the historian to reinterpret the shock of the bomb and Japan's decision to surrender.

The Atomic Bomb as an "External Pressure"

On August 7, one day after Hiroshima, a San Francisco broadcast carried the announcement by President Truman that the United States had dropped an atomic bomb on Japan. As soon as Foreign Minister Tōgō learned of this through the Foreign Ministry's shortwave receiver, he tried to get the facts from the Army Ministry. (Aerial bombings were a purely military matter, and the heads of the armed services exercised sole jurisdiction over reports of air-raid damages.) The army denied that there was any atomic bombing, maintaining that "although the United States claims it to be an atomic bomb, it actually appears to be a conventional bomb with extraordinary destructive power."[27] While Tōgō recognized the possibility that the United States had exaggerated the bomb for propaganda purposes, he was nonetheless impressed that American radio broadcasting was "rampant" and "massive." He probably recalled that the Potsdam Declaration of July 26, 1945, had threatened Japan with "prompt and utter destruction." Galvanized by a sense of urgency, he took the initiative in convening an emergency meeting of key cabinet ministers on the afternoon of August 7.[28]

Deliberations at this cabinet meeting can be reconstructed from Tōgō's memoirs and volume 4 of *Shūsen shiroku*. The bombing of Hiroshima was the subject of discussion. Tōgō tried to find a breakthrough to surrender by

26. Tōgō, *Jidai no ichimen*. Simon and Schuster released an English translation of Tōgō's work in 1956 entitled *The Cause of Japan*.

27. Gaimushō, *Shūsen shiroku*, 4:57; Tōgō, *Jidai no ichimen*, 341–42; Tōgō, *The Cause of Japan*, 314–15; Kurihara and Hatano, eds., *Shūsen kōsaku*, 2:354–55.

28. Tōgō, *Jidai no ichimen*, 342; Tōgō, *The Cause of Japan*, 315; Tōgō Shigenori, May 18, 1949, in U.S. Army, Far Eastern Command, "Statements of Japanese Officials on World War II" (hereafter cited as "Statements"), U.S. Army Center of Military History, Washington, D.C.; Gaimushō, *Shūsen shiroku*, 4:58; Sakomizu Hisatsune, April 21, 1949, in U.S. Army, Far Eastern Command, "Interrogations of Japanese Officials on World War II" (hereafter cited as "Interrogations"), U.S. Army Center of Military History, Washington, D.C.

quoting at great length American radio reports about the bomb. The U.S. government claimed that it had now "added a new and revolutionary increase in destruction," and that, unless Japan surrendered, the United States would keep dropping atomic bombs until Japan was extinct. Tōgō was resorting to the time-honored device of making the most of "external pressure"—the atomic bomb—to counter the army, which was adamant for a "decisive battle on the homeland" against an American invasion. In a line of argument that was to be repeated by the peace party, Tōgō reasoned that "the introduction of a new weapon, which had drastically altered the whole military situation, offered the military ample grounds for ending the war." According to Kurihara Ken, the Foreign Ministry archivist par excellence who compiled *Shūsen shiroku*, Tōgō at this cabinet meeting proposed that surrender be considered at once on the basis of the terms of the Potsdam Declaration. (When the peace party talked about "accepting the Potsdam terms," they always and firmly meant acceptance with one crucial condition: retention of the emperor system.) However, the military authorities refused to concede that the United States had used an atomic weapon. Given the army's intransigence, it was impossible for the cabinet to take up Tōgō's proposal.[29]

About noon on August 7, Kido Kōichi, the emperor's most important adviser ("the eyes and ears of the Throne"),[30] received a report that "the United States had used an atomic bomb against Hiroshima, causing extremely serious damage and 130,000 casualties." In an audience with Hirohito at 1:30, Kido noted how worried the emperor was. Hirohito, a scientist specializing in marine biology, was quick to grasp the destructive power of the atomic bomb, and he peppered Kido with questions about it.[31] He had been apprised by court attendants of the Hiroshima bomb on the afternoon of August 6 and was informed the following morning that it was an atomic bomb. He demanded more details from the government and the army about the devastation of Hiroshima and was strongly displeased that he was not getting enough information.[32]

According to Kido's postwar recollections, Hirohito told him, "Now that things have come to this impasse, we must bow to the inevitable. No matter what happens to my safety, we should lose no time in ending the war so as not to have another tragedy like this."[33] After Kido departed, Hirohito

29. Tōgō, *Jidai no ichimen*, 342; Gaimushō, *Shūsen shiroku*, 4:57–58, 60; Kurihara and Hatano, eds., *Shūsen kōsaku*, 2:355–56.

30. Butow, *Japan's Decision to Surrender*, 12.

31. Kido, ed., *Kido nikki*, 2:1222; *Kido nikki: Tokyo saibanki*, 421; *Kido kankei bunsho*, 84.

32. Fujita Hisanori, *Jijuchō no kaisō* [Memoirs of a Grand Chamberlain], 126.

33. Kido, ed., *Kido nikki: Tokyo saibanki*, 421.

asked his military aide-de-camp almost every hour about the extent of the damage in Hiroshima.[34] The emperor, who had already concluded in June 1945 that the war must end soon, was from this time forward Japan's foremost peace advocate, increasingly articulate and urgent in expressing his wish for peace.

The first to take concrete action to terminate the war was Foreign Minister Tōgō, a dour-faced, outspoken, and resolute man. On the morning of August 8, with Prime Minister Suzuki's approval, Tōgo took it upon himself to visit the Imperial Palace and make a direct appeal to the emperor in his underground air-raid shelter. According to his postwar account in September 1945, Tōgō reported in detail that American and British broadcasts were "most enthusiastically" repeating news of the atomic bomb. Characteristically, he invoked the enemy's broadcast to buttress his case for a prompt surrender. "The atomic bomb," Tōgō said, "has not only revolutionized modern warfare but has also brought about a great social upheaval and transformation of the daily lives of ordinary individuals as well." It was apparent that Tōgō felt not only the shock of the bomb's physical devastation but also a profound culture shock as the nuclear age dawned. He urged that the occasion be used as the turning point to bring an end to the war—on condition, of course, that the emperor system be retained. Emphasizing the urgency of the situation, Tōgō said that the United States would continue to drop atomic bombs on Japanese cities, as President Truman had warned, unless Japan surrendered at once. He emphasized that Japan had no choice but to accept the terms stipulated in the Potsdam Declaration. As Tōgō recalled in his memoirs, Hirohito emphatically concurred. "That is just so," he replied, and went on to divulge his own firm determination:

> Now that such a new weapon has appeared, it has become less and less possible to continue the war. We must not miss a chance to terminate the war by bargaining for more favorable conditions now. Besides, however much we consult about [surrender] terms we desire, we shall not be able to come to an agreement. So my wish is to make such arrangements as will end the war as soon as possible.[35]

In these words the emperor expressed his conviction that a speedy surrender was the only feasible way to save Japan. Hirohito urged Tōgō to "do his utmost to bring about a prompt termination of the war" and commanded him to apprise Prime Minister Suzuki of his wish. The emperor had deep

34. Yomiuri, ed., *Shōwashi no tennō*, 4:310–11.
35. Tōgō, *Jidai no ichimen*, 342; Tōgō, *The Cause of Japan*, 315–16; Gaimushō, *Shūshen shiroku*, 4:60; Kurihara and Hatano, eds., *Shūsen kōsaku*, 2: 356; Fujita, *Jijūchō no kaisō*, 126.

trust in Suzuki, a seventy-eight-year-old retired admiral, who had served as his grand chamberlain from 1929 to 1936. In compliance with the imperial wish, Tōgō met Suzuki and proposed that, "given the atomic bombing of Hiroshima, the Supreme War Council be convened with all dispatch." This council was Japan's inner war cabinet, consisting of the "Big Six"—the prime minister, foreign minister, army and navy ministers, and chiefs of the Army and Naval General Staffs. However, there was one full day's delay because some of the military members of the Supreme War Council had prior engagements—a strange excuse when time was so urgent.[36]

On the late night of August 8, Suzuki told Sakomizu Hisatsune, the chief cabinet secretary, "Now that we know it was an atomic bomb that was dropped on Hiroshima, I will give my views on the termination of the war at tomorrow's cabinet meeting." Suzuki asked Sakomizu to prepare for a cabinet meeting and to draft the prime minister's statement for that meeting.[37] After the war Suzuki recalled, "The atomic bomb provided an additional reason for surrender as well as an extremely favorable opportunity to commence peace talks. I believed such an opportunity could not be afforded by B-29 bombings alone."[38] Suzuki, who had been privately confiding his views favoring peace, now made up his mind to take the leadership for peace advocacy. It is important to note that Suzuki did so *before* he was informed of the Soviet entry into the war at dawn the following day.[39] Sakomizu also felt that "the army will admit that now that the atomic bomb has come into existence, it precludes war between a nation that possesses the atomic bomb and one that does not."[40] However, the army was not to be so easily swayed.

Japan's "Longest Day"—and Night

At dawn on August 9, Tokyo intercepted a TASS broadcast that the Soviet Union had declared war on Japan. Within hours the Red Army's mechanized forces bypassed or overwhelmed Japanese units on the Manchurian border and threw the Kwantung Army into confusion. The Japanese government's panic was now complete. Despite Tōgō's advocacy of speedy

36. Kurihara and Hatano, eds., *Shūsen kōsaku,* 2:356; Gaimushō, *Shūsen shiroku,* 4:98.
37. Sakomizu, *Dai Nippon teikoku saigo no yonkagetsu* [The Last Four Months of the Japanese Empire], 185.
38. *GS,* Vol. 39, *Taiheiyō sensō* 5 [The Pacific War], 756.
39. Sakomizu, May 3, 1949, "Interrogations."
40. Sakomizu Hisatsune, "Shūsen no shōsho: Fu shūsen hiwa" [Imperial Rescript on the War's End and the Taped Recording of Sakomizu's Talk].

peace on the basis of the Potsdam terms, until the moment of the Soviet entry, Tokyo had been trying to obtain Soviet mediation for favorable surrender terms from the United States. Now this last hope was dashed. Prime Minister Suzuki's military estimate was that Japan would be able to hold out against the Soviets in Manchuria for at least two months.[41] However, Lieutenant General Ikeda Sumihisa, who had been transferred from vice chief of staff of the Kwantung Army to head the cabinet's Comprehensive Planning Bureau just two weeks earlier, flabbergasted Suzuki by stating that "Chaochou [capital of Manchukuo] will fall into Russian hands in two weeks." Since the latter part of 1944 the Kwantung Army had been reduced to a skeleton after its best troops had been redeployed to the homeland for a decisive battle against invading American troops.[42]

The effects of the "twin shocks"—the atomic bombing and the Soviet Union's declaration of war—were profound. Early that morning, Tōgō visited Suzuki to inform him that the Soviets had entered the war. Suzuki concurred that the government must end the war at once by accepting the Potsdam terms. On his way back to the Foreign Ministry, Tōgō stopped at the Navy Ministry and told Navy Minister Yonai what he had just said to Suzuki.[43]

Hirohito, having been apprised of the Soviet entry by Suzuki, summoned Lord Privy Seal Kido to his underground air-raid shelter at 9:55 a.m. In light of the Soviet entry, Hirohito said, it was all the more urgent to find means to end the war promptly. He commanded Kido to "have a heart-to-heart talk" with Prime Minister Suzuki at once. Coincidentally, Suzuki had just arrived at the palace, so Kido immediately conveyed the imperial wish to him, emphasizing the importance of immediately accepting the Potsdam terms. Suzuki assured Kido of his determination to end the war speedily, and at 10:55 Kido again had an audience with the emperor to assure him that "the prime minister agrees there is no other way."[44]

Meanwhile, the Supreme War Council had convened at 10:30 a.m., August 9, in an atmosphere of "impatience, frenzy, and bewilderment," as recalled by Fujita Hisanori, the grand chamberlain.[45] It was arguably Japan's most fateful day—and night. All the members of the council recognized that

41. Gaimushō, *Shūsen shiroku*, 4:100; Suzuki Hajime, ed., *Suzuki Kantarō jiden* [Autobiography of Suzuki Kantaro], 294–95.

42. Ikeda Sumihisa, *Nihon no magarikado* [Japan at the Crossroads], 208–9; "Statements" (italics mine).

43. Tōgō, *Jidai no ichimen*, 342; Tōgō, *Cause of Japan*, 316.

44. Kido, ed., *Kido kankei bunsho*, 87; *Kido nikki*, 2:1223; Kido Kōichi, May 17, 1949, "Statements."

45. Fujita, *Jijūchō no kaisō*, 129.

it was impossible to continue the war much longer and that the terms of the Potsdam Declaration would have to be accepted in one form or another. But would they be able to come to a consensual decision for surrender? To reach that decision, the government machinery required that the Supreme War Council and the cabinet achieve unanimity of views. If any military member(s) chose to oppose, either no decision would be reached or the Suzuki cabinet would collapse; in either case, a swift surrender would be aborted.

Prime Minister Suzuki opened the meeting by observing, "Just when we were smarting from the extremely great shock of the Hiroshima bomb, the Soviet Union entered the war. Continuation of the war is totally impossible, and whether willing or not we have no choice but to accept the Potsdam terms." Foreign Minister Tōgō, known for his logical mind, forcefully stated that Japan must immediately accept the Potsdam terms with the sole condition being that the Allies "guarantee the emperor's position." He informed the council members of the emperor's conviction that, since the atomic bomb had made its appearance, continuation of the war had become utterly impossible.[46]

What the peace party had been worrying about most was how many more atomic bombs the United States had in readiness. Nonetheless, at the beginning of the Supreme War Council meeting, "a rather bullish atmosphere" prevailed, as Admiral Toyoda Soemu, the chief of the Naval General Staff, recalled in his memoirs. "To be sure, the damage of the atomic bomb is extremely heavy, but it is questionable whether the United States will be able to use more bombs in rapid succession."[47] For one thing, he argued, the United States would have to heed to world public opinion, which would be revolted by such an inhuman weapon.[48] Although the proceedings of the council meeting do not exist, it appears that Army Minister Anami indulged in wishful thinking when he said that the bomb dropped on Hiroshima was the sole atomic bomb the United States possessed.

At precisely this moment, just before 1:00 p.m., news reached the cabinet meeting that a second atomic bomb had been dropped on Nagasaki. The impact of another set of "twin shocks"—Hiroshima and Nagasaki—was devastating. Suzuki now began to fear that "the United States, instead of staging the invasion of Japan, will keep on dropping atomic bombs."[49] Although Japan had measures to cope with the American invasion, nothing could be done about the continuation of atomic bombings.

---

46. Gaimushō, *Shūsen shiroku*, 4:107–12.
47. Toyoda, *Saigo no teikoku kaigun*, 206–7.
48. Ibid., 207; Gaimushō, *Shūsen shiroku*, 4:107.
49. *GS*, Vol. 39, *Taiheiyō sensō* 5, 756.

We must pause here to ask whether the Nagasaki bomb was necessary. The Hiroshima bomb had already jolted Japan's peace party to move toward surrender. The strategic value of a second bomb was minimal. With all land communications severed between Tokyo and Hiroshima, the full extent of the Hiroshima disaster had not yet sunk in among leaders in Tokyo; there had been an interval of only three days between the two bombs. On the other hand, from the standpoint of its shock effect, the political impact of the Nagasaki bomb cannot be entirely denied. Army Minister Anami's wishful thinking was shattered; if two bombs were available, then maybe there were three or even four.[50] In fact, rumor had it that Tokyo would be atomic-bombed on August 12 and that many more cities would be incinerated. The Nagasaki bomb, which instantly killed approximately thirty-five thousand to forty thousand people, was unnecessary to induce Japan to surrender, but it probably had confirmatory and hastening effects.[51]

However, the news of the Nagasaki bombing did not materially affect the heated argument that continued at the Supreme War Council. Tōgō, who strongly urged acceptance of the Potsdam terms, with the one condition regarding the emperor system, was supported by Navy Minister Yonai, a taciturn admiral known for his liberal views and avowed connections with the navy's "peace maneuvers" (behind-the-scenes political activities centering on aged Admiral Okada Keisuke and Rear Admiral Takagi Sōkichi). But Army Minister Anami remained intransigent.

It is difficult to grasp Anami's position. In Bernstein's apt expression, he was "the keystone in the arch of power that could lead to peace or prolonged war." Anami was a straightforward man, a typical samurai warrior and a master at archery and swordsmanship. His loyalty to the emperor was unquestioned; he had served as Hirohito's military aide-de-camp from 1929 through 1933. And he knew the emperor wished the war brought to an end at once. It is on record that he had met Tōgō at the army minister's official residence on the evening of August 7 from 6:30 to 9:00, had had a heart-to-

---

50. Surprisingly, Army Minister Anami seems to have given some credence to the make-believe account that the United States had a stockpile of one hundred atomic bombs and that Tokyo would be the target for the next atomic bombing. The source of this fabrication was a "confession" by a P-51 fighter pilot by the name of Marcus McDila who had been downed and captured on August 8. (The United States, of course, had completed only two bombs at that time.) Gaimusho, *Shūsen shiroku*, 4:119–20; BBK, *Daihon'ei rikugunbu*, 10:418, 437. Ōkura Kimmochi, the president of the Technological Research Mobilization Office, also heard a similar rumor (Naisei Kenkyūkai and Nihon Kindai Shiryō Kenkyūkai, eds., *Ōkura Kimmochi nikki* [Diaries], 4:321).

51. There was no separate decision to use the second bomb; the local commander was ordered to use additional bombs as they became ready.

heart talk with Tōgō, and had conceded that "defeat was a matter of time."[52] However, when he left his office on the morning of August 9 to attend the Supreme War Council meeting, he told Deputy Chief of the Army General Staff Kawabe Torashirō, "Upon my word I assure you it is going to be a hell of a stormy meeting!"[53]

At the Supreme War Council, Anami in his calmer moments seemed almost ready to accept the Potsdam terms "in principle" but with certain conditions. At his more belligerent moments, he cried out for a decisive homeland battle. The fact was that Anami, "the darling of the army," commanded the full confidence of hot-blooded young officers, and he was now under strong pressure from these fire-eating subordinates. Whatever his inner thoughts, Anami insisted not only on the preservation of the imperial institution but also on the "three additional conditions": (1) that there be no military occupation of the homeland by the Allies; (2) that the armed forces be allowed to disarm and demobilize themselves voluntarily; and (3) that war criminals be prosecuted by the Japanese government. These were "absolute" conditions, Anami said, and Chief of the Army General Staff Umezu Yoshijirō and Chief of the Naval General Staff Toyoda supported Anami. These military chiefs contended that retention of the emperor system (Japan's national polity) was inconceivable if Japan's homeland were occupied by foreign troops and the Japanese forces disbanded by the Allied powers.[54] In reality, however, they were trying to save their own skins. Of course, the "three additional conditions" flew in the face of the Potsdam Declaration, and it was apparent that the United States, its resolve bolstered by the atomic bombs and the Soviet entry into the war, would have rejected these additional conditions. Insisting on them would have meant fighting to the last.[55]

Tōgō then spoke up: there was no hope of obtaining the "three additional conditions." Anami fiercely opposed Tōgō and Suzuki. In fact, Anami's utterances became almost irrational. As recalled by those who attended the meeting, Anami proclaimed, "The appearance of the atomic bomb does not spell the end of war. . . . We are confident about a decisive homeland battle against American forces." He did admit that "given the atomic bomb

52. Matsutani Makoto, *Dai Tōa Sensō shūshū no shinsō* [The Truth about Terminating the Greater East Asian War], 172–73; Kurihara and Hatano, eds., *Shūsen kōsaku,* 2: 365.

53. Kurihara and Hatano, eds., *Shūsen kōsaku,* 2:365; Toyoda, *Saigo no teikoku kaigun,* 207–9; Suzuki, ed., *Suzuki jiden,* 295–96.

54. Gaimushō, *Shūsen shiroku,* 4:119–20, 122–23; Toyoda, *Saigo no teikoku kaigun,* 207–9; Shigemitsu, *Shōwa no dōran,* 2:285–86.

55. Gaimushō, *Shūsen shiroku,* 4:118–24; Shimomura Kainan, *Shūsen hishi* [The Secret History of the Termination of the War], 96–103.

and the Soviet entry, there is no chance of winning on the basis of mathe-matical calculation," but he nevertheless declared that "there will be some chance as long as we keep on fighting for the honor of the Yamato race. . . . If we go on like this and surrender, the Yamato race would be as good as dead spiritually." Such was the mentality of the Japanese military. Urged by middle-echelon and young officers who were "half mad," Anami would not retreat from making the last sacrificial homeland battle.[56]

The deadlock remained unbroken at the first cabinet meeting, which was opened at 2:30 p.m. During the second cabinet meeting in the evening of August 9, Navy Minister Yonai bluntly stated that Japan had no chance and urged a rational decision, pointing out that Japan had lost the battles of Saipan, Luzon, Leyte, Iwo Jima, and Okinawa. Anami retorted that, although Japan had lost battles, it had not yet lost the war. Now on the defensive, Anami said that all he could promise was one massive blow against the first wave of invading American forces; what he counted on was that American casualties would be so heavy as to shake American morale and induce a compromise peace. But Anami made no promise about Japan's chance after the initial blow. Again, the three-to-three stalemate totally par-alyzed the government's decision making.[57]

As the last measure, Suzuki—in accordance with a scenario that had been worked out between Kido, former foreign minister Shigemitsu Mamoru, and former prime minister Konoe Fumimaro—requested shortly before midnight that an imperial conference be convened in the underground air-raid shelter of the Imperial Palace.[58] Suzuki and Tōgō, of course, knew where the imperial wish lay. Attending the conference were the members of the Supreme War Council and the president of the Privy Council, Hiranuma Kiichirō, with Suzuki presiding. Dressed in full army uniform and wearing white gloves, the emperor sat in front of a table covered with a gold-colored tablecloth. In his presence, Tōgō and Anami reenacted their confrontation. Hirohito patiently heard out the heated arguments for some two hours. Once again, a deadlock ensued.[59]

Then, in an act unprecedented in modern Japanese history, the prime min-ister stepped up to the emperor's seat, bowed deeply, and submitted the matter for an imperial decision. Hirohito saw that only his direct interven-

56. Sanbō Honbu, comp., *Haisen no kiroku*, 283; Gaimushō, *Shūsen shiroku*, 4:118–19, 121–15; Ikeda, *Nikon no magarikado*, 174; Hattori, *Daitōa sensō zenshi*, 8:102; Ōki Misao, *Ōki nikki: Shūsenjino Teikoku* [Ōki Diaries], 335.
57. Gaimushō, *Shūsen shiroku*, 4:124.
58. Hata Ikuhiko, *Shōwa tennō itsutsu no ketsudan* [The Five Decisions of the Showa Emperor], 71.
59. Gaimushō, *Shūsen shiroku*, 4:122–42, 139, 142.

tion could save the situation. Breaking his customary silence, he made the "sacred decision." Speaking with emotion but in a quiet tone of voice, Hirohito said he agreed with Tōgō, ruling that the Potsdam terms must be accepted. "Especially since the appearance of the atomic bomb," he said, continuation of the war spelled needless suffering for his subjects and Japan's ruin as a nation. He reprimanded the army and pointed out the discrepancy between its promise and performance, referring to the army's failure to complete defense preparations for the Kujūkuri coastal plain, a key point to repel an American invasion of the Kantō (Tokyo) Plain. Thus at 2:30 a.m. on August 10, the "sacred decision" was made to accept the Potsdam terms on one condition: the "prerogative of His Majesty as a Sovereign Ruler."[60] The decision was subsequently ratified by the cabinet. Later the same day, the Foreign Ministry relayed the message of conditional surrender to the American government through the Swiss and Swedish governments.

As is well known, however, a second intervention by the emperor became necessary on August 14 to resolve the deadlock over the American government's intentionally ambiguous reply, stating that the "authority" of the emperor "shall be subject to" the supreme commander of the Allied powers.[61] Tōgō insisted on acceptance of the American condition, which he said protected the imperial institution, but Anami opposed it most strenuously and demanded a last-ditch homeland battle rather than accepting the American reply. To break the impasse, Hirohito intervened once again, concurring with Tōgō's view.[62] Finally, at noon on August 15, the emperor broadcast to the nation and to the world at large the rescript of surrender. This rescript stated in part that the surrender was forced by a "new and most cruel bomb, the power of which to do damages is indeed incalculable, taking the toll of many innocent lives." The war was finally over.[63]

The Atomic Bomb as a "Gift from Heaven"

In a postwar interview in November 1945, Kido explained the decision to surrender in the following words:

---

60. Ibid., 139, 142; Sanbō Honbu, comp., *Haisen no kiroku*, 362.

61. On the Japanese reaction, see Hatano, "'Kokutai goji' to Potsudamu sengen" [The "National Polity" and the Potsdam Declaration], 28–35. For the American side, see Bernstein, "Perils and Politics of Surrender," 7, 26.

62. Gaimushō, *Shūsen shiroku*, 5:17–56; Kido, ed., *Kido nikki: Tokyo saibanki*, 443; Tōgō, *Jidai no ichimen*, 350–58; Toyoda, *Saigo no teikoku kaigun*, 218–22; Sakomizu, *Dai Nippon teikoku saigo no yonkagetsu*, 233–42.

63. Butow, *Japan's Decision to Surrender*, 248.

The feeling that the emperor and I had about the atomic bombing was that the psychological moment we had long waited for had finally arrived to resolutely carry out the termination of the war. . . . We felt that if we took the occasion and utilized the *psychological shock* of the bomb to follow through, we might perhaps succeed in ending the war.[64]

In the same interview Kido went so far as to say that the U.S. government, by using the atomic bomb, actually intended to "assist" Japan's peace party:

I surmise that the atomic bomb was dropped with the intention of posing a grave threat to Japanese leaders and the people at large, forcefully compelling them to end the war. And certainly the bomb had that effect. However, we of the peace party had already been scheming for a termination of the war, and it is not correct to say that we were driven by the atomic bomb to end the war. Rather, *it might be said that we of the peace party were assisted by the atomic bomb in our endeavor to end the war.*[65]

Unknowingly, Kido proved correct about the intentions of Secretary of War Henry L. Stimson, who considered the bomb a "profound psychological shock." In his memoirs, Stimson wrote that the American leaders had expected the bomb to "produce exactly the kind of shock on the Japanese ruling oligarchy, strengthening the position of those who wished peace, and weakening that of the military party."[66] This "strategy of shock" worked, for it encouraged the peace party to redouble its efforts to bring about the decision for surrender. That Stimson held a high view of Japanese "liberals"—a word that he used interchangeably with the "peace party" and "moderates"—is clear from an important memorandum he submitted to President Truman on July 2, 1945. In it he wrote that Japanese "liberals [had] yielded [to the militarists] only at the point of the pistol" and that after the war they could be "depended upon for [Japan's] reconstruction as a responsible member of the family of nations."[67]

Aside from its terrible destructive power at ground zero, then, the bomb was effective in the hands of Japan's peace party as a political expedient. Prime Minister Suzuki called it "a most convenient pretext" for ending the war immediately. In that the peace party needed and obtained America's

64. Kido, ed., *Kido nikki: Tokyo saibanki,* 444 (italics added).

65. Ibid. (italics added).

66. Stimson and Bundy, *On Active Service in Peace and War,* 626. Stimson and his colleagues had been following the power struggle within the Japanese government through intercepted Japanese cable messages, "Magic."

67. Ibid., 620–24, 630–32; Diary of Henry L. Stimson, entries of June 18 and July 2, 1945, on microfilm, original in Yale University Library; *FRUS, 1945 (Potsdam),* 1:888–92.

"assistance" in its struggle against the military to end the war, it may perhaps be said that there was a tacit political "linkage" and understanding
between conservative American statesmen such as Stimson and Japan's
"peace party," which, in Stimson's mind, broadly included such leaders as
Tōgō, Kido, Yonai, and Konoe. What both groups had in common was the
unquestioning acceptance of the atomic bomb as an instrument for terminating the war, and this linkage rested on the atomic devastation of Hiroshima and Nagasaki. Thus viewed, it is understandable that the destruction
visited by the bombs did not provoke anti-American feelings or a strong
sense of victimization among the Japanese leaders in the months immediately following the surrender.

The atomic bomb also saved Japan's ruling elite from an impending
domestic upheaval. On August 12 Navy Minister Yonai unburdened himself to his trusted subordinate, Rear Admiral Takagi Sōkichi, who had been
involved in the navy's peace maneuvers:

> Perhaps the way I am putting this is inadequate, but I think that *the use of
> the atomic bomb and the Soviet entry into the war are gifts from Heaven.* . . .
> The main reason I have been insisting on saving the situation [surren-
> dering] is neither fear of an enemy attack nor even the atomic bomb and
> the Soviet entry into the war. Above all, it is the alarming state of domes-
> tic affairs. It is good fortune that we can now save the situation without
> bringing such domestic affairs into the open.[68]

To call the atomic bombings, which took so many lives, a "gift from
Heaven" would seem perverted. Callous as this may sound, Yonai was more
alarmed about an impending domestic crisis, popular revolt, even a military coup d'état (like the Uprising of February 26, 1936), than about the
atomic bomb.[69] After the war Kido stated that "a large-scale revolt by the
military could easily have been anticipated." Peace advocates such as Kido
and Yonai found in the bombs the "external pressure" needed to forestall
a domestic commotion. Former prime minister Konoe dreaded a communist revolution if the war continued and the decisive homeland battle took
place.[70] Such fears were widespread among the ruling elites. To avoid this
eventuality, the peace party used the two sets of "twin shocks"—the atomic

68. Takagi, *Takagi kaigun shōshō oboegaki* [Memoranda of Rear Admiral Takagi], 351;
Takagi and Sanematsu Yuzuru, eds., *Kaigun taishō Yonai Mitsumasa oboegaki* [Memoranda
of Admiral Yonai Mitsumasa], 153–54.
    69. Takagi, *Takagi oboegaki*, 227.
    70. *GS*, Vol. 39, *Taiheiyō sensō* 5, 743, 745; Takagi, *Takagi oboegaki*, 180, 198, 227.

bomb and the Soviet entry into the war, Hiroshima and Nagasaki—to bring about speedy acceptance of the Potsdam terms.

The Vacillating Emperor

It must be stressed again that the bomb did not "produce the decision" to end the war, nor did it set in motion the political process that led to Japan's surrender. Japan's informal, secret "peace maneuvers" had begun as early as March 1943, when Hirohito first intimated to Kido his wish for peace.[71] But, in the absence of any clear directions from above, nothing came of the various uncoordinated, hesitant "peace feelers" through various foreign channels.[72] In fact, Hirohito himself was vacillating. During the battle of Leyte Gulf in October 1944 he hoped to "give a telling blow to the enemy so that we can find room for a compromise peace."[73] In mid-February 1945 he told Konoe that there still was a chance; he expected to negotiate peace terms after having given the enemy one final blow.[74] By early May, however, he had reversed himself and almost embarrassed Kido by urging a prompt peace: "The sooner the better," he said.[75]

Kido's diary entry of June 9, 1945, contains the first clear indication that Hirohito had decided to think seriously of peace.[76] Distressed by the debacle of the battle of Okinawa, the emperor took an unprecedented step on June 22 when he told the Supreme War Council, "I desire that *concrete plans* to end the war, unhampered by existing policy, be speedily studied and that efforts be made to implement them."[77] This meant a significant turnabout,

71. Kido, ed., *Kido nikki,* 1:28–29, 2:1020; *Kido kankei bunsho,* 46. The position of Hirohito is critically treated in the following works: Tanaka Nobumasa, *Dokyumento Shōwa tennō,* Vol. 5: *Haisen* [A Documentary History of Showa Emperor, Vol. 5: Defeat 2]; Yamada Akira and Kōketsu Atsushi, *Ososugita seidan: Shōwa tennō no sensō shidō to sensō sekinin* [The Sacred Decision That Came Too Late: Showa Emperor's War Guidance and War Responsibility]; and Yoshida Yutaka, *Shōwa tennō no shūsenshi* [A History of Showa Emperor's War Termination]. Bix's "Japan's Delayed Surrender" relies heavily on these works.

72. Tōgō, *Jidan no ichimen,* 329–30; Tōgō, *Cause of Japan,* 299; Hayashi, ed., *Nihon shūsenshi,* vol. 2, passim.

73. Terasaki Hidenari and Mariko Terasaki Miller, eds., *Shōwa tennō dokuhakuroku, Terasaki Hidenari goyōgakari nikki* [Monologues of Showa Emperor and the Diaries of Terasaki Hidenari], 101–2.

74. Takagi, *Takagi oboegaki,* 227–28.

75. Ibid., 228–29; Hosokawa Morisada, *Jōhō tennō ni tassezu* [Information That Never Reached the Emperor], 2:385.

76. Kido, ed., *Kido nikki,* 2:1209–10; *Kido kankei bunsho,* 75–77; Gaimushō, *Shūsen shiroku,* 3:91–94.

77. Kido, ed., *Kido nikki,* 2:1212–13 (italics added).

but the "Big Six" failed to reach an agreement because Anami, Umezu, and Toyoda insisted that Japan had not yet lost the war and pinned their last hope on a decisive homeland battle.[78] In the end it was the Hiroshima bomb that compelled them to face the stark reality of defeat.

Thus, the atomic bombing was crucial in accelerating the peace process. The impact of the bomb was such that it brought further urgency to the governmental machinery for achieving peace, enabling the prime minister to bring Hirohito directly into a position where his "sacred decision" for surrender could override the diehards. In the apt words of Robert Butow, the atomic bombing, followed by the Soviet entry, had created "that unusual atmosphere in which the heretofore static power of the emperor could be made active in such an extraordinary way as to work what was virtually a political miracle."[79]

Missed Opportunities

Some historians have argued that if the United States had only modified its "unconditional surrender" formula and explicitly guaranteed the retention of the imperial institution, Japan would have surrendered earlier, before the use of the atomic bomb. This was the view held by Acting Secretary of State Joseph C. Grew, who urged President Truman to include an announcement to this effect in the Potsdam Declaration. An early draft of the proclamation, submitted to Truman on July 2, contained an explicit assurance of "a constitutional monarchy under the present dynasty." However, this passage was deleted from the final Potsdam Declaration for fear of domestic backlash in the United States and also of strengthening the hands of the military diehards in Japan.[80]

After the war Grew maintained that, had his advice been followed, Japan would have surrendered without suffering from atomic devastations, and Stimson agreed in his memoirs.[81] In time the Grew-Stimson view came to be firmly accepted by some American and Japanese historians. For example, Sherwin and Alperovitz, revisionist historians, argue that the decision to use the bomb "delayed the end of war." They contend that, because of the availability of the bomb, Washington delayed modification of the unconditional

---

78. Sakomizu, *Dai Nippon teikoku*, 28.
79. Kido, ed., *Kido nikki: Tokyo saibanki*, 444; Butow, *Japan's Decision to Surrender*, 231.
80. Akira Iriye, *Power and Culture: The Japanese-American War, 1941–1945*, 253–54.
81. Joseph C. Grew, *Turbulent Era: A Diplomatic Record of Forty Years, 1904–1945*, 2:1425–28; Stimson and Bundy, *On Active Service*, 628.

surrender formula.[82] However, as has been noted, Japan's military chiefs were intransigent about the "three additional conditions" even after the two bombs and the Soviet entry into the war. Most likely there was no missed opportunity for an earlier peace on this account.

Another case for an alleged missed opportunity relates to Truman's "failure" to exploit Japan's bumbling efforts in July to seek Soviet mediation for favorable surrender terms. The United States had been eavesdropping on telegraphic exchanges between Foreign Minister Tōgō and Ambassador Satō Naotake in Moscow through intercepted cable messages, "Magic." Alperovitz makes much of Tōgō's cable to Satō dated July 12, which conveyed Hirohito's message "that the war be concluded speedily."[83] In a similar vein, Nishijima Ariatsu contends that Truman, knowing of the Tokyo-Moscow exchanges, lost "a golden opportunity for a negotiated peace with Japan" and instead dropped the bombs.[84]

What the deciphered Japanese dispatches reveal, however, were indecision and contradictions in Tokyo; the Japanese government could never agree on surrender terms. The cable messages went round and round: Tōgō, under pressure from the military, repeated that Japan could never accept an unconditional surrender, while the more realistic Satō entreated for "specific" mediation terms and "a concrete plan for terminating the war." As was to be expected, the Soviet response was chilly: Solomon A. Lozovsky, the deputy foreign commissar, replied that the emperor's message "contained mere generalities and no concrete proposal." In the end the Soviet government flatly rejected the Japanese proposal to send the emperor's special emissary, Konoe Fumimaro, to Moscow on the ground that the Japanese proposal was too "opaque" regarding surrender conditions.[85] Through these efforts Japan merely wasted valuable time. There is thus very little likelihood of any missed opportunity here.

If any opportunity was missed, it may have been Japan's failure to accept the Potsdam Declaration of July 26. Tōgō at once noted from its wording ("The following are our terms . . .") that it actually amounted to a "conditional surrender." Although it said nothing about the emperor system, he interpreted the declaration as offering the basis of a negotiated peace. The

---

82. Gar Alperovitz and Robert L. Messer, "Marshall, Truman, and the Decision to Drop the Bomb," 204–14; Alperovitz, *Decision to Use the Atomic Bomb*, 634; Alperovitz, *Atomic Diplomacy* (1985 edition), 27–32 (italics mine).

83. Alperovitz, *Decision to Use the Atomic Bomb*, 165, 233–37, 248, 412, 519, 536. For Ambassador Satō's negative reaction to this telegram, see Satō Naotake, *Kaiko hachijū-nen*, 490–91.

84. Nishijima, *Gembaku wa naze tōka saretaka*, 224–26.

85. Satō, *Kaiko hachijūnen*, 481–97; Gaimushō, *Shūsen shiroku*, 3:136–204.

upper echelons of the Foreign Ministry agreed that the Potsdam terms be accepted at once.[86] However, the Japanese military found the Potsdam terms totally unacceptable because they amounted to unconditional surrender and did not contain the "three additional conditions": they rejected an Allied trial of Japanese war criminals, demobilization and disarmament of Japanese forces by the Allies, and an Allied military occupation of Japan. Japan's military chiefs had been watching with increasing concern the Allies' stern treatment of Nazi leaders and German war criminals. Likewise, the Potsdam terms demanded the eradication of Japanese "militarism" and the elimination of military leaders.[87]

Apprehensive about the military's opposition, Tōgō took pains to persuade the Supreme War Council and the cabinet on July 27 that nothing be done pending Moscow's reply to Tokyo's mediation proposal. Tōgō's wait-and-see policy notwithstanding, Prime Minister Suzuki, under pressure from the army and navy command, floundered and announced, to Tōgō's great dismay, that the Japanese government would "ignore" (*mokusatsu*) the Potsdam terms. (The unfortunate word has been variously translated as "withhold comment," "treat with silent contempt," "ignore with contempt," "unworthy of public notice," and even "reject").[88] The consequences were swift and devastating: Japan's seeming rejection gave the United States the pretext for dropping the atom bomb.

The Bomb or Soviet Entry?

As to the relative weight of the atomic bombing compared with the Soviet entry in forcing Japan's surrender, there has been lively controversy among historians. While Robert Butow, Herbert Feis, and Barton Bernstein have tended to regard the bomb as the decisive factor in Japan's surrender, Gar Alperovitz and Robert L. Messer have emphasized the Soviet entry.[89] Japanese historians, particularly those on the left, generally regard the entry of the

---

86. Gaimusho, *Shūsen shiroku*, 4:4–5, 13–14, 18; Tōgō Shigehiko, *Sofu Tōgō Shigenori no shōgai* [The Life of My Grandfather Tōgō Shigenori], 373–75.

87. Gaimushō, *Shūsen shiroku*, 4:5, 13–17; Kurihara and Hatano, eds., *Shūsen kōsaku*, 2:334–37.

88. Gaimushō, *Shūsen shiroku*, 4:19–24.

89. For example, Alperovitz and Messer, "Marshall, Truman, and the Decision to Drop the Bomb," 204–6. Among American scholars, Paul Kecskemeti has persuasively argued that the Soviet entry was "the main factor that determined the *timing* of Japan's surrender" (*Strategic Surrender*, 198–99 [italics mine]); Hasegawa's *Racing the Enemy* is the most expressive of this view.

Soviet Union into the war as having had "the greatest impact."[90] It is difficult to determine precisely which factor was more important. Because the Soviet entry came on the heels of the Hiroshima bomb, it is hard to separate the shocks of the two events; their impacts were cumulative. The foregoing analysis, however, would suggest the primacy of the Hiroshima bomb; the Soviet entry, coming as it did when the Hiroshima bomb had already shaken Japan's ruling elite, served as a confirmation and coup de grace.

From a political and diplomatic viewpoint the Soviet entry was indeed a serious blow to Japan; it dashed the last hope of Soviet peace mediation. But it did not come as a total surprise, which the atomic bomb assuredly was. When he received the report of the Soviet declaration of war, Army Minister Anami was heard to remark, "The inevitable has come at last."[91] The army had been aware since the German surrender in May that the Soviets had been transferring powerful forces with offensive equipment to Siberia.

The truth of the matter is that the Soviet entry spelled the strategic bankruptcy of Japan. In late June and early July 1945 the members of the Supreme War Council agreed that Soviet entry into the war would "determine the fate of our Empire."[92] In a similar vein, Kawabe Torashirō, the deputy chief of the Army General Staff, had categorically stated at the imperial conference that "the absolute maintenance of peace in our relations with the Soviet Union is one of the fundamental conditions for continuing the war with the United States."[93] This notwithstanding, when Kawabe was faced with the reality of the Soviet entry, he wrote in his diary that "To save the honor of the Yamato race, there is no way but to keep on fighting. At this critical moment, I don't even want to consider peace or surrender."[94] From the viewpoint of the shock effect, then, it may be argued that the bomb had greater immediate impact on Japanese leaders than did the Soviet entry into the war. After all, the Soviet invasion of Manchuria gave them only an *indirect* shock, whereas the use of the atomic bomb on their homeland gave them the *direct* threat of the atomic extinction of the Japanese people.[95]

90. Rekishigaku Kenkyūkai, comp., *Taiheiyō sensōshi*, 5:364, 366–69; Arai, *Gembaku tōka*, 254–56, 266; Nishijima, *Gembaku wa naze tōka saretaka*, 235, 237–38; Arai Shin'ichi, *Dainiji sekai taisen* [World War II], 177.

91. Kurihara and Hatano, eds., *Shūsen kōsaku*, 2:360–61.

92. Sanbō Honbu, comp., *Haisen no kiroku*, 272, 276, 278; Kurihara and Hatano, eds., *Shūsen kōsaku*, 2:360–61; BBKS, *Senshi sōsho: Kantōgun* [War History Series: The Kwantung Army], 3:329.

93. Sanbō Honbu, comp., *Haisen no kiroku*, 276; Miyazaki Diary, December 29, 1949, "Interrogations"; Kurihara and Hatano, eds., *Shūsen kōsaku*, 2:361.

94. Kawabe, *Kawabe Torashirō kaikoroku* [Memoirs of Kawabe Torashirō], 154–55; Kawabe, August 23, 1948, "Statements"; Kurihara and Hatano, eds., *Shūsen kōsaku*, 2:342–43; Oki, *Ōki nikki*, 334.

95. On this point, see Lawrence Freedman and Saki Dockrill, "Hiroshima: A Strategy of Shock," 205, 207.

The shock of the bomb was all the greater because it came as a "surprise attack" and because it contained the element of a profound culture shock. Kawabe later admitted that, although "we have long worried about the question of the Soviet entry, a surprise attack with this new [atomic] weapon was beyond our wildest dreams." Ōki Misao, the chief secretary of the House of Representatives, wrote in his diary, "There is nothing we can do about the appearance of the atomic bomb. That nullifies everything. All our efforts until now have come to naught."[96]

As noted, even the hitherto equivocal Suzuki said *before* the Soviet entry that he had made up his mind for surrender. In addition, we have Kido's postwar testimony: "I believe that with the atomic bomb alone we could have brought the war to an end. But the Soviet entry into the war made it that much easier."[97] Going a step further, Sakomizu Hisatsune, the chief cabinet secretary, later testified, "I am sure we could have ended the war in a similar way if the Russian declaration of the war had not taken place at all."[98] The foregoing testimonies would seem to suggest the relative importance of the bomb's shock.

The A-Bomb Saves the Army's "Face"

From the beginning the army tried to minimize the A-bomb's damage, and Army Minister Anami even denied that it was an atomic bomb. At the cabinet meeting on the morning of August 7, he asked, "Is it not a matter of common knowledge among Japanese physicists that it will take several more years before an atomic bomb can be developed?" Even the representatives of the Technology Board, whose task it was to mobilize the nation's scientific and technological resources, stated, "No matter how advanced American technology may be, it is quite impossible for the Americans to bring such an unstable weapon as an atomic device to Japan, across the Pacific."[99]

However, from the beginning some army leaders were aware that an atomic bomb had been dropped. As noted before, Miyazaki, the head of the Operations Division, wrote in his diary on August 6, "it may be the so-called atomic bomb."[100] Lieutenant General Kawabe, one of the few army men familiar with Japanese atomic research, suspected that the weapon was an

96. Kawabe, *Kaikoroku,* 155; Ōki, *Ōki nikki,* 334.
97. Kido, ed., *Kido nikki: Tokyo saibanki,* 444.
98. Sakomizu, May 3, 1949, "Interrogations."
99. Sakomizu, *Dai Nippon teikoku,* 183; Ikeda Sumihisa, December 23, 1949, "Statements."
100. Miyazaki Diary, August 6, 1945; Kurihara and Hatano, eds., *Shūsen kōsaku,* 2:343.

atomic bomb even before he learned of Truman's statement. He recalled having heard about the atomic bomb from Dr. Nishina Yoshio, the leader of the Japanese A-bomb project, and could not help shuddering.[101]

It was hastily decided by the Imperial General Headquarters to dispatch to Hiroshima an investigative commission with Dr. Nishina as an expert member. On the evening of August 8, Nishina reported, "We regret to say that it certainly was an atomic bomb."[102] The full, official report reached the Imperial General Headquarters on August 10. The question then became whether or not to acknowledge the A-bomb publicly. The Cabinet Board of Information and the Foreign Ministry were for announcing the truth, but the military flatly opposed this idea for fear that such an announcement would shake the morale of the people. In the end, the government equivocated and announced that it was just a "new type of bomb"; only after the end of the war did the Japanese people learn the truth about the atomic bomb.[103]

Despite the "twin shocks" of the Hiroshima and Nagasaki bombs, the army men still insisted on a fight to the finish. In the end they accepted surrender partly because the atomic bomb paradoxically helped them save "face." There was a strong feeling among the army's leaders that Japan had been "overwhelmed by America's scientific prowess." On August 8 Miyazaki wrote, "Technically Japan seems about half a century behind" the United States.[104] Colonel Ogata Ken'ichi, the military aide-de-camp to the emperor, unburdened himself in his diary: "Our foe must be given credit for the great power of the atomic bomb and remarkable progress in science and technology. I admit I must admire their achievement."[105]

By saving the army men's "face," such attitudes toward America's scientific achievements smoothed their acceptance of surrender. At the cabinet meeting of August 9, Ishiguro Tadaatsu, the minister of agriculture and commerce, tried to persuade the military: "We have lost a scientific war. The people may be dissatisfied with the military for the defeat. But if we say we lost a scientific war, the people will understand."[106]

After the war Kido stated, "If military leaders could convince themselves that they were defeated by the power of science but not because of lack of

101. Kawabe, *Kaikoroku*, 154; Kawabe Diary, August 23, 1948; Kawabe's "Statements"; Kurihara and Hatano, eds., *Shūsen kōsaku*, 2:342–43.
102. Arisue Seizo, *Shūsen hishi: Arisue kikanchō no shuki* [A Secret History of the Termination of the War: A Memoir of Lieutenant General Arisue], 26–33; Sakomizu, *Dai Nippon teikoku*, 183.
103. Gaimushō, *Shūsen shiroku*, 4:65–66.
104. Miyazaki Diary, August 8, 1945.
105. Yomiuri, ed., *Shōwashi no tennō*, 4:310.
106. Ikeda, *Nihon no magarikado*, 178; Yomiuri, ed., *Shōwashi no tenno*, 4:309–10.

spiritual power or strategic errors, this could save their face to some extent."[107] In fact, some army men accepted the argument that "the Japanese military would never lose a war, but now that Japanese science has been beaten, we must end the war just as soon as possible." Along the same lines, Sakomizu, the chief cabinet secretary, recalled,

> The atomic bomb was a golden opportunity given by Heaven for Japan to end the war. There were those who said that the Japanese armed forces were not defeated. It was in science that Japan was defeated, so the military will not bring shame on themselves by surrendering.

He added that "in ending the war, the idea was to put the responsibility for defeat solely on the atomic bomb, not on the military. This was a clever pretext." From that viewpoint, the endeavor to end the war may be said to have been "a search for ways to save the military's face," although such a face-saving argument was not needed for the highest army officials, Anami and Umezu.[108]

As Sakomizu recollected, "It was commonly understood at that time that the invention of the atomic bomb spelled the end of the war. The power that possessed the atomic bomb will win the war."[109] In point of fact, the Japanese government and the military had embarked on research on the bomb. Prime Minister Tōjō Hideki took a personal interest in the Japanese bomb project, believing that "the atomic bomb would spell the difference between life and death in this war." There was a consensus among Japan's nuclear physicists, however, that no country would be able to develop an atomic bomb during the course of the war. Since government officials believed this forecast, the Hiroshima bomb caught them completely off their guard.[110]

There is no doubt that the Japanese military would not have hesitated to use the atomic bomb in the unlikely event that Japan had developed one. In his diary, Colonel Ogata confided,

> Is there not somehow a way to invent a new weapon that would forestall the enemy? If we had such a weapon, it will be no problem to attack [and recapture] Iwo Jima, the Ryukyus, and the Marianas. It would then be possible to annihilate the enemy's task force and attack the mainland of the

107. Kido, ed., *Kido nikki: Tokyo saibanki*, 443.
108. Sakomizu Hisatsune, *Shūsen no shinsō* [The Truth about Surrender]; and "Kōfukuji no shinsō" [The Truth about Surrender], 60–61.
109. Sakomizu, *Shūsen no shinsō*, 36.
110. BBK, *Senshi sōsho: Hondo bōkū sakusen* [War History Series: Air Defense of the Homeland], 632.

United States, thus turning the tables and affording a golden opportunity to reverse the tide of war. Oh, what a pity![111]

Ogata was engaging in pure fantasy, but what underlies this diary entry is the stark military logic that did not question the legitimacy of using the atomic bomb as a winning weapon.

Conclusion

The above analysis has shown that in August 1945 Japan's peace party made the maximum political use of the atomic bomb to end the war. To them the bomb was "a gift from Heaven," "a golden opportunity," and "a psychological moment" to end the war. They saw the bomb as "assisting" their peace efforts and as a means of saving the military's face. But such a utilitarian viewpoint, which regarded the atomic bomb merely as an expedient for inducing surrender, hardly prompted an awareness of the transformation wrought in the fabric of international society by the appearance of the nuclear weapon. Regarding the bomb as if it were a natural calamity also inhibited soul-searching reflection on the war that Japan had started and lost. An embodiment of scientific advances that went beyond their imagination, the superbomb protected Japan's ruling elite from squarely facing the agonies of their nation's unprecedented surrender.

On August 15, 1945, the day the emperor's rescript of surrender was broadcast, Morobuse Kōshin, a liberal journalist of the old generation, lamented that all "responsibility" had been placed on two "unexpected events," the atomic bomb and the Soviet entry into the war. "Nothing is said about the government's ignorance, mistakes, and impotence."[112] The government's responsibility for the war and defeat was thus conveniently shelved.

Although most observers pondered the meaning of the atomic bomb in terms of Japan's surrender, Ōkura Kimmochi, the president of the Technological Research Mobilization Office, recorded on August 7 his thoughts on the bomb's impact for the next several decades to come:

As far as I am concerned, I think it is better for our country to suffer a total defeat than to win a total victory in the present Greater East Asian War. During the past ten years the military domination of our country has been flagrant, and the reins of government have been totally controlled by the military. What would happen if Japan were to win the war in such a sit-

111. Yomiuri, ed., *Shōwashi no tennō*, 4:310.
112. Morobuse, *Senso shisho* [Private Wartime Journal], 330.

uation? Inevitably Japan would come under both internal and external attacks and the nation would go to pieces. On the other hand, in case of Japan's total defeat, the armed forces will be abolished, but the Japanese people will rise to the occasion during the next several decades to reform themselves into truly a splendid people. . . . I believe that the great humiliation [of the atomic bomb] is nothing but an admonition administered by Heaven to our country.[113]

Ōkura was already envisaging the future of a peaceful postwar Japan immediately after he learned about the Hiroshima bomb. However, his vision, which reminds one of Stimson's prospect for a "liberal" postwar Japan, was a minority view. On September 9 an *Asahi* correspondent reported that in America and England there was a rising distrust toward Japan: "Does Japan truly realize that it has been defeated?" "Japanese statements, both at home and abroad, do not refer to Japan's war responsibility, attributing the cause of its defeat solely to the atomic bomb."[114] A year later, on August 15, 1946, Mark Gayn, an American newsman and eyewitness reporter, shrewdly observed in his diary:

> In vain, on this historic day for Japan, I looked for soul-searching, for penitence, for a sign that the lessons of defeat had been taken to heart. The Premier has issued a statement filled with generalities. The press has contented itself with pious phrases. . . . This would have been a good day for the Japanese press to begin telling the people the real and complete story of the war and defeat.[115]

Today, sixty-odd years after Hiroshima and Nagasaki, the question of Japan's "war responsibility" still remains with the nation.[116]

Perhaps no account of Japan's surrender decision is complete without counterfactuals, however risky they may be. This essay has shown that conventional bombing by B-29s alone would not have driven Hirohito to say "we must bow to the inevitable and surrender as speedily as possible." The crucial actor here was the Japanese military, and only the shock of the bombs followed by the Soviet entry could have thrown them off balance and led to surrender—and this very narrowly.

We must then ask this question: Without the use of the atomic bomb, but *with Soviet entry* and with heavy strategic bombing and a strangling blockade,

113. *Ōkura Kimmochi nikki,* 4: 3
114. Hayashi, ed., *Nihon shūsenshi,* 3:195.
115. Gayn, *Japan Diary,* 269–71.
116. Ian Buruma, *Wages of Guilt: Memories of War in Germany and Japan.*

would Japan have surrendered before November 1—the day scheduled for the U.S. invasion of Kyushu? Available Japanese data do not provide a conclusive answer.[117] In June 1945 Japanese leaders agreed that food shortages would become critical in the autumn and toward the onset of the cold season; the country had suffered a "disastrous" failure of its rice crop.[118] On the other hand, we must consider that fanaticism was not restricted to the military; the men and women in the street were thoroughly indoctrinated. This author remembers how women practiced facing American tanks with bamboo spears. Perhaps civilian morale had not deteriorated as much as the ruling elite had feared. In all probability Japan could not have endured the winter of 1945–1946, but there was a possibility that Japan would not have surrendered before November 1. Most assuredly, Japanese sources do not support the *ex post facto* contention of the U.S. Strategic Bombing Survey (1946) that "in all probability" Japan would have surrendered before November 1 "even if the atomic bombs had not been dropped, even if Russia had not entered the war, and even if no invasion had been planned or contemplated."[119]

To repulse the landing of American forces, the Sixteenth Area Army in Kyushu had been built up to nine hundred thousand troops. They were to give a crushing blow to the first wave of American invasion.[120] In the process, they were to die glorious deaths on the beaches and in the interior—in kamikaze planes as human rockets, in midget submarines as human torpedoes, and in suicide charges by ground units. On the American side, the army chief of staff, General George C. Marshall, began to fear such massive Japanese attacks, causing huge American casualties, and came to consider the tactical use of atomic bombs (six to nine) to assist and support the invading American forces.[121] It may be said that Japan's surrender, coming as it did in August, forestalled sacrifices on both sides far surpassing those at Hiroshima and Nagasaki.

This essay suggests that, given the intransigence of the Japanese military, there were few "missed opportunities" for earlier peace and that the alter-

117. Record of the imperial conference of June 8, 1945, in Sanbō Honbu, comp., *Haisen no kiroku*, 256–77; Kido, ed., *Kido nikki*, 2:1208–9.

118. Gaimushō, *Shūsen shiroku*, 3:135, 208–9, 4:120.

119. Cited in Feis, *Atomic Bomb and the End of World War II*, 191. For a detailed critique, see Barton J. Bernstein, "Compelling Japan's Surrender," 113–48. See also Robert P. Newman, "Ending the War with Japan: Paul Nitze's 'Early Surrender' Counterfactual."

120. Edward J. Drea, *MacArthur's ULTRA: Codebreaking and the War against Japan*, 216–25; John Ray Skates, *The Invasion of Japan: Alternative to the Bomb*.

121. Barton J. Bernstein, "Eclipsed by Hiroshima and Nagasaki: Early Thinking about Tactical Nuclear Weapons"; Marc Gallicchio, "After Nagasaki: General Marshall's Plan for Tactical Nuclear Weapons in Japan."

natives available to President Truman in the summer of 1945 were limited, fewer than we may imagine today. In the end, Japan needed "external pressure" in the form of the atomic bombs for its government and military to decide to surrender. Whether or not the atomic bombing of Hiroshima and Nagasaki was *morally justified* is the question that has been debated ever since in Japan and the United States—in fact, the world over—but this is a question that is beyond the scope of this essay and better discussed in the ethical context of just and unjust wars, moral and immoral wars.[122]

Addendum: A Note on Hasegawa's Racing the Enemy[123]

Few recent works in diplomatic history have been greeted with such acclaim. Prominent academics, scholarly journals, and major newspapers have all praised the book as "groundbreaking," "a tour de force," "a landmark book," and a model of multiarchival research. The book won the Robert H. Ferrell Prize of the Society for Historians of American Foreign Relations, and its Japanese version, *Antō* [A Battle behind the Scene], was awarded the even more prestigious Yomiuri-Yoshino Sakuzo Prize.

First, let us examine Hasegawa's use of archives. He did not conduct research in the Russian archives because they are closed. The original sources that he used seem to have been "provided" by the late Boris Slavinsky. As for Japanese sources, there are no "Japanese archives" for this period, and Hasegawa relied mostly on printed sources. As for American sources, he used the standard materials, but he often misquoted and distorted them.

Hasegawa's choice of interpretive framework for the endgame of the Pacific War was unfortunate. According to Hasegawa, President Truman was engaged in a "race" with Stalin to force Japan's surrender with the

---

122. Michael Walzer, *Just and Unjust Wars: A Moral Argument with Historical Illustrations,* contends, "In the summer of 1945, the victorious Americans owed the Japanese People an experiment in negotiations. To use the atomic bomb . . . without even attempting such an experiment, was a double crime" (263–68). Would such an "experiment" have met conditions demanded by the Japanese military? Obviously not. Martin Sherwin's "Hiroshima at Fifty" offers yet another scenario: Stimson could have declared that "our nation is too moral" to use the atomic weapon and dissuaded President Truman from using it. Would this have induced Japan to surrender?

The moral ambiguities in the use of the atomic bomb are more judiciously treated by Melvyn P. Leffler, "Truman's Decision to Drop the Atomic Bomb." The psychological— and moral—implications of the bomb are discussed in Lifton and Mitchell, *Hiroshima in America.*

123. This note is a summary of an extended review article that appeared in the Japanese journal *Shokun* (September 2006): 138–49.

atomic bomb, before the Soviets could enter the war. Hasegawa implies that Truman intended to use the bomb for the political purpose of restraining Soviet expansion in Manchuria. This interpretation has been an article of faith among left-wing Japanese historians. Hasegawa's thesis is also squarely in the revisionist tradition of P. M. S. Blackett's *Fear, War, and the Bomb* (1949) and Gar Alperovitz's *Atomic Diplomacy* (1965). Looked at this way, Hasegawa's thesis is a rehash of an old revisionism.

It will be recalled that Truman's foremost reason for going to Potsdam was to secure Soviet entry into the war. Hasegawa quotes Truman's diary (entry of July 17): "He'll [Stalin] be in the Jap war on August 15th. Fini Japs when that comes about." This entry does not betray any urgency on Truman's part about "the race to see who could force Japan to surrender." On the contrary, the president seemed pleased with Stalin's promise to join the war in mid-August. Again, Hasegawa quotes from Truman, this time from a letter to his wife, Bess, which was written about the same time: "I've gotten what I came for—Stalin goes to war August 15 with no strings on it." Both entries show that military considerations were uppermost in Truman's mind.

Hasegawa argues that "the race between Soviet entry into the war and atomic bomb *now reached its climax*" (*Racing*, 140 [italics added]). But he immediately contradicts himself with the following quote: on July 23 the president instructed Stimson to find out "whether [General George C.] Marshall felt that we [needed] the Russians in the war." Even at this date, Truman was wondering whether Soviet entry was necessary. This fact undermines Hasegawa's assertion that the race with the Soviets had "reached its climax." The following day Truman was told that Soviet entry was no longer needed because of the atomic bomb. So only on July 24 could a "race" with the Soviets possibly start, if it ever did. Since the Soviets entered the war on August 9, the so-called race lasted a mere two weeks. When I pointed out in a review in the *Journal of Strategic Studies* (*JSS*) that a period of two weeks was not long enough to sustain the entire book, Haswgawa rather incoherently answered, "Whether a 100-meter dash, or a marathon, a race is a race, irrespective of the duration."

Turning to the question of the atomic bomb, Hasegawa quotes from Secretary of State James Byrnes's memoirs to the effect that "had the Japanese government surrendered unconditionally, it would not have been necessary to drop the atomic bomb." Then Hasegawa says, "this statement can best be read in reverse": "If we insisted on unconditional surrender, we could justify the dropping of the atomic bomb" (*Racing*, 135). This is a distortion of Byrnes. And on the basis of this misreading, Hasegawa argues that the Potsdam Declaration was an "alibi" to "justify" the use of the atomic bomb. As Robert Ferrell's studies make clear, President Truman simply did not think justification was needed for the bomb. His all-consuming purpose was to bring Japan to surrender as soon as possible with the minimum cost in American lives.

Hasegawa minimizes the impact of the bomb on Japan, repeatedly asserting that the Hiroshima bomb did not have "a direct and immediate impact" on Japan's political process. But he ignores Foreign Minister Tōgō's initiative at the cabinet meeting of August 7 for surrender on the basis of the Potsdam terms and his appeal to the emperor to the same effect on the following day.

What was most crucial here was the shock the bomb gave to the emperor. According to Lord Keeper of the Privy Seal Kido Kōichi's postwar recollections, the emperor told him that "Now that things have come to this impasse, we must bow to the inevitable. No matter what happens to my safety, we should lose no time in ending the war so as not to have another tragedy like this." Hasegawa dismisses Hirohito's statement as a "myth" cultivated by Kido (possibly in collusion with the emperor) after the war to prevent Hirohito from being tried as a war criminal (*Antō*, 374). If Kido's account is suspicious, there is a statement the emperor made to Tōgō on the 8th: "Now that such a new weapon has appeared, it has become less and less possible to continue the war. . . . So my wish is to make such arrangements as will end the war as soon as possible." This notwithstanding, Hasegawa states that "the emperor never positively participated in the political process until the Soviets entered the war" (*Antō*, 517). He repeats ad nauseam without supportive evidence that the Hiroshima bomb did not change the political situation.

What was the position of Prime Minister Suzuki Kantatō? Late at night of August 8 he summoned Chief Cabinet Secretary Sakomizu Tsunehisa and asked him to make preparations since "I would give my views on the termination of the war at tomorrow's Supreme War Council." It is significant that *before* the news of Soviet entry reached Tokyo on the early morning of August 9, Suzuki, too, had decided that the war must end. Despite Hasegawa's contention that it was the entry of the Soviet Union into the war, not the atomic bomb, that was decisive, it is important to bear in mind that the army leaders doggedly insisted on fighting to the finish even *after* the Soviet entry. Military leaders ultimately accepted surrender only after the "sacred decision" was made by the emperor, and it was the shock of the atomic bomb that prompted Hirohito's decision.

I have never argued, as Hasegawa charges, that the Soviet entry was not an important factor. In my *Pacific Historical Review* (*PHR*) article I emphasized the "*double* shock" of the bomb and Soviet entry. As I stated, it is "difficult to determine precisely which factor was more important," and I pointed out the differences between the two shocks. The shock of the atomic bomb was all the greater because it came as a total "surprise attack," and nothing could be done about it. On the other hand, the Japanese army had been aware that the Soviets had been transferring powerful forces to the Russian Far East. I argued that to the extent that the Soviet attack could be anticipated, it reduced the shock effect. But Hasegawa declared that the Imperial General Headquarters did not expect Soviet entry "right up to the moment of attack" and that it "caught the army by complete surprise" (*Racing*, 199). When I challenged Hasegawa's contention, to my surprise he withdrew his statement, admitting that "there was a division [about Soviet entry] within the Army General Staff."

What I emphasized in my *PHR* essay was the *cumulative* effect of the bomb and Soviet entry on the decision to surrender. As I wrote in my *PHR* article, "the Soviet entry, coming as it did when the bomb had already shaken Japan's ruling class, served as a confirmation and coup de grace." In his rejoinder in the *JSS*, Hasegawa "agree[ed] on the cumulative effect," thus weakening his central thesis that Soviet entry was *the* "decisive" factor in Japan's surrender.

Hasegawa's counterfactuals are far-fetched, contradictory, and incredible. On the one hand, he says "even without the atomic bombs, the war most likely would have ended *shortly* after Soviet entry into the war—before November 1," which was the scheduled date for the Allied invasion of Japan's homelands. (Are the intervening eighty-five days to be regarded as a "short" time span?) On the other hand, "Without the Soviet entry into the war [but with the two bombs], the Japanese would have continued to fight until numerous atomic bombs, a successful Allied invasion of the home islands, or continued aerial bombardments, combined with a naval blockade, rendered them incapable of doing so" (*Racing*, 298). In the former case, Hasegawa minimizes Japan's reserve fighting strength; in the latter case, he maximizes it, and these are contradictory statements.

Hasegawa's conclusion is the most dogmatic and vulnerable portion of the book. While he raises "the question of moral responsibility" on the part of the United States, he refers to Japan's wartime atrocities as merely "moral lapses" (*Racing*, 298–99). He concludes by suddenly taking on an Olympian posture: "Thus this is a story with no heroes but no real villains, either—just men" (*Racing*, 302–3) In my *JSS* review I wrote, "This comes close to placing President Harry S. Truman, a plain-speaking 'man from Missouri,' on the same moral plane as Generalissimo Joseph Stalin (and Japanese warlords), and I for one find it difficult to identify with such a moral equation.'"

The Mushroom Cloud and National Psyches

Japanese and American Perceptions of the Atomic Bomb Decision—A Reconsideration, 1945-2006

Japan's strongly felt national identity as the first and only country to have undergone atomic bombings gives a unique stamp to its perspective on the atomic bomb. Not surprisingly, the Japanese view of the decision to use the bomb is markedly different from the American perspective. In Japan opinions on the atomic bomb have been understandably surrounded by historical myths and strong emotionalism stemming from its victimization. In the United States, until very recently, the exigencies of nuclear strategy, especially deterrence, often defined perceptions of the atomic bomb in narrowly military terms, clouding the broader significance of Hiroshima and Nagasaki in human history. Gaps in Japanese and American perceptions of the atomic bombings continue to widen and the psychological and cognitive dissonance has been such that it has constituted a serious irritant and obstacle in relations between the two peoples, as well as in their official governmental dealings.[1]

This state of affairs was suddenly dramatized in 1994–1995 by the controversy over the proposed exhibit of the fuselage of the *Enola Gay*, the B-29 bomber that dropped the atomic bomb on Hiroshima, together with historical materials and artifacts from Hiroshima, at the National Air and Space

This essay expands and updates the article that appeared in the *Journal of American-East Asian Relations* 4 (Summer 1995): 95–116. It was reprinted in Laura Hein and Mark Selden, eds., *Living with the Bomb: American and Japanese Cultural Conflicts in the Nuclear Age.* I am grateful to the following friends for commenting on earlier drafts of this essay: Robert J. C. Butow, Robert H. Ferrell, Mark Fitzpatrick, Marc S. Gallicchio, Ishii Osamu, Michael Kort, Charles E. Neu, Robert P. Newman, and Allan M. Winkler.

1. See, for example, Asada, "Busshu daitōryō to gembaku tōka mondai" [President Bush and His View on Dropping the Atomic Bomb], the *Sankei Shinbun,* December 4, 1991.

Museum (NASM) of the Smithsonian Institution.[2] Well-organized veterans of World War II, who strongly supported the atomic bombings, brought fierce pressures on the museum to eliminate from the exhibit materials on atomic victimization and demanded that its script be heavily censored. In the end, the projected exhibition was cancelled. What could have been an excellent occasion for a dialogue on the historical and moral significance of Hiroshima and Nagasaki thus turned into the "history war" that rocked the nation.

After the Smithsonian debacle the American mass media lost interest in the issue of the atomic bomb. It is tempting to call 1995–2005 a lost decade, but there have been signs that the perceptual gaps between the Japanese and Americans were gradually narrowing. According to a Gallup poll, announced in March 1995, 44 percent of American respondents replied that if the atomic bomb decision had been theirs to make, they "would have dropped the atomic bomb," and as many as 49 percent said they would have "tried some other way" to force Japan to surrender.[3] This contrasts with the 86 percent who approved the bombing in the fall of 1945.

In Japan, too, public opinion seems to be moving away from exclusively blaming the United States for the bomb. According to a large-scale survey of surviving atomic victims (*hibakusha*) held in July 2005, nearly half responded that "the responsibility of atomic damages" lay with *both* the American and Japanese governments. Only 28 percent believed that the responsibility lay solely with the U.S. government.[4] This contrasts with past polls that showed a large majority blaming the United States exclusively.

Such were the perceptions in recent years, and I shall trace the changes in attitudes toward the atomic bombings over the past sixty years to examine what caused them, pointing to the fallacies and pitfalls of collective memory. Only such a long-term and comparative perspective will afford us the historical background for the ongoing dialogue about the use of the atomic bomb and, by implication, about the danger of its future use.

Japan in the Early Postwar Period

The earliest statistics available about Japanese attitudes toward the bomb are in the United States Strategic Bombing Survey, undertaken just three

---

2. A well-documented recent study of the abortive Smithsonian exhibition is Waldo H. Heinrichs, "The Enola Gay and Contested Public Memory." See also Paul Boyer, "Whose History Is It Anyway?"

3. Cited in Kai Bird and Lawrence Lifschultz, eds., *Hiroshima Shadow: Writings on the Denial of History and the Smithsonian Controversy*, xlvi.

4. *Asahi Shimbun*, July 17, 2005. More than forty thousand were polled; among them about 60 percent resided in Hiroshima.

months after Japan's surrender. Questioning five thousand people in Japan about the bombings, the survey team found an unexpectedly low level of hostility toward the United States. Only 19 percent of Hiroshima and Nagasaki residents (and 12 percent of the Japanese people as a whole) registered hatred of Americans for having used the bomb. Instead, they tended to turn their anger against their own leaders, especially the military leaders, who led Japan to war. When asked where the responsibility lay for the atomic bombing, 35 percent of respondents replied it was Japan's fault; another 29 percent said neither side was responsible, believing it to be a consequence of war.[5]

As the survey's report frankly admitted, these figures probably underestimated hostility toward the United States. The stupor caused by the shock of defeat, the immediate postwar lethargy, and a fatalistic attitude toward war all influenced Japanese attitudes.[6] Many respondents refrained from disclosing their true feelings for fear of offending the Americans. The International Military Tribunal for the Far East, which began its investigation in the spring of 1946, exposing one war crime after another, reinforced the blaming of the atomic tragedy on Japan's military leaders who not only started the war but refused to surrender long after it was defeated.

In the early postwar years the Japanese people, on the verge of starvation, were in no condition to give much thought to the question of the atomic bomb. Even if they had wished to do so, the occupation authority's press code (a euphemism for censorship) that went into effect in September 1945 banned newspapers, magazines, or other print media from publishing anything that might invite "mistrust or resentment" of the United States and its occupation forces. The policy included the censorship films and photographs relating to the atomic devastation and all opinions suggesting that the atomic bomb was barbarous or a crime against humanity. Literature by atomic victims was not allowed. As the historian Imabori Seiji has noted, because the voices of atomic victims were thus silenced, an important opportunity to have decisive influence on world affairs was lost.

Yet censorship was by no means total, consistent, or even effective,[7] and as the years passed and the occupation neared its end, Japanese translations

5. The breakdown of the reaction of Hiroshima-Nagasaki residents to the atomic bombing was as follows: Fear—terror, 47 percent; fear for own life, 16 percent; admiration—impressed by the scientific power behind the bomb, 26 percent; jealousy—why couldn't Japan make such a bomb? 3 percent; anger—bomb is cruel, inhuman, barbarous, 17 percent; hatred of U.S. because of the atomic bomb, 2 percent; and no response, 11 percent (United States Strategic Bombing Survey, *Effects of Strategic Bombing on Japanese Morale, Report on the Pacific War,* 3, 91–97).

6. A superb recent account of the Japanese after defeat is John W. Dower's prizewinning *Embracing Defeat: Japan in the Wake of World War II.*

7. Monica Braw, *The Atomic Bomb Suppressed,* 92, 102–3, 151. In 1994 the former members of the Civil Censorship Division of the General Headquarters met in a reunion and

of foreign publications relating to the bomb began to appear. The translation of John Hersey's best- selling book, *Hiroshima*, was issued in April 1949.[8] In 1951 the translation of P. M. S. Blackett's early revisionist book, *Fear, War, and the Bomb*, came out and soon became the oracle for Japan's left-wing historians and peace activists.

Reversal of Japanese Perceptions

The year Japan regained independence under the peace treaty signed in San Francisco, 1952, saw a spate of books and films about the bomb. Changes in the international environment—the intensification of the Cold War, Soviet acquisition of a nuclear capability, the development of the hydrogen bomb, the Korean War and President Harry S. Truman's slip in a press conference about the possible use of the atomic bomb in Korea, the conclusion of the U.S.-Japan Security Treaty in 1952 by which Japan became America's ally—all affected perceptions of the atomic bomb. Fear of becoming involved in a nuclear war came to the fore in Japanese opinion.

Then in 1954 Japanese fishermen aboard the *Lucky Dragon* were exposed, with one fatality, to fallout from an American hydrogen bomb test conducted at the Bikini Atoll in the Marshall Islands. The boat was well outside the official danger zone. But the fish brought in by the *Lucky Dragon* were radioactive.[9] This incident came as a profound culture shock to the Japanese and unlocked their anti-American feelings that had lain hidden since 1945 and touched off an antinuclear furor. The movement originated with a group of middle-class Tokyo housewives who were concerned about fallout, and it spread like wildfire across the nation. Now not only the Hiroshima-Nagasaki survivors but the entire Japanese people could see themselves as nuclear victims. This was, so to speak, the third nuclear attack they suffered.[10]

A decade later, in the 1960s, the war in Vietnam gave credence to a racial interpretation of the atomic bomb. Instances of reported American atrocities in Vietnam, such as the killing that took place in the village of My Lai

---

testified that there were relatively few instances of deletion by the occupation authorities. The Japanese media, they said, practiced self-control (*Asahi Shimbun*, May 15, 1994; Lawrence S. Wittner, *One World or None: A History of the World Nuclear Disarmament Movement through 1953*, 39–46).

8. Hersey's work was translated by Ishikawa Kin'ichi as *Hiroshima* (Tokyo: Hōsei Daigaku Shuppankyoku, 1949).

9. Chūgoku Shinbunsha, ed., *Nenpyō Hiroshima: Kaku jidai 50-nen no kiroku* [Chronology Hiroshima: Fifty-Year Record of the Nuclear Age], 164–69.

10. Robert P. Newman, *Enola Gay and the Court of History*, 86.

in 1968, and "body counts" intensified the sense of racial victimization; these events seemed to confirm the view that the United States dropped the bomb on the Japanese because of racial hatred against Asians. By then the Japanese people had long since abandoned their immediate postwar attitude of blaming their leaders. In time, the new nationalism that accompanied Japan's rise to an economic superpower further embittered Japan's perception of the atomic bomb decision.

According to a 1970 poll, 61 percent of Japanese respondents said that the atomic bomb should never have been used for any reason whatsoever. Including those who were moderately opposed, 75 percent registered disapproval. Eighteen percent expressed anger toward the Japanese government.[11] A year later a survey of Hiroshima residents by *Chūgoku Shinbun* showed that 31 percent singled out the U.S. president of the time, Harry S. Truman, for denunciation. Only 10 percent held the Japanese government and military responsible. There had been a definite reversal of Japanese attitudes.

American Perceptions of the A-Bomb Decision

Compare Japanese with American perceptions. On August 9, 1945, the day of the Nagasaki bomb, President Truman publicly stated that the bombs had been used to end the war promptly and to save "thousands and thousands of lives" that would have been lost in an invasion of Japan's home islands.[12] (He later said "half a million lives" were saved.) This "official" view—the so-called Truman orthodoxy—which held that his decision was necessary and justified for military reasons—has become the standard line for American presidents since Truman, and it has been the majority view of the American people, at least until very recently.

When the Pacific War—a "good war" for Americans[13]—came to an end in mid-August 1945, few people in America talked about the guilt incurred by the bombing of noncombatants, with the exception of church leaders, liberal or radical intellectuals, and a handful of pacifists. A soldier's reaction to Hiroshima, as recalled by Paul Fussell, was "Thank God for the atom bomb."[14] In a Gallup poll conducted on August 16, 1945, the day after Japan surren-

11. Odagiri Hideo, ed., *Shinbun shiryō genbaku* [Newspaper Materials on the Atomic Bomb], 1:213.
12. Truman, *Public Papers of the Presidents: Harry S. Truman,* 1945, 203–14. See Karl T. Compton, "If the Atomic Bomb Had Not Been Used," 54–56, reprinted in Robert H. Ferrell, ed., *Harry S. Truman and the Bomb,* 89–94.
13. Studs Terkel, *"The Good War": An Oral History of World War Two.*
14. Fussell, "Thank God for the Atom Bomb—Hiroshima: A Soldier's View."

dered, as many as 85 percent of American respondents expressed support for "using the new atomic bomb on Japanese cities," as compared with 10 percent who stated their opposition. The following month another poll found overwhelming approval: 43 percent would have used the bombs on one city at a time; 24 percent would have tried to wipe out as many cities as possible; 27 percent would have used them only after a demonstration on an unpopulated area; and 4 percent would have refused to use the bomb. In the autumn of that year, a Roper poll registered American feelings on the subject:

1. We should have used the two bombs on cities, just as we did. (53.5 percent)
2. We should have quickly used many more of the bombs before Japan had a chance to surrender. (22.7 percent)
3. We should have dropped one on some unpopulated region, to show the Japanese its power, and dropped the second one on a city only if they hadn't surrendered after the first one. (13.8 percent)
4. We should not have used any atomic bombs at all. (4.5 percent)
5. Don't know. (5.5 percent)[15]

In 1946, John Hersey's "Hiroshima" first appeared in a single issue of the *New Yorker*, before it became a best-selling book, bringing a human dimension to the devastation of the atomic bomb. In a cool, understated, and for that reason all the more poignant style, he re-created the Hiroshima bombing from the standpoint of the victims by portraying six survivors. It was a profoundly moving report. But Hersey's article did not precipitate a wave of petitions to President Truman denouncing his decision. Because Hersey refrained from raising the ethical question, readers could seek catharsis, yet were not required to change their political view on the dropping of the bomb. As Michael J. Yavenditti wrote, "Indeed, for many, the very act of reading [*Hiroshima*] seems to have provided release from stressful and complex emotions. It was like the funeral rituals that provide a socially sanctioned outlet for grief and mourning."[16]

From the beginning of the atomic era, Americans were haunted by nightmares that one day they might become atomic victims themselves—a fear that became pressing when the Soviet Union successfully detonated a nuclear device in August 1949. With President Truman's decision in January

15. Paul S. Boyer, *By the Bomb's Early Light: American Thought and Culture at the Dawn of the Atomic Age*, 183–84, 209; Spencer R. Weart, *Nuclear Fear: A History of Images*, 106–9. See also Allan M. Winkler, *Life under a Cloud: American Anxiety about the Atom*, which was translated into Japanese under Asada's supervision as *Americajin no kaku ishiti* (Kyoto: Mineruva Shobō, 1999).

16. Yavenditti, "The American People and the Use of Atomic Bombs on Japan: The 1940s"; Yavenditti, "John Hersey and the American Conscience: The Reception of

1950 to proceed with the development of the hydrogen bomb, a weapon with a thousand times the power of the Hiroshima bomb, a nuclear arms race was obviously under way. The Japanese press anxiously followed Truman's decision. The U.S. embassy in Tokyo reported that this and other Cold War developments added up "in the Japanese view to the frightening prospect of a super atomic war."[17] In the United States, Truman's decision produced a "nuclear nightmare."

Nuclear deterrence became American policy. With the occasional talk of preemptive or preventive nuclear strikes, the meanings of Hiroshima and Nagasaki seemed to have become overpowered by the rhetoric of megaton overkill.[18] American air force leaders, who had justified Hiroshima and Nagasaki, said the atomic bomb was just another more powerful weapon.[19] Until the late 1960s images of human suffering in Hiroshima and Nagasaki were hard to find in the United States.[20] It was as if the American people and their leaders were suffering from "psychic numbness," a phrase coined by the psychiatrist Robert Lifton.[21]

Given this background, it is not surprising that there was a dearth of data on American perceptions of the A-bomb decision during the 1950s and 1960s. According to the 1965 nationwide survey conducted by Louis Harris, 70 percent agreed that the United States was "right" in dropping the bomb to save American lives; only 17 percent "regretted" it.[22] The figures had not changed much from the 1945 polls. In 1971, when the *Asahi Shimbun* (in cooperation with Harris) conducted its first poll on American attitudes toward the bombings, 64 percent of respondents asserted that dropping the bomb "could not have been helped," and 21 percent said it was a "mistake."

Cognitive Dissonance

These findings came as a "great surprise"—a culture shock—to the Japanese people, an *Asahi* editorial writer commented. They had expected a much larger

---

'Hiroshima.'"; Peter Schwenger, "America's Hiroshima," 240. The 1950 Japanese translation of *Hiroshima,* under the same title, was a best seller in Japan.

17. Quoted in Wittner, *One World or None,* 53.

18. Sheila K. Johnson, *American Attitudes toward Japan, 1941–1975,* 37- 39; Boyer, *By the Bomb's Early Light,* 204–10; Michael S. Sherry, *The Rise of American Air Power: The Creation of Armageddon,* 245, 351.

19. Bret J. Cillessen, "Embracing the Bomb: Ethics, Morality, and Nuclear Deterrence in the US AIR FORCE, 1945–1955," 115–20.

20. Tom Englehardt, "The Victors and the Vanquished," in *History Wars: The Enola Gay and Other Battles for the American Past,* ed. Edward T. Linenthal and Tom Englehardt, 235.

21. Lifton and Mitchell, *Hiroshima in America,* 337–40.

22. *Asahi Shimbun,* August 5, 1965.

percentage of Americans to disapprove of the atomic bombings of Hiroshima and Nagasaki.[23] The editorial reflected that the Japanese people had not fulfilled the great responsibility to themselves and to the world to tell the truth about atomic devastation.[24] Japanese remained bitter about atomic bombings.

In Japan, the assertion that the atomic bomb was dropped to end the war quickly was regarded not as a statement of fact or even a historical interpretation but as a moral justification of the act, and as such evoked revulsion. Yamada Setsuo, the mayor of Hiroshima, said in March 1971 that such a statement was "a political utterance, in which there is not one iota of humanity, and the American people must understand this."[25] In August 1983 the well-known Japanologist and former ambassador to Japan, Edwin O. Reischauer, created a furor in Japan by writing in the *Boston Globe* that but for the bomb the Japanese would have "fought on to extinction"; the bomb not only saved millions of lives but also preserved Japan as a nation.[26] The Japanese people overwhelmingly took umbrage, remarking that "even Reischauer," trusted as a friend of Japan, "is justifying the atomic bomb!"[27] To refute Reischauer, Kawaguchi Kazuko, a Sophia University professor, and two other Japanese political scientists, then residing in Boston, interviewed fifteen professors at Harvard, the Massachusetts Institute of Technology, and the Fletcher School of Law and Diplomacy. To their surprise, however, they found that "most of the scholars interviewed seemed to agree with Reischauer and tended to approve of the dropping of the bomb to hasten Japan's surrender." Kawaguchi's reaction is revealing: "I experienced at first a certain amount of culture shock. I recognized how differently the same historical facts could be interpreted by U.S. and Japanese scholars and individuals."[28]

A-Bomb Stamp Controversy

Another example of cognitive dissonance occurred in December 1994, when it was announced that the U.S. Postal Service would issue, as a part of World War II commemorative series, a stamp showing the *Enola Gay*, with

23. Asahi Shimbunsha, ed., *Nihon to Amerika* [Japan and the United States], 430–32; Asahi Shimbunsha Yoron Chōsashitsu, ed., *Shiryō Beikoku ni okeru tai-Nichi yoron chōsa* [U.S. Public Opinion Survey Regarding Japan], 9–10.
24. *Asahi Shimbun*, August 6, 1965.
25. Ibid., March 18, 1971.
26. Reischauer, "Hiroshima Bomb Saved Japan from a Worse Fate." Reischauer repeated the same view in his memoirs, *My Life between Japan and America*, 101.
27. *Asahi Shimbun*, December 16, 1983.
28. Hirose Kazuko et al., "Did Hiroshima Save Japan? 'Reischauer's Interpretation' Reexamined," unpublished manuscript, in the author's possession. Portions of this report were published as Hirose, "Hiroshima wa Nihon o sukutta ka: 'Raishawā kenkai'

the caption, "Atom bombs hasten war's end, August 1945."[29] The design and caption, wrote an American reporter, "irritated the rawest nerve in the Japanese psyche, triggering a shock, anger, outrage," and even a diplomatic incident.[30] Japan's mass media and political leaders, not to mention the mayors of Hiroshima and Nagasaki, joined the nationwide chorus denouncing the stamp as "heartless," saying that it was being used to justify the use of the bomb.[31] But the Japanese were more offended by the caption than by use of the picture of the *Enola Gay*. White House press secretary Dee Dee Myers said that this wording had the president's approval, thus confirming the U.S. government's traditional view. But Japanese newspapers and Hiroshima mayor Hiraoka Takashi asserted that the caption actively endorsed the atomic bombings. For the first time the Japanese government took action, requesting through diplomatic channels that the stamp be withdrawn. After President Bill Clinton made his distaste known, the U.S. Postal Service hastily withdrew the stamp.

A philatelist, I wrote an article on the A-bomb stamp for the *Sankei Shinbun* that stated, "Looking on the bright side, we can say that the flap exposed the extent of the Japan-U.S. gap with regard to the atomic bombings and dramatically underscored the need to bridge it." I urged the Japanese people not to be overemotional, stating that the words on the stamp "represented the consensus general outside Japan."[32] In the United States the withdrawal of the problematic stamp brought forth a few howls of indignation. The *Chicago Tribune* charged that the withdrawal was tantamount to foisting a perversion of history on the United States. The *Houston Post* shrilled that the president had surrendered to Japan—and on Pearl Harbor Day at that. However, most Americans remained levelheaded. "Who wants to send a birthday card with an A-bomb stamp on the envelope?" someone asked.

Changing American Perceptions

It is clear that since the first *Asahi* poll of Americans in 1971, feelings about the bomb remained static until the mid-1990s. In a 1986 poll, 67 percent of

e no Amerika no kyōjutachi no iken" [Did Hiroshima Save Japan? American Professors' Views on the "Reischauer Thesis"], 22–27.

29. A perceptive account on the A-bomb stamp is found in Boyer, "Whose History Is It Anyway?" 117.

30. *Chicago Tribune,* December 2, 1994.

31. This question is treated in the present volume in "The Shock of the Atomic Bomb and Japan's Decision to Surrender—A Reconsideration."

32. *Sankei Shinbun,* December 21, 1994. Its English translation appeared as Asada, "The Flap over A-Bomb Stamp: How the Japanese and American Historical Perceptions Differ," 79.

respondents replied that the bombings could not have been helped, and 24 percent said they were a mistake. Women were slightly more critical than men. Middle-aged and elderly respondents were more likely to approve of the use of the bomb than were the younger participants. Nonwhites were more critical than whites. The generational difference clearly came out in a Harris poll announced in December 1986: in the age bracket of 21–24, those who disapproved of the atomic bombings were 33 percent; for the age group 40–49, only 12 percent disapproved.[33]

A September 1991 survey of Californians showed 60 percent approved of the bombing for ending the war, whereas 28 percent disapproved.[34] Compare this with a poll conducted in both Japan and the United States in December of that same year: as many as 64 percent of Japanese respondents called the bombing a wanton act of mass slaughter, while 29 percent accepted the atomic bombing as a measure for ending the war. The American response was precisely the opposite: 63 percent approved and 29 percent disapproved.

More important, since the 1970s a significant minority of Americans have disapproved of the bombing, and over the years this minority has been on the increase. The 1971 *Asahi* survey found that only about 20 percent of Americans considered the atomic bombing a mistake.[35] But in a *New York Times* poll conducted in November 1991, 39 percent expressed their disapproval.[36]

This trend accelerated in the mid-1990s. As has been mentioned, a Gallup poll from March 1995 showed that while 44 percent of respondents said "they would have dropped the atomic bomb," a larger percentage, 49 percent, would have "tried some other way."[37] In an August 1998 Gallup–*USA Today* survey, half of Americans polled believed that President Truman should have pursued alternatives. Obviously, the American people were having difficulty coming to terms with Hiroshima and Nagasaki toward the end of the century.

Truman and the Japanese

It is significant that the Japanese, especially atomic survivors of the bombings, have tended not to direct resentment toward the American people as

33. *Asahi Shimbun,* December 17, 1986.
34. Ibid., November 3, 1991.
35. Asahi Shimbunsha, ed., *Nihon to Amerika,* 432.
36. The *New York Times*/CBS News/Tokyo Broadcasting System Poll, November 26, 1991.
37. Cited in Bird and Lifschultz, eds., *Hiroshima's Shadow,* xlvi.

a whole but to an individual, President Truman. A 1971 poll by *Chūgoku Shinbun* showed that 31 percent of respondents singled out Truman. As the psychiatrist Robert Lifton has suggested, this may have been "a means of avoiding wider and more malignant forms of hatred."[38] But the Japanese people were baffled, offended, and even outraged by Truman's repeated public disavowals of any remorse. For more than a quarter century, until his death in 1972, he repeated the "Truman orthodoxy" that the bomb was necessary to save American lives. "I never lost any sleep over that decision," he said. When Edward R. Murrow asked him in a February 1958 CBS television interview if he had "Any regrets?" Truman responded, "Not the slightest—not the slightest in the world." He added that to possess a weapon that could win a war but not use it would be foolish. Then Truman made one of the most somber forecasts of his career.[39] Expressing hope that the hydrogen bomb would never be used, he added a warning: "If the world gets into turmoil, it will be used. You can be sure of that."[40]

Truman's statement about the hydrogen bomb enraged the Japanese. The chairman of the Hiroshima City Council denounced the remark as "a gross defilement committed on the people of Hiroshima and their fallen victims."[41] Truman said that the use of the atomic bomb was an "urgent and necessary measure. . . . The need for such a fateful decision, of course, never would have arisen, had we not been shot in the back by Japan at Pearl Harbor in December, 1941." Truman wondered why the citizens of Hiroshima could not understand that wartime Japanese leaders were to blame for the American use of the atomic bomb.[42] The governor of the Hiroshima Prefecture, Ōhara Hiroo, issued his own statement: "At a time when tens of thousands of atomic victims are facing the danger of death, Truman's remark that the hydrogen bomb will be used in case of need is to turn against the public opinion of the world and cannot be forgiven." The Hiroshima City Council was angered that there was no remorse for having killed noncombatants in Hiroshima "solely on account of retributive feelings" about the Pearl Harbor attack.[43]

In his *Memoirs*, published in 1955 and translated into Japanese in 1966, Truman flatly stated, "Let there be no mistake about it. I regarded the bomb

38. Robert J. Lifton, *Death in Life: Survivors of Hiroshima*, 323–24.
39. *Asahi Shimbun*, February 3, 1958. Taking this opportunity, Truman revised sharply downward the numbers of American lives that the use of the atomic bomb might have saved to 250,000. Earlier he had said that the bombs "saved half a million."
40. Ferrell, ed., *Harry S. Truman and the Bomb*, 111.
41. *Asahi Shimbun*, February 14, 1958.
42. Ferrell, ed., *Harry S. Truman and the Bomb*, 113–15; *New York Times*, February 3, 1958; *Asahi Shimbun*, February 3, March 15, April 9, and August 5, 1958.
43. *Chūgoku Shinbun*, February 7, and March 21, 1958.

as a military weapon and never had any doubt that it should be used." He added that under similar circumstances he would do it again.[44]

On May 5, 1964, an occasion arose for visiting atomic survivors to meet with Truman, who was about to celebrate his eightieth birthday, to ascertain his "real feelings" about the bomb. He was to receive the Hiroshima-Nagasaki delegation at the Truman Library in Independence, Missouri. The Japanese world-peace pilgrims had been led by some close to him to believe that Truman would perhaps admit that the bombing was a mistake. Since they had been told that the former president was suffering from a sense of guilt, they were all the more disappointed by his reiteration of the Truman orthodoxy about half a million American lives saved.[45]

Given their national psychology, the Japanese people wanted and waited Truman just to express his *regret*, above anything else. In Japan a sincere apology has a magical power to bring about reconciliation, whereas Americans do not as easily take to apologizing. The Japanese people felt that if there was to be true forgiveness, it behooved Americans, Truman in particular, to take the initiative. For Truman to apologize, however, was out of the question, because it would have meant not only an admission of an official and moral responsibility—culpability—on the part of the U.S. government but also a negation of the policy of nuclear deterrence that underlay its Cold War strategy.

Contrary to his resolute public image, however, Truman was acutely sensitive to the charge of heartlessness. He had written Senator Richard B. Russell on August 9, 1945, the day of the Nagasaki bombing, that "For myself, I certainly regret the necessity of wiping out whole populations because of the 'pig-headedness' of the leaders of a nation." He added, "I also have a human feeling for the women and children in Japan."[46] When Truman issued an order on August 10 not to use a third bomb, he told the cabinet that he "didn't like the idea of killing all those kids."[47] On the following day he wrote Samuel McCrea Cavert, the general secretary of the Federal Council of Churches, "Nobody is more disturbed over the use of atomic bombs."[48]

---

44. *Asahi Shimbun,* February 3, March 14, and April 9, 1958; *Tokyo Shinbun,* February 3, 1958; *Sankei Shinbun,* February 8, 1958; Harry S. Truman, *Memoirs,* 1:419.

45. Chūgoku Shinbunsha, ed., *Honoo no hi kara 20-nen* [Twenty Years since the Day of the Flame], 197.

46. Truman to Russell, August 9, 1945, Official File, box 685, Harry S. Truman Papers, Harry S. Truman Library, Independence, Mo.

47. John Morton Blum, ed., *The Price of Vision: The Diary of Henry A. Wallace, 1942–1946,* 474.

48. Ferrell, ed., *Harry S. Truman and the Bomb,* 72.

In public Truman used to say, "It was just the same as getting a bigger gun than the other fellow had to win a war."[49] Privately, he understood that the atomic bomb had revolutionized warfare and was uneasy about the vast power he had unleashed. When he was informed of the successful test of the bomb in the New Mexico desert while attending the Potsdam Conference on July 25, 1945, he wrote in his diary, "We have discovered the most terrible bomb in the history of the world. It may be the fire destruction prophesied in the Euphrates Valley Era, after Noah and his fabulous Ark."[50]

The Hiroshima–Pearl Harbor Syndrome

For Truman, the stumbling block to any conciliatory gesture toward Japan was the memory of Pearl Harbor. On August 11 he wrote to Cavert, "I was greatly disturbed over the unwarranted attack by the Japanese on Pearl Harbor. The only language they seem to understand is the one that we have been using to bombard them."[51] This motif of revenge had been equally blunt in his statement announcing the dropping of the Hiroshima bomb on August 6, 1945: "Japan started the war at Pearl Harbor; she has been repaid many times over."[52]

The attack on Pearl Harbor and the bombings of Hiroshima and Nagasaki are often equated in the saying, "No More Hiroshimas, But Remember Pearl Harbor!" In the 1986 Harris poll, 43 percent of Americans said they entertained ill feelings about the Pearl Harbor attack.[53] The survey conducted in 1995 by the ABC News Polling Unit and NHK (Japan Broadcasting Corporation) revealed that "despite the passage of time 39 percent of Americans say they feel anger toward the Japanese on account of the Pearl Harbor attack." The persistent ill feelings jumped up to 60 percent among Americans more than sixty years old. This showed the spell cast on Americans by the wartime slogan "Remember Pearl Harbor."[54]

In Japan the outlook is different. The Japanese indignantly reject the "Pearl Harbor–Hiroshima syndrome." To them the atomic annihilation of Hiroshima and Nagasaki by the "absolute weapon" is not in the same category as the raid against warships and army and navy installations at Pearl

---

49. Harry S. Truman, *Truman Speaks: Lectures and Discussions Held at Columbia University on April 27, 28, and 29, 1959*, 93.
50. Robert H. Ferrell, ed., *Off the Record: The Private Papers of Harry S. Truman*, 55–56.
51. Ferrell, ed., *Harry S. Truman and the Bomb*, 72.
52. Ibid., 48.
53. *Asahi Shimbun*, December 17, 1986.
54. Asahi Shimbunsha, *Amerikajin no Nihonkan*, 66; *Asahi Shimbun*, November 3, 1991.

Harbor—these attacks were different not only because of the sheer number of civilian casualties, but also because of the nature and length of the suffering and the symbolic significance for the survival of humankind.[55]

The demand of many Japanese that the United States must apologize for the atomic bombings grew stronger in the 1980s, as Japan became an economic superpower with its attendant nationalism and self-assertive stance in trade conflict with the United States. But, as if to rub it in, Truman's successors have time and again repeated the "Truman orthodoxy." On August 5, 1985, on the fortieth anniversary of Hiroshima, President Ronald Reagan stated in a press interview, "We cannot now say that those who made the solemn decision were foolish." He reiterated the argument of "more than one million American lives saved,"[56] doubling Truman's earlier fatalities estimate.

As one might have expected, the fiftieth anniversary of Pearl Harbor in 1991 once again brought into bold relief the Pearl Harbor–Hiroshima syndrome by raising the question of apology. According to a November 1991 *New York Times* survey, 73 percent of the Japanese respondents said, "the United States government should formally apologize to Japan and its people for dropping the atomic bombs"; but only 16 percent of Americans agreed. The American respondents were asked, "If Japan apologizes for the attack on Pearl Harbor, then do you think the United States government should apologize to Japan for dropping the atomic bombs?" In response, 34 percent said the United States should, while 42 percent replied it should not.[57]

On December 1, 1991, in a televised interview President George H. W. Bush categorically stated he did not intended to apologize. "No apology is required, and it will not be asked of this President, I can guarantee you. I was fighting over there!" (During the Pacific War he was the youngest navy pilot and his torpedo bomber *Barbara* was shot down in 1944 near Chichi Jima in the Bonin Islands.) Dismissing the idea of an apology to Japan as "rank revisionism," Bush said that Truman "made a tough, calculating decision, and it was right, because it spared *millions* of Americans lives."[58] He had thereby increased Truman's estimated number of American casualties tenfold. Again, the Japanese took umbrage at Bush's statement, consider-

55. For a personal exposition of the "Pearl Harbor–Hiroshima syndrome," see Akiba Tadatoshi, *Shinju to sakura* [Pearl and Cherry]; Robert H. Ferrell, ed., *Truman in the White House: The Diary of Eben A. Ayers*, 57.

56. *Sankei Shinbun*, August 6, 1985; *Asahi Shimbun*, August 6, 1985 (evening edition).

57. The *New York Times*/CBS News/Tokyo Broadcasting System Poll, November 26, 1991.

58. USIS Press Office, December 2, 1991 (italics added); *New York Times*, December 2, 1991; *Asahi Shimbun*, December 2 (evening edition), and December 6, 1991; *Mainichi Shinbun*, December 2, 1991; *Nikkei Shinbun*, December 2, 1991 (evening edition); *Sankei Shinbun*, December 2 (evening edition), and December 3, 1991.

ing it to be just another American "justification." Hiroshima's atomic survivors said that President Bush "failed to understand the historic meaning of the atomic bombing." There were sit-ins in front of the cenotaph in Hiroshima's Peace Park.[59]

The Pearl Harbor–Hiroshima syndrome surfaced again in June 1994 when Emperor Akihito took a two-week tour of the United States. His original itinerary, submitted to Washington, had included a stopover at the USS *Arizona* Memorial at Pearl Harbor. However, it was canceled because of a domestic backlash from Diet members who questioned why the emperor must apologize for Pearl Harbor when no American president had visited and apologized for Hiroshima and Nagasaki.[60]

A reiteration of the "Truman orthodoxy" came again when President Clinton in April 1995 stated that "the United States owes no apology to Japan for having dropped the atomic bombs." Concerning President Truman's decision to use the bomb, Clinton carefully chose his words and said, "Based on the facts he had before him," Truman's decision was the right one for ending the war. As was expected, Japanese political leaders were sharply critical of Clinton's "justification," and Hiroshima's mayor, Hiraoka Takashi, accused him of "following the idea of successive presidents."[61]

The question of apology, involving the cultural gulf separating the two nations, has never been solved.

Paul Tibbets Reenacting Hiroshima

In all of this there was the behavior of Colonel Paul Tibbets, the pilot of the *Enola Gay*, who continued to arouse the Japanese press. The first brush was an air show in Texas in October 1976, staged by a group calling itself the Confederate Air Force, in which Tibbets flew the last air-worthy B-29 bomber and simulated the dropping of the mock atomic bomb, as eighteen thousand spectators looked on. The Japanese were quick to take offense. A leader of a *hibakusha* association in Hiroshima denounced Tibbets's stunt, saying that "We cannot forgive an attempt to reenact 'that moment' by a mockery." Hiroshima mayor Araki Takeshi sent telegrams protesting the air show to Tibbets and the show's sponsors: "To make a show of the atomic

---

59. *Chūgoku Shinbun*, December 2 (evening edition), and December 3 and 4, 1991.

60. Only two presidents have visited Hiroshima, though they did so either before or after being elected to office. Nixon visited Hiroshima during a tour of Japan in 1964. Jimmy Carter stopped in Hiroshima during the late 1980s on one of his many trips to Japan.

61. *Asahi Shimbun*, April 8 (evening edition) and 18, 1995; *Japan Times*, April 9, 1995.

bombing is a defilement of those unnumbered victims who were killed or are still suffering from the aftereffects of this inhumane act." The mayors of Hiroshima and Nagasaki, the Foreign Ministry, and *hibakusha* associations sent telegrams to President Gerald Ford, demanding that the U.S. government make the sponsors of the air show apologize for their act.[62] The sponsors in Texas flatly refused to apologize, justifying the bombing of Hiroshima and Nagasaki.

In response to a Japanese interviewer, Tibbets stated that he simply could not understand why a reenactment of a historic scene was defilement of the dead. He added that he had never lost sleep over having commanded the plane that dropped the atomic bomb.[63] The Japanese critics pointed out that obeying the wartime order to drop the bomb was one thing, reenacting it in a mock show just for amusement quite another.[64] Although the U.S. government expressed regret, the sponsors of the A-bomb air show went ahead with it.[65]

In September of the following year the Confederate Air Force again planned an air show that included a mock atomic bombing. This time Congress, the State Department, and the Defense Department pressured its sponsors to cancel it, "for fear of adversely influencing relations with an allied nation."[66] The Confederate Air Force finally acquiesced, but Tibbets flew the B-29 in the show.

When Tibbets was defending his atomic bombing of Hiroshima, Senator Mike Gravel, a leading "dove" in the Vietnam War and one of the leaders most concerned about nuclear weapons, was visiting Hiroshima and meeting its *hibakusha*. He apologized for Tibbets's behavior in the Texas air show. Emphatically, he urged the need to eradicate nuclear weapons from the face of the earth. By saying "Hiroshima is my spiritual constituency," he won the hearts of atomic victims.[67]

There were moves in the United States to express sincere regrets over Hiroshima and Nagasaki. A leading liberal senator, Mark Hatfield, on the occasion of ratification of SALT II (1979), gave his eyewitness account before the Senate Foreign Relations Committee of what he had seen in Hiroshima in September 1945. Hatfield, a lieutenant junior grade in the U.S. Navy, was one of the first to enter Hiroshima as a member of U.S. occupation troops. "What I saw that day in Hiroshima was not something I could understand with my

62. *Asahi Shimbun*, October 12, 13, and 14 (evening edition), 1976.
63. Ibid., October 16, 1976 (evening edition).
64. *Chugoku Shinbun*, October 11, 1976.
65. Ibid., October 14, 1976.
66. Ibid., September 3 and 30, 1977.
67. *Asahi Shimbun*, November 8, 1976.

mind and heart. As far as I could see, everything had been indiscriminately destroyed." He stated that if the United States were to use all its strategic nuclear warheads in its possession, it could demolish 246,000 Hiroshimas.[68] The atomic devastation he had witnessed in Hiroshima would be "a mere firework in comparison with the destructive power we now possess."[69]

The "Atomic Diplomacy" Thesis in Japan

Thus far we have compared Japanese and American perceptions of the decision to use the atomic bomb in simple terms of approval or disapproval. But the reasons that have been attributed to the decision had much to do with the way the Japanese and Americans have reacted to it. Without going into the familiar historiographical controversy, we may simply identify two schools of interpretations.[70] One is the so-called orthodox school, led by the late Herbert Feis, a noted diplomatic historian, who argued that the bomb was dropped for military reasons, to force a prompt Japanese surrender.[71] The other is "Cold War revisionism," led by the New Left historian Gar Alperovitz, who claimed that the bomb was used to intimidate the Soviet Union in the emerging Cold War.[72] The thesis of his *Atomic Diplomacy* gained popularity among Americans as the anti-Vietnam War movement mounted.

My own view is close to that of Barton J. Bernstein, who maintains that the United States dropped the bombs primarily to hasten the end of the war, but that the bombs had the "bonus effect" of pressuring the Soviet Union.[73] But atomic diplomacy or no atomic diplomacy, my understanding is that President Truman's policy was to end the war as soon as possible with the least sacrifice to American lives.

The atomic diplomacy thesis has carried much appeal in Japan. This is not because Alperovitz's *Atomic Diplomacy* has been widely read,[74] but because P. M. S. Blackett's book, which preempted Alperovitz's main thrust,

68. In 1995 Robert S. McNamara wrote, "Today, there are 40,000–50,000 nuclear warheads in the world, with a total destructive power more than one million times greater than that of the bomb that flattened Hiroshima" (*In Retrospect: The Tragedy and Lessons of Vietnam*, 337).

69. *Asahi Shimbun*, September 19, 1979 (evening edition).

70. See Walker, "Decision to Use the Bomb: A Historiographical Update," 97–114.

71. Feis, *Japan Subdued*; Feis, *Atomic Bomb and the End of World War II*.

72. See Alperovitz's *Atomic Diplomacy*.

73. Asada, "Reisen no kigen to shūseishugi kenkyū—Amerika no baai" [The Origins of the Cold War and Revisionist Studies in the United States], 170.

74. Alperovitz, *Decision to Use the Atomic Bomb*.

was translated in 1951 and has been very popular among Japanese intellectuals, especially those on the left.[75] A British physicist, Nobel laureate, and political radical, Blackett presented his 1949 book as a mere "hypothesis." In the United States his book was angrily dismissed by reviewers and was totally ignored. But many Japanese intellectuals have accepted Blackett as an oracle.

There have been few public opinion surveys regarding the reasons that the bombs were dropped. Therefore, I conducted four surveys of undergraduates at Doshisha University (in January 1976, December 1991, June 1994, and November 2005). Students were asked, "What do you think were the reasons for dropping the atomic bomb?" Supplying seven reasons in my questionnaires, I asked the respondents to rank them in order of importance. The most frequently chosen reasons were political considerations vis-à-vis the Soviet Union: "To pressure the Soviet Union by a demonstration of power" and "to end the war against Japan before the Soviet Union could enter it."

How can we account for Japanese students' preference for the atomic diplomacy thesis? One obvious answer, already mentioned, is the influence of Blackett's *Fear, War, and the Bomb*. In point of fact, these students were exposed to the Blackett theory in their junior high school textbooks. The atomic diplomacy thesis began to appear in Japanese history texts in the 1960s and continued to dominate them. A typical passage read, "as the Soviet Union's entry into war became imminent, the United States dropped the atomic bomb to gain supremacy over the Soviet Union after the war."[76]

Among widely read books on contemporary Japanese history, *Shōwashi* [A History of the Shōwa Period] by Tōyama Shigeki and others approvingly quoted from Blackett.[77] In a similar vein, in *Taiheiyō sensō-shi* [A History of the Pacific War], a group of left-wing historians charged, "*500,000 citizens* [of Hiroshima and Nagasaki] were utterly meaninglessly sacrificed for America's cruel political purposes." Here, the sense of victimization takes command over rational analysis, especially in the number of the alleged dead.[78]

To cite another example, the historian Nishijima Ariatsu's frequently quoted book, *Gembaku wa naze tōka saretaka?* recapitulated Blackett's thesis, arguing that "the most important thing" was that Hiroshima-Nagasaki residents were "killed as human guinea pigs for the sake of [America's] anti-

75. For an early citation from Blackett, see Osada Arata, "Genshi bakudan wa naze tōka saretaka" [Why Were the Atomic Bombs Dropped?], 181, which appeared in 1953.

76. We shall cite only the representative texts: Kodama et al., *Chūgaku shakai: Rekishiteki bun'ya*, 297; Kawata et al., *Atarashii shakai: Rekishi*, 24; Blackett, *Fear, War, and the Bomb*, 127.

77. Tōyama, Imai, and Fujiwara, *Shōwashi*, 366.

78. Rekishigaku Kenkyūkai, comp., *Taiheiyō sensōshi*, 5:363–66 (italics added).

Communist, hegemonic policy." He stressed that the atomic bombing of Hiroshima and Nagasaki did not result from the Pacific War but rather from America's own global anti-Soviet policy, concluding with a political appeal that "the deaths and sufferings of the atomic devastation, caused by the cruelty of [American] imperialism, were in vain and that cognizance of this fact must be the starting point for any anti-nuclear movement in Japan."[79] Such a reasoning gave no comfort to atomic victims and only fanned anti-American sentiment.

The above is not to say that Japanese historical scholarship is dominated by the atomic diplomacy thesis. Although perhaps more than half of general historians unthinkingly subscribe to this thesis, specialists in diplomatic history are fully au courant with ongoing research in the United States. Historians Yamagiwa Akira and Tachibana Seiitsu edited and translated into Japanese a massive documentary volume on the Manhattan Project, which is based on extensive archival research.[80] But Japanese scholars have had a hard time countering the atomic diplomacy thesis, which prevails in the mass media.

For example, in serialized articles on the atomic bomb an *Asahi* reporter stated in 1975, "It is now a commonly accepted view that the real purpose of the United States in dropping the atomic bombs was not so much to force Japan's surrender as to coerce the Soviet Union."[81] The atomic diplomacy thesis even found its way into the most complete scientific study on the subject, *Hiroshima-Nagasaki no gembaku saigai* [Disasters of Hiroshima and Nagasaki], prepared under the sponsorship of the two battered cities in 1979.[82] It included the following passage: "The atomic bombings were needed not so much against Japan—already on the brink of surrender and no longer capable of mounting an effective counteroffensive—as to establish clearly America's post-war international position and strategic supremacy in the anticipated Cold War setting." An American reviewer critically commented that the study "clings to the questionable theory that the attacks were mainly intended to awe Joseph Stalin and the Soviet Union."[83]

---

79. Nishijima, *Gembaku wa naze tōka saretaka*, 383; Nishijima Ariatsu, "Nihon kōfuku no sekaishiteki haikei" [The World Historical Background of Japan's Surrender], 103.

80. Yamagiwa and Tachibana, eds., *Shiryō Manhattan keikaku*.

81. *Asahi Shimbun*, July 30, 1975.

82. Hiroshimashi-Nagasakishi Gembaku Saigaishi Henshū Iinkai [Committee for the Compilation of Materials on the Damage Caused by the Atomic Bombs in Hiroshima and Nagasaki], ed., *Hiroshima-Nagasaki no gembaku saigai*, 411–12, quotes from Blackett and Nishijima. The English translation of this work is *Hiroshima and Nagasaki: The Physical, Medical, and Social Effects of the Atomic Bombings*.

83. *Time*, August 17, 1981, 56.

It is important, however, to bear in mind that the atomic diplomacy thesis that has dominated in the press and academia has not reached the grass
roots. As *Asahi*'s large-scale poll of 1975 revealed, only 13 percent of respondents believed that the bomb was dropped to "assure America's superior
position vis-à-vis the Soviet Union in the postwar world."[84]

This notwithstanding, Japanese textbook writers, left-wing historians,
peace activists, and the media continue to quote from Blackett's 1949 book,
a book that did not even pretend to be a work of historical scholarship. One
explanation may be that dissociating the atomic bomb from the Pacific War
helps extricate the Japanese from the moral symmetry of the Pearl Harbor-
Hiroshima syndrome and tips the balance in their favor. While the atomic
diplomacy thesis heightens their sense of victimization, it accords with
Japanese unwillingness to come to grips with their responsibility for and
the consequences of the war. Suffering from what is sometimes called "historical amnesia," the Japanese are reluctant to view the atomic bomb in the
context of the Pacific War. They often assert that their country was already
prostrate and on the verge of surrender when the United States dropped
the bombs. Have they forgotten that their military leaders had vowed to
fight to the death against the invading American forces?

Thus viewed, the popularity of the atomic diplomacy thesis among the
Japanese people has a great deal to do with their unwillingness to come to
terms with the Pacific War. Ironically, Mayor Hiraoka of Hiroshima, who had
emphasized the importance of reflecting on Japan's wartime record, made
a statement in his speech at the City University of New York in April 1993
blaming the United States for having dropped the bomb "to maintain its
supremacy in the postwar world."[85] This kind of uninformed talk from the
mayor of Hiroshima makes the city's appeal to world peace less credible.

The Racial Factor and the A-bomb

Racism toward Asians often enters into Japanese discussions about the
factors that influenced the decision to use the atomic bomb,[86] and on college campuses much credence is given to this racial interpretation. In our

---

84. *Asahi Shimbun*, July 23, 1975; *Chūgoku Shinbun*, July 23, 1971.
85. *Chūgoku Shinbun*, April 24, 1993.
86. In other parts of the world, especially in Asia, the atomic bomb had come to be
seen as a racist instrument. The impression was developing, Saudi Arabia's UN delegate told Eleanor Roosevelt, that the bomb was intended to use against "colored people." Indian prime minister Jawaharlal Nehru warned of the "widespread feeling in Asia
that the atomic bomb is a weapon used only against Asiatics" (Gaddis, *Long Peace*, 119).

surveys of 1976, 1991, and 1994, as many as 50.5 percent, 44.7 percent, and 49.6 percent of respondents at Doshisha University respectively replied that "even if the atomic bomb had been completed while war against Germany was still continuing, the United States would *not* have used it in Germany." According to a joint poll conducted by the *New York Times*, CBS News, and Tokyo Broadcasting System in 1985, 33 percent of Japanese agreed with the proposition that the United States was willing to drop the bomb because Japan is nonwhite. (Among Americans only 7 percent disagreed.)[87]

The racial interpretation made its first appearance at the dawn of the atomic age. As early as August 14, 1945, the day *before* Japan's surrender, a respected legal authority, Kiyose Ichirō, wrote that "Americans regard the Japanese as an alien and inferior people and little more than apes, so this racial prejudice explains why they cruelly used the atomic bomb on Japan."[88]

Because this racial interpretation has become more pronounced since the mid-1960s, it seems to represent an extrapolation backward of the perception in Japan that American policies and actions in Vietnam had definite racist overtones—the My Lai massacre of 1968 and the bombing of hospitals, schools, civilian centers, and other reported instances of racial brutalities in Vietnam.[89]

The more extreme of Japanese polemicists have approvingly quoted Noam Chomsky, an American linguist and radical thinker, on "official racism" associating the policy of "genocide" in Vietnam with the nuclear "holocausts" of Hiroshima and Nagasaki; both, they claimed, stemmed from the same racist attitude of treating Asians as "less than human beings."[90] In the above cited book Nishijima stated that the Hiroshima-Nagasaki victims and Vietnam War victims were "two of a kind."[91]

Interestingly, the United States government was sensitive to the fact that in other parts of the world, especially in Asia, the atomic bombing of Hiroshima and Nagasaki was seen as a racial instrument. This awareness had a restraining influence on the use of nuclear weapons in Korea, Dien Bien Phu, and the Taiwan Strait. As John L. Gaddis observes, "one can hardly deny the clearly devastating effect their use once again against Asians would have on the American position in that part of the world."[92]

87. *New York Times*, August 6, 1985.

88. *Asahi Shimbun*, August 14, 1945.

89. Even the respected Japanologist at Yale University, John W. Hall, wrote, "What are the racial implications of Hiroshima and Nagasaki?" ("Pearl Harbor Thirty Years After—Reflections on the Pathology of War and Nationalism," 12).

90. Chomsky, "On War Crimes," 298–99; Honda Katsuichi, *Korosareru gawa no ronri* [The Logic of Being Killed], 17, 33, 156.

91. Nishijima, *Gembaku wa naze tōka saretaka*, 384.

92. Gaddis, *Long Peace*, 119, 142.

Significantly, one of the strongest denials of the racial interpretation for the atomic bombings came from Brigadier General Leslie R. Groves, the chief of the Manhattan Project, who gave an interview to a *Sankei Shinbun* reporter on Veterans Day (November 11) in 1968. He said he was making an important statement so that future historians would not misunderstand why the United States decided to use the atomic bomb against Japan.

> There are those who say the United States harbored racial prejudices because it used the atomic bomb on Japan but not on Germany. From the beginning, however, the United States made preparations to use the atomic bomb on Germany but did not do so because the war in Europe came to an end.[93]

As evidence, Groves recalled the meeting he and Secretary of War Henry L. Stimson had with President Roosevelt in the White House on December 30, 1944. Discouraged by the setback in the Battle of the Bulge, Roosevelt told Groves that he thought the war might be prolonged and that "we should be prepared to use the bomb against Germany." The evidence that the United States would have used the atomic bomb against Germany—which is what the U.S. intended to do in the first place—is compelling.

There is no doubt that Truman made his decision in a wartime climate saturated with crudely racist portrayals of the Japanese as subhuman monsters or vermin, as historian John W. Dower has shown in his 1986 book, *War without Mercy: Race and Power in the Pacific War.*[94] Yet it is difficult to find any direct evidence linking such pervasive racism to the specific decision to drop the atomic bombs on Japan. One might detect racial nuances in Truman's statement a few days after Nagasaki: "When you have to deal with a beast you have to treat him as a beast."[95] But this hardly substantiates the racial interpretation.

On the other hand, Stimson—an admirer of Japanese culture who loved Kyoto—was hardly a crude racist in the summer of 1945. On the contrary, he wrote in an important memorandum to Truman on July 2:

> I think she [Japan] has within her population enough liberal leaders (although now submerged by the terrorists) to be depended upon for her reconstruction as a responsible member of the family of nations. I think

---

93. *Sankei Shinbun,* November 11, 1968.
94. Dower's *War without Mercy* is silent on the racial implications of the atomic bombing of Japan.
95. Cited in Barton J. Bernstein, "Roosevelt, Truman, and the Atomic Bomb," 61.

she is *better in this last respect than Germany* was. Her liberals yielded only at the point of the pistol.[96]

According to a 1991 poll conducted by the *New York Times*, 38 percent of the Japanese respondents but only 8 percent of the Americans supported the racial interpretation.[97] In 1994 the curators of the Smithsonian were roundly criticized for implying in their script that racism motivated the use of the atomic bomb on Japan.[98] In Japan, as the survey of Doshisha University students would seem to indicate, the racial interpretation is gradually losing support as memories of the Vietnam War fade. (Those who registered opposition to the racial interpretation were 17 percent in 1976, 30.8 percent in 1991, and 31.3 percent in 1994.)

The Human Guinea-Pig Interpretation

A corollary of the racial interpretation is the "human guinea-pig theory." The establishment of the Atomic Bomb Casualty Commission in Hiroshima by the U.S. government at the beginning of 1947 gave this concept wide currency. The commission collected scientific data about the victims of the atomic bomb attacks but never gave them medical attention,[99] creating an impression that it was treating these patients as experimental objects. The human guinea-pig theory has been surprisingly persistent in Japan. As late as 1999, the former director of the Hiroshima Peace Museum, Takahashi Akihiro, wrote,

The use of the atomic bomb was obviously a human experiment. The strategy of the United States was to drop a uranium bomb on Hiroshima and then a plutonium bomb on Nagasaki, to test which type of bomb had more destructive power, and to use the results to develop the nuclear weapon, so that the United States would obtain supremacy over the Soviet Union.[100]

96. *FRUS*, 1:891 (italics added).

97. The *New York Times* / CBS News / Tokyo Broadcasting System Poll, November 26, 1991.

98. National Air and Space Museum, Smithsonian Institution, "The Crossroads: The End of World War II, the Atomic Bomb, and the Origins of the Cold War," 1994, printed in Philip Nobile, ed., *Judgment at Smithsonian*, 1–126.

99. All the data gathered by ABCC were brought back to the United States and were not shared with Japanese medical researchers.

100. Takahashi, "Fukugan de miru genbaku higai to sensō kagai" [Dual Perspective: Atomic Devastations], 7:391.

From England, Bertrand Russell—a Nobel laureate, a famous philosopher, and an anti-Vietnam activist—argued, "The use of two different kinds of atomic bombs on the two cities suggests a calculated experimentation, at the cost of thousands of lives."[101] Behind the atomic bombings of Hiroshima and Nagasaki, Russell stated, was American racism that regarded the Japanese as less than human. More recently, the human guinea-pig theory was given voice by Mayor Hiraoka of Hiroshima, who, in his 1993 address at the City University of New York, stated the United States was responsible for dropping bombs for the sake of human experiment.[102] On August 6, 1994—the forty-ninth anniversary of the Hiroshima bombing—the Japan Congress against Atomic and Hydrogen Bombs (led by the Japan Socialist Party) adopted a public appeal that the atomic bombings had been "an experiment on human bodies."[103]

Japanese Textbooks: Rote Memory

Sheila K. Johnson, a cultural anthropologist knowledgeable about Japan, wrote in 1975 that as the World War II generation dies off, "the number of Americans who believe the use of the atomic bomb on Japan to have been 'necessary and proper' will continue to diminish." This seems to be precisely what is gradually happening today.[104]

Frances FitzGerald, who has made a useful study of secondary schoolbooks in American history, points out that it is often the version of events presented in history textbooks that students remember for the rest of their lives.[105] Japanese textbooks fail miserably in comparison.

During the occupation, the subject of the atomic bomb was not allowed to appear in textbooks, but as soon as Japan regained independence in 1952 a rich variety of excerpts from "A-bomb literature," written by *hibakusha*, found their way into schoolbooks. These books also contained statistics on damages and casualties and photographs of mushroom clouds and atomic desolation.[106] But after 1961, reflecting the Education Ministry's tightening authorization policy, the coverage of Hiroshima and Nagasaki dwindled,

101. Russell, *War Crimes in Vietnam*, 20.
102. *Chūgoku Shinbun*, April 24, 1993.
103. *Asahi Shimbun*, August 6, 1994 (evening edition).
104. Johnson, *American Attitudes toward Japan*, 45.
105. FitzGerald, *America Revised: History Schoolbooks in the Twentieth Century*.
106. Ishida Akira, "Sengo kyōiku ni okeru 'Genbaku mondai' no ketsujo" [The "Atomic Bomb Question" Missing in Postwar Education], 13; Ishida, *Hibaku kyōshi* [A-Bombed Teacher], 215–29; Ishida, *Chūtō shakaika* [Junior High School Social Studies], 74–76.

from several pages to just a few *lines* in extreme instances.[107] The treatment of the bomb in high school history textbooks (1965, 1985, 1990) was almost perfunctory. The briefest textbook accounts laconically stated, "In August 1945 atomic bombs were dropped on Hiroshima and then on Nagasaki,"[108] without even saying which country had dropped the bombs or mentioning the scale of destruction and human suffering.[109] (It is no wonder that 20 percent of primary and junior high school students, polled in 1969 and 1970, did not know that the United States had dropped the atomic bombs on Hiroshima and Nagasaki.[110]) And the generation of teachers who were atomic victims disappeared from the classroom.

The schoolbooks lacked intellectual content and a call to moral reflection, indicating how effective the government's authorization and self-censorship were. (The policy of the Education Ministry until very recently has been to downplay the horrors of war, including the atomic bombings.[111]) Students were required to memorize bare facts. Strikingly lacking were efforts to make the students think for themselves and discuss different perspectives. Meanwhile, students were getting their information about the atomic bomb from comic books.[112]

In 1980–1981, educational experts and editors of schoolbooks undertook a joint "Japanese-American project on social studies textbooks." The American members pointed out that Japanese texts "omit all explanations of the ethical and moral significance of the atomic bombing,"[113] and they questioned the atomic diplomacy thesis. Japanese textbooks seemed almost devoid of nationality.

The textbooks being used in Japanese classrooms today have improved, although they are still far from satisfactory. The interpretations in better schoolbooks are eclectic, combining "orthodox" and "revisionist" interpretations:

> The United States in an attempt to minimize military damages, obtain supremacy in the postwar world, and force Japan to surrender before the Soviet Union entered the war against Japan, dropped the atomic bomb on

107. *Asahi Shimbun*, July 27 and August 2, 1970.

108. Nakamura Hidekazu et al., *Sekaishi* [World History], 330; Besshi Atsuhiko, *Sensō no oshiekata: Sekai no kyōkasho ni miru* [How to Teach about War: Textbooks around the World], 131–32.

109. *Nagasaki Shinbun*, July 20, 1977.

110. *Asahi Shimbun*, May 27 and August 5, 27, 1970.

111. Ienaga Saburō, "The Glorification of War in Japanese Education," passim.

112. *Mainichi Shinbun*, August 2, 1970.

113. Kyōkasho kenkyū sentā, *Shakaika kyōkasho no Nichi-Bei hikaku* [Comparison of Japanese and American Social Studies Textbooks], 59.

Hiroshima on 6 August which killed about 120,000 persons. On the 8th the Soviet Union declared war against Japan, and on the 9th the United States dropped the atomic bomb in Nagasaki, destroying 70,000 persons.[114]

American Textbooks: The Decision-Making Approach

How do American textbooks fare? They devote far more space than do Japanese schoolbooks to the atomic bombing of the two cities.[115] But until well into the 1970s their treatments of the bombings were, with a few outstanding exceptions, dull and monotonic recitations of facts. Perhaps not surprisingly, only 44 percent of American high school students knew that the United States had bombed Hiroshima and Nagasaki, according to the *Washington Post*. Similarly, the survey conducted by Akiba Tadatoshi, then associate professor at Tufts University (and present mayor of Hiroshima), revealed that about one-half of high school students did not know about the atomic bombings.[116]

As early as 1971 the great historian Richard Hofstadter in collaboration with Clarence L. Ver Steeg had written a critical textbook, *A People and a Nation*. The authors asked, "Which would you choose, military advantages and the loss of confidence in the United States or a feeling of horror relative to the use of the bomb? Was that the only choice connected with the decision regarding the use of the bomb?" Hofstadter and Ver Steeg wrote, "Many persons have wondered whether it was really necessary to drop a first and then even a second atomic bomb on Japan. Certainly the decision to use this weapon was among the major tragedies of history."[117] In textbooks in the 1980s, there was an increased emphasis on the ethical implications of the atomic bombing. Lew Smith, in *American Dream* (1983), asked, "And what of the moral dilemma of the United States which had developed and used the atomic bomb?"[118]

114. Sanseidō, *Shōkai Nihonshi B, kaiteiban* [Detailed Japanese History: B, Revised], 316; Sanseidō, *Nihonshi A* [Japanese History A], 124. *Nihonshi B* [Japanese History B] states that the United States dropped the atomic bomb "in order to secure leadership in postwar [international politics] and force Japan to surrender before the Soviet entry into the war" (336).

115. Carol Berkin, Robert A. Divine, Alan Brinkley, and others, *American Voices: A History of the United States*, 649–65; Henry W. Bragdon, Samuel P. McCutchen, and Donald A. Ritchie, *History of a Free Nation*, 875–76.

116. *Chūgoku Shinbun*, February 21, 1984, and August 6, 1980.

117. Ver Steeg and Hofstadter, *A People and A Nation*, v, 710, 711.

118. Smith, *American Dream*, 557–59.

Then, almost suddenly, in the early 1990s new and exciting textbooks began to appear. How can we account for this? My explanation is that as the Cold War was ending so was the "Cold War consensus" of history. This released a variety of perspectives that enriched American schoolbooks. While about half of the textbooks still subscribe to the "Truman orthodoxy," the better ones tend to show a liberal outlook; in fact, they almost lean over backward to include alternative revisionist interpretations for student discussion. For example, Paul Boyer, in his *Todd and Curti's American Nation* (1994), maintains that some historians have suggested that the Japanese were desperately seeking to end the war in the summer of 1945, that the war could have been won without nuclear weapons and without an invasion of Japan, and that Truman and his advisers wanted to demonstrate the power of atomic weapons to the Soviet Union.[119] Boyer's *The American Nation* (1998) contains an even more explicit citation from the Blackett-Alperovitz thesis.[120] As I have made clear, I do not agree with the atomic diplomacy thesis, but I am in favor of introducing it for student discussion.

Gary B. Nash's *American Odyssey* (1991) asked students to consider a variety of opinions expressed during the summer of 1945: first, Henry Stimson's argument for the use of the bomb; second, Supreme Allied commander General Dwight D. Eisenhower's alleged statement to Stimson that "It wasn't necessary to hit them [the Japanese] with that awful thing"[121]; third, Undersecretary of the Navy Ralph A. Bard's opposition to the use of the atomic bomb because of humanitarian reasons; and fourth, Chicago physicists' opposition on the ground of world public opinion and the fear of starting an arms race. Students were required to discuss the "conflict in values" found in these quotations.

The 1999 edition of Nash's textbook presented five "options" that President Truman had to consider and asked the students to judge whether the bombings were "unnecessary, even immoral" and whether Truman and his advisers were "naïve" and failed to take into account the long-term effects of dropping the bomb, such as the arms race and the Cold War.[122] The decision-making approach, already suggested in Nash's textbook, found its most explicit formulation as a teaching tool in John A. Garraty's *Story of America* (1994).[123] This work asks students to consider whether

---

119. Boyer, *Todd and Curti's American Nation*, 769.

120. Boyer, *The American Nation*, 769.

121. Eisenhower did not actually say this (Robert Maddox, *Weapons for Victory: The Hiroshima Decision Fifty Years Later*, 121–22).

122. Gary B. Nash, *American Odyssey: The United States in the Twentieth Century*, 415–21.

123. Garraty, *Story of America*, 972–73.

Truman made the correct decision. Overall, perhaps the best account of the Manhattan Project and the decision to drop the bomb is in *America: Pathways to the Present* (the 1995 edition) by Andrew Clayton, Elisabeth Israels Perry, and Allan M. Winkler—this is not surprising since Winkler had written a fine book on America's nuclear anxiety.[124] After ritualistically asking whether atomic diplomacy and racism were possible factors in the atomic bombing, the book offers a model treatment of "the lasting impact of the Atomic Bomb."[125]

Pervading these liberal textbooks is a genuine lamentation over the Japanese lives lost in atomic bombings. Several textbooks ponder how mankind can control this absolute weapon and avoid future war, a war that would spell the end of civilization. What characterizes American textbooks is their variety, richness, vividness, and, above all, critical viewpoints that stand in sharp contrast to drab Japanese textbooks. It is these textbooks that will to a large extent shape the perceptions of young Americans. As far as text-books are concerned, then, it appears that Americans are doing a much better job of educating their school-age children about the atomic bomb than the Japanese are.[126] And this has already had definite effects on the perceptions of the younger generation in the United States, as we shall shortly see.

Smithsonian Controversy

The Smithsonian controversy has produced an avalanche of books, and it will not be necessary to dwell on it. Only salient points related to the perceptions of the atomic bomb will be briefly noted here.

The scripts of the National Air and Space Museum were similar to the liberal interpretations that had appeared in the better high school textbooks. But by injecting Alperovitz's "atomic diplomacy" thesis and early-surrender scenarios, the curators shifted the ground to revisionism.[127] The script took every opportunity to suggest alternative interpretations and raise doubts about "orthodox" views. It is unfortunate that in planning for the exhibit Michael Neufeld, the curator in charge, found "particularly helpful" J. Samuel Walker's 1990 historiographical article that declared, "The consensus among scholars is that the bomb was not needed to avoid any invasion of Japan and to end the war within a relatively short time. It is clear that

124. See Winkler, *Life under a Cloud*. Its Japanese translation by Asada appeared in 1999.
125. Clayton, Perry, and Winkler, *America: Pathways to the Present*, 682–87.
126. Of course, textbooks are not the only media used in Japanese schools: Japanese children are often taken on school trips to Hiroshima or Nagasaki.
127. Nobile, *Judgment at the Smithsonian*, 41.

alternatives to the bomb existed and that Truman and his advisors knew it."[128] In actuality, no such "consensus" exists among historians. Walker's habit of imposing "consensus" and his pleas for "a centrist view" can have stifling effects on lively historical exchanges.[129]

It was not so much historical details but the total concept of the exhibit that infuriated veterans. Veterans demanded it focus on how heroically they fought the Pacific War and on how the atomic bomb saved hundreds of thousands of American lives. Instead, the NASM's scripts concentrated on the atomic slaughter of noncombatants and the origins of the Cold War, in which America's future was under a cloud. In short, the veterans reacted so strongly because the Smithsonian went against their memory of the "Good War," the Norman Rockwell image. As Robert J. Lifton and Greg Mitchell noted, after years of refusing to look in the face of the human devastation of the atomic bomb—a collective form of "psychic numbness"—any reopening of the scar would have made Americans uneasy.

My greatest criticism was directed at both the curators and the historians on the advisory board of the NASM for their America-centered parochialism. They almost completely ignored the Japanese situation—Tokyo's badly divided government; the intransigence, fanaticism, and even irrationality of Japan's military leaders; and the powerlessness of the "peace party." Thus the curators argued about whether the United States could have induced Japan to surrender earlier, but Japanese documents clearly show that diplomatic settlement was simply not in the cards. None of the historians consulted by the NASM had expertise on the end of the Pacific War. The curators should have tapped the brains of experts, starting perhaps with Robert Butow who is still actively writing.[130]

If I had been consulted by the Smithsonian, I would have advised roughly as follows: (1) Japanese military leaders were driven by a fanaticism that cried for a decisive battle and certain death in the mainland struggle; (2) given their intransigence, even irrationality, there were few, if any, "missed opportunities" for earlier peace, and the alternatives available to President Truman were severely limited; and (3) an assurance of constitutional monarchy would not have satisfied Japan because its military leaders absolutely insisted on three additional conditions (no military occupation, demobilization, and prosecution of war criminals by the Japanese).

128. Walker, "Decision to Use The Bomb: An Historiographical Update," 110; Heinrichs, "*Enola Gay* and Contested Public Memory."

129. Walker, "Recent Literature on Truman's Atomic Bomb Decision: A Search for Middle Ground," 333–34.

130. Butow, *Japan's Decision to Surrender.*

Truman and his principal advisers believed the shock of the atomic bomb was necessary to force Japan to promptly surrender. In the end, Japan needed "external pressure" in the form of two bombs to decide to surrender. If the atomic bombs had not been dropped on Hiroshima and Nagasaki, it is possible that far greater sacrifices would have likely resulted on both the American and the Japanese sides on account of the Allied landings in Japan scheduled for November 1, a tightened blockade, and intensified conventional bombings.

Yet, it is difficult to morally justify the killing of hundreds of thousands of noncombatants, and here is a moral dilemma from which policy makers were unable to escape. The great American theologian Reinhold Niebuhr once wrote, "Politics will, to the end of history, be an area where conscience and power meet, where the ethical and coercive factors of human life will interpenetrate and work out their tentative and uneasy compromises."[131] In an essay, "Tragic Element in Modern Conflict," the British historian Herbert Butterfield also wrote about "this condition of absolute predicament or irreducible dilemma."[132] The problem of the atomic bomb will have to be understood in terms of terrible conflict between power, absolutized by the atomic bomb, and morality, as formulated by Saint Augustine in his "just war" theory. It is in this sense that Hofstadter said that the decision to use this weapon was "among the major tragedies of history."[133]

From my perspective, the saddest thing about the whole Smithsonian fiasco was that an ideal opportunity to engage in meaningful Japanese-American dialogue about the atom bomb and nuclear danger was lost. To his credit, the Smithsonian's director, Martin Harwit, had visited Hiroshima in April 1993 with his staff and had met with Mayor Hiraoka to carefully prepare for the exhibition. Causing offense to Japan was Harwit's constant worry, and he understood that "cultural differences can easily lead to serious misunderstandings." In fact, Hiraoka had worried that the Peace Memorial Museum's atomic relics that were to be loaned to the Smithsonian might be used to glorify the destructive power of the atomic bomb.[134] Harwit dispelled such fears. Hiraoka took this occasion to try out the Pearl Harbor-Hiroshima syndrome on Harwit, telling Harwit that "he felt Japan owes the U.S. an apology for Pearl Harbor, and that [the United States] owed one to Japan for the atomic bombings. Would our exhibition do that?" Harwit diplomatically replied that apologies were not as important as try-

131. Niebuhr, *Moral Man and Immoral Society: A Study in Ethics and Politics*, 4.
132. Butterfield, *History and Human Relations*, 20.
133. Ver Steeg and Hofstadter, *A People and a Nation*, 710.
134. *Chōgoku Shinbun*, March 18, 1993, and April 6, 1993.

ing to learn lessons.[135] On this note, the Japanese were happy to cooperate with the Smithsonian.

The Japanese people were disappointed and confused by the cancellation of the Smithsonian exhibit, but they soon took some comfort in a much smaller private exhibit held at American University in the summer of 1995. NHK conducted polls about the cancellation of the Smithsonian exhibit. Fifty-three percent of the Japanese respondents (67 percent of Hiroshima residents) considered the cancellation to be a mistake, whereas only 30 percent of Americans felt so.[136]

The Hiroshima-Victimizer Syndrome

Those Americans who justify the atomic bombings in strongest terms were those who most fiercely attack Japan's aggressions and atrocities—the Rape of Nanjing, the Bataan Death March, the killing of POWs. More generally, for many years, Americans (and Asians) have been critical of Japan's cabinet ministers, educators (history textbooks), and press for downplaying Japan's record of aggression and atrocities, in sharp contrast to Germany's leaders who apologized for the criminal deeds of Hitler's state.

But as the fiftieth anniversary of Hiroshima and Nagasaki approached, Japan's historical stance began to change. Under pressure from internal critics, the Socialist Party, and peace groups, Japan took significant steps toward publicly and officially apologizing for having launched the war and for having committed atrocities. Prime Minister Murayama Tomiichi called for a parliamentary apology to the Asian countries that Japan victimized. While visiting Beijing in the spring of 1995, he said, "I recognize anew that Japan's actions, including aggression and colonial rule, at one time in history, caused unbearable suffering and sorrow for many people in your country and other Asian neighbors."[137] In Hiroshima, Mayor Hiraoka argued that "when we think about the atom bomb, we should think about the aggression and atrocities we committed in war, too." Finally on August 15, 1995, during the fiftieth anniversary commemorations of the war's end, Murayama made the most explicit declaration yet. Recalling the damages and suffering caused by Japan, he expressed his "feeling of deep remorse" and gave his "heartfelt apology."

These Japanese apologies for past aggressions were not, however, sufficiently noted in the United States (and Asia), and in the absence of an

---

135. Harwit, *An Exhibit Denied: Lobbying the History of the Enola Gay*, 156, 170.
136. Nihon Hōsō Kyōkai (NHK) [Japan Broadcasting Corporation], (1995.11), 8.
137. Quoted in Bird and Lifschultz, *Hiroshima Shadow*, 337.

American expression of regret for Hiroshima and Nagasaki, they seem one-sided. The Hiroshima-victimizer syndrome still remains in the minds of many Asians.

Perspectives Sixty Years Later

Sixty years is a long time. Those who can recall the war have mostly retired. A large-scale public opinion survey conducted by NHK in 2005 both in Japan and in the United States registered significant perceptual changes.[138] Although Americans who replied that dropping the bomb was "based on right judgment" amounted to 56 percent of the respondents, there were generational differences: 70 percent of those over age sixty said that it was "right," whereas only 42 percent of people in their twenties and thirties thought so.

If the present trend continues, it is expected that perceptual differences between the Japanese and Americans, especially the younger generations, will narrow. When the American *and* Japanese respondents who said they believed that the bombings were "based on right judgment" were asked why they thought so, 60 percent replied, "because it hastened the end of the war." This marks a clear departure for the Japanese, for as late as 1994 (remember the controversy over the atomic bomb stamp) it was a taboo for Japanese to admit this.

A large-scale poll conducted by *Asahi Shimbun* in July 2005, on the sixtieth anniversary, among *hibakusha* yielded significant results. One of the largest polls of atomic survivors (72.4 years old on average) ever attempted, it elicited responses from 13,204 persons.[139] This poll asked survivors which government they thought was "responsible for atomic bomb damages." More than half replied that *both* the Japanese and the American governments were responsible; those who said the U.S. government alone was responsible remained only 28 percent. The old habit of solely blaming the American government alone is disappearing.

As for the younger generation, who will shape future perceptions of the atomic bomb, in a 1989 poll of fifth and six graders and junior high school students in Hiroshima, 55 percent believed, "The atomic bomb could not be forgiven for humanitarian reasons"—fifteen points less than the figures obtained in the 1987 survey (70 percent). Those who answered that "the atomic bombing could not be helped because it was wartime" or "because it

---

138. Kobayashi Toshiiki, "Usureru hibaku no kioku, Takamaru kakusensō eno fuan" [Fading Memories of Atomic Victimization, Rising Anxiety for Nuclear Warfare], 18–25.
139. *Asahi Shimbun*, July 17, 2006.

was needed to hasten the end of the war" amounted to 21 percent, which is a six-point increase over the previous survey.[140] These subtle changes seem to indicate a more down-to-earth attitude toward the use of the atomic bomb. The most recent poll of junior and senior high school students and college students, conducted in July 2005, reveals that 25 percent accepted or approved of the atomic bombing "because it could not be helped as a wartime measure."[141] Compared to earlier surveys, the 25 percent acceptance of the atomic bomb is significantly higher than, say, ten or fifteen years ago.

College Surveys in Japan and the United States, 2005–2006

To obtain up-to-date comparative data on college students, I conducted polls of 332 Japanese students at Doshisha University in November 2005 and 232 American students at Miami University in Oxford, Ohio, in February 2006. Among Doshisha students only 17 percent (about the same as the 1994 survey) agreed that "to save American lives, the atomic bombing could not be helped," whereas 71 percent of American students thought so. On the other hand, the racial interpretation is obviously on the decline. Doshisha students who felt that the United States would *not* have dropped the atomic bomb on Germany constituted 44.5 percent (5 points lower than in 1994). In contrast, 34.7 percent of American students felt this way.

The most interesting finding was the striking difference between the two groups concerning the reasons for dropping the atomic bomb. Students were asked to list what they considered to be the reasons in order of importance. Doshisha students cited "to test the destructive power of the atomic bomb" as the most important consideration. This came as something of a surprise to us. But their second and third choices concerned the Soviet Union: "To pressure the Soviet Union by a display of power" and "to end the war before Soviet entry." In sharp contrast, American students overwhelmingly ranked "to avoid U.S. casualties" as the most important reason. The second reason was "to pay back for Pearl Harbor." (For detailed data, see the addendum.[142]) Among Japanese students anti-Soviet motives were still given considerable credence, though less so than in the 1991 survey. Apparently, the end of the Cold War accounts for this. In contrast, American students, as might be expected, voiced the "Truman orthodoxy." In the questionnaire to American students we asked if the U.S. should apologize for the use of the atomic

---

140. Takahashi, "Fukugan de miru genbaku higai to sensō kagai," 390.
141. *Chūgoku Shinbun*, July 23, 2005.
142. I am indebted to Allan M. Winkler of Miami University for the American poll.

bomb. As many as 38.8 percent of respondents said that "the U.S. should apologize to Japan," and another 32 percent replied it should do so "if Japan apologizes for Pearl Harbor." It is significant that a total of 70.8 percent of American students favored apologizing to Japan. This is about the same percentage as that of Japan's atomic victims (62 percent).[143]

Lessons of Hiroshima and Nagasaki

Recent polls indicate that a large majority, 90 to 91 percent, of Hiroshima-Nagasaki citizens believe it is their duty to transmit to the next generation the experiences of atomic victimization.[144] When asked "how much the actual damages and sufferings of *hibakusha* are being made known to the world," 41 percent in Hiroshima and 49 percent in Nagasaki replied that they are being made known. They believe the efforts are very important for the prevention of nuclear war.

The end of the Cold War has lessened the fear of an all-out nuclear war, but as McGeorge Bundy, William J. Crowe Jr., and Sidney D. Drell reminded us in 1993, "it would be dangerously wrong to suppose that the end of the Cold War means an end of nuclear danger, and it would be a grave error for our people or our government to let nuclear fear be replaced by nuclear complacency."[145] The Pugwash Conference of scientists, held in Hiroshima in July 2005, declared that compared to ten years ago the world is a less safe place, citing the lack of progress of nuclear disarmament, proliferation of nuclear nations such as India and Pakistan, and the danger of terrorist use of nuclear weapons. Reflecting this situation, those who feel there is the danger of a nuclear war in the near future has increased both in Hiroshima and in the United States by more than ten points (56 percent), according to a recent NHK poll. Fifty percent of Japanese (and 43 percent of Americans) replied that "the nuclear weapon would be used as long as it exists." This led to the next question, "What should we do with the nuclear weapons we have on earth?" Those who replied "all nuclear weapons must be abolished" amounted to 44 percent among Japanese but only 20 percent among Americans.[146]

143. *Asahi Shimbun*, July 17, 2005.
144. NHK, "Sengo 50-nen: Sensō no tsumeato—Hiroshima, Nagasaki, Okinwa" [Fifty years since the End of the War: The War's Scratches—Hiroshima, Nagasaki, and Okinawa], 6.
145. Bundy, Crowe, and Drell, *Reducing Nuclear Danger: The Road Away from the Brink*, 2.
146. Kobayashi, "Usureru hibaku no kioku," 25–26.

Then there was a related question: "Do you think that Japan's anti-nuclear peace movement has contributed to world peace or prevention of nuclear warfare?" The percentage of Japanese who replied in the affirmative increased to 66 percent, as compared to 49 percent in 1975 and 57 percent in 1987.[147] The poll conducted in July 2005 among youth in Hiroshima yielded even more positive results. As many as 76.7 percent responded that they thought "the experience of using atom-bomb in Hiroshima and Nagasaki has influenced prevention of nuclear war and contributed to peace."

Hiroshima and the *hibakusha* have rightly led the world in appealing for the abolition of nuclear weapons, but on this issue the lessons of Hiroshima and Pearl Harbor are antipodal. Those who take to heart the lesson of Hiroshima argue that nuclear weapons must be abolished because they will destroy the world and wonder why most Americans do not understand this. On the other hand, Americans who emphasize the lesson of Pearl Harbor argue that military preparedness is essential to deter war and wonder why the Japanese have not learned that only early intervention against aggressors can prevent armed conflict. The Japanese feel that the lesson of Hiroshima has not as yet been accepted by a majority of Americans.

Conclusions

As long as we are trapped in the "victim-victimizer syndrome" and the habit of mutual recrimination, we will never reach a consensus on the issues discussed in this essay. What we need is a view of history that does not seek sanctuaries in moral self-righteousness, a view of history that is free from the ideological thesis of atomic diplomacy and emotional racial interpretation. Many years have passed since the end of the Cold War, and "Cold War revisionism" à la Alperovitz has lost much of its relevance, although its grip is still strong in Japan.

The Japanese must guard against "A-bomb nationalism," which claims for Japan a morally superior position because of its atomic victimization. Ian Burma has described the pitfall of self-righteousness in the following words: "Having learned their lesson through their unique suffering, having been purified through hellfire and purgatory, so to speak, the Japanese people have earned the right . . . to sit in judgment of others, specifically the United States."[148] Such an attitude can only militate against the universal appeal for nuclear disarmament.

147. Ibid., 21–23.
148. Buruma, *Wages of Guilt*, 98.

The sixty years since Hiroshima and Nagasaki have been a period of international tension, local conflicts and limited wars, crises and provocations, and an abundance of ethnic and religious violence that in the preatomic age may well have triggered a third world war. There have been genuine scares: in 1948 and 1961 because of Berlin; in 1950 and 1953 because of the Korean War; in 1954 because of Indochina; in 1954–1955 because of the Taiwan Strait crisis; in 1962 because of the Cuban missile crisis; in 1968 because of the battle of Khe Sanh in the Vietnam War; and in 1967 and 1973 because of Arab-Israeli wars. With the hindsight of history it can be argued that the use of the "absolute weapon" against Hiroshima and Nagasaki in August 1945, by offering a horrifying precedence, played its role in helping deter a thermonuclear war. In this sense, the lesson of Hiroshima and Nagasaki has contributed to the prevention of a third world war.

This, I hasten to add, is not to evoke the logic of nuclear deterrence ex post facto to justify the bombing of Hiroshima and Nagasaki. The "long peace," built on nuclear deterrence, was at best a fragile and unstable affair, hanging as it did on an uncontrolled nuclear arms race. The end of the Cold War has brought a sea change from nuclear deterrence to nuclear disarmament. Robert S. McNamara, once a consummate practitioner of nuclear strategy, made a rather surprising statement in October 1992 on the thirtieth anniversary of the Cuban missile crisis:

> The lesson I draw from the Cuban Missile Crisis is that as long as we combine human fallibility with nuclear weapons, the world runs a high risk of use of these weapons with the likely destruction of nations and perhaps the risk of survival of civilizations. And there is only one way we can avoid it and that is to return insofar as achievable to a non-nuclear world.[149]

We may very well call McNamara's reflection the "lesson of Hiroshima and Nagasaki." Physicist Ralph Lapp, the Manhattan Project physicist who later became a vigorous critic of the nuclear arms, protested at the height of the Cold War: "If the memory of things is to deter, where is that memory? Hiroshima has been taken out of the American conscience—eviscerated, extirpated."[150] One may hope that the events of the sixtieth anniversary, proving this is no longer the case, will reaffirm modern mem-

---

149. Robert S. McNamara's statement is from a NHK television program on the Cuban missile crisis, which aired on October 28, 1992. For an earlier articulation of this view, see McNamara, *Out of the Cold: New Thinking for American Foreign and Defense Policy in the Twenty-First Century*, 97–99, 102–4.

150. *Los Angeles Times*, August 3, 1994.

ory. As recent polls have shown, younger generations in both countries are more akin to each other in their perceptions of Hiroshima and Nagasaki. And there is ground for hope in the future.

Addendum: University Student Polls on the A-Bomb Decision

Questionnaires: January 1976, sample size 95; December 1994, sample size 209; July 1994, sample size 310; November 2005, sample size 332. Miami questionnaire: February 2006, sample size 232.

I. Concerning the American decision to drop the atomic bomb, please indicate your support or opposition to the following views:

A. It was right to drop the atomic bomb to save the lives of many American lives who would die in an American invasion of Japan.

	1976	1991	1994	2005	Miami U (2006)
Strongly support	0.0	0.0	0.9	0.3	12.5
Support	1.1	5.7	12.2	11.2	42.9
Oppose	25.2	25.4	41.7	42.6	16.6
Strongly oppose	62.1	43.5	31.3	28.7	4.4
Neither	7.4	22.5	9.6	14.2	15.2
Don't know	4.2	2.9	4.3	3.0	8.4
Total	100.0	100.0	100.0	100.0	100.0

B. For the same reason, the atomic bombing could not be helped.

	1976	1991	1994	2005	Miami U (2006)
Strongly support	0.0	1.0	0.9	0.9	6.1
Support	2.1	14.4	16.5	16.1	28.4
Oppose	30.5	21.5	44.3	36.8	31.1
Strongly oppose	51.6	36.5	26.1	31.6	5.1
Neither	8.4	23.7	11.3	11.2	18.6
Don't know	7.4	2.0	0.9	3.4	10.7
Total	100.0	100.0	100.0	100.0	100.0

II. Even if the atomic bomb had been completed while war against Germany was still continuing, the United States would *not* have used it against Germany.

	1976	1991	1994	2005	Miami U (2006)
Strongly support	16.8	13.0	14.8	10.8	8.2
Support	33.7	31.7	34.8	33.7	26.5
Oppose	16.8	13.5	26.1	15.4	26.5
Strongly oppose	1.0	17.3	5.2	4.8	6.1
Neither	1.7	3.3	2.6	4.2	12.2
Don't know	20.0	21.2	16.5	30.9	20.5
Total	100.0	100.0	100.0	100.0	100.0

III. What do you think were the reasons for dropping the atomic bomb? What do you think were the important reasons to the American leaders? Please circle them and then list them in order of importance.
A. To avoid U.S. casualties
B. To avoid further Japanese casualties also
C. To end the war against Japan before Soviet entry
D. To pressure the Soviet Union by a display of power
E. To test the destructive power of the atomic bomb
F. To pay back for Pearl Harbor
G. To justify to the American public the $2 billion spent on the Manhattan Project

	Student Responses				(Miami	University)	
Order	A	B	C	D	E	F	G
No. 1	21.5	4.2	33.0	22.5	39.7	6.4	7.1
	(21.8)	(0)	(12.2)	(4.1)	(0)	(16.3)	(2.0)
No. 2	20.4	6.6	25.6	35.3	19.5	10.2	15.3
	(19.7)	(6.7)	(25.5)	(35.3)	(8.2)	(11.3)	(15.6)
No. 3	17.8	10.7	20.7	22.6	15.7	16.8	21.7
	(17.6)	(10.8)	(16.3)	(20.5)	(22.5)	(17.0)	(22.1)
No. 4	14.7	9.8	8.4	10.9	16.1	12.6	21.7
	(14.9)	(10.1)	(8.5)	(11.0)	(16.2)	(12.1)	(21.4)
Others	25.6	68.9	12.4	8.6	8.5	53.2	33.8
	(26.8)	(86.4)	(12.5)	(8.7)	(8.6)	(53.1)	(33.7)
(8.7) N=332	100.0	100.0	100.0	100.0	100.0	100.0	100.0

Bibliography

Archives

Enomoto Juji Papers. Contained in the "Senbi gunshuku" [Naval Armament and Limitation] group. Institute of Defense Studies, Japanese Ministry of Defense

Hori Teikichi Papers. Library, National Maritime Self Defense College, Tokyo

Japan. Ministry of Foreign Affairs, Diplomatic Record Office

————. Ministry of Justice, Senpan Shiryō Shitsu

Library, Institute of Defense Studies, Japanese Ministry of Defense

United States Army, Far Eastern Command. "Interrogations of Japanese Officials" and "Statements of Japanese Officials." U.S. Army Center of Military History, Washington, D.C.

United States, National Archives and Records Administration, Suitland, Md. Department of State Archives

————. General Records of the Department of the Navy, Record Group 80

————. Records of the General Board, Modern Military Records, Record Group 45

Private Papers

Castle, William R., Jr. Hoover Presidential Library, West Branch, Iowa

Fujii Shigeru Diary. In private possession

Gardiner, William Howard. Houghton Library, Harvard Univesity

Ishikawa Shingo Diary. In private possession

Katō Kanji. Institute of Social Science, University of Tokyo

Kobayashi Seizō, Kaisōroku [Manuscript Notes]. BBK

Konoe Fumimaro Papers. Photocopy at BBK

Lodge, Henry Cabot. Massachusetts Historical Society, Boston

Miyazaki Shūichi Diary. BBK
Pratt, William V. Operational Archives, Naval History Division, Washington
      Navy Yard
Saitō Makoto. National Diet Library
Stimson, Henry L., microfilmed diary. Yale University Library
Washburn, Stanley. Washburn Oral History, Butler Library, Columbia
      University

Library of Congress, Washington, D.C.

Anderson, Chandler P.
Hughes, Charles Evans
Johnson, Nelson T.
Lansing, Robert
Mahan, Alfred Thayer
Roosevelt, Theodore, Jr.

Government Publications

Great Britain

Documents on British Foreign Policy, 1919–1939. 1st. ser., vol. 3. Edited by W.
      H. Medlicott, Douglas Dakin, and M. E. Lambert. London: HMSO,
      1970.

Japan

Gaimushō. *Nihon gaikō nenpyō narabini shuyō bunsho, 1840–1945* [Chronology
      and Major Documents of Japanese Diplomacy, 1840–1945]. 2 vols.
      Reprint, Tokyo: Hara Shobō, 1966.
————. *NGB: 1930-nen Rondon kaigun kaigi* [1930 London Naval Conference].
      2 vols. 1983–1984.
————. *NGB: Juvēvu kaigun gunbi seigen kaigi* [Geneva Naval Conference].
      1982.
————. *NGB: Washinton kaigi.* 2 vols. 1977–1978.
————. *NGB: Washinton kaigi gunbi seigen mondai* [Washington Conference:
      The Problem of Naval Limitation]. 1974.
————. *NGB: Washinton kaigi kyokutō mondai* [Washington Conference: Far
      Eastern Questions]. 1976.
————. *NGB: Shōwa jidai I.* Vol. 4 (1927–1931), pt. 2. 1991.

———. *Shūsen shiroku*. 6 vols. 1952. Expanded ed., Tokyo: Hokuyōsha, 1977–1978.

United States

Congress. *Hearings before the Joint Committee of Investigation of the Pearl Harbor Attack*. 79th Cong., 1st sess., pt. 12.

Department of State. *Conference on the Limitation of Armament: Washington, November 12, 1921–February 6, 1922.*

———. *Foreign Relations of the United States, 1921*. 2 vols. (1938); *1922*, Vol. 1 (1938); *1927*, Vol. 1 (1942); *1929*, Vol. 1 (1943); *1930*, Vol. 1 (1945).

———. *Foreign Relations of the United States: The Conference of Berlin (Potsdam), 1945*. 2 vols. (1960).

Senate. *Japanese Immigration Legislation, Hearings before the Committee on Immigration*. 68th Cong., 1st sess., March 11–15, 1924.

Strategic Bombing Survey. *Effects of Strategic Bombing on Japanese Morale, Report on the Pacific War.*

Interviews and Oral History

Records of Interviews

Fukudome Shigeru (BBK); Hashimoto Shōzō (JMJ); Inoue Shigeyoshi (BBK); Maeda Minoru (BBK); Miyo Kazunari (JMJ and BBK); Oka Takazumi (JMJ); Shiba Katsuo (BBK); Takada Toshitane (BBK); Takahashi Sankichi (BBK); Toyoda Teijirō (BBK); Yokoi Tadao (BBK).

Interviews with Author

Enomoto Jūji, July and August 1975
Hornbeck, Stanley K., February 1961
Roosevelt, Mrs. Theodore, Jr., March 1961
Tomioka Sadatoshi, November 1968

Books, Articles, and Unpublished Studies

In English

Adler, Selig. *The Isolationist Impulse: Its Twentieth-Century Reaction*. New York: Collier Books, 1961.

Agawa Hiroyuki. *Reluctant Admiral: Yamamoto and the Imperial Navy.* Tokyo: Kodansha International, 1979.

Albion, Robert G. *Makers of Naval Policy.* Annapolis: Naval Institute Press, 1980.

Allen, Frederick L. *Only Yesterday: An Informal History of the Nineteen-Twenties.* New York: Harper and Brothers, 1931.

Allen, H. C. "Samuel Flagg Bemis." In *Pastmasters : Some Essays on American Historians,* edited by Marcus Cunliffe and Robin W. Winks. New York: Harper and Row, 1969.

Alperovitz, Gar. *Atomic Diplomacy: Hiroshima and Nagasaki, the Use of the Atomic Bomb and the American Confrontation with Soviet Power.* New York: Simon and Schuster, 1965. Updated and expanded ed. Elizabeth Shifon Books, 1985. Boulder, Colo.: Westview Press, 1995.

———. *The Decision to Use the Atomic Bomb and the Architecture of an American Myth.* New York: Knopf, 1995.

Alperovitz, Gar, and Robert L. Messer. "Marshall, Truman, and the Decision to Drop the Bomb." *International Security* 16 (Winter 1991/1992).

Asada, Sadao. "Between the Old Diplomacy and New, 1918–1922: The Washington System and the Origins of the Japanese-Rapprochement." *Diplomatic History* 30 (April 2006).

———. "The Flap over A-Bomb Stamp: How the Japanese and American Historical Perceptions Differ." *Japan Echo* (Summer 1995).

———. *From Mahan to Pearl Harbor: The Imperial Japanese Navy and the United States.* Annapolis: Naval Institute Press, 2006.

———. "From Washington to London: The Imperial Japanese Navy and the Politics of Naval Limitation, 1921–1922." *Diplomacy and Statecraft* 4 (November 1993). Reprinted in *The Washington Conference, 1921–1922.* Edited by Erik Goldstein and John Maurer. Ilford, Essex, UK: Frank Cass, 1994.

———. "Japan and the United States, 1915–1925." Ph.D. diss., Yale University, 1963.

———, ed. *Japan and the World, 1853–1952: A Bibliographic Guide to Japanese Scholarship in Foreign Relations.* New York: Columbia University Press, 1989.

———. "Japanese Admirals and the Politics of Naval Limitation: Katō Tomosaburō vs. Katō Kanji." In *Naval Warfare in the Twentieth Century: Essays in Honour of Arthur Marder,* edited by Gerald Jordan. London: Croom Helm, 1977.

———. "The Japanese Navy and the United States." In *Pearl Harbor as History: Japanese-American Relations, 1931–1941,* edited by Dorothy Borg and Shumpei Okamoto. New York, Columbia University Press, 1930.

———. "Japanese Perceptions of the A-Bomb Decision." In *The American Military and the Far East: Proceedings of the Ninth Military History Symposium,* edited by Joe C. Dixon. United States Air Force Academy, 1–3 October 1980. Washington, D.C.: Government Printing Office, [1981].

———. "Japan's 'Special Interests' and the Washington Conference, 1921–1922." *American Historical Review* 67 (1961). Reprinted in *Japan and North America.* Vol. 1. Edited by Ellis Krauss and Benjamin Nyblade. London: RoutledgeCurzon, 2004.

———. "The Mushroom Cloud and National Psyches: Japanese and American Perceptions of the A-Bomb Decision, 1945–1995." *Journal of American-East Asian Relations* 4 (Summer 1995). Reprinted in *Living with the Bomb: American and Japanese Culture Conflicts in the Nuclear Age,* edited by Laura Hein and Mark Selden. Armonk, N.Y.: E. M. Sharp, 1997.

———. "The Revolt against the Washington Treaty: The Imperial Japanese Navy and the Politics of Naval Limitation, 1921–1927." *Naval War College Review* 46 (Summer 1993): 82–97.

———. "The Shock of the Atomic Bomb and Japan's Decision to Surrender: A Reconsideration." *Pacific Historical Review* 67 (November 1998): 477–512. Reprinted in *Japan and North America.* Vol. 1. Edited by Ellis Krauss and Benjamin Nyblade. London: RoutledgeCurzon, 2004. Also reprinted in *Hiroshima in History: The Myths of Revisionism.* Edited by Robert James Maddox. Columbia: University of Missouri Press, 2007.

Austin, Clyde N., ed. *Cross-Cultural Reentry: A Book of Readings.* Abilene, Tex.: Abilene Christian University, 1986

Baer, George W. *One Hundred Years of Sea Power: The U.S. Navy, 1890–1990.* Stanford: Stanford University Press, 1994.

Bemis, Samuel Flagg. *Guide to the Diplomatic History of the United States, 1775–1921.* Washington, D.C.: Government Printing Office, 1935.

———. *John Quincy Adams and the Foundations of American Foreign Policy.* New York: Knopf, 1949.

———. *John Quincy Adams and the Union.* New York: Knopf, 1956.

———. *A Short History of American Foreign Policy and Diplomacy.* New York: Henry Holt, 1959.

Beard, Charles A. "The Issues of Pacific Policy." *Survey Graphic* (May 1, 1926).

———. "War with Japan: What Shall We Get Out of It?" *Nation* (March 25, 1925).

Beard, Charles, and Mary Beard. "Our View of Japanese-American Relationships." *Survey Graphic* (May 1, 1926).

―――. "Our War Advertising Campaign." *Nation* (March 25, 1925).

Beck, A. Adams. "Unbroken Ways in South Japan." *Asia* (April 1923).

Bell, Ronald, ed. *The Japan Experience.* New York: Weatherhill, 1973.

Benedict, Ruth. *The Chrysanthemum and the Sword: Patterns of Japanese Culture.* Boston: Houghton Mifflin, 1946.

Bennett, John W., Herbert Passin, and Robert K. McKnight. *In Search of Identity: The Japanese Overseas Scholar in America and Japan.* Minneapolis: University of Minnesota Press, 1958.

Beisner, Robert L. *From the Old Diplomacy to the New, 1865–1900.* 2nd ed. Arlington Heights, Ill.: Harlan Davidson, 1986.

Berkin, Carol, Robert A. Divine, Alan Brinkley, and others. *American Voices: A History of the United States.* Teacher's annotated ed. Glenview, Ill.: Scott Foresman, 1992.

Bernstein, Barton J. "The Atomic Bombings Reconsidered." *Foreign Affairs* 74 (January–February, 1995): 135–52.

―――. "Eclipsed by Hiroshima and Nagasaki: Early Thinking about Tactical Nuclear Weapons." *International Security* 15 (Spring 1991): 149–73.

―――. "The Perils and Politics of Surrender: Ending the War with Japan and Avoiding the Third Atomic Bomb." *Pacific Historical Review* 46 (November 1977): 1–27.

―――. "Roosevelt, Truman, and the Atomic Bomb, 1941–1945: A Reinterpretation." *Political Science Quarterly* 90 (Spring 1975).

―――. "The Struggle over History: Defining the Hiroshima Narrative." In *Judgment at the Smithsonian,* edited by Philip Nobile, 127–256. New York: Marlowe and Company, 1995.

―――. "Understanding the Atomic Bomb and the Japanese Surrender: Missed Opportunities, Little Known Near Disasters, and Modern Memory." In *Hiroshima in History and Memory,* edited by Michael J. Hogan, 38–79. New York: Cambridge University Press, 1996.

Bird, Kai, and Lawrence Lifschultz, eds. *Hiroshima Shadow: Writings on the Denial of History and the Smithsonian Controversy.* Stony Creek, Conn.: The Pamphleteer's Press, 1998.

Bix, Herbert P. *Hirohito and the Making of Modern Japan.* New York: Harper Collins, 2000.

―――. "Japan's Delayed Surrender: A Reinterpretation." *Diplomatic History* 19 (Spring 1995): 197–225.

Blackett, P. M. S. *Fear, War, and the Bomb: Military and Political Consequences of Atomic Energy.* New York: Whittlesey House, 1949. Japanese translation published in 1951 by Hōsei Daigaku Shuppankyoku, Tokyo.

Blum, John Morton. *A Life with History.* Lawrence: University Press of Kansas, 2004.

————, ed. *The Price of Vision: The Diary of Henry A. Wallace, 1942–1946.* Boston: Houghton Mifflin, 1973.

Borg, Dorothy, and Shumpei Okamoto. *Pearl Harbor as History: Japanese-American Relations, 1931–1941.* New York: Columbia University Press, 1973.

Bostert, Russell H., and John A. DeNovo. "Samuel Flagg Bemis." *Proceedings of the Massachusetts Historical Society* 85 (1973).

Boulding, Kenneth E. *The Image: Knowledge in Life and Society.* Ann Arbor, Mich.: University of Michigan Press, 1961.

Boydston, Jo Ann, ed. *John Dewey: The Middle Works, 1899–1924, Vol. 2: 1918–1919.* Carbondale: Southern Illinois University Press, 1982.

Boyer, Paul S. *The American Nation.* Austin: Holt, 1998.

————. *By the Bomb's Early Light: American Thought and Culture at the Dawn of the Atomic Age.* New York: Pantheon, 1985.

————. *Fallout: A Historian Reflects on America's Half Century.* Columbus: Ohio State University Press, 1998.

————. *Todd and Curti's American Nation.* Austin: Holt, 1994.

————. "Whose History Is It Anyway? Memory, Politics, and Historical Scholarship." In *History Wars: The Enola Gay and Other Battles for the American Past,* edited by Edward T. Linenthal and Tom Engelhardt, 115–39. New York: Henry Holt, 1996.

Bragdon, Henry W., Samuel P. McCutchen, and Donald A. Ritchie. *History of a Free Nation.* Lake Forest, Ill.: Glencoe/McGraw Hill, 1992.

Braisted, William R. "On the United States Navy's Operational Outlook in the Pacific, 1919–1931." Unpublished paper (in the author's possession), presented to the Kauai Island Conference on the history of Japanese-American relations (1918–1931), January 1976.

————. *The United States in the Pacific, 1897–1909.* Austin: University of Texas Press, 1958.

————. *The United States Navy in the Pacific, 1909–1922.* Austin: University of Texas Press, 1971.

Braw, Monica. *The Atomic Bomb Suppressed.* Reprint, Armonk, N.Y.: M. E. Sharpe, 1991.

Bundy, McGeorge, William J. Crowe Jr., Sidney D. Drell. *Reducing Nuclear Danger: The Road Away from the Brink.* New York: Council on Foreign Relations, 1993.

Buruma, Ian. *Wages of Guilt: Memories of War in Germany and Japan.* New York: A Meridian Book, 1995.

Butow, Robert J. C. *Japan's Decision to Surrender.* Stanford: Stanford University Press, 1954. Japanese edition, *Shūshen gaishi: Mujōken kōfuku made no keii.* Translated by Ōi Atsushi. Tokyo: Jiji Tsūshinsha, 1958.

Butterfield, Herbert. *History and Human Relations.* New York: Macmillan, 1952.

Bywater, Hector C. *The Great Pacific War: A History of the American-Japanese Campaign of 1931–1933.* London: Constable, 1925. Japanese edition, *Nihon wa hatashite yabururuka.* Tokyo: Senshinsha, 1931.

———. *Sea Power in the Pacific: A Study of Japanese-American Problems.* Boston: Houghton Mifflin, 1921.

Carlton, David. "Great Britain and the Coolidge Naval Disarmament Conference of 1927." *Political Science Quarterly* 83, no. 4 (December 1968).

Carpenter, Frank G. *Carpenter's Geographical Reader: Asia.* New York: American Book Company, 1897.

Chisolm, Lawrence W. *Fenollosa: The Far East and American Culture.* New Haven: Yale University Press, 1963.

Chomsky, Noam. "On War Crimes." In *At War with Asia.* New York: Vintage Books, 1970.

Cillessen, Bret J. "Embracing the Bomb: Ethics, Morality, and Nuclear Deterrence in the US AIR FORCE, 1945–1955." *Journal of Strategic Studies* 21 (March 1998).

Clark, Rosamond H. "Getting Home." *Missionary Herald* (January 1925).

Clarke, Joseph I. C. *Japan at First Hand.* New York: Dodd, Mead, 1919.

Clayton, Andrew, Elisabeth Israels Perry, and Allan M. Winkler. *America: Pathways to the Present.* Englewood Cliffs, N.J.: Prentice Hall, 1995.

Cohen, Warren I. *The American Revisionists: The Lessons of Intervention in World War I.* Chicago: University of Chicago Press, 1967.

Compton, Karl T. "If the Atomic Bomb Had Not Been Used." *Atlantic Monthly* (December 1946).

Crow, Carl. *Japan and America: A Contrast.* New York: Robert M. McBride, 1916.

Crowl, Philip A. "Alfred Thayer Mahan: The Naval Historian." In *Makers of Modern Strategy from Machiavelli to the Nuclear Age,* edited by Peter Paret. Princeton: Princeton University Press, 1986.

Crowley, James B. *Japan's Quest for Autonomy: National Security and Foreign Policy, 1930–1938.* Princeton: Princeton University Press, 1966.

Danelski, David J., and Joseph S. Tulchin, eds., *The Autobiographical Notes of Charles Evans Hughes.* Cambridge: Harvard University Press, 1973.

Davis, Vincent. *The Admirals Lobby.* Chapel Hill: University of North Carolina Press, 1967.

Dewey, John. "Highly Colored White Lies." *New Republic* (April 22, 1925).

———. "Japan and America." *Dial* (May 17, 1919).

———. *Letters from China and Japan.* New York: E. P. Dutton Company, 1920.

———."Liberalism in Japan, II." *Dial* (October 8, 1919).

Dingman, Roger. "Japan and Mahan." In *Proceedings of a Conference Marking the Centenary of Alfred Thayer Mahan's "The Influence of Sea Power upon History, 1660–1783,"* edited by John B. Hattendorf. Newport, R.I.: Naval War College Press, 1991.

———. *Power in the Pacific: The Origins of Naval Arms Limitation, 1914–1922.* Chicago: University of Chicago Press, 1976.

Dockrill, Saki, ed. *From Pearl Harbor to Hiroshima: The Second World War in Asia and the Pacific, 1941–1945.* London: Macmillan, 1994.

Dower, John W. "The Bombed: Hiroshima and Nagasaki in Japanese Memory." In *Hiroshima in History and Memory,* edited by Michael J. Hogan, 200–232. New York: Cambridge University Press, 1996.

———. *Embracing Defeat: Japan in the Wake of World War II.* New York: W. W. Norton, 1999.

———. *War without Mercy: Race and Power in the Pacific War.* New York: Pantheon Books, 1986.

Drea, Edward J. *MacArthur's ULTRA: Codebreaking and the War against Japan, 1942–1945.* Lawrence: University Press of Kansas, 1992.

———."Previews of Hell: The End of the War with Japan." *Military History Quarterly* 7, no. 3 (Spring 1995).

Ellicott, J. M. "Japanese Students at the United States Naval Academy." United States Naval Institute *Proceedings* 73 (March 1947).

Evans, David C., and Mark R. Peattie. *Kaigun: Strategy, Tactics, and Technology in the Imperial Japanese Navy, 1887–1941.* Annapolis: Naval Institute Press, 1997.

Feis, Herbert. *The Atomic Bomb and the End of World War II.* Princeton: Princeton University Press, 1966.

———. *Japan Subdued: The Atomic Bomb and the End of the War in the Pacific.* Princeton: Princeton University Press, 1961.

Ferrell, Robert H., ed. *Dear Bess: The Letters from Harry to Bess Truman, 1910–1959.* New York: Norton, 1983.

———. *Harry S. Truman and the Bomb.* Warland, Wyo.: High Plains Publishing, 1996.

———, ed. *Off the Record: The Private Papers of Harry S. Truman.* New York: Harper and Row, 1980.

———, ed. *Truman in the White House: The Diary of Eben A. Ayers.* Columbia: University of Missouri Press, 1991.

FitzGerald, Frances. *America Revised: History Schoolbooks in the Twentieth Century.* Boston: Little, Brown, 1979.

Fitzgerald, F. Scott. *This Side of Paradise.* Reprint , New York: Penguin, 1963.

Flowers, Montaville. *The Japanese Conquest of American Opinion.* New York: G. H. Doran, 1917.

Frank, Harry. *Glimpses of Japan and Formosa.* New York: Century Co., 1924.

Frank, Richard B. *Downfall: The End of the Imperial Japanese Empire*. New York: Random House, 1999.

Freedman, Lawrence, and Saki Dockrill. "Hiroshima: A Strategy of Shock." In *From Pearl Harbor to Hiroshima*, edited by Saki Dockrill. London: Longman, 1994.

Freidel, Frank. *Franklin D. Roosevelt: The Apprenticeship*. Boston: Little, Brown, 1952.

Friedman, George, and Meredith LeBard. *The Coming War with Japan*. New York: St. Martin's Press, 1991.

Fussell, Paul. "Thank God for the Atom Bomb—Hiroshima: A Soldier's View." *New Republic* (August 1981).

———. *Thank God for the Atomic Bomb and Other Essays*. New York: Ballantine Books, 1988.

Gaddis, John Lewis. *The Long Peace: Inquiries into the History of the Cold War*. New York: Oxford University Press, 1987.

Gallicchio, Marc. "After Nagasaki: General Marshall's Plan for Tactical Nuclear Weapons in Japan." *Prologue* 23 (Winter 1991): 396–404.

Gardiner, William H. "America's Responsibility in the Far East." *Harper* (June 1924).

Garraty, John A. *The Story of America*. Austin: Holt, 1991, 1994.

Gayn, Mark. *Japan Diary*. Reprint, Rutland, Vt.: C. E. Tuttle, 1981.

Geoffrey, Theodore. *An Immigrant in Japan*. Boston: Houghton Mifflin, 1926.

Gibbs, A. Hamilton. "Moral Preparedness for the Next War." *Survey* (April 1, 1927).

Glad, Betty. *Charles Evans Hughes and the Illusion of American Innocence: A Study in American Diplomacy*. Urbana, Ill.: University of Illinois Press, 1966.

Glazer, Nathan. "From Ruth Benedict to Herman Kahn: The Postwar Japanese Image in the American Mind." In *Mutual Images: Essays in American-Japanese Relations*, edited by Akira Iriye. Cambridge: Harvard University Press, 1975.

Gleason, John H. *Genesis of Russophobia in Great Britain: A Study in the Interaction of Policy and Opinion*. Cambridge: Harvard University Press, 1950.

Goldman, Emily O. *Sunken Treaties: Naval Arms Control between the Wars*. University Park: Pennsylvania State University Press, 1994.

Goldstein, Erik, and John Maurer, eds. *The Washington Conference, 1921–1922: Naval Rivalry, East Asian Stability, and the Road to Pearl Harbor*. Essex, UK: Frank Cass, 1994.

Gow, Ian. *Military Intervention in Pre-War Japanese Politics: Admiral Katō Kanji and the "Washington System."* London: RoutledgeCurzon, 2004.

Greenbie, Sydney. *Japan, Real and Imaginary.* New York: Harper and Brothers, [1920].

Grew, Joseph C. *Ten Years in Japan.* New York: Simon and Schuster, 1944.

———. *Turbulent Era: A Diplomatic Record of Forty Years, 1904–1945.* 2 vols. Boston: Houghton Mifflin, 1952.

Griffith, William E. "Japan's Progress in Rebuilding an Empire." *Current History* (December 1921).

———. "The Sorrow of a Non-Partisan." *Missionary Herald* (September 1919).

Griswold, Arthur Whitney. *Far Eastern Policy of the United States.* Reprint, New Haven: Yale University Press, 1962.

Gulick, Sidney L. *The East and the West: A Study of Their Psychic and Cultural Characteristics.* Rutland, Vt.: C. E. Tuttle, 1963.

———. *The Winning of the Far East: A Study of the Christian Movement in China, Korea, and Japan.* New York: George H. Doran, 1923.

Guypt, Arnold H. *The Geographical Reader and Primer: A Series of Journeys Round the World.* New York: American Book Company, 1881.

Hacker, Louis. "The Incendiary Mahan: A Biography." *Scribner Magazine* 64 (April 1934).

Hagan, Kenneth J. "Alfred Thayer Mahan: Turning America Back to the Sea." In *Makers of American Diplomacy: From Benjamin Franklin to Alfred Thayer Mahan,* edited by Frank J. Merle and Theodore A. Wilson. New York: Charles Scribner's Sons, 1974.

Halberstam, David. *The Fifties.* New York: Fawcett Columbine, 1993.

Hall, John W. "Pearl Harbor Thirty Years After—Reflections on the Pathology of War and Nationalism." *FUKUOKA UNESCO* 10 (1975).

Handlin, Oscar. *The Uprooted.* New York: Grosset and Dunlap, 1951.

Harwit, Martin. *An Exhibit Denied: Lobbying the History of Enola Gay.* New York: Springer-Verlag, 1996.

Hasegawa Tsuyoshi. *Racing the Enemy: Stalin, Truman, and the Surrender of Japan.* Cambridge: Harvard University Press, 2005.

Hatano Sumio, and Asada Sadao. "The Japanese Decision to Move South." In *Paths to War: New Essays on the Origins of the Second World War,* edited by Robert Boyce and Esmonde M. Robertson. London: Macmillan, 1989.

Hattendorf, John D., ed. *Mahan on Naval Strategy: Selections from the Writings of Alfred Thayer Mahan.* Newport, R.I.: Naval War College Press, 1986.

Hattendorf, John D., and Lynn C. Hattendorf. *A Bibliography of the Works of Alfred Thayer Mahan.* Newport, R.I.: Naval War College Press, 1986.

Hein, Laura, and Mark Selden, eds. *Living with the Bomb: American and Japanese Cultural Conflicts in the Nuclear Age.* Armonk, N.Y.: M. E. Sharpe, 1997.

Heinrichs, Waldo H. "The *Enola Gay* and Contested Public Memory." In *The Unpredictability of the Past: Memories of the Asia-Pacific War in U.S.-Eastern Relations,* edited by Marc S. Gallicchio. Durham: Duke University Press, 2007.

Hersey, John. *Hiroshima.* New York: Penguin Books, 1946.

Hervey, Harvey. "The Heavenly City." *Century* (September 1924).

Hewlett, Richard G., and Oscar E. Anderson. *The New World: A History of the United States Atomic Energy Commission,* Vol. 1: 1939–1946. University Park: Pennsylvania State University Press, 1962.

Hoffman, Frederick J. *The 1920s: American Writing in the Postwar Decade.* Rev. ed. New York: Free Press, 1962.

Hofstadter, Richard, and Clarence L. Ver Steeg. *A People and a Nation.* New York: Harper and Row, 1977.

Hogan, Michael J., ed. *Hiroshima in History and Memory.* New York: Cambridge University Press, 1996.

Holsti, Ole R. "Theories of Crisis Decision Making." In *Diplomacy: New Approaches in History, Theory, and Policy,* edited by Paul Gordon Lauren. New York: Free Press, 1979.

Hoover, Herbert C. *Memoirs of Herbert Hoover: The Cabinet and the Presidency, 1920–1933.* New York: Macmillan, 1952.

Hughes, Charles Evans. "The Foreign Policy of the United States." *Current History* (January 1924).

———. *The Pathway of Peace.* New York: Harper, 1925.

Huntington, Ellsworth. *Asia: A Geography Reader.* 1912. Reprint, New York: Rand McNally, 1923.

Ichihashi, Yamato. *The Washington Conference and After.* Stanford: Stanford University Press, 1928.

Ienaga Saburō, "The Glorification of War in Japanese Education." *International Security* 18 (Winter 1993/1994).

Ike Nobutaka, ed. and trans. *Japan's Decision for War: Records of the 1941 Policy Conferences.* Stanford: Stanford University Press, 1967.

Iriye, Akira. "Japan as a Competitor, 1895–1917." In *Mutual Images: Essays in American-Japanese Relations,* edited by Akira Iriye. Cambridge: Harvard University Press, 1975.

———. ed. *Mutual Images: Essays in American-Japanese Relations.* Cambridge: Harvard University Press, 1975.

———. *Pacific Estrangement: Japanese and American Expansion, 1897–1911.* Cambridge: Harvard University Press, 1972.

————. *Power and Culture: The Japanese-American War, 1941–1945.* Cambridge: Harvard University Press, 1981.

Irvine, William. "Hybrid Soul of Japan." *Current History* (March 1924).

Irving National Bank. *Trading with the Far East.* New York: Irving National Bank, 1920.

Isaacs, Harold. *Scratches on Our Minds: American Views of China and India.* New York: John Day, 1958. Reprinted in 1962 as *Images of Asia: American Views of China and India.*

Janis, Irvin. *Groupthink: Psychological Studies of Policy Decisions and Fiascoes.* 2nd ed. Boston: Houghton Miflin, 1982.

Jessup, Philip. *Elihu Root.* 2 vols. New York: Dodd, Mead, 1938.

Johnson, Sheila K. *American Attitudes toward Japan, 1941–1975.* Washington, D.C.: American Enterprise Institute for Public Policy Research, 1975.

————. *The Japanese through American Eyes.* Stanford: Stanford University Press, 1988.

Jordan, Gerald, ed. *Naval Warfare in the Twentieth Century, 1900–1945: Essays in Honour of Arthur Marder.* London: Croom Helm, 1977.

Karsten, Peter. "The Nature of 'Influence': Roosevelt, Mahan, and the Concept of Sea Power." *American Quarterly* 23 (October 1971).

————. *Naval Aristocracy: The Golden Age of Annapolis and the Emergence of Modern American Navalism.* New York: Free Press, 1972.

Kase Toshikazu. *Journey to the Missouri.* Edited by David Nelson Rowe. New Haven: Yale University Press, 1950.

Kaufman, Robert Gordon. *Arms Control during the Pre-Nuclear Era: The United States and Naval Limitation between the Two World Wars.* New York: Columbia University Press, 1990.

Kecskemeti, Paul. *Strategic Surrender: The Politics of Victory and Defeat.* Stanford: Stanford University Press, 1958.

Kennan, George F. *The Cloud of Danger: Some Current Problems of American Foreign Policy.* London: Hutchinson and Co., 1977.

————."The Future of Soviet Communism." *The New Leader* (June 18, 1956).

Kennedy, Thomas C. *Charles A. Beard and American Foreign Policy.* Gainesville: University Press of Florida, 1975.

Kirtland, L. S. *Samurai Trails: A Chronicle of Wanderings on the Japanese High Road.* New York: George H. Doran, 1918.

Knock, Thomas J. *To End All Wars: Woodrow Wilson and the Quest for a New World Order.* Princeton: Princeton University Press, 1992.

Knudsen, L. T. "A Note on Walter LaFeber, Captain Mahan, and the Use of Historical Sources." *Pacific Historical Review* 40 (November 1971).

Kuehl, Warren F. *Hamilton Holt: Journalist, Internationalist, Educator.* Gainesville: University of Florida Press, 1960.

LaFeber, Walter. *The New Empire: An Interpretation of American Expansionism, 1860–1898*. Ithaca: Cornell University Press, 1963.

———. "A Note on the 'Mercantilistic Imperialism' of Alfred Thayer Mahan." *Mississippi Valley Historical Review* 48 (March 1962).

Langer, William L., and S. Everett Gleason. *The Undeclared War: The World Crisis and American Foreign Policy*. New York: Harper, 1953.

Lauren, Paul Gordon, ed. *Diplomacy: New Approaches in History, Theory, and Policy*. New York: Free Press, 1979.

Leffler, Melvyn P. "Truman's Decision to Drop the Atomic Bomb." *IHJ Bulletin* [A Quarterly Publication of the International House of Japan] 15 (1995): 1–7.

Leopold, Richard W. *Elihu Root and the Conservative Tradition*. Boston: Little, Brown, 1954.

Leuchtenberg, William. *Perils of Prosperity, 1914–1932*. Chicago: University of Chicago Press, 1959.

Levine, N. Gordon, Jr. *Woodrow Wilson and World Politics: America's Response to War and Revolution*. New York: Oxford University Press, 1968.

Levy, Morris. "Alfred Thayer Mahan and United States Foreign Policy." Ph.D. diss., New York University, 1963.

Lifton, Robert J. *Death in Life: Survivors of Hiroshima*. Reprint, Chapel Hill: University of North Carolina Press, 1991.

Lifton, Robert J., and Greg Mitchell. *Hiroshima in America: Fifty Years of Denial*. New York: Grosset/Putnam, 1995.

Linenthal, Edward T., and Tom Engelhardt. *History Wars: The Enola Gay and Other Battles for the American Past*. New York: Henry Holt, 1996.

Lippmann, Walter. *Public Opinion*. New York: Harcourt, Brace, 1922.

Livezey, William E. *Mahan on Sea Power*. Norman: University of Oklahoma Press, 1947.

Love, Robert W. *History of the United States Navy*. Vol. 1. Harrisburg, Pa.: Stackpo Books, 1992.

Maddox, Robert, ed. *Hiroshima in History: The Myths of Revisionism*. Columbia: University of Missouri Press, 2007.

———. *Weapons for Victory: The Hiroshima Decision Fifty Years Later*. Columbia: University of Missouri Press, 1995.

Mahan, Alfred Thayer. *From Sail to Steam: Recollections of Naval Life*. New York: Harper, 1907.

———. "Hawaii and Our Future Sea Power." *The Forum* (March 1893).

———. *The Influence of Sea Power upon History, 1660–1783*. Boston: Little, Brown, 1945.

———. *The Interest of America in International Conditions*. Boston: Little, Brown, 1910.

————. *The Interest of America in Sea Power, Present and Future.* Boston: Little, Brown, 1897. Japanese edition, *Taiheiyō kaikenron.* Tokyo: Senryūdō, 1900.

————. *Letters and Papers of Alfred Thayer Mahan.* Edited by Robert Seager II. Annapolis: Naval Institute Press, 1975.

————. *Naval Strategy: Compared and Contrasted with the Principles and Practices of Military Operations on Land.* Boston: Little, Brown, 1911.

————. "Open Door." In *The Interest of America in International Conditions.* Boston: Little, Brown, 1910.

————. "Preparedness for Naval War." *Harper's Monthly* (September 1897).

————. *The Problem of Asia and Its Effects upon International Policies.* Boston: Little, 1900.

————. "A Twentieth-Century Outlook." *Harper's* (September 1897).

————. "The United States Looking Outward." *Atlantic Monthly* (December 1890).

Mahan, Lyle Evans. "My Parents, Rear Admiral and Mrs. Alfred Thayer Mahan." *Naval War College Review* 43 (Autumn 1990).

Marcosson, Isaac. "The Changing East." *Saturday Evening Post* (August 12, 1922, and September 30, 1922).

Marder, Arthur. *Old Friends, New Enemies: The Royal Navy and the Imperial Japanese Navy: Strategic Illusions, 1936–1941.* New York: Oxford University Press, 1981.

May, Henry, ed. *The Discontent of the Intellectuals: A Problem of the Twenties.* Chicago: Rand McNally, 1963.

McCormick, Frederick. *The Menace of Japan.* Boston: Little, Brown, 1917.

McGray, Douglas. "Japan's Gross National Cool." *Foreign Policy* (May / June 2002).

McMurray, Frank M. *Third Book: Europe and Other Continents.* New York: Macmillan, 1906.

McMurray, Frank M., and A. E. Parkins. *Elementary Geography.* New York: Macmillan, 1921.

McNamara, Robert S. *In Retrospect: The Tragedy and Lessons of Vietnam.* New York: Times Books, 1995.

————. *Out of the Cold: New Thinking for American Foreign and Defense Policy in the Twenty-First Century.* New York: Simon and Schuster, 1989.

Michener, James. *Sayonara.* Rutland, Vt.: C. E. Tuttle, 1954.

Miller, Edward S. "War Plan Orange, 1897–1941: The Blue Thrust through the Pacific." In *Naval History: The Seventh Symposium of U.S. Naval Academy,* edited by William B. Cogar. Wilmington, Del.: Scholarly Resources, 1988.

————. *War Plan Orange: The U.S. Strategy to Defeat Japan, 1897–1945.* Annapolis: Naval Institute Press, 1991.

Miner, Earl. *The Japanese Tradition in British and American Literature.* Princeton: Princeton University Press, 1958.

Morison, Eltin E., ed. *Letters of Theodore Roosevelt.* Cambridge: Harvard University Press, 1951.

Morley, James W., ed. *The Deterrent Diplomacy: Japan, Germany, and the USSR, 1935–1940.* New York: Columbia University Press, 1976.

————. *The Fateful Choice: Japan's Advance into Southeast Asia, 1939–1941.* New York: Columbia University Press, 1980.

————. *The Final Confrontation: Japan's Negotiations with the United States, 1941.* Translated by David Titis. New York: Columbia University Press, 1994.

————. *Japan Erupts: The London Naval Conference and the Manchurian Incident, 1928–1932.* New York: Columbia University Press, 1984.

Mowry, George E., ed. *The Twenties: Fords, Flappers, and Fanatics.* Englewood Cliffs, N.J.: Prentice Hall., 1963.

Nash, Gary B. *American Odyssey: The United States in the Twentieth Century.* Lake Forest, Ill.: Glencoe, 1991.

Neumann, L. William. *America Encounters Japan: From Perry to MacArthur.* Baltimore: Johns Hopkins University Press, 1963.

————. "Franklin Delano Roosevelt: A Disciple of Admiral Mahan." United States Naval Institute *Proceedings* 78 (July 1952).

Newman, Robert P. "Ending the War with Japan: Paul Nitze's 'Early Surrender' Counterfactual." *Pacific Historical Review* 64 (May 1995): 167–94.

————. *Enola Gay and the Court of History.* New York: Peter Lang, 2004.

Nichols, Wilber. *Topics in Geography.* Boston: D. C. Heath, 1889.

Niebuhr, Reinhold. *Moral Man and Immoral Society: A Study in Ethics and Politics.* New York: Scribner, 1932.

Nish, Ian. *Alliance in Decline: A Study in Anglo-Japanese Relations, 1908–1923.* London: Athlon, 1972.

————. *Japanese Foreign Policy, 1869–1942: From Kasumigaseki to Miyakezaka.* London: Routledge and Kegan Paul, 1977.

————. *Japanese Foreign Policy in the Interwar Period.* Westport, Conn.: Praeger, 2002.

Nobile, Philip, ed. *Judgment at the Smithsonian.* New York: Marlowe, 1995.

Oberg, Kalervo. "Culture Shock: Adjustment to New Cultural Environments." *Practical Anthropology* 7 (July–August 1969): 177–82.

Okimoto, Daniel I. *American in Disguise.* New York: Walker / Weatherhill, 1971.

Osgood, Robert Endicott. *Ideals and Self-Interest in America's Foreign Relations: The Great Transformation of the Twentieth Century.* Chicago: University of Chicago Press, 1953.

Osborne, Sidney. *The New Japanese Peril.* New York: Macmillan, 1921.

Peattie, Mark R. "Akiyama Saneyuki and Emergence of Modern Japanese Naval Doctrine." United States Naval Institute *Proceedings* 103 (January 1977).

———. *Sunburst: The Rise of Japanese Naval Air Power, 1909–1941.* Annapolis: Naval Institute Press, 2001.

Pederson, Paul. *The Five Stages of Culture Shock: Critical Incidents around the World.* Westport, Conn.: Greenwood Press, 1995.

Pelz, Stephen E. *Race to Pearl Harbor: The Failure of the Second London Naval Conference and the Onset of World War II.* Cambridge: Harvard University Press, 1974.

Pitkin, Walter B. *Must We Fight Japan?* New York: The Century Co., 1921.

Porter, David H., and Merrill E. Jarchow, eds. *Carleton Remembered, 1909–1986.* Northfield, Minn.: Carleton College, 1987.

Prange, Gordon W., in collaboration with Donald M. Goldstein and Katherine V. Dillon. *At Dawn We Slept: The Untold Story of Pearl Harbor.* New York: McGraw Hill, 1981.

Pratt, Julius W. *Expansionists of 1898: The Acquisition of Hawaii and the Spanish Islands.* Baltimore: Johns Hopkins University Press, 1936.

Puleston, William D. *Mahan: The Life and Work of Captain Alfred Thayer Mahan, U.S.N.* New Haven: Yale University Press, 1939.

Redway, Jacques W. *All around Asia: Redway's Geography Readers.* New York: Scribner's, 1910.

Reischauer, Edwin O. "Hiroshima Bomb Saved Japan from a Worse Fate." *Boston Globe* (August 30, 1983).

———. *My Life between Japan and America.* New York: Harper, 1986.

Roosevelt, Eleanor B. *Day before Yesterday: The Reminiscences of Mrs. Theodore Roosevelt Jr.* Garden City, N.Y.: Doubleday, 1959.

Roosevelt, Theodore. *Letters of Theodore Roosevelt.* Vol. 1. Edited by Eltin E. Morison. Cambridge: Harvard University Press, 1951.

Russell, Bertrand. *War Crimes in Vietnam.* London: Allen and Unwin, 1967.

Saloutus, Theodore. *They Remembered America: The Story of Repatriated Greek-Americans.* Berkeley: University of California Press, 1956.

Schilpp, Paul Arthur, ed. *The Philosophy of John Dewey.* New York: Tudor Publishing Co., 1939.

Schwantes, Robert S. *Japanese and Americans: A Century of Cultural Relations.* New York: Harper, 1955.

Schwenger, Peter. "America's Hiroshima." *Boundary* 2 (Spring 1994).

Seager, Robert II. *Alfred Thayer Mahan: The Man and His Letters.* 3 vols. Annapolis: Naval Institute Press, 1977.

———. "Alfred Thayer Mahan: Navalist and Historian." In *Quarterdeck and Bridge: Two Centuries of American Naval Leadership,* edited by James Bradford. Annapolis: Naval Institute Press, 1997.

Sedgwick, Ellery. "The Japanese Mystery." *Atlantic Monthly* (September 1930).

———. "Made in Japan." *Atlantic Monthly* (October 1930).

Sherry, Michael S. *The Rise of American Air Power: The Creation of Armageddon.* New Haven: Yale University Press, 1987.

Sherwin, Martin. "Hiroshima at Fifty: The Politics of History and Memory." *IHJ Bulletin* [A Quarterly Publication of the International House of Japan] 15 (1995): 1–10.

Sigal, Leon V. *Fighting to a Finish: The Politics of War Termination in the United States and Japan, 1945.* Ithaca: Cornell University Press, 1988.

Skates, John Ray. *The Invasion of Japan: Alternative to the Bomb.* Columbia: University of South Carolina Press, 1994.

Small, Melvin, ed. *Public Opinion and Historians: Interdisciplinary Perspectives.* Detroit: Wayne State University Press, 1970.

Smalley, William A. "Culture Shock, Language Shock, and the Shock of Self-Discovery." *Practical Anthropology* 10 (May–April 1963): 49–56.

Smith, Mary Cate. *The World and Its People, Book 6: Life in Asia.* New York: Silver Burdett, 1889.

Spector, Ronald H. *Eagle against the Sun: The American War with Japan.* New York: Free Press, 1985.

———. *Professors of War: The Naval War College and the Development of the Naval Profession.* Newport, R.I.: Naval War College Press, 1977.

———. *War at Sea: Sailors and Naval Combat in the Twentieth Century.* New York: Viking, 2001.

Sprout, Harold, and Margaret Sprout. *The Rise of American Naval Power, 1776–1918.* Princeton: Princeton University Press, 1959.

———. *Toward a New Order of Sea Power: American Naval Policy and the World Scene, 1918–1922.* Princeton: Princeton University Press, 1943.

Sprout, Margaret T. "Mahan, Evangelist of Sea Power." In *Makers of Modern Strategy: Military Thought from Machiavelli to Hitler.* Edited by Edward Mead Earle. Princeton: Princeton University Press, 1942.

Stearns, Harold, ed. *Civilization in the United States: An Inquiry by Twenty Americans.* New York: Harcourt, Brace, 1922.

Steiner, Jesse F. *The Japanese Invasion.* Reprint, New York: Arno Press, 1978.

Stevenson, Elizabeth. *Henry Adams: A Biography.* New York: Collier Books, 1955.

Stimson, Henry L., and McGeorge Bundy. *On Active Service in Peace and War.* New York: Harper, 1948.

Stoddard, Lothrop. "The East Tucks in Its Shirt." *Reader's Digest* (April 1929).

———. *The Rising Tide of Color against White World Supremacy.* New York: Scribner, 1920.

Street, Julian. *Mysterious Japan.* Garden City, N.Y.: Doubleday, 1922.

Sullivan, Mark. *Our Times: The Twenties.* New York: Scribner, 1925.

Sumida, John Tetsuro. *Inventing Grand Strategy and Teaching Command: The Classic Works of Alfred Thayer Mahan Reconsidered.* Baltimore: Johns Hopkins University Press, 1977.

Sunderland, Jabez T. *Rising Japan: Is She a Menace or a Comrade to Be Welcomed in the Fraternity of Nations?* New York: G. P. Putnam's Sons, 1918.

Talbot, Melvin F. "Thoughts on Leaving the Orient." *Atlantic Monthly* (June 1931).

Tarbell, Ida M. "That War with Japan." Editorial. *Outlook* (March 17, 1920).

Tarr, Ralph S., and Frank M. McMurray. *Third Book: Europe and Other Continents.* New York: Macmillan, 1906.

Taylor, Charles C. *The Life of Admiral Alfred Thayer Mahan, Naval Philosopher, Rear Admiral United States Navy.* London: George H. Doran, 1920.

Taylor, Sandra C. *Advocate of Understanding: Sidney Gulick and the Search for Peace with Japan.* Kent: Kent State University Press, 1984.

Terkel, Studs. *"The Good War": An Oral History of World War Two.* New York: Pantheon Books, 1984.

Thompson, Richard Austin. *The Yellow Peril, 1890–1924.* New York: Arno Press, 1978.

Tōgō Shigenori. *The Cause of Japan.* Edited and Translated by Tōgō Fumihiko and B. B. Blakeney. New York: Simon and Schuster, 1956.

Truman, Harry S. *Memoirs.* 2 vols. Garden City, N.Y.: Doubleday, 1955–1956.

———. *Public Papers of the Presidents: Harry S. Truman, 1945.* Washington, D.C.: Government Printing Office, 1961.

———. *Truman Speaks: Lectures and Discussions Held at Columbia University on April 27, 28, and 29, 1959.* New York: Columbia University Press, 1960.

Tuleja, Thaddeus V. *Statesmen and Admirals: Quest for a Far Eastern Naval Policy.* New York: Norton, 1963.

Turk, Richard W. *The Ambiguous Relationship: Theodore Roosevelt and Alfred Thayer Mahan.* New York: Greenwood Press, 1987.

Utley, Jonathan G. *Going to War with Japan.* Knoxville: University of Tennessee Press, 1985.

Villard, Oswald Garrison. "Japan—Enemy or Friend?" *Nation* (May 17, 1919).

Vinson, John Chalmers. "Charles Evans Hughes." In *An Uncertain Tradition: American Secretaries of State in the Twentieth Century*, edited by Norman A. Graebner. New York: McGraw-Hill, 1961.

Vlahos, Michael. "The Naval War College and the Origins of War-Planning against Japan." *Naval War College Review* 33 (July–August 1980).

Walker, J. Samuel. "The Decision to Use the Bomb: A Historiographical Update." *Diplomatic History* 14 (Winter 1990).

———. "Recent Literature on Truman's Atomic Bomb Decision: A Search for Middle Ground." *Diplomatic History* 29 (April 2005).

Wallace, Mike. "The Battle of the Enola Gay." In *Hiroshima Shadow: Writings on the Denial of History and the Smithsonian Controversy*, edited by Kai Bird and Lawrence Lifschultz. Stony Creek, Conn.: The Pamphleteer's Press, 1998.

Walzer, Michael. *Just and Unjust Wars: A Moral Argument with Historical Illustrations*. New York: Basic Books, 1977.

Weart, Spencer R. *Nuclear Fear: A History of Images*. Cambridge: Harvard University Press, 1988.

Weigley, Russell F. *The American Way of War: A History of United States Military Strategy and Policy*. Bloomington: Indiana University Press, 1973.

Wheeler, Gerald E. *Admiral William Veazie Pratt, U.S. Navy*. Washington, D.C.: Naval History Division, Department of the Navy, 1974.

———. *Prelude to Pearl Harbor: The United States Navy and the Far East, 1921–1931*. Columbia: University of Missouri Press, 1963.

———. "The United States Navy and the Japanese 'Enemy.'" *Military Affairs* 21 (Summer 1957).

White, Theodore. "The Danger from Japan." *New York Times Magazine*, July 28, 1985.

Wilson, Hugh. *Diplomat between Wars*. New York: Longmans, Green, 1941.

Winkler, Allan M. *Life under a Cloud: American Anxiety about the Atom*. New York: Oxford University Press, 1993.

Wittner, Lawrence S. *One World or None: A History of the World Nuclear Disarmament Movement through 1953*. Stanford: Stanford University Press, 1993.

Wolfers, Arnold. *Discord and Collaboration: Essays on International Politics*. Baltimore: Johns Hopkins University Press, 1962.

Wolferen, Karel van. *The Enigma of Japanese Power: People and Politics in a Stateless Nation*. New York: Macmillan, 1989.

Yavenditti, Michael J. "The American People and the Use of Atomic Bombs on Japan: The 1940s." *Historian* 36 (February 1974).

————. "John Hersey and the American Conscience: The Reception of 'Hiroshima.'" *Pacific Historical Review* 43 (February 1974).

In Japanese

Agawa Hiroyuki. *Yamamoto Isoroku.* Tokyo: Shinchōsha, 1969.

Akiba Tadatoshi. *Shinju to sakura.* Tokyo: Asahi Shimbunsha, 1986.

Akiyama Saneyuki. *Senjutsu ronshū* [Collected Treatises on Tactics]. Edited by Todaka Kazushige. Tokyo: Chūō Kron Shinsha, 2005.

Akiyama Saneyuki Kai. *Akiyama Saneyuki.* Akiyama Saneyuki Kai, 1933.

Andō Yoshio, ed. *Shōwa keizaishi e no shōgen.* Tokyo: Mainichi Shinbunsha, 1966.

Arai Shin'ichi. *Dainiji sekai taisen.* Tokyo: Tokyo Daigaku Shuppankai, 1973.

————. *Gembaku tōka e no michi.* Tokyo: Tokyo Daigaku Shuppankai, 1985.

Arima Kaoru. "Takarabe denki shiryō." Materials for biography, BBK.

Arisue Seizo. *Shūsen hishi: Arisue kikanchō no shuki.* Tokyo: Fuyō Shobō, 1976.

Aritake Shūji. *Saitō Makoto.* Tokyo: Jiji Tsūshinsha, 1958.

Asada Sadao. "Amerika no tai-Nichi kan to 'Washinton taisei'" [American Images of Japan and the "Washington System"]. In *Kokusai seiji: Nichi-Bei kankei no imēji.* Tokyo: Yūhikaku, 1966.

————. ed. and trans. *Arufureddo T. Mahan.* Tokyo: Kenkyūsha, 1977.

————. "Genbaku tōka o meguru Nichi-Bei ishiki no gyappu, 1945–1992." *Gaikō fōramu,* 47 (August 1993).

————, trans. *Gurū taishi to Nichi-Bei gaikō,* by Waldo H. Heinrichs. Tokyo: Grew Foundation, 2000. Originally published in English as *American Ambassador: Joseph C. Grew and the Development of the United States Diplomatic Tradition.* Boston: Little, Brown, 1966.

————. "Jinshu to bunka no sōkuō:Imin mondai to Nichi-Bei kankei" [Race and Culture: The Immigration Question and Japanese-American Relations]. In *Nihon to America 2: Demokurasī to Nichi-Bei kankei,* edited by Saito Makotō. Tokyo: Nan'undō, 1973.

————. "Kaigun seisaku no hen'yō to ta-Bei kaisen e no michi." In *Ryōtaisenkan no Nichi-Bei kankei* [Transformations of Japanese Naval Policy and the Road to the War with the United States]. Tokyo: Tokyo Daigaku Shuppankai, 1993.

————. "Karuchā shokku no gaikōshi. *Chūō kōron* (November 1994): 325–26.

————. "Kyū gaikō to shin gaikō no hazama, 1918–1922: Nichi-Bei detanto to Washinton taisei no seiritsu" [Between the Old Diplomacy and the New, 1918–1922: Japanese-American Détente and the Emergence of the Washington System]. In *Senkanki no Nihon gaikō,* edited by Iriye Akira and Aruga Tadashi. Tokyo: Tokyo Daigaku Shuppankai, 1984.

———. "Nichi-Bei kankei no imēji (Senzen)." In *Sōgō kōza Nihon no shakai bunkashi,* edited by Miwa Kimitada. Tokyo: Kōdansha, 1974.

———. "Nihon kaigun to gunshuku: Tai-Bei seisaku o meguru seiji katei" [The Japanese Navy and Naval Limitation: Political Process of Policy toward the United States]. In *Washington taisei to Nichi-Bei kankei,* edited by Hosoya Chihiro and Saitō Makoto. Tokyo: Tokyo Daigaku Shuppankai, 1978.

———. "Nihon kaigun to Tai-Bei seisaku oyobi senryaku" [The Japanese Navy's Policy and Strategy toward the United States]. In *Nichi-Bei kankeishi,* vol. 2, edited by Hosoya Chihiro et al. Tokyo: Tokyo Daigaku Shuppankai, 1971.

———. "1920-nendai ni okeru America no Nihonzō: Imēji kenkyū no ichi shiron" [American Images of Japan during the 1920s: An Approach to "Image Studies"]. *Doshisha Amerika kenkyū* 2 (1965).

———. "Reisen no kigen to shūseishugi kenkyū: Amerika no baai." *Kokusai mondai,* no. 170 (May 1974).

———. *Ryotaisenkan no Nichi-Bei kankei: Kaigun to seisaku kettei katei.* Tokyo: Tokyo Daigaku Shuppankai, 1993.

———. "Washinton kaigi o meguru Nichi-Bei seisaku kettei katei no hikaku." In *Taigai seisaku kettei katei no Nichi-Bei hikaku,* edited by Hosoya Chihiro and Watanuku Jōji. Tokyo: Tokyo Daigaku Shuppankai, 1977.

———. "Washinton kaigun gunshuku no seiji katei: Futarino Katō o megutte" [The Politics of Washington Naval Limitation Focusing on the Two Katōs]. *Doshisha hōgaku* 49 (March 1998).

Asahi Shimbunsha, ed. *Nihon to Amerika.* Tokyo: Asahi Shimbunsha, 1971.

Asahi Shimbunsha Yoron Chōsashitsu, ed. *Shiryō Beikoku ni okeru tai-Nichi yoron chōsa.* Tokyo: Asahi Shimbunsha, 1982.

Besshi Atsuhiko. *Sensō no oshiekata: Sekai no kyōkasho ni miru.* Tokyo: Shinchōsha, 1983.

Bōeichō Bōei Kenshūjo. *Shiryōshū: Kaigun nendo sakusen keikaku* [Collected Documents: The Navy's Annual Operational Plans]. Asagumo Shinbunsha, 1986.

Bōeichō Bōei Kenshūjo Senshibu. *Senshi sōsho: Daihon'ei kaigunbu: Rengō kantai.* Vol. 1. Tokyo: Asagumo Shinbunsha, 1975.

———. *Senshi soshō: Daihon'ei kaigunbu: Daitōa sensō kaisen keii.* 2 vols. Tokyo: Asagumo Shinbunsha, 1979.

———. *Senshi sōsho: Daihon'ei rikugunbu.* Vol. 1. Tokyo: Asagumo Shinbunsha, 1975.

————. *Senshi soshō: Daihon'ei rikugunbu: Daitōa sensō kaisen keii.* 5 vols. Tokyo: Asagumo Shinbunsha, 1973–1974.

————. *Senshi sōsho: Hawai sakusen.* Tokyo: Asagumo Shinbunsha, 1967.

————. *Senshi sōsho: Hondo bōkū sakusen.* Tokyo: Asagumo Shinbunsha, 1968.

————. *Senshi sōsho: Kaigun gunsenbi.* Vol. 1. Tokyo: Asagumo Shinbunsha, 1969.

————. *Senshi sōsho: Kantōgun* [War History Series: The Kwantung Army]. Tokyo: Asagumo Shinbunsha, 1969.

————. *Senshi sōsho: Sensuikanshi.* Tokyo: Asagumo Shinbunsha, 1979.

Chihaya Masataka, *Nihon kaigun no senryaku hassō.* Tokyo: Purejidentosha, 1982.

Chūgoku Shinbunsha, ed. *Honoo no hi kara 20-nen.* Tokyo: Miraisha, 1966.

————, ed. *Nenpyō Hiroshima: Kaku jidai 50-nen no kiroku.* Hiroshima: Chūgoku Shinbunsha, 1995.

Daihon'ei Rikugunbu Sensō Shidōhan. *Kimutsu sensō nisshi* [Confidential War Journal]. Edited by Gunjishi Gakkai. 2 vols. Tokyo: Kinshōsha, 1998.

Fujita Hisanori. *Jijūchō no kaisō.* Tokyo: Chūō Kōronsha, 1987.

Fukudome Shigeru. *Kaigun no hansei.* Tokyo: Nihon Shuppan Kyodō, 1951.

————. *Shikan: Shinjuwan kōgeki.* Tokyo: Jiyū Ajiasha, 1955.

Fukui, Shizuo. *Nihon no gunkan.* Tokyo: Shuppan Kyōdōsha, 1956.

Gendaishi shiryō. Vol. 7, *Manshū jihen.* Edited by Kobayashi Tatsuo and Shimada Toshihiko. Misuzu Shobō, 1964.

————. Vol. 8, *Nitshū jihen,* 1 [China War 1]. Edited by Shimada Toshihiko and Inaba Masao. 1964.

————. Vol. 10, *Nitchū sensō,* 3. Edited by Tsunoda Jun. 1964.

————. Vol. 11, *Zoku Manshū jihen* [Sequel Volume on the Manchurian Incident]. Edited by Inaba Masao, Kobayashi Tatsuo, and Shimada Toshihiko. 1965.

————. Vol. 12, *Nitchū sensō,* 4. Edited by Kobayashi Tatsuo, Inaba Masao, Shimada Toshihiko, and Usui Katsumi. 1965.

Hara Keiichirō, ed. *Hara Kei nikki.* Vol. 5. Tokyo: Fukumura Shuppan, 1965.

Hara Shirō. *Senryaku naki kaisen: Kyū Daihon'ei Rikugunbu ichi bakuryō no kaisō.* Tokyo: Fukumura Shoter, 1987.

Harada Kumao. *Saionjikō to seikyoku.* 8 vols. Tokyo: Iwanami Shoten, 1950–1952.

Hasegawa Nyozekan. "Minzoku shugi to kokusaishugi." *Warera* (March 1919).

————. "Osaka *Asahi* kara *Warera.*" *Warera* (February 1919).

————. "Risō seiji oyobi genjutsu seiji no nidai seiryoku no shōtotsu" [Clash of Realistic Politics and Realpolitik]. *Chūō kōron* (August 1918).

Hasegawa Tsuyoshi. *Antō: Sutārin Torūman to Nihon kōfuku*. Tokyo: Chūō Kōron Shinsha, 2006.

Hata Ikuhiko. "Kantaiha to jōyakuha: Kaigun no habatsu keifu" [The Fleet Faction and the Treaty Faction: Genealogy of Naval Factionalism]. In *Shōwashi no gunbu to seiji, Vol. 1: Gunbu shihai no kaimaku*, edited by Miyake Masaki et al. Tokyo: Daiichi Hōki, 1983.

———*Shōwashi no gunjintachi* [Military and Naval Leaders during the Showa Period]. Tokyo: Bungei Shunjū, 1982.

———. *Shōwa tennō itsutsu no ketsudan*. Tokyo: Bungei Shunjū, 1994.

———. "Suetsugu Nobumasa—Kantaiha to yū" [Suetsugu Nobumasa: The Hero of the Fleet Faction]. *Keizai Ōrai* (June 1979).

Hatano Masaru, ed. *Kaigun no gaikōkan Takeshita Isamu nikki*. Tokyo: Fuyō Shobō, 1998.

Hatano Sumio. "'Kokutai goji' to Potsudamu sengen." *Gaikō jihō*, no. 1320 (July / August 1995).

Hattori Takushirō. *Daitōa sensō zenshi*. Vols. 1 and 8. Tokyo: Hara Shobō, 1965.

Hayashi Kiroku. "Kafu kaigi to waga teikoku." *Gaikō jihō* (1 May 1922).

Hayashi Shigeru, ed. *Nihon shūsenshi*. 3 vols. Tokyo: Yomiuri Shinbunsha, 1962.

Hirama Yōichi. "A. T. Mahan ga Nihon Kaigun Seiji." *keizai shigaku*, no. 220 (February 1993).

———. "Mahan no Nihonkan to Nichi-Bei kankei e no eikyō" [Mahan's Views of Japan and Their Influence on Japanese-American Relations]. *Kokusai Seiji, Vol. 102: Kan Taiheiyō kokusai kankei no imēji* (1993).

Hirose Kazuko. "Hiroshima wa Nihon o sukutta ka: 'Raishawā kenkai' e no Amerika no kyōjutachi no iken." *Asahi Jānaru* (December 16, 1983).

Hiroshimashi-Nagasakishi Gembaku Saigaishi Henshū Iinkai, ed. *Hiroshima- Nagasaki no gembaku saigai*. Tokyo: Iwanami Shoten, 1979.

Hirota Kōki Denki Kankōkai, ed. *Hirota Kōki*. Tokyo: Hirota Kōki Denki Kankōkai, 1966.

Honda Katsuichi. *Korosareru gawa no ronri* [The Logic of Those Who Get Killed]. Tokyo: Asahi Shimbunsha, 1971.

Honjō Shigeru. *Honjō nikki*. Tokyo: Hara Shobō, 1967.

Horikawa Jun'ichirō. *Jufu sangoku kaigi to sonogo* [The Junēva Conference and After]. Tokyo: Hōbunkan, 1929.

Hoshina Zenshirō. *Daitōwa sensō hishi*. Tokyo: Hara Shobō, 1975.

Hosokawa Morisada. *Jōhō tennō ni tassezu*. 2 vols. Tokyo: Dōkōsha Isobe Shobō, 1953.

Hosoya Chihiro et al. *Kioku to shite no Pāru hābā* [Pearl Harbor as Memory]. Kyoto: Mineruva Shobō, 2004.

———— et al., eds. *Taiheiyō sensō no shūketsu: Ajia Taiheiyō no sengo keisei* [The Close of the Pacific War: The Emergence of the Postwar Asia-Pacific]. Tokyo: Kashiwa Shobō, 1997.

Hosoya Chihiro, and Saitō Makoto, eds. *Washinton taisei to Nichi-Bei kankei.* Tokyo: Tokyo Daigaku Shuppan kai, 1978.

Ienaga Soshō Shien Shimin no Kai, ed. *Taiheiyō senso to kyōkasho* [The Pacific War and Textbooks]. Tokyo: Shisō no Kagakusha, 1970.

Ikeda, Kiyoshi. *Kaigun to Nihon.* Tokyo: Chūō Kōronsha, 1981.

————. *Nihon no kaigun.* Tokyo: Shiseidō, 1967.

————. "Rondon gunshuku jōyaku to tōsuiken mondai." *Hōgaku zasshi* 15, no. 2 (1968).

Ikeda Sumihisa. *Nihon no magarikado.* Tokyo: Chishiro Shuppan, 1968.

Ikei Masaru, Hatano Masaru, and Kurosawa Fumitaka, eds. *Hamaguchi Osachi nikki, zuikanroku.* Tokyo: Misuzu Shobō, 1991.

Inoue Shigeyoshi Denki Kankō Kai, ed. *Inoue Shigeyoshi.* Tokyo: Editor, 1982.

Ishida Akira. *Hibaku kyōshi.* Tokyo: Hitotsubashi Shobō, 1976.

————. "Sengo kyōiku ni okeru 'Genbaku mondai' no ketsujo." *Gendai kyōiku kagaku,* no. 173 (March 1972).

Ishii Itarō. *Gaikōkan no isshō.* Tokyo: Yomiuri Shinbunsha, 1972.

Ishii Kikujirō. *Gaikō yoroku.* Tokyo: Iwanami Shoten, 1930.

Ishii Osamu. "Pāru hāba no zanshō: Nichi-Bei no keizai, shakai, bunka masatsu, 1982–1992." In *Kioku to shite no pāru hāba* [Pearl Harbor as Memory], edited by Hosoya Chihiro et al. Kyoto: Mineruva Shobō, 2004.

Ishikawa Shingo. *Shinjuwan made no keii.* Tokyo: Jiji Tsūshinsha, 1960.

Ishikawa Yasushi. *Satō Tetsutarō kaigun chūjō den* [Biography]. Tokyo: Hara Shobō, 2000.

Itō Kinjirō. *Ikiteiru kaishō Katō Kanji.* Tokyo: Shōwa Shobō, 1942.

Itō Kōbun. "Satō Tetsutarō no kokubō riron [National Defense Theory of Satō Tetsutarō]. *Kaikankō hyōron* 4 (September 1966).

Itō Masanori. *Gunshuku?* Tokyo: Shun'yōdō, 1939.

————. *Rengō kantai no saigo.* Reprint, Tokyo: Bungei Shunjū, 1969.

Itō Takashi. *Shōwa shoki seijishi kenkyū: Rondon kaigun gunshuku mondai o meguru sho seiji shūdan no taikō to teikei* [A Study of the Political History of the Early Showa Period: Conflicts and Alignments of Political Groups over the Question of the London Naval Limitation]. Tokyo: Tokyo Daigaku Shuppankai, 1969.

Kaigun Daigakkō. "Taishō 4 naishi 9-nen sen'eki kaigun senshi furoku dai-6 hen kimitsu hoshū." Naval Staff College, unpublished study, n.d. BBK.

Kaigun Daijin Kanbō, ed. *Kaigun gunbi enkaku.* 1934. Reprinted by Gannandō, 1970.

Kaigunshō Kaigun Gunji Fukyūbu. *Kokumin no seikatsu to gunshuku.* (October 1934). BBK.

Kaikoku Hyakunen Kinen Bunka Jigyō Kai, ed. *Nichi-Bei bunka kōshōshi, 2: Tsūshō sangyō-hen.* Tokyo: Yōyōsha, 1954.

Kanazawa Masao. *Waga kaigun to Takahashi Sankich.* Tokyo: Takahashi Shin'ichi, 1970.

Katō Kanji Taishō Denki Kankōkai, comp. *Katō Kanji taishō den.* Tokyo: Denki Hensankai, 1941.

Katō Kanji. *Zoku gendaishi shiryō, Vol. 5: Kaigun, Katō Kanji nikki.* Edited by Itō Takashi et al. Tokyo: Misuzu Shobō, 1994.

Kawabe Torashirō. *Kawabe Torashirō kaikoroku.* Tokyo: Mainichi Shinbunsha, 1979.

Kawanishi Susumu, and Takita Yoshiko, eds. and trans. *Amerikajin no Nihonkan.* Tokyo: Kenkyūsha, 1975.

Kawata Tadashi et al. *Atarashii shakai: Rekishi.* Tokyo: Tokyo Shoseki, 1992.

Kaya Okinori. *Senzen sengo 80-nen* [Eighty Years before and after the War]. Tokyo: Roman, 1975.

Kiba Kōsuke. *Nomura Kichisaburō.* Tokyo: Denki Kankōkai, 1961.

Kido Kōichi Kenkyūkai, ed. *Kido Kōichi kankei bunsho.* Tokyo: Tokyo Daigaku Shuppankai, 1966.

———. ed. *Kido Kōichi nikki.* 2 vols. Tokyo: Tokyo Daigaku Shuppankai, 1966.

———. ed. *Kido Kōichi nikki: Tokyo saibanki.* Tokyo: Tokyo Daigaku Shuppankai, 1980.

Kobayashi Seizō. *Kaigun taishō Kobayashi Seizō oboegaki.* Edited by Itō Takashi and Nomura Minoru. Tokyo: Yamakawa Shuppansha, 1981.

Kobayashi Tatsuo, ed. *Suiusō nikki: Rinji Gaikō Chōsa Iinkai kaigi hikki nado.* Tokyo: Hara Shobō, 1966.

Kobayashi Toshiiki, "Usureru hibaku no kioku, Takamaru kakusensō e no fuan." *Hōsō kenkyū to chōsa* (December 2005).

Kodama Kōta et al. *Chūgaku shakai: Rekishiteki bun'ya.* Tokyo: Nihon Shoseki, 1986.

Ko Matsudaira Tsuisōkai, comp. *Matsudaira Tsuneo tsuisōroku.* Tokyo: Editor, 1961.

Konoe Fumimaro. "Ei-Bei hon'i no heiwashugi o haisu." *Nihon oyobi Nihonjin* (December 15, 1918).

Koyama Hirotake. *Zōho gunji shisō no kenkyū.* Enlarged ed., Tokyo: Shinshensha, 1977.

Kurihara Hirota, ed. *Gensui Katō Tomosaburō den.* Tokyo: Miyata Mitsuo, 1928.

Kurihara Ken, and Hatano Sumio, eds. *Shūsen kōsaku no kiroku.* 2 vols. Tokyo: Kōdansha, 1975.

Kurono Taeru. *Teikoku kokubō hōshin no kenkyū* [A Study of the Imperial National Defense Policy]. Tokyo: Sōwasha, 2000.

Kusumi Tadao. "Akiyama Saneyuki to Nihonkai kaisen." *Chūō kōron* (August 1965).

Kyōkasho Kenkyū Sentā. *Shakaika kyōkasho no Nichi-Bei hikaku* [Comparison of Japanese and American Social Studies Textbooks]. Tokyo: Daiichi Hōki, 1981.

Makino Nobuaki. "Kokusai renmei to Nihon no taido." *Taiyō* (May 1920).

———. *Makino Nobuaki nikki* [Diary]. Edited by Itō Takashi. Tokyo: Chūō Kōronsha, 1990.

Makino Yōko. *Rafukadio Hān: Ibunka taiken no hateni.* Tokyo: Chūō Kōronsha, 1992.

Matsutani Makoto. *Dai Tōa sensō shūshū no shinsō.* Tokyo: Fuyō Shobō, 1980.

Mitani Taichirō. "'Tenkanki' (1918–1921) no gaikō shidō: Hara Kei oyobi Tanaka Giichi o chūshin to shite." In *Kindai Nihon no seiji shidō,* vol. 2, edited by Shinohara Hajime and Mitani Taichirō. Tokyo: Tokyo Daigaku Shuppankai, 1965.

Mizuno Hironori. "Ā Akiyama kaigun chūjō." *Chūō kōron* (March 1918).

Mori Shōzō, *Sempū nijūnen.* Reissued, Tokyo: Kōjinsha, 1968.

Moriyama, Atsushi. *Nichi-Bei kaisen no seiji katei* [The Political Process of Commencement of the Japanese-American War]. Tokyo: Yoshikawa Kōbunkan, 1998.

Morobuse Kōshin. *Sensō shisho.* Tokyo: Chūō Kōronsha, 1990.

Murakami Teiichi, ed. *Kaigun shōsho Akiyama Saneyuki: Gundan* [Rear Admiral Akiyama Saneyuki, A War Story]. Tokyo, 1917.

Nagai Kansei. "Katō Kanji Shōshō ikkō no hō-Doku chōsa" [Rear Admiral Katō's Visit to Germany for Military investigations]. *Hatō* 23 (September 1977); 23 (November 1997).

Nagai Sumitaka. "Kokubō hōshin to kaigun yōhei shisō no hensen." (May 1962), pt. 13. Staff Study. BBK.

Nakahara Yoshimasa. "Dainiji sekai taisenshi." Unpublished history. BBK.

Nakamura Hidekazu et al. *Sekaishi.* Tokyo: Shoseki, 1988.

Nakamura Kikuo, ed. *Shōwa kaigun hishi.* Tokyo: Banchō Shobō, 1969.

Nakamura Takafusa et al., eds. *Gendai o tsukuru hitobito.* Tokyo: Mainichi Shinbunsha, 1971.

Nakazawa Tasuku Kankō Kai, ed. *Kaigun chūjō Nakazawa Tasuku: Sakusen buchō, jinji kyokuchō.* Tokyo: Editor, 1979.

Neu, Charles E. "Higashi Ajia ni okeru Amerika gaikōkan." In *Washinton taisei to Nichi-Bei kankei.* Edited by Hosoya Chihiro and Saitō Makoto. Tokyo: Tokyo Daigaku Shuppankai.

NHK (Nihon Hōsō Kyōkai). "Dokyumento Shōwa" Shuzaihan. *Dokyumento Shōwa 5: Orenji sakusen* [Documentary on the Shōwa Era, 5: War Plan Orange]. Tokyo: Kadokawa Shoten, 1986.

―――. "Sengo 50-nen: Sensō no tsumeato—Hiroshima, Nagasaki, Okinawa." *Hōsō kenkyū to chōsa* (November 1995).

Nihon Dewey Gakkai, ed. *Dewey rai-Nichi 50-shūnen kinen ronbunshū: Dewey kenkyū.* Tokyo: Tamagawa Daigaku Shuppanbu, 1969.

Nihon Kokusai Seiji Gakkai [Japan Association of International Relations], ed. *TSM, Vol. 1: Manshūjihen Zen'ya* [The Eve of the Manchurian Incident]. Tokyo: Asahi Shimbunsha, 1963.

―――. *TSM, Vol. 5: Sangoku Dōmei, Nisso Chūritsu Jōyaku* [The Tripartite Pact, Soviet-Japanese Neutrality Treaty].

―――. *TSM, Vol. 6: Nanpō shinshutsu* [Southward Advance].

―――. *TSM, Vol. Nichi-Bei kaisen* [The Japanese-American Hostilities].

―――. *TSM: Bekkan shiryōhen* [Separate Volumes of Documents].

Nishijima Ariatsu. *Gembaku wa naze tōka saretaka: Nihon kōfuku o meguru senryaku to gaikō.* Tokyo: Aoki Shoten, 1968, 1985.

Nomura Minoru. *Nihon kaigun no rekishi* [A History of the Japanese Navy]. Tokyo: Yoshikawa Kōbunkan, 2002.

―――. *Rekishi no naka no Nihon kaigun.* Tokyo: Hara Shobō, 1980.

―――."Tai-Bei-Ei kaisen to tai-Bei 7-wari shisō." *Gunji shigaku* 9, no. 3 (1973).

―――. *Tennō, Fushimi no miya to Nihon kaigun.* Tokyo: Bungei Shunjū, 1988.

―――. *Yamamoto Isoroku saikō* [Yamamoto Isoroku Reconsidered]. Tokyo: Chūō Kōronsha, 1996.

Odagiri Hideo. *Shinbun shiryō genbaku.* Tokyo: Nihon tosho sentā, 1987.

Ogata Taketora. *Ichi gunjin no shōgai.* Tokyo: Bungei Shunjū Shinsha, 1955.

Okada Sadahiro, ed. *Okada Keisuke kaikoroku.* Tokyo: Mainichi Shinbunsha, 1977.

Okada Taishō Kiroku Hensankai, ed. *Okada Keisuke.* Tokyo: Editor, 1956.

Oka Yoshitake, ed. *Yoshino Sakuzō hyōronshū.* Tokyo: Iwanami Bunko, 1975.

Ōki Misao. *Ōki nikki: Shūsenjino teikoku.* Tokyo: Asahi Shimbusha, [1969].

Ōkubo Tatsumasa et al., eds. (Doi Akira, supervisor). *Shōwa shakai keizai shiryō shūsei: Kaigunshō shiryō.* 12 vols. Tokyo: Ochanomizu Shobō, 1978–1987.

Ōkubo Toshiaki, ed. *Gaikokujun no mita Nihon, 3: Meiji.* Tokyo: Chikuma Shobō, 1961.

Ōkura Kimmochi. *Ōkura Kimmochi nikki.* Edited by Naisei Kenkyūkai and Nihon Kindai Shiryō Kenkyūkai. Tokyo: Editor, 1971.

Ōmae Toshikazu. "Kyū Nihon kaigun no heijutsuteki hensen to koreni tomonau gunbi narabini sakusen, 1: Daitōa sensō kaisen made." Unpublished staff study. BBK.

Osada Arata. "Genshi bakudan wa naze tōka saretaka." *Sekai* (September 1953).

Ōsumi Taishō Denki Kankōkai, ed. *Danshaku Ōsumi Mineo den.* Tokyo: Kaigun Yūshū Kai, 1943.

Ōta Yūzō. *Rafukadio Hān: Kyozō to jitsuzō.* Tokyo: Iwanami Shoten, 1994.

Ōya Hayato [Ishikawa Shingo]. *Nihon no kiki* [Japan's Crisis]. Moriyama Shoten, 1931.

Pelz, Stephen E. "Rondon gunshuku kaigi to yoron" [London Naval Disarmament Conference and Public Opinion]. *Nihon Kokusai seiji: Nihon gaikōshi kenkyū—Gaikō to yoron.* Tokyo: Yūhikaku, 1970.

Rekishigaku Kenkyūkai, comp. *Taiheiyō sensōshi.* Vol. 6. Tokyo: Aoki Shoten, 1971–1973.

Saitō Shishaku Kinenkai, ed. *Shishaku Saitō Makoto Den.* Tokyo: Editor, 1942.

Sakomizu Hisatsune. *Dai Nippon teikoku saigo no yonkagetsu.* Tokyo: Oriento, 1973.

————. "Kōfukuji no shinsō." *Jiyū kokumin* (February 1946).

————. *Shūsen no shinsō.* Tokyo: privately printed, [1955].

Sakamoto Yoshikazu, ed. *Kaku to ningen: Kaku to taiketsu suru 20-seiki* [Confronting Nuclearism: The Twentieth-Century World Crisis]. Tokyo: Iwanami Shoten, 1999.

————, and Shōno Naomi, supervisors. *Nihon genbakuron taikei, Vol. 7: Rekishi ninshiki to shiteno genbaku* [A Survey of A-Bomb Studies, Vol. 7: The Atomic Bomb as Historical Knowledge]. Tokyo: Nihon Tosho Sentā, 1999.

Sakurai Masakiyo. *Teitoku Akiyama Saneyuki.* Tokyo: Iwanami Shoten, 1934.

Sanbō Honbu, comp. *Haisen no kiroku.* Tokyo: Hara Shobō, 1979.

————, ed. *Sugiyama memo: Daihon'ei-seifu renraku kaigi nado hikki* [Sugiyama Memo: Record of Imperial Headquarters-Government Liaison Conferences, etc.]. Tokyo: Hara Shobō, 1967.

Sanseidō. *Nihonshi A.* Tokyo: Sanseidō, 2004.

————. *Nihonshi B.* Tokyo: Tokyo Shoseki, 2005.

————. *Shōkai Nihonshi B (kaiteiban).* Tokyo: Sanseidō, 2003.

Satō Ichirō. *Satō Ichirō gunshuku kaigi kaisōroku, shōgai* [Memoirs of Naval Arms Conference and My Life]. Edited by Satō Tama and Satō Shintarō. Privately printed, 1991.

Satō Motoei and Kurosawa Fumitaka, eds. *GHQ Rekishika jutsuroku: Shūsenshi shiryō.* 2 vols. Tokyo: Hara Shobō, 2002.

Satō Naotake. *Kaiko hachijū-nen.* Tokyo: Jiji Tsūshinsha, 1964.

Satō Seizaburō. "Kyōchō to jiritsu to no aida: Nihon." *Nenpō seijigaku 1969: Kokusai kinchō kanwa no seiji katei* [The Annual of the Japanese Political Science Association], (1969).

Satō Tetsutarō. "Kokubō sakugi." Secret, Navy Ministry, 1912. BBK.

———. *Teikoku kokubōron.* Tokyo: Satō Tetsutarō, 1902.

———. *Teikoku kokubō shiron.* 1908. Reprint, Tokyo: Hara Shobō, 1979.

———. *Teikoku kokubō shironshō.* Tokyo: Saikōsha, 1912.

Satō Tetsutarō et al. *Kokubō mondai no kenkyū.* Navy Ministry, 1913. BBK.

Sawamoto Yorio. "Sawamoto Yorio kaigun jikan nikki: Nichi-Bei kaisen zen'ya." *Chūō kōron* (January 1988).

Shibusawa Seien Kinen Zaidan Ryūmonsha, ed. *Shibusawa Eiichi denki shiryō.* Tokyo: Ryūmonsha, 1960.

Shidehara Heiwa Zaidan, ed. *Shidehara Kijūrō.* Tokyo: Editor, 1955.

Shidehara Kijūrō. *Gaikō 50-nen.* Tokyo: Yomiuri Shinbunsha, 1951.

Shigemitsu Mamoru. *Shōwa no dōran.* 2 vols. Tokyo: Chūō Kōronsha, 1952.

Shimada Kinji. *Amerika ni okeru Akiyama Saneyuki.* Tokyo: Asahi Shimbunsha, 1969.

———. *Roshia sensō zen'ya no Akiyama Saneyuki.* Tokyo: Asahi Shimbunsha, 1990.

Shimada Shigetarō. "Shimada Shigetarō taishō kaisen nikki." *Bungei shunjū* (December 1976).

Shimanuki Takeharu. "Daiichiji sekai taisen igo no kokubō hōshin, shoyō heiryoku, yōhei kōryō no hensen." *Gunji shigaku* 9 (1973).

———. "Nichi-Ro sensō ikō ni okeru kokubō hōshin,shoyō heiryoku, yōhei kōryō no hensen" [The Development of National Defense Policy, the Naval Strength Requirement, and General Plan for Strategy since the Russo-Japanese War]. *Gunji shigaku* 8 (March 1973).

Shimomura Kainan. *Shūsen hishi.* Tokyo: Kōdansha, 1985.

Shinmyō Takeo, ed. *Kaigun sensō kentō kaigi kiroku: Taiheiyō sensō kaisen no keii.* Tokyo: Mainichi Shinbunsha, 1976.

Shinohara Hiroshi. *Kaigun Sōsetsushi: Igirisu gunji komondan no kage.* Tokyo: Eibupōto, 1986.

Shiryō Chōsa Kai, ed. *Taiheiyō sensō to Tomioka Sadatoshi* [The Pacific War and Tomioka Sadatoshi]. Tokyo: Gunji Kenkyūkai, 1971.

Sorimachi Eiichi. *Ningen Yamamoto Isoroku: Gensui no shōgai.* Tokyo: Kōwadō, 1964.

Suekuni Masao. "Katō Tomosaburō: Washinton gunshyuku jōyaku teiketsu no eidan" [Katō Tomosaburō: Decision for the Conclusion of the Washington Naval Treaty]. In *Nihon kaigun no meishō to meisanbō,* edited by Yoshida Toshio. Tokyo: Jinbutsu Ōraisha, 1986.

Sugimura Yōtarō. *Hatashite kyōkoku wa sametariya.* Tokyo: Kokusai Rengō Kyōkai, 1922.

Suzuki Hajime, ed. *Suzuki Kantarō jiden.* Tokyo, 1985.

Takagi Sōkichi. *Jidenteki Nihon kaigun shimatsuki* [Autobiographical Account of the Japanese Navy]. Tokyo: Kōjinsha, 1971.

———. *Nikki to jōhō* [Diary and Reports]. 2 vols. Edited by Itō Takashi et al. Tokyo: Misuzu Shobō, 2000.

———. *Shikan Taiheiyō sensō.* Tokyo: Bungei Shunjū, 1969.

———. *Taiheiyō sensō to rikukaigun no kōsō* [The Pacific War and the Army-Navy Conflict]. Tokyo: Keizai Ōraisha, 1967.

———. *Takagi kaigun shōshō oboegaki.* Tokyo: Mainichi Shinbunsha, 1979.

———. *Takagi Sōkichi nikki: Nichi-Doku-I sangoku dōmei to Tōjō naikaku datō.* Tokyo: Mainichi Shinbunsha, 1985.

———. *Yamamoto Isoroku to Yonai Mitsumasa.* Tokyo: Bungei Shunjū, 1967.

Takagi Sōkichi and Sanematsu Yuzuru, eds. *Kaigun taishō Yonai Mitsumasa oboegaki.* Tokyo: Kōjinsha, 1978.

Takahashi Akihiro. "Fukugan de miru genbaku higai to sensō kagai." In *Nihon genbakuron taikei, Vol. 7,* edited by Iwadara Hiroshi and Nakajima Tatsumi. Tokyo, Nohon Tosho Sentā, 1999.

Tanaka Nobumasa. *Dokyumento Shōwa tennō,* Vol. 5: *Haisen,* pt. 2. Tokyo: Ryokufū Shuppan, 1988.

Terasaki Hidenari and Mariko Terasaki Miller, eds. *Shōwa tennō dokuha-kuroku, Terasaki Hidenari goyōgakari nikki.* Tokyo: Bungei Shunjū, 1991.

Terashima Ken Denki Kankōkai, ed. *Terashima Ken den.* Tokyo: Terashima Ken Denki Kankō Kai, 1973.

Tōgō Shigehiko. *Sofu Tōgō Shigenori no shōgai.* Tokyo: Bungei Shunjū, 1993.

Tōgō Shigenori. *Jidai no ichimen.* Tokyo: Kaizōsha, 1952.

Tokutomi Sohō. *Jimu ikkagen.* Tokyo: Min'yōsha, 1913.

Tomioka Sadatoshi. *Kaisen to shūsen: Hito to kikō to keikaku.* Tokyo: Mainichi Shinbunsha, 1968.

———. "Taiheiyō sensō zenshi." Vols. 1–4. Unpublished study. Shiryō Chōsa Kai., n.d.

Toyama Saburō. *Daitōa sensō to senshi no kyōkun.* Tokyo: Hara Shobō, 1978.

Tōyama Shigeki, Imai Seiichi, and Fujiwara Akira, *Shōwashi.* Rev. ed. Tokyo: Iwanami Shinsho, 1959.

Toyoda Soemu. *Saigo no teikoku kaigun.* Tokyo: Sekai no Nihonsha, 1950.

Tsukishima Kenzō. *Rafukadio Hān no Nihonkan.* Tokyo: Keisō Shobō, 1964.

Tsunoda Jun. *Manshū mondai to kokubō hōshin: Meiji kōki ni okeru kokubō kankyō no hendō.* Tokyo: Hara Shobō, 1967.

Uchida Yasuya Denki Hensan Iinkai, ed. *Uchida Yasuya.* Tokyo: Kashima Kenkyūsho Shuppankai, 1969.

Ugaki Kazushige. *Ugaki Kazushige nikki.* Edited by Tsunoda Jun. Tokyo: Misuzu Shobō, 1968.

Ugaki Matome. *Sensō roku* [War Diary]. Tokyo: Hara Shobō, 1968.

Ujita Naoyoshi. *Shidehara Kijūrō.* Tokyo: Jiji Tsūshinsha, 1958.

Ukita Kazutami. "Beikoku daitōryō no kyōsho o yomu." *Taiyō* (January 1918).

———. "Daitōryō Wiruson to gaikō no daikakumei." *Taiyō* (June 1917).

Unno Yoshirō. *Nihon gaikōshi, Vol. 16: Kaigun gunshuku kōshō, fusen jōyaku.* Tokyo: Kashima Kenkyūsho Shuppankai, 1973.

Wakatsuki Reijirō. *Kofūan kaikoroku.* Tokyo: Yomiuri Shinbunsha, 1950.

Yabe Teiji. *Konoe Fumimaro.* 2 vols. Tokyo: Kōbundō, 1952.

Yamada Akira and Koketsu Atsushi. *Ososugita seidan: Shōwa tennō no sensō shidō to sensō sekinin.* Tokyo: Shōwa Shuppan, 1991.

Yamagiwa Akira and Tachibana Seiitsu, eds. *Shiryō Manhattan keikaku.* Translated by Okada Ryōnosuke. Tokyo: Ōtsuki Shoten, 1993.

Yamaji Kazuyoshi. *Nihon kaigun no kōbō to sekininsha tachi.* Tokyo: Tsukudo Shobō, 1959.

Yamamoto Eisuke, comp. *Danshaku Ōsumi Mineo* [Biography of Baron Ōsumi Mineo]. Tokyo: Kaigun Yūshūkai, 1943.

Yamanashi Katsunoshin. *Katō Tomosaburō gensui o shinobu.* Tokyo: Suikōsha, 1967.

Yamanashi Katsunoshin Sensei Kinen Shuppan Iinkai, ed. *Yamanashi Katsunoshin ihōroku.* Tokyo: Editor, 1968.

Yasui Sōmei. "Yo no mitaru Akiyama Saneyuki kaigun chūjō." *Taiyō* (March 1918).

Yokoyama Ichirō. *Umi e kaeru: Kaigun shōshō Yokoyama Ichirō kaikoroku.* Tokyo: Hara Shobō, 1980.

Yomiuri Shinbunsha, ed. *Shōwashi no tennō.* 30 vols. Tokyo: Yomiuri Shinbunsha, 1968.

Yoshida Toshio. *Kaigun sanbō.* Tokyo: Bungei Shunjū, 1989.

Yoshida Yutaka. *Shōwa tennō no shūsenshi.* Tokyo: Iwanami Shinsho, 1992.

Yoshino Sakuzō hakase minshushugi ronshū. Vol. 4. Tokyo: Shin Kigensha, 1946.

Yoshino Sakuzō. "Jiron." *Chūō kōron* (March 1922).

———. "Sekai kaizō no risō." *Chūō kōron* (March 1919).

———."Sensō no eikyō to shite no dōtokuteki kakusei." In *Yoshino Sakuzō hakase minshushugi ronshū.* Vol. 4. Tokyo: Shinkigensha, 1946.

———. "Taigaiteki ryōshin no hakki." *Chūō kōron* (April 1919).

Yoshizawa Minami. *Sensō kakudai no kōzu: Nihongun no Futsu-in shinchū.* Tokyo: Aoki Shoten, 1986.

Index

Abbott, Lyman, 42
Abe Katsuo, 169
Abo Kiyokazu, 128, 129, 133
A-bomb. *See* Atomic bomb
A-bomb nationalism, 241
Adams, Henry, 32
Adams, John Quincy, 12
Aguinaldo, Emilio, 61
Akiba Tadatoshi, 232
Akihito, Emperor, 221
Akiyama Saneyuki, 72–75
Allen, Frederick L., 50*n*81
Allen, H. C., 11
Alperovitz, Gar, 25, 177, 193–95, 204,
  223–24, 233, 234, 241
America: Pathways to the Present (Clayton
  et al.), 234
American Dream (Smith), 232
American Historical Association, 25
American Historical Review, 15
American in Disguise (Okimoto), 20
The American Nation (Boyer), 233
American Odyssey (Nash), 233
Amherst College, 19
Anami Korechika, 175, 185–89, 193, 197,
  199
Anderson, Chandler P., 94
Anglo-Japanese Alliance, 88, 102, 139
Anti-Comintern Pact, 139
Arab-Israeli wars, 242
Arai Shin'ichi, 178
Araki Takeshi, 221–22
Armacost, Michael, 4, 52
Asada Benji, 5
Asada Sadao: Americanization of, during
  college and graduate school, 6–8, 10,
  16, 17; and atomic bomb controversy,
  25–26, 179, 204–6; at Carleton College,
  2–10, 13, 19, 25; childhood of, during

World War II, 1–2; decision by, to return to Japan, 16–17; dissertation by,
  15–16, 23; as Doshisha University political science professor, 22–26; as executive secretary of Doshisha University
  Center for American Studies, 17–21; at
  Harvard's Charles Warren Center for
  Study in American History, 21; and
  historical revisionism, 1–2; honors thesis and graduation of, from Carleton
  College, 9–10; Kyoto University
  courses taught by, 22; lectures and
  writing by, in Japanese language, 20–
  21; and naval history, 23–25; publications by, 22–25; and reverse culture
  shock, 16–22; summer vacations and
  summer jobs of, during college and
  graduate school, 6–8, 13; in
  Washington, D.C., 13–15; at Yale
  University for graduate training, 11–16
Asahi, 201, 213–14, 215, 216, 225, 226
Atomic bomb: Asada's papers and writings on, 25–26, 179, 204–6; and "atomic
  diplomacy" thesis, 25, 176*n*11, 177–78,
  203–4, 223–26, 233, 234; casualties
  from, 174, 181, 186, 229, 232; college
  student surveys on, 224, 227, 229, 239–
  40, 243–44; description of, 174; as "external pressure" for Japan's surrender,
  175, 176, 180–83, 186, 189–93, 200, 214,
  236; as "gift from heaven," 189–92, 200;
  and Hirohito, 181–83, 189, 205;
  Hiroshima-Nagasaki survivors' reac-
  tions to, 209, 209*n*5, 211, 238; and
  Hiroshima–Pearl Harbor syndrome,
  219–21, 226, 236–37; and Hiroshima-
  victimizer syndrome, 237–38, 241; human guinea-pig interpretation of,
  224–25, 229–30; and Japanese army,

About the Author

Sadao Asada is Professor Emeritus of Diplomatic History at Doshisha University in Kyoto, Japan. His *Japanese-American Relations between the Wars* (in Japanese) won the coveted Yomiuri Yoshino Sakuzo Book Prize. For his essays, he has been awarded the Edward S. Miller History Prize by the U.S. Naval War College and the Louis Knott Koontz Memorial Award by the American Historical Association. His other books include *Japan and the World, 1853–1952: A Bibliographic Guide to Japanese Scholarship in Foreign Relations* and *From Mahan to Pearl Harbor: The Imperial Japanese Navy and the United States.*